MW01199286

Daily Wisdom
VOLUME TWO

DAILY WISDOM

VOLUME TWO

*Inspiring Insights on the Torah Portion
from the Lubavitcher Rebbe*

Rabbi Menachem M. Schneerson
זצוקללה"ה נבג"מ זי"ע

TRANSLATED AND ADAPTED BY
Rabbi Moshe Yaakov Wisnefsky

KEHOT PUBLICATION SOCIETY
770 Eastern Parkway, Brooklyn, NY 11213

CHABAD HOUSE
PUBLICATIONS

DAILY WISDOM

VOLUME TWO

*Inspiring Insights on the Torah Portion
from the Lubavitcher Rebbe*

Copyright © 2018 by
CHABAD HOUSE PUBLICATIONS
Los Angeles, California
info@chabadhousepublications.org
www.chabadhousepublications.org
First printing, Compact Edition, August 2018

Published by
KEHOT PUBLICATION SOCIETY
770 Eastern Parkway, Brooklyn, NY 11213
+1-718-774-4000 / Fax +1-718-774-2718
editor@kehot.com

ORDER DEPARTMENT:
291 Kingston Avenue, Brooklyn, NY 11213
+1-718-778-0226 / Fax +1-718-778-4148
www.kehot.com

Typesetting: Raphaël Freeman, Renana Typesetting

ISBN: 978-0-8266-0894-9

Manufactured in the United States of America

About the Weisblum/Spodek Edition

THE GREAT CHASIDIC MASTER, RABBI DOVBER (THE MAGGID) of Mezeritch, was the disciple and spiritual successor to the founder of the Chasidic movement, the holy Rabbi Yisrael Baal Shem Tov (1698–1760).

The Maggid of Mezeritch's inner circle of disciples, known as the *Chevraya Kadisha* ("the sacred fellowship"), included the legendary brothers Rabbi Elimelech Weisblum of Lizhensk and Rabbi Zusha of Hanipol; Rabbi Levi Yitzchak of Berditchev; and the founder of the Chabad movement, Rabbi Schneur Zalman of Liadi, ancestor of the Rebbe, Rabbi Menachem Mendel Schneerson.

This group of saintly luminaries dedicated every fiber of their being to revealing the esoteric light of the Torah and spreading it throughout the world in order that all could learn to serve their Creator with love and joy. Their efforts were met with extraordinary success and they transformed the Jewish landscape to this day.

Now, more than 200 years later, their descendants – Gil Avraham Weisblum, a descendant of Rabbi Elimelech Weisblum of Lizhensk; Rabbis Levi and Chaim Cunin, descendants of Rabbi Zusha of Hanipol; Asher David Milstein, a descendant of Rabbi Levi Yitzchok of Berditchev; Avi Spodek; and Yuri Pikover, patron of the Rebbe's Chumash Project – have joined together to publish *Daily Wisdom* volume 2. With it, they continue the mission of their forefathers by spreading the light of the Torah throughout the world in the form of these precious and profound teachings on the weekly Torah portion.

It is our fervent hope that the light that emanates from these teachings will bring inspiration and love to all, and usher in the era of ultimate light and peace, when "the world will be filled with the knowledge of G-d as the waters cover the ocean floor" (Isaiah 11:9).

This book is a celebration of our fathers Zev Weisblum and Lenny Spodek, two men who began their lives as victims of hatred, and who out of despair emerged as strong, courageous, determined men – dedicated to their families and the preservation of a Jewish way of life.

Their examples of sacrifice, hard work, and perseverance are what drives us to succeed each and every day. These life-lessons that our fathers taught are their legacy and our guiding light in all that we strive to do.

I HUMBLY PAY TRIBUTE TO MY HEROES

In honor and memory of my father

Leonard Spodek ז״ל

Thank you for your wisdom, guidance, and inspiration.

To my beloved grandparents

Sarah Elbaum Spodek ז״ל
Israel Spodek ז״ל
Lillian Bernhajm Tyras ז״ל
Irving Tyras ז״ל

*Their ideals and selfless devotion are the strength that
moves us forward generation after generation.*

*In loving memory of the Elbaum, Spodek, Bernhajm, and
Tyras family members who perished in the Holocaust*

Great-Grandparents ז״ל
Aunts ז״ל
Uncles ז״ל
Cousins ז״ל

We are forever indebted to you for your sacrifice on our behalf.

In honor of my mother

Rosalind Spodek תחי׳

To our children

Isaac Spodek שי׳
David Spodek שי׳
Jack Spodek שי׳

You are our future, our legacy and our blessings!

AVI AND EVELYN SPODEK

Dedicated in honor of our children

Nathan,
Yitzchok,
Moshe Lev,
and Gilana

*May you continue to grow in the ways
of our holy Torah*

YURI AND DEANA PIKOVER

A PROJECT OF Chabad House Publications

DIRECTOR AND GENERAL EDITOR Rabbi Chaim N. Cunin

EDITOR IN CHIEF Rabbi Moshe Yaakov Wisnefsky

RABBINIC CONSULTANTS
Rabbi Yosef Friedman
Rabbi Dovid Olidort
Rabbi Aaron Leib Raskin
Rabbi Leizer Shemtov
Rabbi Asi Spiegel
Rabbi Avraham D. Vaisfiche

SENIOR EDITOR Yaakov Ort

CHIEF COPY EDITOR Reuven Abish Macales

PROOFREADING Rabbi Shmuel Rabin

COVER ART Yossi Belkin

DESIGN AND LAYOUT Raphaël Freeman, Renana Typesetting

SPECIAL THANKS TO Rabbi Baruch Shlomo Eliyahu Cunin,
Rabbi Yehuda Krinsky, Rabbis Danny Cohen, Levi
Yitzchak Cunin, Yosef Cunin, Zushe Cunin, Michoel
Goldman, Yankel Kagan, Baruch Kaplan, Betzalel
Lifshitz, Shalom Lipskar, Zalman Lipskar, Moishe Meir
Lipszyc, Chaim Marcus, Yosef Marcus, Ezzy Rappoport,
Moshe Pinson, Dov Wagner, and Aryeh Wuensch

Odel Miriam Cunin, Tova Cunin, Asher David
and Michal Milstein, Gil and Jessica Weisblum,
Avi and Evelyn Spodek, Yuri and Deana Pikover,
Michael and Vivian Perez, David Suissa, and the
dedicated staff of Kehot Publication Society

Preface

WITH GRATITUDE TO G-D, AND IN RESPONSE TO THE OVER-
whelming acclaim that we received for the first volume of *Daily
Wisdom*, we are pleased to present this second anthology of
inspirational lessons on the Torah portion from the teachings
of the Lubavitcher Rebbe, Rabbi Menachem M. Schneerson, of
righteous memory.

Daily Wisdom is a distillation of the Rebbe's complex analyses of the Torah's text, adapting them into brief teachings that
invite the reader to live inspired by the daily section of the Torah.
The first edition has been enthusiastically received by tens of
thousands of readers worldwide. Since it was first published a
mere four years ago, it has been reprinted over 20 times, including translations into Hebrew, French, Spanish, Russian, and
Portuguese.

We are blessed by the encouragement and support of Yuri and
Deana Pikover, visionaries and patrons of the Rebbe's Chumash
Project, who generously sponsored the development of *Daily
Wisdom*.

We extend our sincere thanks to Gil and Jessica Weisblum and
Avi and Evelyn Spodek. Gil and Avi, who are dearest of friends,
have devoted themselves to illuminating the world with the light,
love, and study of the Torah.

The present volume contains 378 new insights, one for each day
of the yearly cycle of Torah-study. By studying the appropriate
selection each day, the reader can follow the daily course of Torah-
study and be inspired by the Rebbe's teachings on a daily basis.

The Rebbe stresses in his teachings that the world as we know
it is incomplete and broken; that our job is to correct and refine
this world, thereby hastening the coming of the Messiah, who
will usher in the final Redemption; that we do this through acts
of loving kindness. The inner meaning of these concepts and how

they are rooted in the Torah is found in the teachings presented in this book.

It is our hope that through studying the Rebbe's teachings, we will very soon merit to the fulfillment of the Rebbe's ultimate goal, the promise of the immediate redemption.

CHABAD HOUSE PUBLICATIONS

19 KISLEV 5779

Contents

DEUTERONOMY

Introduction

THE WORD *TORAH* IN HEBREW MEANS "INSTRUCTION."[1] JEWISH tradition, over 3,000 years old, informs us that G-d[2] not only created the universe but taught His creatures how to live in it. This Divine teaching is the Torah, G-d's "user's manual" for the world.

After G-d communicated His teachings to the original human beings, these teachings were transmitted through the generations, being studied by select individuals in each generation and eventually by the patriarchs of the Jewish people. G-d's teachings took their final, authoritative form as a written document and its interpretation. The written document consists of the "Five Books of Moses" – Genesis, Exodus, Leviticus, Numbers, and Deuteronomy – which G-d dictated directly to Moses, who wrote them down before his death.[3] The oral interpretation is known as the "Oral Torah."[4]

---

1. Rabbi David Kimchi on Psalms 19:8 and in *Sefer HaShorashim, s.v. yud-reish-hei*; *Zohar* 3:53b.

2. As an expression of respect to the Creator, it is customary (in certain contexts) to write "G-d" with a hyphen in place of the letter "o" (*Urim veTumim* 27:1, *Urim* 2; *Kitzur Shulchan Aruch* 6:3; *Igrot Kodesh*, vol. 7, p. 26; ibid., vol. 9, p. 62). For the same reason, G-d's proper Name (יהו-ה) is referred to as "the Name *Havayah*" and abbreviated as 'ה (in the citations from the Torah in Hebrew) and the word for "G-d" (אלהי-ם) is transliterated at *Elokim* and spelled אלקים.

3. *Bava Batra* 15a; *Mishneh Torah*, Introduction.

4. The Oral Torah was also eventually written down, and is preserved principally in the Talmud and Midrashim. The *Talmud* ("learning") consists of the *Mishnah* ("repetition"), the basic compendium of Jewish law and lore, recorded by Rabbi Yehudah the Prince in the second century CE, and the *Gemara* ("study"), which elucidates the Mishnah with the help of the extra-mishnaic material Rabbi Yehudah did not include in the Mishnah, and which includes many more teachings. The process of elucidating the Mishnah took place both in the academies of the Land of Israel and those of Babylonia, and thus there are two Talmuds: the Jerusalem Talmud and the Babylonian Talmud. A *Midrash* ("exegesis") is a compilation of teachings derived by comparing and contrasting Scriptural passages. There are both legal and homiletic Midrashim. The Babylonian Talmud includes much midrashic material, while the midrashic teachings of the academies of the Land of Israel are recorded separately, in the *Midrash Rabbah* series.

Thus, in its broadest sense, the word "Torah" refers to the totality or any part of G-d's teachings; specifically, however, it refers to the Five Books of Moses and its oral interpretation.

After Moses' death, the Jewish people's successes and failures in fulfilling the teachings of the Torah in their land resulted in the expansion of the Written Torah to include books of the Prophets (*Nevi'im*)[5] and the Writings (*Ketuvim*).[6] Nonetheless, the Five Books of Moses remain the primary repository of G-d's teachings. They are complete by themselves, containing all the legal and homiletical material necessary for humanity to live as G-d intends. The Prophets and Writings form an essential complement to the Five Books, but add no *new* legal or philosophical content.[7]

Inasmuch as the Torah embodies G-d's instructions concerning how we are to live our lives, it is essential for everyone to be conversant in the Torah's text and teachings. Moses instituted the practice of reading publicly from a Torah scroll on Sabbath and Festival mornings as well as on Monday and Thursday mornings.[8] In order to complete the reading of the whole Torah in a year, the Torah is divided into 54 sections. Since the Jewish calendar comprises both regular years (of 12 months) and leap years (of 13 months), two sections are sometimes read on the same Sabbath. Moses further instituted that the Torah reading on the Sabbath be divided among seven people. For this purpose, each of the 54 sections were divided into seven sub-sections.

---

5. Comprising the books of Joshua, Judges, Samuel, Kings, Isaiah, Jeremiah, Ezekiel, Hosea, Joel, Amos, Obadiah, Jonah, Micah, Nahum, Habakkuk, Zephaniah, Haggai, Zechariah, and Malachi.

6. Comprising the books of Psalms, Proverbs, Job, The Song of Songs, Ruth, Lamentations, Ecclesiastes, Esther, Daniel, Ezra-Nehemiah, and Chronicles.

7. See *Torah Or* 60a–d. It is therefore taught that "had the Jewish people never sinned, there would have been no need for any books other than the Five Books of Moses and the Book of Joshua" (*Nedarim* 22b).

8. *Soferim* 10:1–2; *Megilah* 3:6; *Bava Kama* 82a; *Megilah* 31b; *Yerushalmi Megilah* 4:5; *Mishneh Torah, Tefilah* 12:1; *Kesef Mishneh* ad loc. The custom of reading the beginning of the following Sabbath morning's reading on the Sabbath afternoon was instituted by Ezra (ibid.).

The teachings of the Chasidic movement, founded by Rabbi Yisrael Ba'al Shem Tov (1698–1760), revealed how the Torah describes the connection between G-d and creation in general and each individual in particular. In this spirit, the founder of the Chabad branch of Chasidism, Rabbi Shneur Zalman of Liadi (1745–1812) once told his followers to "live with the times," by which he meant to live throughout the year with the section of the Torah that is studied at the time.[9] Thus, the law and lore of the Torah is studied not only as legal and historical information, but also personally, as if we are experiencing the spiritual growth processes implicit in them. In this way, the Torah becomes our own personal story; the chronicle of our developing relationship with G-d. Rabbi Shneur Zalman also instituted the practice of studying each day the corresponding sub-section of the weekly Torah section.[10] In this context, Rabbi Shneur Zalman's exhortation to "live with the times" came to mean not only living with the Torah section of the week but with the sub-section of the day.

In addition to continuing to develop the teachings of his predecessors, the seventh Lubavitcher Rebbe,[11] Rabbi Menachem Mendel Schneerson, devoted considerable time to elucidating both the basic meaning of the Torah's text and the Torah's inner lessons. In his public discourses, his private audiences, and his voluminous correspondence, spread over the 44 years of his public leadership, the Rebbe demonstrated how the Torah's teachings are eternally relevant and applicable to every aspect of life, even those that have come to existence only in modern times.

This book contains a concise insight from teachings of the Rebbe or his predecessors for each of the seven sub-sections of the 54 sections of the Torah – one for each day of the week, for the full year of Torah study. Of course, in order to know which insight to read for any given day, the reader will need to know

---

9. *Sefer HaSichot 5702*, pp. 29–30; *HaYom Yom*, 2 Cheshvan.

10. *Sefer HaSichot 5702*, p. 27; *HaYom Yom*, 19 Tevet.

11. Lubavitch is the name of the town in White Russia where the Chabad movement flourished. The various branches of the Chasidic movement are usually known by the name of the locale in which they developed.

which section of the Torah is being studied that week. We have provided a calendar for this purpose on p. 444; in addition, any Jewish calendar, as well as numerous online resources, can provide this information.

Thus, the impact of the insights presented in this book will be felt to the greatest extent when the reader reads each insight on the day it is meant to be read, rather than by reading the book, say, cover to cover, or by browsing through it. Since the Rebbe emphasized certain key lessons repeatedly, seeing them alluded to over and over again in the Torah, these lessons are also highlighted numerous times throughout this book.

We have prefaced each weekly section with a short summary of the entire section, and each daily sub-section with a synopsis of the portion of the Torah's narrative leading up to the verse being expounded. For the chronology provided in these synopses, we have used the traditional Jewish reckoning of time, i.e., from the creation of the world, and the Jewish months. A table of these months and their approximate correspondence to Gregorian months is given on p. 443.

We have given the sources for each insight in published Chasidic texts. We should point out, however, that in many cases we have fleshed out the original sources with material culled from other sources in the Rebbe's teachings.[12] Also, we have presented the Rebbe's or his predecessors' teachings often in a somewhat "digested" form, i.e., the way the teachings have spoken to us and how we think they could speak to the reader. Whenever anyone attempts to convey another person's thoughts in his own words, he runs the risk of inadvertently distorting them; we hope this has been minimal in our case.

Our goal of providing insights that would be accessible to the widest possible readership has precluded the inclusion of many of the Rebbe's profound insights, simply because doing them justice

---

12. In accordance with the Talmudic sages' statement that "the teachings of the Torah are poor in their place but enriched in another place" (*Yerushalmi Rosh HaShanah* 3:5).

would have required more space. We hope that the glimpse that this work provides will inspire its readers to seek further and deeper knowledge of the Rebbe's empowering teachings.

We further hope that this work inspires its readers to live with the Torah's ultimate message, as highlighted by the Rebbe: to actualize the Messianic imperative to make this world into G-d's ultimate home.

THE EDITORIAL STAFF

GENESIS

Bereishit

Creation, Adam and Eve, and Humanity's Early History
Genesis 1:1–6:8

THE NAME OF THE FIRST SECTION OF THE BOOK OF GENESIS is taken from its first words, "In the beginning" (*Bereishit*, in Hebrew), and opens with G-d's creation of the world. Humanity was created with the ability to choose between good and evil, but the first humans, Adam and Eve, misused this gift, launching humanity onto a path of increasing moral degeneration. Eventually, it became necessary to establish a new order and give the world a fresh start.

FIRST READING
Genesis 1:1–2:3

The Torah begins with its account of how G-d created the world in six days. On the first day, G-d created the earth, as a core of solid matter submerged in water, and then created light.

Harnessing the Power of Darkness

וַיַּרְא אֱלֹקִים אֶת הָאוֹר כִּי טוֹב וגו': (בראשית א, ד)

G-d saw that the light was good.

"Light" signifies Divine consciousness and "darkness" signifies the lack thereof. G-d created the world inherently "dark" in order for us to transform it into His home by shining the light of Divine consciousness into it.

This pair of opposites – light and darkness – manifests itself in many ways: as knowledge vs. ignorance, positivity vs. negativity, love vs. hatred, order vs. chaos, and so on. In each of these cases, there is an inherent power in the "darkness" that is lacking in the "light." This inherent power of darkness can be harnessed, like the rest of creation, toward the fulfillment of G-d's purpose. Thus, rather than use light to *eliminate* darkness, G-d wants us to use light to *transform* darkness itself into light – to make the darkness itself shine with Divine consciousness.

This is why, when "G-d saw that the light was good," He did not do away with the darkness, leaving daylight to shine throughout the entire 24-hour day. In fact, darkness' purpose is so important that for half the year there is more darkness than light.

Rather, when "G-d saw that the light was good," it was because we can use light to subordinate and guide darkness, to direct darkness' power toward holy purposes.[1]

---

1. *Bereishit Rabbah* 2:5; *Likutei Torah* 2:7d.

SECOND READING
Genesis 2:4–2:19

The atmosphere was created on the second day. The dry land rose above sea level on the third day. The heavenly bodies were placed in outer space on the fourth day. The sea animals populated the oceans on the fifth day. The land animals and first humans populated the dry land on the sixth day. On the seventh day, G-d "rested" from creating. After its account of the creation week, the Torah returns to the events of the sixth day, focusing on the details of the creation of the first human being.

Our Human Potential

בְּיוֹם עֲשׂוֹת ה' אֱלֹקִים אֶרֶץ וְשָׁמָיִם: (בראשית ב, ד)

**[Everything was created] on the day
that G-d made earth and heaven.**

The Torah uses two main Names for G-d. Throughout its account of the creation week, it refers to Him exclusively by the Name *Elokim* (אלקים), which signifies His concealment within creation. This is because only by hiding His existence could G-d create creatures who are conscious of themselves as being separate from Him. This concealment of G-d is known as "nature," the façade that makes us think that the world runs by itself.

But when the Torah begins the story of humanity, it introduces a second Name of G-d, *Havayah* (י-ה-ו-ה), which signifies His revelation, His open intervention in the affairs of the world. This is because humanity's mission is to reveal G-d within the physical world. In order to accomplish this, G-d grants us the unique capacity to connect with Him beyond the limitations of nature.[2]

2. *Likutei Torah* 5:32a; *Sefer HaMa'amarim Melukat*, vol. 1, pp. 346–347; *Hitva'aduyot 5748*, vol. 3, p. 163.

THIRD READING

Genesis 2:20–3:21

The first human couple, Adam and Eve, lived in the Garden of Eden, where they were meant to enjoy G-d's creation in order to enhance their awareness of G-d and His goodness. However, they were seduced by the primordial serpent (who personified the temptation to increase their *self*-awareness) into eating the fruit of the Tree of Knowledge, which G-d had forbidden to them.

Overcoming Evil

וַיֹּאמֶר אֶל הָאִשָּׁה אַף כִּי אָמַר אֱלֹקִים לֹא תֹאכְלוּ מִכֹּל עֵץ הַגָּן: (בראשית ג, א)

[The serpent] said to Eve, "Did G-d really say, 'You may not eat from any of the trees of the garden?'"

Both Eve and the serpent knew that G-d had not forbidden any fruit other than that of the Tree of Knowledge. G-d intended for Adam and Eve to expand their Divine consciousness by enjoying the fruits of the Garden. Thus, the serpent was suggesting that by depriving them of the fruit of this tree, G-d was limiting their ability to accomplish His objective. "If He has denied you this fruit, He may as well have denied you all fruit!" Eating the forbidden fruit, the serpent argued, would be the best way to achieve G-d's purpose.

This is the classic technique of the evil inclination: It does not (initially, at least) attempt to convince us to disobey G-d's will, for we, as logical thinkers, would refuse. It instead convinces us that transgressing G-d's will is a shortcut to accomplishing G-d's purposes.

Thus, at the very dawn of human history, G-d's first lesson to us was to reject our evil inclination's schemes, in order to remain true to our Divine calling.[3]

3. *Torah Or* 5c–6a.

FOURTH READING
Genesis 3:22–4:18

Had Adam and Eve repented properly, G-d would have forgiven them and allowed them to remain in the Garden of Eden. But since they did not rise to the occasion, G-d banished them from it. Their firstborn child, Cain, was presented with a similar opportunity: When G-d accepted his brother Abel's offering and not his, Cain should have understood that this meant that he needed to repent; instead, he chose to kill Abel.

Bringing G-d into Our Lives

וַיָּבֵא קַיִן מִפְּרִי הָאֲדָמָה מִנְחָה לַה': (בראשית ד, ג)

Cain brought some of the produce of the ground as an offering to G-d.

Cain felt that the only acceptable type of Divine consciousness is the awareness that G-d is all that there is. He therefore purposely did not offer up the best specimen of his crop, for if everything is really G-d, there is no "best," "average," or "worst."

The problem with this outlook is that denying the reality of the world thwarts the purpose of creation: to spread Divine consciousness where *the world's* existence – not G-d's existence – is self-evident. It makes us seek G-d only in "otherworldly" pursuits: the intrinsically spiritual activities of prayer and religious observance.

In contrast, Abel understood the advantage of the lower type of Divine consciousness – the realization that G-d manifests Himself *within* creation. He therefore offered up the finest of his flock in order to acknowledge the diversity of creation – that we feel G-d's presence more in some aspects of creation than in others. It is then our task to make G-d felt in the "lower," mundane aspects of reality, as well.[4]

4. *Likutei Sichot*, vol. 15, pp. 22–25.

FIFTH READING
Genesis 4:19–22

The generations following Adam and Eve began to worship the forces of nature and the idols they fashioned to represent or channel them. Forgetting about G-d, their moral behavior also began to degenerate.

Being True to Our Inner Selves

וַתֵּלֶד עָדָה אֶת יָבָל הוּא הָיָה אֲבִי יֹשֵׁב אֹהֶל וּמִקְנֶה: (בראשית ד, כ)

Adah gave birth to Yaval; He was the forerunner of all those who live in tents and keep herds.

The Hebrew word for "and keep herds" also means "and provoke"; indeed, Yaval was the first person who provoked G-d by building shrines for idolatry.[5]

Idolatry arose from the mistaken notion that since G-d has chosen to channel His control of the world through various natural forces, it is fitting for us to respect and honor these forces. This seemingly harmless notion eventually led people to worship the forces of nature exclusively, forgetting about G-d.[6]

In our own lives, it is tempting to think that in order to secure the blessings of happiness, wealth, social acceptance, etc., we have to obey the mundane laws of nature, devoting excessive efforts to our jobs, our bodies, and our social circles. Of course, G-d wants us to live our lives naturally, but at the same time to realize that true success is only possible with His blessings.

In contrast, ascribing absolute power to the forces of nature and therefore "serving" them is a subtle form of idolatry. Only by serving G-d do we accrue all the true blessings in life.[7]

5. Rashi on this verse, citing Ezekiel 8:3.
6. *Mishneh Torah, Avodah Zarah* 1:1–2.
7. *Sefer HaMa'amarim 5685*, pp. 98–99; *Sefer HaMa'amarim 5705*, pp. 85–86; *Hitva'aduyot 5723*, vol. 2, p. 228.

SIXTH READING

Genesis 4:23–5:24

In addition to their sons Cain and Abel, Adam and Eve had a third son, Seth. One of Seth's fifth-generation descendants was Enoch, who resisted the degeneration into which the rest of humanity was sinking, and lived a righteous life.

The Purpose of Idealism

וַיּוֹלֶד אֶת חֲנוֹךְ: (בראשית ה, יח)

[Seth's great-grandson Yered] had a son, Enoch.

Cain rejected the physical world, yearning to unite with G-d. Consequently, all but one of his descendants later perished in Noah's Flood. In contrast, Seth used the physical world to express how G-d is not limited by it. Consequently, it was Seth's descendants who rebuilt the world after the Flood.

Both Cain and Seth had descendants named Enoch who were their opposite.[8] Cain's son Enoch was a Seth-like person: the first city was built in his name,[9] and a city is built in order to promote civilization. In contrast, Seth's descendant Enoch was a Cain-like person, who shunned the world – and G-d validated his disposition by taking him from the physical world before his time.

This teaches us that while both ideals are necessary – a person must yearn inwardly to soar to spiritual heights, yet remain conscious of the fact that G-d's purpose is served in expressing Divinity in *this* world – each ideal must complement the other. The ultimate concern of the mystic within us must be the practical application of the Torah in *this* world, while the pragmatic servant of G-d within us must also yearn for the mystical experience, rising beyond ordinary life.[10]

---

8. This verse is part of the genealogy of Seth. Cain's first son was Enoch (Genesis 4:17).
9. Genesis 4:17.
10. *Likutei Sichot*, vol. 35, pp. 11–13.

SEVENTH READING
Genesis 5:25–6:8

Despite Enoch's positive example, humanity continued in its downward spiral of moral degeneration. Eventually, G-d saw that the only remedy was to give humanity a fresh start, and decided to wipe out the world with a flood, after which He would repopulate the world from Noah, the only righteous individual of that generation.

The Power of Resolve

וְנֹחַ מָצָא חֵן בְּעֵינֵי ה': (בראשית ו, ח)

Noah found favor in the eyes of G-d.

Noah was the only righteous person of his generation, yet his uniqueness incredibly did not negatively affect his morality or ethics.

This thought can serve to inspire us whenever an inner voice torments us: "Why do you even bother to pursue the path of spirituality and holiness, studying the Torah and fulfilling G-d's commandments? After all, you are just one very small person in a very big world that is often cold and even hostile to goodness and holiness."

The story of Noah provides a fitting response to this inner voice: Noah resolved to behave properly, living a moral life despite the antagonistic behavior of his contemporaries, and furthermore, his conduct brought salvation to the entire world. If Noah, who was truly on his own, was capable of this, certainly we today, who are *not* alone in our commitment to G-d's Torah, can courageously withstand the moral challenges of our contemporary world.[11]

11. *Hitva'aduyot 5743*, vol. 1, pp. 412–413.

Noach

Noah, the Flood, and Beyond

Genesis 6:9–11:32

THE SECOND SECTION OF THE BOOK OF GENESIS IS NAMED after its central character, Noah (*Noach*, in Hebrew), and begins with the account of the great Flood that washed the world clean of the depravity and degeneration into which humanity had sunk since the creation of the world. This is followed by the account of how the world was divided up between Noah's sons, the dispersion of humanity brought about by the incident of the Tower of Babel, and the prelude to the upcoming sections' account of humanity's next great hero, Abraham.

FIRST READING
Genesis 6:9–22

Noah, in contrast to the degeneration that characterized his times, remained faithful to the traditions of morality that had been inherited from Adam and Eve. G-d therefore chose Noah to survive the Flood and repopulate the world in its aftermath.

Raising Children

אֵלֶּה תּוֹלְדֹת נֹחַ נֹחַ אִישׁ צַדִּיק תָּמִים הָיָה וגו': (בראשית ו, ט)

The following are the descendants of Noah. Noah was a righteous man; he was flawless.

By mentioning Noah's righteousness before discussing his children, the Torah teaches us that our truest "offspring" are first and foremost our own good deeds. Our children should thus sense that our greatest aspiration for them is that they excel in good deeds, which carry on our lineage in the spiritual sense.

Blessed with such an upbringing, our children will follow the right path in their relationship with G-d, with their fellow human beings, and especially with us, their parents. Such an atmosphere will unite the entire family under the common goal of excelling in acts of goodness and kindness.[1]

---

1. *Likutei Sichot*, vol. 9, pp. xiv–xv.

SECOND READING
Genesis 7:1–16

G-d told Noah to build an ark in order that he, his family, and representatives of all forms of animal life survive the Flood.

Responsibility

בֹּא אַתָּה וְכָל בֵּיתְךָ אֶל הַתֵּבָה וְגוֹ': (בראשית ז, א)

**[G-d told Noah,] "Come into the ark, you
and your entire household."**

Allegorically, "entering the ark" means that we should immerse ourselves in the study of the Torah and in prayer, in order to protect ourselves from the "flood" of worldly distractions that threaten to "drown" us in materialism.

This does not mean, however, that when we do this we should become unconcerned about the needs of others. We must not be content with our own self-preservation alone. We are empowered to bring our families, our children, and ultimately the entire world into a wholesome, safe haven of Torah study and prayer. The plight of our fellow person should give us no rest, for we are all like one body – if one of us is spiritually ill, we are all affected, and the health of our collective self positively affects the health of each one of us.[2]

2. *Likutei Sichot*, vol. 1, pp. 8–10.

TUESDAY

The rain lasted 40 days, after which the earth remained submerged for another five months until the water began to subside. It then took almost six more months for the water to recede completely. During this entire year, Noah and his family tended the animals in the ark.

Devotion to Others

וַיִּשָּׁאֶר אַךְ נֹחַ וַאֲשֶׁר אִתּוֹ בַּתֵּבָה: (בראשית ז, כג)

Only Noah and those who were with him in the ark survived.

Noah and his family took care of the animals faithfully and humanely throughout their year in the ark, even though feeding all of them was an exhausting task. Even when one of the lions struck Noah for delivering their meal late, this only strengthened Noah's concern for his charges.

Like Noah and his family, we are all responsible for providing for needs of those together with us in this world, our "ark." This applies to their material needs, of course, but also and especially to their spiritual needs. Like Noah and his family, we can persevere in our task despite its difficulty.

The incident with the lion teaches us the importance of being acutely sensitive to the discomfort of others, providing for their needs promptly. If we are tempted to consider their necessities mere luxuries,[3] we should recall that we have no way of estimating another person's true, inner worth; each might possess a lofty soul and therefore be a "lion," a "king."[4] Moreover, while we should indeed assume that whenever *we* suffer it is because we deserve to, we should always assume that *others* deserve only the best.[5]

3. *Ketubot* 67b.
4. See *Pesachim* 50a.
5. *Likutei Sichot*, vol. 5, pp. 53–56.

FOURTH READING

Genesis 8:15–9:7

After the Flood, Noah built an altar and sacrificed animals to G-d. G-d then decided that He would never again wipe out humanity.

Overcoming Judgment with Mercy

יֵצֶר לֵב הָאָדָם רַע מִנְּעֻרָיו וגו': (בראשית ח, כא)

[G-d thought,] "The inclination of a person's heart is evil from his youth."

This statement is part of G-d's explanation why He would never again destroy humanity. Yet when G-d examined humanity's behavior before the Flood,[6] He used the very same statement for precisely the opposite purpose – to explain why humanity *should* be destroyed!

It was Noah's sacrificial offerings that caused the same argument that had previously invoked G-d's attribute of strict judgment to now invoke His attribute of kindness and mercy. We see here the incredible spiritual power of sacrifices.

It is the same in our own personal lives. When we "sacrifice" ourselves by forgoing our own needs and desires in favor of doing G-d's will, we elicit the same kind of treatment from Him: He will forgo the dictates of His strict justice in order to fulfill our needs and desires. When our behavior is examined in the heavenly court, mitigating factors and rationalizations will be found to either lessen or do away with any punishment for our misdeeds. Evidence that would normally be used against us will be used in our favor, enabling G-d's attribute of mercy to overrule His attribute of strict judgment.[7]

6. Genesis 6:5.
7. *Sefer HaMa'amarim* 5700, pp. 5, 12–13.

THURSDAY

FIFTH READING
Genesis 9:8–17

Noah hesitated to fulfill G-d's command to procreate and repopulate the earth, fearing that his descendants might one day be wiped away in another Flood. G-d therefore swore to Noah that there would be no future Flood.

Helping the World

וַאֲנִי הִנְנִי מֵקִים אֶת בְּרִיתִי אִתְּכֶם וגו': (בראשית ט, ט)

[G-d told Noah,] "I am setting up My covenant with you."

This covenant did not just ensure that the world and its population would continue to exist physically. Its deeper intention was that the world be spiritually receptive to being transformed into G-d's home, thereby fulfilling the purpose for which it was created.[8]

On account of this covenant, the world is indeed receptive to Divine consciousness. Nonetheless, this promise has not yet been fulfilled in its entirety, and will not be until the Messianic Redemption. On the contrary, we have sadly suffered far too much religious and physical persecution throughout our prolonged exile.

Nevertheless, by clinging to our heartfelt hopes and fervently praying that we should never again undergo or witness the horrors we have experienced in the past, while at the same time dedicating ourselves to our Divine mission with joy and inspiration, we hasten the advent of the final Redemption. At that time, G-d's intention that the world assist us in our Divine mission will be finally fulfilled.[9]

---

8. *Likutei Sichot*, vol. 20, p. 34.
9. *Sefer HaMa'amarim 5740*, p. 41.

SIXTH READING
Genesis 9:18–10:32

Adam and Eve had misused wine (the fruit of the Tree of Knowledge) by using it to achieve self-awareness. Noah tried to rectify this by using it to lose himself in Divine joy. But because this selflessness was artificial, it backfired, and Noah exposed himself indecently. Seeing this, Noah's youngest son, Ham, told his older brothers, Shem and Japheth, about the incident. Ham's two brothers immediately proceeded to cover Noah up.

The Pursuit of Spiritual Profit

וְחָם הוּא אֲבִי כְנָעַן: (בראשית ט, יח)

Ham was the father of Canaan.

Ham in Hebrew means "hot." Allegorically, Ham alludes to the soul's burning desire to draw near and cleave to G-d.

Canaan is sometimes translated as "merchant,"[10] and thus alludes to the soul's pursuit of the "profit" it earns by studying the Torah and observing G-d's commandments – its increased connection to G-d.

In this context, then, the allegorical meaning of the verse "Ham was the father [i.e., progenitor] of Canaan" is:

Our Divine soul is *Ham* ("hot") from the moment it descends into this world; clothed in the body and the animating soul, it experiences a burning desire for G-d's presence. This longing inspires it to become *Canaan* ("a merchant"). It seeks to increase its connection to G-d in reward for studying the Torah and performing the commandments.

Thus, whereas Ham misused his innate passion to focus on his father's inappropriate behavior, we can use our innate passion to fan the flames of our desire to increase G-d's presence in our lives.[11]

10. See Isaiah 23:8.
11. *Torah Or* 27a.

SEVENTH READING
Genesis 11:1–32

After the Flood, the original traditions of morality and monotheism were only preserved by select individuals; foremost among these was Abraham (who was initially known as Abram). Abram's beliefs angered the king of his native Babylonia, so his family set out toward Canaan (the future Land of Israel), settling in the meantime in Aram (present-day Syria and southeast Turkey), in the city of Charan.

Emulating Abraham

וַיָּבֹאוּ עַד חָרָן וַיֵּשְׁבוּ שָׁם: (בראשית יא, לא)

[Abram's family] came as far as Charan, settling there.

The word *Charan* means "anger." Allegorically, then, this verse implies that Abraham was able to appease G-d's anger. Although humanity continued to rebel against G-d after the Flood, Abraham – unlike Noah – prayed for his contemporaries and befriended them, working to improve their beliefs and behavior. G-d therefore was merciful to them.

Similarly, the accomplishments and suffering of preceding generations have prepared the world for the coming Messianic Era, when the purpose of all of creation will be realized.[12] Having gone through enough "floods" throughout history, our remaining task is to emulate Abraham, lovingly befriending all people and awakening their innate connection to G-d. In this way, we can guide the world toward its ultimate purpose: the true and complete Redemption.[13]

12. *Tanya*, chapter 36.
13. *Likutei Sichot*, vol. 3, pp. 756–757; ibid., vol. 15, pp. 70–74.

Lech Lecha

Abraham's Calling

Genesis 12:1–17:27

THE THIRD SECTION OF THE BOOK OF GENESIS BEGINS THE chronicle of Abraham (who was initially named Abram). Abram was selected by G-d to found the Jewish people, whose task it would be to reverse the process of moral degeneration that humanity had been locked into since their expulsion from the Garden of Eden. The name of this section (*Lech Lecha*) is taken from G-d's first words to Abram: "Go...," in which He told him to leave his native Mesopotamia (modern-day Iraq) and settle in the Promised Land of Israel. Throughout his journeys, Abram challenged paganism, spreading awareness of all reality's source and continuous dependence on the one G-d.

FIRST READING

Genesis 12:1–13

Responding to Abram's efforts to restore monotheism and morality to the world, G-d informs him that He has selected him to found the Jewish people, whose mission it will be to inspire and instruct the world in G-d's ways. In order to have a setting in which to demonstrate the beauty of G-dly life to the rest of humanity, G-d also promises the Land of Israel to Abram and his descendants, and instructs him to settle there.

Traveling Liberators

וַיֹּאמֶר ה' אֶל אַבְרָם לֶךְ לְךָ וְגוֹ': (בראשית יב, א)

G-d said to Abram, "Go."

Rabbi Shalom DovBer of Lubavitch once said:

From the very moment G-d instructed Abram to leave his homeland and set out on his journey, the process of spiritually refining the world began. Sparks of Divinity lay embedded in the materiality of the physical world, awaiting us to redeem them by revealing their potential to be utilized for holy purposes.

Saintly individuals, who possess clear spiritual vision, can perceive just where the captive sparks they are meant to refine are located and go there on their own.

The rest of us are led by Divine providence to places or situations in which the sparks we are meant to liberate await us. Every moment in our lives and every place we go is charged with spiritual potential, challenging us to transform it into something holy.[1]

---

1. *HaYom Yom*, 1 Marcheshvan.

SECOND READING
Genesis 12:14–13:4

The first challenge Abram faced in the Promised Land of Israel was a famine that began immediately upon his arrival, forcing him to temporarily relocate to neighboring Egypt. In Egypt, his wife Sarah (who was initially named Sarai) was abducted by Pharaoh. Sarai resisted Pharaoh's overtures, and G-d miraculously protected her.

Righteous Inspiration

וַתֻּקַּח הָאִשָּׁה בֵּית פַּרְעֹה: (בראשית יב, טו)

The woman [Sarai] was taken to Pharaoh's palace.

Sarai's resistance to the Egyptian king's overtures gave her descendants, the Jewish women enslaved in Egypt in Moses' time, the spiritual fortitude to resist the lure of illicit behavior even in the midst of the depraved Egyptian culture.[2] The sages point out that the righteous behavior of the Jewish women in Egypt was one of the merits in which the Exodus occurred.[3]

We too, can draw strength from the examples of our matriarch Sarai and the righteous Jewish women in Egypt, as well as the examples of all righteous Jewish women throughout history. When confronted with the depravity of the society we live in, we must recall that we possess the spiritual fortitude to resist its temptations. And just as our forefathers were redeemed from Egypt in the merit of the righteous women's dedication to Jewish morality and modesty, so will we witness the true and final Redemption in the merit of following their examples.[4]

---

2. *Vayikra Rabbah* 32:5; *Shir HaShirim Rabbah* 4:25. See also *Tzeror HaMor* on Genesis 12:1.
3. *Shir HaShirim Rabbah* 4:12.
4. *Likutei Sichot*, vol. 5, p. 61.

THIRD READING
Genesis 13:5–18

In the course of his travels throughout the Promised Land, Abram built altars to G-d in three different locations.

Unity

וַיָּבֹא וַיֵּשֶׁב בְּאֵלֹנֵי מַמְרֵא אֲשֶׁר בְּחֶבְרוֹן וַיִּבֶן שָׁם מִזְבֵּחַ לַה': (בראשית יג, יח)

**[Abram] came and settled in the plains of Mamrei,
in Hebron. There, he built an altar to G-d.**

The name *Hebron* (*Chevron*) is related to the word for "connect" (*chaber*).[5] The city of Hebron, both allegorically and physically, expresses the unity of the Jewish people, as well as their unity with G-d.[6]

This is why King David was crowned in Hebron.[7] Of all Biblical figures, he personified our constant and absolute unity with G-d. His psalms, the source of many of our prayers, speak of his unwavering love and devotion to G-d, throughout both the successes and tribulations of his life. Furthermore, King David is the ancestor of the Messiah, who will usher in the Redemption, in which we will all live with the constant awareness of our unity with G-d.

This is the deeper reason why Abram built his third and final altar in Hebron. He built this altar – unlike the first two – neither to thank G-d for something nor to forestall some future calamity. He built it simply to express his oneness with G-d and his desire to spread Divine consciousness.

By internalizing these values, living in unity with one another and with G-d, we can hasten the advent of the Redemption, when both these unities will be fully actualized.[8]

---

5. *Zohar* 1:122b and 125a.
6. See below, on 23:2.
7. 2 Samuel 5:3.
8. *Likutei Sichot*, vol. 30, pp. 41–43.

FOURTH READING

Genesis 14:1–20

Abram's nephew Lot had accompanied him to the Promised Land. Abram was too idealistic for Lot, so Lot left him, settling in Sodom, near the Dead Sea. When the Land of Israel was invaded by a coalition of nations who captured Lot, Abram pursued them in Lot's defense.

Perseverance

וַיִּשְׁמַע אַבְרָם כִּי נִשְׁבָּה אָחִיו וַיָּרֶק אֶת חֲנִיכָיו וְגוֹ': (בראשית יד, יד)

When Abram heard that his kinsman had been taken captive, he armed his attendants.

We would have expected Lot, Abram's kinsman and companion, to become his foremost disciple. Yet Lot eventually rejected both Abram and G-d, and even chose to live in Sodom, the center of immorality and corruption.

Nonetheless, even when Abram had no choice but to send Lot away, he assured him that he would always remain close enough to protect him should the need arise. When it did, Abram did not hesitate to risk his own life to save Lot's.

Abram's perseverance with Lot paid off: Lot maintained some of the praiseworthy practices Abram taught him. For example, Lot insisted on providing hospitality to visitors in Sodom even though it was a capital offense there. Ultimately, Lot became the ancestor of Ruth, King David, and the Messiah.

Following Abram's example, we should realize that our efforts to inspire others, even if they appear to be in vain, will have positive results that we cannot always foresee.[9]

9. *Sefer HaSichot 5750*, vol. 1, pp. 100–102.

FIFTH READING
Genesis 14:21–15:6

Abram was concerned that his miraculous victory over Lot's captors was his full compensation for his accrued merits. G-d therefore reiterated His promise to give Abram the Land of Israel and, with it, material bounty. But Abram replied that all this was useless unless G-d would give him a child who would continue his work of spreading Divine consciousness.

The Purpose of Wealth

וַיֹּאמֶר אַבְרָם ה' אֱלֹקִים מַה תִּתֶּן לִי וְאָנֹכִי הוֹלֵךְ עֲרִירִי וְגו': (בראשית טו, ב)

**Abram said, "G-d, what can You give
me, seeing that I am childless?"**

Abram, who was dedicated to giving to others and teaching them, was not content with a blessing that would merely ensure his personal well-being and good fortune. He sought to perpetuate his spiritual legacy as well.

Similarly, Rabbi Shneur Zalman of Liadi (founder of the Chabad movement) once wanted to bless one of his students with great wealth. But the student refused the blessing, explaining that material wealth would only distract him from pursuing his spiritual studies and refining himself. When the Rebbe then wished to bless him with longevity, he replied: "But not with 'empty' years, in which I will be insensitive to G-dliness."

Thus, we see that while there is nothing wrong with material wealth or aspiring to obtain it, our focus should always be, as was Abram's, on the spiritual ends that material means can serve.[10]

---

10. *Sefer HaSichot 5702*, p. 103; *HaYom Yom*, 6 Marcheshvan.

SIXTH READING
Genesis 15:7–17:6

After promising him offspring, G-d reiterated to Abram His promise of the Land of Israel. Abram requested a sign from G-d that his offspring would inherit the land.

Making the Spiritual Physical

וַיֹּאמַר ה' אֱלֹקִים בַּמָּה אֵדַע כִּי אִירָשֶׁנָּה: (בראשית טו, ח)

**[Abram] said [to G-d], "By what sign
can I know that I will inherit it?"**

It seems incomprehensible that Abram, whose trust in G-d had already been proven many times, would question G-d's promise by asking for a sign. And indeed, this is not really what his question meant. Rather, Abram knew that G-d's blessings do not necessarily manifest themselves in our physical world; they can be equally fulfilled on a spiritual plane. He was therefore concerned that G-d's promise to give the Land of Israel to his offspring might occur only in a spiritual sense, in which case only spiritually attuned people would be able to perceive and appreciate it. Abram therefore insisted on ensuring that the fulfillment of G-d's promise would manifest itself in physical reality.

From Abram's insistence, we learn that the true goal of our efforts toward spiritual growth – praiseworthy as they may be in and of themselves – should be to elevate the physical world, and particularly those who are not yet spiritually attuned.[11]

---

11. *Or HaTorah, Bereishit*, vol. 1, 82a.

SEVENTH READING
Genesis 17:7–27

Despite G-d's promise, Abram and Sarai had not yet had children. Sarai therefore had her Egyptian bondwoman, Hagar, bear a child by Abram. When Hagar quickly conceived, she mocked Sarai, and Abram sent her away. Hagar miscarried, but was told by G-d to return to Sarai. Hagar obeyed and gave birth to Abram's first son, Ishmael. Thirteen years later, G-d told Abram that it was now time for him to have a son with Sarai, and in preparation for this, He was going to change their names to Abraham and Sarah.

Direct and Indirect Influence

לֹא תִקְרָא אֶת שְׁמָהּ שָׂרָי כִּי שָׂרָה שְׁמָהּ: (בראשית יז, טו)

[G-d said,] "She will no longer be called Sarai, for Sarah is [now] her name."

Whereas Abraham's name change proclaimed him to be the "*father* of nations," Sarah's proclaimed her to be a "*sovereign*." Sovereigns remain aloof and detached from their subjects, wielding their influence by virtue of this very aloofness. Parents, by contrast, are personally involved with their children's daily lives.

Abraham influenced people by interacting with them directly, inducing them to keep G-d's laws and behave ethically. Sarah, in contrast, influenced people indirectly, via personal example and by virtue of her awe-inspiring righteousness.

Similarly, in our own lives, although we should always aim to inspire others directly, we should not overlook our own spiritual growth, which will ultimately serve to inspire others indirectly, as well.[12]

12. *Likutei Sichot,* vol. 35, pp. 97–100.

Vayeira

Founder of the Faith

Genesis 18:1–22:24

THE FOURTH SECTION OF THE BOOK OF GENESIS CONTINUES the chronicle of Abraham. The name of this section (*Vayeira*, "He appeared") is its first word, describing G-d's revelation to Abraham after his circumcision. This revelation is followed by the visit of three angels, who inform Abraham of his son Isaac's imminent birth. We then follow Abraham as he argues with G-d over the destruction of Sodom and Gomorrah, migrates to Philistia, banishes Hagar and Ishmael after Isaac is born, and is finally tested by G-d's directive to sacrifice Isaac.

FIRST READING
Genesis 18:1–14

On the third day of Abraham's recovery after his circumcision, G-d appeared to him, paying a visit to the sick.

Earning Divine Revelation

וַיֵּרָא אֵלָיו ה' וגו': (בראשית יח, א)

G-d appeared to [Abraham].

When, as a young boy, Shalom DovBer of Lubavitch (the future fifth Rebbe of the Chabad movement) learned this verse for the first time, he came in tears to his grandfather, Rabbi Menachem Mendel of Lubavitch (the third Rebbe). He cried, "If G-d appeared to Abraham, why doesn't He appear to me, as well?"

Rabbi Menachem Mendel replied: Abraham had indeed refined himself enough to attain a very elevated level of Divine consciousness. However, he knew that G-d is infinite, and that therefore there were still an infinite number of levels of Divine consciousness to attain. This left Abraham feeling woefully inadequate, as though he were still encrusted by layers of insensitivity to Divine awareness that still needed to be removed – to be "circumcised" – in order to sensitize himself to G-d. In recognition of this humble attitude, G-d revealed Himself to Abraham.

From the child's impassioned question and from his grandfather's answer, we learn firstly that we must yearn – even cry out – for G-d to reveal His presence to us. Secondly, we learn that we, too, can merit to see G-d's presence if we realize that no matter how much we may have achieved spiritually, we still need to "circumcise" ourselves – to remove "the foreskin of the heart"[1] – which prevents us from attaining yet higher levels of Divine consciousness.[2]

---

1. See Deuteronomy 10:16.
2. *Likutei Sichot*, vol. 1, pp. 23–27.

SECOND READING
Genesis 18:15–33

The kindness and hospitality practiced by Abraham in Hebron stood in stark contrast to the wickedness and inhospitality of the nearby cities of Sodom, Gomorrah, and their neighbors. When their cruelty reached the point that they had to be eliminated, G-d first informed Abraham. Knowing that Abraham practiced righteousness and justice, He wanted to give him the opportunity to plead on behalf of these cities.

Mercy and Justice

וְשָׁמְרוּ דֶּרֶךְ ה' לַעֲשׂוֹת צְדָקָה וּמִשְׁפָּט וְגוֹ': (בראשית יח, יט)

[G-d said, "I know that Abraham teaches others] to keep G-d's ways by acting with righteousness and justice."

The Name of G-d used in this verse (יהו-ה, *Havayah*) indicates G-d's mercy. Thus, the deeper meaning of "keeping G-d's ways" means ensuring that G-d will sustain the world through His attribute of mercy. This ensures, in turn, that the world will be blessed with an abundance of spiritual and material beneficence.

We "motivate" G-d to bless us to sustain the world through His attribute of mercy by "acting with righteousness" (*tzedakah*), which means showing mercy and generosity toward others.

But besides motivating G-d to treat the world with mercy, we must also motivate Him to employ His attribute of justice. Without justice, mercy would act indiscriminately, sustaining negative forces as well. We awaken G-d's attribute of justice by exercising justice on ourselves, evaluating candidly how much of what G-d has blessed us with we really need for our own sustenance – spiritually and materially – and then sharing the surplus with others.[3]

3. *Torah Or* 63b. See *Likutei Sichot*, vol. 25, p. 84; ibid., vol. 5, p. 148.

THIRD READING
Genesis 19:1–20

Despite Abraham's pleas, the wickedness of Sodom and its neighbors was so great that it could not be overlooked. The angels arrived at Lot's house in order to rescue him from the impending destruction. Hearing that Lot had invited guests into his home, the people of Sodom stormed the house.

Defending Humanity

וְאַנְשֵׁי הָעִיר אַנְשֵׁי סְדֹם נָסַבּוּ עַל הַבַּיִת מִנַּעַר

וְעַד זָקֵן כָּל הָעָם מִקָּצֶה: (בראשית יט, ד)

The men of the city, of Sodom, surrounded [Lot's] house, young and old, all the people from every quarter.

Despite the wickedness of the inhabitants of Sodom, Abraham tried to defend them before G-d. In fact, Abraham was the first person in history to speak up in defense of others.

G-d was very pleased when Abraham spoke up in defense of humanity, for in doing so, he was imitating G-d's own ways. As King David expressed it, "G-d is good to all, and His mercy extends to all His creatures."[4] For this reason, the Midrash teaches us that the world is sustained – and was even created – in the merit of Abraham.[5]

Similarly, by defending other people's behavior, finding mitigating factors and reasons for their misdeeds as Abraham did, we become partners in sustaining the world. Moreover, we thereby sustain our own personal "worlds" – the circles of family, friends, students, and co-workers among whom we live – arousing G-d's mercy on them and on us.[6]

---

4. Psalms 145:9.
5. *Bereishit Rabbah* 12:9.
6. *Sefer HaMa'amarim 5686*, p. 108.

FOURTH READING

Genesis 19:21–21:4

After the overthrow of Sodom and Gomorrah, Abraham moved from Hebron to Philistia. The agents of the Philistine king, Avimelech, asked Abraham if Sarah was his wife or his sister. Seeing that they wanted to take her to the king, Abraham feared for his life and told them that she was his sister. When the truth was discovered, the king accused Abraham of lying. Abraham replied that since Sarah was his niece, she technically was a sort of "sister" of his, and that he had to call her his "sister" in order to save his own life.

The Foundation of Civilization

וַיֹּאמֶר אַבְרָהָם כִּי אָמַרְתִּי רַק אֵין יִרְאַת אֱלֹקִים בַּמָּקוֹם
הַזֶּה וַהֲרָגוּנִי עַל דְּבַר אִשְׁתִּי: (בראשית כ, יא)

**Abraham said, "Because there is simply no fear of G-d
in this place, they will kill me on account of my wife."**

In this statement, Abraham voiced the two principles underlying his life's work: The first was that making the world into a home for G-d means, above all, encouraging virtue and the practice of justice. The second was that it is impossible to encourage virtue and the practice of justice unless they are based on the belief in G-d as the creator and master of the world. History has proven Abraham right: We have unfortunately seen all too many failed attempts to base morality on any other foundation.

Belief in G-d must therefore be the underlying foundation both of our own morals and ethics as well as of the education of our children. Only when we and our children know that G-d created the world and wants it to be made into His home through righteous and just behavior can we be assured that both we and our children will behave virtuously and justly.[7]

---

7. *Hitva'aduyot 5743*, vol. 2, pp. 899–900.

FIFTH READING
Genesis 21:5–21

When Abraham was 100 years old and his wife Sarah was 90, Sarah gave birth to their son Isaac.

Ignoring the Scoffers

וַתֹּאמֶר שָׂרָה צְחֹק עָשָׂה לִי אֱלֹקִים כָּל הַשֹּׁמֵעַ יִצֲחַק לִי: (בראשית כא, ו)

Sarah said, "G-d has brought me happiness. Whoever hears will be happy *for* me and happy *with* me."

The literal meaning of Sarah's words is "whoever hears will laugh *at* me," for it is unbelievable that a man of 100 and a woman of 90 could have a child.

This is exactly how our people's detractors have scoffed at us throughout the ages. "It is ridiculous to think that your young people will continue to abide by your old-fashioned, outdated values and practices. How can you be so old (-fashioned) and hope to have a child (that is, someone who will perpetuate *your* life-style)? Do you really think your children will lay down their lives rather than engage in idolatry, as Abraham did? Or that they will remain true to their beliefs even in an immoral environment, as Sarah did in Egypt?"

Yet, history has proven that if we dedicate ourselves to educating our youth uncompromisingly, as Abraham and Sarah educated Isaac, we too will be able to raise offspring selflessly dedicated to our ideals.

Furthermore, by furthering Abraham and Sarah's goal of spreading Divine consciousness, we can even change those who laughed "at" us to friends who laugh "for" us and "with" us.[8]

---

8. *Sichot Kodesh 5731*, pp. 462 ff.

SIXTH READING
Genesis 21:22–34

After the birth of Isaac, Abraham concluded a treaty with the local Philistine king and opened an inn in Beersheba, where he taught wayfarers about monotheism.

Being a Positive Influence

וַיִּקְרָא שָׁם בְּשֵׁם ה' אֵל עוֹלָם: (בראשית כא, לג)

**There, [Abraham] induced others to
proclaim the name of G-d.**

Abraham at first tried to teach his guests about G-d through explanations and parables, but some of them remained unimpressed by his words. With these doubters, Abraham resorted to a bolder approach, designed to break down their spiritual wall of resistance. All people believe in G-d on some level, yet some are so spiritually detached that they are in need of added encouragement to awaken their dormant knowledge of G-d.[9]

From Abraham's example, we can learn to motivate others to ascend to a heightened level of spiritual connection, even when doing so requires the occasional use of added encouragement. For example, some might argue: "Why approach someone with the suggestion to put on *tefillin* or light Shabbat candles when they may agree only because someone else prompted them to do so? Is the fulfillment of a commandment in this way of any value?"

The answer to this is that fulfilling a Divine commandment, even at the encouragement of others, is a great achievement in and of itself, and can awaken the individual's latent desire to fulfill the commandment. Since "one good deed leads to another,"[10] that person will very likely eventually come to observe more and more commandments, joyfully and on his own initiative.[11]

---

9. See on Numbers 14:40.
10. *Avot* 4:2.
11. *Likutei Sichot*, vol. 15, pp. 122–128.

SEVENTH READING
Genesis 22:1–22:24

Abraham's greatest challenge came 37 years after his son Isaac was born. G-d commanded him to sacrifice Isaac.

Tests

וַיְהִי אַחַר הַדְּבָרִים הָאֵלֶּה וְהָאֱלֹקִים נִסָּה אֶת אַבְרָהָם: (בראשית כב, א)

After these words, G-d tested Abraham.

G-d tests us in order to bring our deepest, most essential spiritual powers to the fore.

In fact, life itself – the very descent of the soul into this world – is such a test. Before descending into this world, our soul has no need to *yearn* for G-d, since it is constantly basking in the revelation of G-d's presence. Once our soul has been encased in a physical body, however, it is challenged by a materialistic world that is by nature antagonistic to spirituality. In order to remain faithful to G-d despite our daily trials and tribulations, we must summon our innate, intense longing for our lost Divine consciousness, and access our deepest, innermost spiritual strengths.

By virtue of our newfound, passionate dedication to G-d, we forge a far more profound relationship with G-d than our soul experienced before its descent into our body.[12]

12. *Sefer HaMa'amarim 5700*, p. 37.

Chayei Sarah

The Burial of Sarah and the Marriage of Isaac and Rebecca

Genesis 23:1–25:18

THE NAME OF THE FIFTH SECTION OF THE BOOK OF GENESIS is taken from its first words, "The Life of Sarah" (*Chayei Sarah*, in Hebrew), and begins with Sarah's death and burial. We then follow Abraham's servant, Eliezer, as he betroths Abraham's grandniece Rebecca to Abraham's son Isaac. This account is followed by that of Isaac and Rebecca's marriage and the closing phases of Abraham's life: his remarriage to Hagar, his death, and his son Ishmael's departure from Abraham's family and its Divine mission.

FIRST READING
Genesis 23:1–16

When the news reached Sarah that Isaac was almost sacrificed, the shock of his near loss, coupled with the relief of his life being spared, was too much for her to bear, and she died.

Integrating the Divine

וַתָּמָת שָׂרָה בְּקִרְיַת אַרְבַּע הִוא חֶבְרוֹן וְגוֹ׳: (בראשית כג, ב)

Sarah died in Kiryat Arba, which is Hebron.

Both Abraham and Sarah knew that sacrificing Isaac would threaten the success of their Divine mission. Even if they were to train a disciple to carry on their work after their death, such a disciple would not compare to their son Isaac, who carried their idealism and devotion in his very blood and bones. Yet, whereas Abraham was willing to sacrifice his son, Sarah could not even bear to *hear* about such a possibility.

This is because Abraham was sufficiently detached from the physical world to imagine his and Sarah's Divine mission being fulfilled on a purely spiritual plane. Sarah, in contrast, was so focused on integrating Divine spirituality into the physical world that such a prospect was unimaginable.

The events immediately following Sarah's death vindicated her approach. First, Abraham purchased the Machpeilah Cave in order to bury her. This began the process of transforming the physical Land of Israel into the setting where G-d's chosen people would become a light to all nations. After this, Abraham arranged Isaac's marriage to Rebecca, thereby ensuring the continuity of his and Sarah's mission through their physical progeny.

Thus, we can learn from Sarah the primacy of integrating Divinity into our physical world, rather than being satisfied with spiritual growth alone.[1]

---

1. *Sefer HaSichot 5748*, vol. 1, pp. 85–87, and note 45 ad loc.

SECOND READING
Genesis 23:17–24:9

In order to bury Sarah, Abraham purchased the Machpeilah Cave and the surrounding field in Hebron from the local Hittites for a family burial ground. He did not protest the inflated price that Ephron the Hittite requested of him.

Elevating the Mundane

וַיָּקָם שְׂדֵה עֶפְרוֹן אֲשֶׁר בַּמַּכְפֵּלָה וגו' וְהַמְּעָרָה אֲשֶׁר
בּוֹ וגו' לְאַבְרָהָם לְמִקְנָה וגו': (בראשית כג, יז-יח)

Ephron's field of Machpeilah . . . and the cave in it . . . was confirmed as Abraham's purchase.

The Hebrew word for "was confirmed" literally means "arose." This teaches us that just as the Machpeilah Cave rose from mundane to holy status when Abraham purchased it, so do we elevate physical objects when we use them for a holy purpose. In fact, our mere *intention* of using an object for spiritual purposes uplifts it – even *before* we use it – just as the Machpeilah field was lifted out of its former mundane status even before Abraham buried Sarah there.[2]

Just as Abraham was not fazed by the highly inflated price he paid for the Machpeilah Cave, we too should not be deterred by apparently excessive expenditures of either money or effort when fulfilling our mandate to elevate the physical world. We should never underestimate the potential positive impact of our actions.[3]

Furthermore, just as Abraham purchased the Machpeilah Cave permanently, establishing it as Jewish property for all time, we too should realize that when we elevate our personal portion of the world, we do so permanently and absolutely.[4]

2. *Hitva'aduyot 5746*, vol. 1, pp. 582–583; *Likutei Sichot*, vol. 35, p. 87.
3. *Sichot Kodesh 5733*, vol. 1, pp. 128–132.
4. *Likutei Sichot*, vol. 35, pp. 84–86.

THIRD READING
Genesis 24:10–26

After burying Sarah, Abraham sent his servant Eliezer to his family's household in Aram to select a suitable wife for his son Isaac. Abraham sent a sizeable gift along with Eliezer, as well as a document showing that he was transferring all his wealth to Isaac. All this was in order to impress the girl that Eliezer would ultimately choose, together with her family, with the fact that Abraham had designated Isaac as his exclusive heir, as well as to induce the girl's family to allow her to return with him to the Land of Israel and marry Isaac.

The Extent of Parenthood

וַיִּקַּח הָעֶבֶד עֲשָׂרָה גְמַלִּים מִגְּמַלֵּי אֲדֹנָיו וַיֵּלֶךְ
וְכָל טוּב אֲדֹנָיו בְּיָדוֹ וְגוֹ': (בראשית כד, י)

The servant took ten of his master's camels and set out, with all his master's wealth in his hand.

Although Isaac was already 40 years old at the time, Abraham nevertheless went unhesitatingly to all extremes for his son's benefit, for he knew that his role and responsibility as a parent never ends.

Indeed, there is no age limit to the parent-child bond. The unique, spiritual connection between parents and children enables fathers and mothers to remain positive forces in their children's lives forever.

Of course, part of our job as parents is to teach our children to take responsibility for their own lives. But even then, as parents, we remain obligated to be involved, guiding and helping them in their journey through life.[5]

---

5. *Sichot Kodesh 5730*, vol. 1, pp. 209–210.

FOURTH READING
Genesis 24:27–52

Eliezer prayed that G-d guide him toward Isaac's proper match by having her respond generously to his request that she provide water for him and his entourage. And indeed, Abraham's grandniece Rebecca gave water to Eliezer and his caravan. After having betrothed Rebecca to Isaac, Eliezer met Rebecca's family and told them about the miraculous details of his trip and his mission.

Exploring the Torah's Depths

וַיֹּאמַר עֶבֶד אַבְרָהָם אָנֹכִי: (בראשית כד, לד)

[Eliezer began his speech,] saying, "I am Abraham's servant."

The Torah is generally quite terse, even when conveying its most crucial laws. We must study the text very closely even just to understand it properly, and all the more so if we want to uncover its underlying, infinite levels of meaning.

Yet the Torah is strikingly detailed in narrating Eliezer's mission, first relating the episode at length and then recounting Eliezer's repetition of the events to Rebecca's family.[6]

This is so because the Torah wishes to impress us with Eliezer's selfless commitment and devotion in carrying out his master Abraham's mission, even identifying himself not by name but simply as Abraham's servant. Eliezer's example of selflessness is meant to be the foundation of our own spiritual lives.

This selflessness enables us to approach the Torah unencumbered by preconceived notions and biases, and even allows us to rise above the finite nature of our human intellect. Thus, selflessness is the prerequisite to grasping the infinite meanings latent in all the Torah's laws.[7]

6. See Rashi on Genesis 24:42.
7. *Likutei Sichot*, vol. 1, p. 37.

FIFTH READING
Genesis 24:53–67

Eliezer set out with Rebecca back to Canaan to meet Isaac. They happened upon Isaac in the late afternoon, as he was praying.

Transforming the Field

וַיֵּצֵא יִצְחָק לָשׂוּחַ בַּשָּׂדֶה לִפְנוֹת עָרֶב וגו': (בראשית כד, סג)

Isaac went out to pray in the field toward evening.

We recite the morning prayer before beginning our workday and the evening prayer after completing our day's activities. In contrast, the afternoon prayer requires us to stop in the midst of our mundane affairs and focus on G-d.

Our daily, mundane affairs are symbolized by "the field," the area outside the city limits, which is untamed and uncultivated. Through praying in the afternoon, Isaac transformed "the field" into a place of prayer to G-d.

The morning prayer undeniably serves as our principal daily renewal of Divine consciousness. Nonetheless, afterward, it remains to be seen how we will fare when we go out into "the field." Will the secular and material influences of "the field" cause us to lose the spiritual awareness and closeness to G-d that we achieved during the morning prayer? By pausing in the middle of our mundane affairs in order to recite the afternoon prayer, we demonstrate that our involvement in material affairs does not separate us from G-d.[8]

---

8. *Sichot Kodesh 5715*, p. 260. *HaYom Yom*, 22 Adar I; *Igrot Kodesh*, vol. 4, pp. 182–183.

SIXTH READING
Genesis 25:1–11

Hagar adopted monotheism when she first became Sarah's bond-woman, but after she and her son Ishmael were banished from Abraham's household, she lapsed back into her former practice of idolatry. Shortly after Sarah's death and Isaac's marriage to Rebecca, Abraham remarried Hagar (who had by then perma-nently renounced idolatry), eventually having six additional sons through her.

G-d's Pleasure in Our Return

וַיֹּסֶף אַבְרָהָם וַיִּקַּח אִשָּׁה וּשְׁמָהּ קְטוּרָה: (בראשית כה, א)

**Abraham remarried [Hagar, the] woman
who was [now also] named Keturah.**

Hagar was renamed *Keturah* (which means "incense") because, having permanently renounced idolatry, her deeds were now as pleasing to G-d as incense.[9]

One of the ingredients of the incense that was offered up in the holy Temple was musk, which was derived from the blood of a non-kosher animal.[10] This demonstrates the incense's unique capability to elevate even entities on the lowest rung of spirituality to the heights of holiness. Hagar/Keturah is therefore compared to the incense, because her return to Abraham and the path of truth after having lapsed into idolatry mirrors this unique char-acteristic of the Temple's incense.

From this we learn how great is the pleasure we can give G-d by returning to Him after any lapse in our own behavior.[11]

9. Rashi on this verse.
10. *Mishneh Torah, Kelei HaMikdash* 1:3.
11. *Likutei Sichot*, vol. 15, pp. 174–179.

SEVENTH READING
Genesis 25:12–18

Abraham died when he was 175 years old. After chronicling Abraham's death, the Torah lists the descendants of Ishmael before continuing with the chronicle of Isaac in the next section.

Proper Roles

עַל פְּנֵי כָל אֶחָיו נָפָל: (בראשית כה, יח)

[Ishmael] dwelt in the company of all his descendants.

This statement echoes G-d's earlier promise to Abraham that Ishmael would "dwell in the company of all his descendants,"[12] but with one significant difference. The literal translation of the word for "he dwelt" used here (*nafal*) is "he fell." The Torah thus informs us that as long as Abraham was alive, Ishmael "dwelt" securely in his father's merit, but once Abraham died, Ishmael "fell" and began to be harassed by his enemies.[13]

On a deeper level, this statement teaches us that Ishmael's well-being depends upon his recognition of his status as Abraham's son. As long as the spirit of Abraham lives within him and he acknowledges Abraham's designation of Isaac as his successor, he is capable of "dwelling" securely and prosperously. As soon as Abraham perishes in Ishmael's mind and he ignores his identity, he "falls" into danger and affliction.

We see here that honoring our Jewish role as Abraham's rightful heirs, G-d's chosen people, is not only not detrimental to other nations, but on the contrary, it is the ultimate way to bring maximum benefit to them.[14]

---

12. Genesis 16:12.
13. Rashi on this verse.
14. *Likutei Sichot*, vol. 15, pp. 152–154.

Toledot

Isaac, Jacob, and Esau

Genesis 25:19–28:9

THE SIXTH SECTION OF THE BOOK OF GENESIS DESCRIBES
the history (*Toledot*, in Hebrew) of Isaac and his twin sons, the
righteous Jacob and wicked Esau. It first chronicles their birth,
which foretells their future conflict. Esau, the firstborn, sells his
birthright to Jacob. The narrative then follows Isaac to Philistia,
focusing on his curious project of digging wells. We then see Esau
marry. Shortly afterward, Rebecca tricks Isaac into conferring his
blessings – and thus the future leadership of the Jewish people –
to Jacob rather than to their actual firstborn, Esau. After realizing
that Rebecca was correct, Isaac sends Jacob to Aram to marry a
daughter of one of his kinsmen.

FIRST READING

Genesis 25:19–26:5

After 20 years of marriage, Isaac and Rebecca had twin sons, Esau and Jacob. Esau was drawn toward sensual thrills while Jacob was drawn toward absorbing the wisdom and traditions transmitted by Abraham and Isaac. Although Esau was the firstborn, Jacob understood that he would be the more faithful steward of the family's ideals, so he offered Esau to trade the right of leadership for a hot meal, to which Esau readily agreed.

How to Discipline

וְאֵלֶּה תּוֹלְדֹת יִצְחָק בֶּן אַבְרָהָם אַבְרָהָם הוֹלִיד אֶת יִצְחָק: (בראשית כה, יט)

**These are the chronicles of Isaac son of
Abraham; Abraham was the father of Isaac.**

In Kabbalah, Abraham was the embodiment of kindness (*chesed*), while Isaac embodied severity (*gevurah*). The wording of this verse alludes to an important lesson both in educating young children as well as in how we are to conduct our personal interactions. The second mention of Abraham's name in this verse occurs immediately after the first, whereas the two mentions of Isaac's name in this verse are separated by several words. This teaches us that although it may occasionally be necessary to employ disciplinary measures, we should never do so twice in succession. There must always be an interval of kindness between every two such occasions.

In fact, Isaac's name never appears twice in succession throughout the entire Torah, in contrast to the names of Abraham (signifying kindness) and Jacob (signifying *tiferet*, "harmony"), which do.[1]

---

1. Abraham: this verse and Genesis 22:11; Jacob: Genesis 46:2. *Likutei Levi Yitzchak* on *Zohar* 1:11 ff.

SECOND READING

Genesis 26:6–12

The Land of Israel was plagued by famine, so Isaac relocated his family to Philistia, which was located within the borders of the Land of Israel.

Inside Out and Outside In

וַיֵּשֶׁב יִצְחָק בִּגְרָר: (בראשית כו, ו)

Isaac settled in Gerar.

Isaac assumed that the famine was meant to induce him to journey outside the Land of Israel in order to disseminate Divine teachings there just as his father Abraham had.[2] But G-d told Isaac not to leave the land, thereby affirming that his particular mode of bringing Divine awareness to the world differed from Abraham's. Abraham travelled to his audiences, tailoring his message to his listeners' ability to grasp it. Isaac, in contrast, was to focus on intensifying his own Divine consciousness and the Divine consciousness of his immediate surroundings. The force, clarity, and vigor of Isaac's spirituality would give him a magnetic charisma that would draw the outside world to him and make them aspire to learn from him.

Abraham personifies those who sanctify the world from within it; Isaac personifies those who sanctify the world from "outside" it, ensconced within synagogues and centers of Torah study. Since we are all descendants of both Abraham and Isaac, each of us must embody both their approaches. Full-time students of the Torah must take time off from their studies to teach and help others, whereas those who are engaged in the material world must take time off from their jobs and other pursuits to study the Torah.[3]

2. Genesis 12:10.
3. *Likutei Sichot,* vol. 25, pp. 124–130.

TUESDAY

THIRD READING
Genesis 26:13–22

Isaac began his life project: digging wells to provide sources of water for new towns and villages. He began by uncovering his father Abraham's wells, which the Philistines had blocked up.

Unstoppable Wells

וַיְסַתְּמוּם פְּלִשְׁתִּים אַחֲרֵי מוֹת אַבְרָהָם: (בראשית כו, יח)

**[Isaac redug the wells] that the Philistines
had blocked up after Abraham's death.**

Allegorically, the Philistines represent uncontrolled materialism, and the wells that Abraham and Isaac dug represent our inner wellsprings of goodness. Abraham was not really a "well digger": although he did inspire others, this inspiration was not enough to uncover their inner wellsprings of goodness, which would have improved their character permanently. Therefore, the Philistines were able to block up Abraham's wells.

In contrast, Isaac's holy charisma forced people to confront their psychological obstacles to living a Divine life. He changed them by making them uncover their own hidden goodness. Therefore, the Philistines could not block up his wells.

Similarly, by praying and meditating, we clear away the mental "dirt" that has blocked up our wellsprings of inspiration. But if we revel in our inspiration rather than focusing on correcting a particular character flaw, our wellsprings can become blocked again by our ingrained obsession for material satisfaction, once we re-enter the world of our mundane affairs.

In contrast, when we focus on improving a specific character trait while praying, we change ourselves, enabling us to retain our inspiration.[4]

4. *Sefer HaMa'amarim 5698*, pp. 147–153; *Likutei Sichot*, vol. 15, p. 194. See *Torah Or* 17a–c; *Likutei Sichot*, vol. 1, pp. 27–29.

FOURTH READING
Genesis 26:23–29

Isaac settled in Beersheba, where he continued to dig wells.

The Merit of the Patriarchs

וַיִּכְרוּ שָׁם עַבְדֵי יִצְחָק בְּאֵר: (בראשית כו, כה)

Isaac's servants dug a well there.

There are three recommended steps we can take to prepare ourselves spiritually for prayer:

- Giving charity[5] inspires G-d to act charitably toward us and to answer our prayers.
- Immersing ourselves in a natural body of water or *mikveh*[6] purifies us from the spiritual defilement of negativity. This frees us to feel the joy that should accompany our prayers.
- Studying the inspirational teachings of the Torah puts us in the mood to commune with G-d.[7]

These three types of preparation are derived from the parallel characteristic behavior of each of the patriarchs:

- Charity is alluded to by Abraham's deeds of kindness.[8]
- Immersion in water is alluded to by Isaac's efforts in digging wells.
- Inspirational Torah study is alluded to by Jacob's devotion to the study of the Torah.[9]

Thus, by following the above-mentioned three types of preparation for prayer, we connect with the patriarchs and elicit their merit to aid us in our meditations.[10]

5. *Bava Batra* 10a.
6. See Leviticus 15:18.
7. *Likutei Torah* 4:43b-c.
8. *Megaleh Amukot* 250; see Genesis 18:19.
9. Genesis 25:27.
10. *Reshimot* 20.

FIFTH READING
Genesis 26:30–27:27

When Esau turned 40, he married two pagan Canaanite women. The smoke from their idolatrous incense offerings gradually caused his righteous father, Isaac, to go blind. Isaac's blindness enabled Rebecca to maneuver him into passing the mantle of leadership to Jacob rather than Esau.

Speaking Positively

וַיְהִי כִּי זָקֵן יִצְחָק וַתִּכְהֶיןָ עֵינָיו מֵרְאֹת וְגוֹ': (בראשית כז, א)

When Isaac was old, his eyesight went dim.

Instead of waiting for Isaac to become blind so that Rebecca could maneuver him into blessing Jacob instead of Esau, G-d could have simply revealed Esau's wickedness and unworthiness to Isaac. G-d would not have been divulging anything to Isaac that he did not already suspect. Isaac already knew that Esau's wives were idolaters and that he paid G-d so little notice that he hardly ever mentioned Him.[11] Yet G-d was reluctant to speak ill of Esau.

Similarly, many years later, G-d refused to divulge to Joshua the identity of the person who had stolen some of the spoils that had been dedicated to G-d after the conquest of Jericho. This lone individual's embezzlement had caused G-d's protection to be removed from the entire Jewish army, exposing them to defeat. Yet when Joshua asked G-d to name the culprit, He responded, "Am I to be a talebearer to you?"[12]

All this teaches us an important lesson: If G-d Himself avoided speaking negatively about these wicked people, how much more must we take extreme care not to speak negatively of others, even if they are not of sterling character.[13]

---

11. See Genesis 27:21, and Nachmanides and commentaries on Rashi ad loc.
12. Joshua 7; *Sanhedrin* 11a.
13. *Likutei Sichot*, vol. 15, pp. 215–216.

SIXTH READING
Genesis 27:28–28:4

Rebecca disguised Jacob as Esau, having him impersonate Esau before Isaac in order to receive Isaac's blessings. Believing that Esau was in front of him, Isaac blessed Jacob.

The Full Reward is Yet to Come

וְיִתֶּן לְךָ הָאֱלֹקִים מִטַּל הַשָּׁמַיִם וּמִשְׁמַנֵּי הָאָרֶץ
וְרֹב דָּגָן וְתִירֹשׁ: (בראשית כז, כח)

[Isaac blessed Jacob,] "May G-d grant you of the dew of heaven and the fat of the land, and an abundance of grain and wine."

There are both spiritual and material rewards for fulfilling G-d's commandments. The spiritual rewards are the sublime levels of Divine consciousness that we would not be able to attain on our own. The physical rewards are the various aspects of our material prosperity.

Until the world is refined sufficiently to enable us to experience our full spiritual reward, all we can receive is a glimmer of inspiration. And since the spiritual and material facets of reality are intertwined, our full material reward is also being delayed; in the meantime, all we can receive is an occasional trickle of it.

When the Messiah comes, however, the physicality of the world will be totally refined, and we will receive both our full spiritual and material rewards for having fulfilled G-d's commandments.[14]

14. *Likutei Sichot*, vol. 1, pp. 58–59.

SEVENTH READING
Genesis 28:5–9

After Esau returned, Isaac realized what had happened, but acknowledged that Jacob deserved the blessings more than Esau. Esau, in contrast, resolved to murder Jacob as soon as Isaac would die. Rebecca therefore convinced Isaac to send Jacob away to Rebecca's brother Laban in Aram, in order to find a wife.

Hidden Purposes

וַיִּשְׁלַח יִצְחָק אֶת יַעֲקֹב ... אֶל לָבָן בֶּן בְּתוּאֵל הָאֲרַמִּי: (בראשית כח, ה)

Isaac sent forth Jacob . . . to Laban
son of Bethuel the Aramean.

Jacob had to shepherd Laban's flocks for 14 years in order to get him to agree to let Jacob marry Laban's daughters. During these years, Laban oppressed Jacob cruelly, and when Jacob eventually fled Laban's house to return home, Laban viciously pursued him.

On the spiritual plane, Jacob was liberating the sparks of holiness that were trapped within Laban's possessions by working for him. And subconsciously, when Laban pursued Jacob, he did so in order to present Jacob with the sparks of holiness that Jacob had failed to liberate on his own![15]

This reflects the truth that all challenges to fulfilling our Divine mission are purposeful and designed to aid us. Once we realize this, we awaken within the apparent obstacle its latent awareness of its Divine purpose, enabling it to aid us in our task of transforming the world into G-d's home.[16]

15. *Or HaTorah, Bereishit*, vol. 5, p. 869a (quoted in *Maggid Devarav LeYa'akov* [ed. Kehot], addendum 7), based on *Or HaMei'ir, Vayeitzei*, s.v. *Vayirdof Acharav*; *Sefer HaMa'amarim 5663*, vol. 1, p. 76.
16. *Likutei Sichot*, vol. 1, p. 80.

Vayeitzei

Jacob in Aram
Genesis 28:10–32:3

THE SEVENTH SECTION OF THE BOOK OF GENESIS BEGINS THE
chronicle of the third and final patriarch, Jacob. It opens as he
leaves (*Vayeitzei*, "he left," in Hebrew) the Land of Israel to find
a wife from among his kinsmen in Aram. He in fact marries
four wives there and fathers a large family, as well as amassing a
considerable fortune with Divine help. After 20 years, he secretly
flees Aram, fearful that his possessive father-in-law, Laban, will
try to prevent him from leaving. But after Laban overtakes him,
they make peace.

FIRST READING
Genesis 28:10–22

Jacob left Beersheba and set out for the city of Charan, in Aram. On the way, Jacob spent the night on Mount Moriah (known today as the Temple Mount in Jerusalem), and in his dream saw a vision of angels ascending and descending a ladder to heaven. When he awoke, realizing the intrinsic holiness of this site, he vowed to consecrate this place as the site of the future Temple.

Living Dangerously

וַיֵּצֵא יַעֲקֹב מִבְּאֵר שָׁבַע וַיֵּלֶךְ חָרָנָה: (בראשית כח, י)

Jacob left Beersheba and set out for Charan.

Jacob left the holy environment of the Land of Israel, descending to the less-than-holy environment of Charan, knowing that he would have to survive the schemes of his future father-in-law, Laban, who was well-known as a deceiver. Yet Jacob faced this challenge and passed his tests heroically.

Jacob's precedent endows us with the spiritual strength to face similar moral and ethical challenges in our daily lives. Our homes should indeed be havens from the materialistic world, permeated with the Torah's wholesome and holy values. However, once we have established such a home, we need not be afraid to venture into the outside world – our personal Charan – in order to refine and elevate reality.

Furthermore, just as Jacob's descent to Charan actually propelled him to great spiritual heights, the same holds true for us: our temporary forays into the non-spiritual milieu of the material world with the aim of elevating it will not only not harm us, but will prove beneficial to our spiritual growth, as well.[1]

1. *Likutei Sichot*, vol. 1, pp. 60–61, vol. 3; ibid., pp. 788–789; *Sefer HaSichot 5752*, vol. 1, p. 139.

SECOND READING

Genesis 29:1–17

Jacob arrived at the well where the local shepherds gathered each day to water their flocks. Because the boulder covering the well was so heavy, the shepherds had to remove it together. But when Jacob's cousin Rachel arrived, shepherding her father Laban's flocks, Jacob removed the boulder by himself.

Uniting Opposites

וְגָלֲלוּ אֶת הָאֶבֶן מֵעַל פִּי הַבְּאֵר וגו': (בראשית כט, ג)

[The shepherds] would together roll the boulder off the opening of the well.

The well represents our inner wellsprings of holiness, the boulder represents the materialism that often blocks these wellsprings, and the "shepherds" are our love and our fear of G-d.

But just as one shepherd alone could not remove the boulder, we cannot unblock our wellspring with only love or only fear of G-d. This is because both love and fear of G-d can easily slip into unhealthy forms if we are not careful. An example of unhealthy love is the love of material indulgence; an example of unhealthy fear is acting harshly toward others.

If, however, we both love *and* fear G-d, our fear of G-d can prevent us from falling into negative forms of love, and our love of G-d can protect us from falling into negative forms of fear.

This is why the "shepherds" were able to remove the "boulder" from the "well" only when working together. Jacob, however, was able to remove the boulder by himself, because he embodied both love and fear of G-d.[2]

2. *Likutei Torah* 4:5a–b; *Ma'amarei Admor HaZakein 5573*, pp. 3–4; *Sefer HaMa'amarim 5628*, pp. 29–34.

THIRD READING
Genesis 29:18–30:13

Rachel introduced Jacob to Laban, who put him in charge of his flocks. Jacob married Laban's two daughters, Leah and Rachel. Leah gave birth to four sons in succession, while Rachel remained childless. Rachel had her bondwoman (and half-sister), Bilhah, marry her husband, hoping that in this merit she would also be blessed with children. After Bilhah had two sons, Leah – who had stopped bearing children by then – had her bondwoman (and half-sister), Zilpah, marry Jacob, with the same hope. Zilpah also had two sons.

The Blessing of Children

וַתַּהַר עוֹד וַתֵּלֶד בֵּן וְגו': (בראשית כט, לג)

[Leah] again conceived and had a son.

Even after Leah had already been blessed with children, she still considered each subsequent child an additional blessing.

The Torah teaches us that our ability to love expands according to the number of our children, as do the Divine blessings of sustenance and livelihood. Thus, the more children we have, the more attention and material benefits we can give to each.

The story of Leah is one of the numerous places in the Torah that emphasize the beauty and blessing inherent in the birth of each additional child. Each child is a unique reflection of G-d's image, and has his or her unique contribution to make both to our lives and to our Divine mission.[3]

3. *Sichot Kodesh 5740*, vol. 3, p. 282.

FOURTH READING

Genesis 30:14–27

Knowing that his mother, Leah, was trying to restore her fertility, Reuben gathered for her some mandrakes, which were considered to promote fertility. G-d indeed restored Leah's fertility, and she had two more sons and a daughter. Rachel then finally conceived and bore her first son, whom she named Joseph.

It's Never Too Early to Educate

וַיֵּלֶךְ רְאוּבֵן בִּימֵי קְצִיר חִטִּים וַיִּמְצָא דוּדָאִים בַּשָּׂדֶה וגו': (בראשית ל, יד)

Reuben was taking a walk during the season of the wheat harvest and found mandrakes in the field.

In the harvest season, cut grain is lying unsupervised in the fields and people can easily get away with taking some for themselves. Yet Reuben gathered only ownerless, wild mandrakes. He knew that it was not right to take wheat that did not belong to him.[4]

Reuben was a mere child in this episode, no more than five years old. Yet he possessed the moral fiber to go against the immoral practices of his society. This demonstrates the quality of training that Jacob and his wives gave their children. Even as children, unable to fully comprehend the precepts of the Torah, they knew to follow the example of Jacob, who was scrupulously honest in all his dealings.

Similarly, we should never think that our children are too young or unsophisticated to notice our behavior or to be taught to be ethical. Rather, we can and should begin their moral education from the youngest age.[5]

4. Rashi on this verse.
5. *Likutei Sichot*, vol. 3, p. 793.

FIFTH READING
Genesis 30:28–31:16

Jacob earned his livelihood primarily by tending sheep. He later used his surplus of sheep to buy bondwomen, bondmen, camels, and donkeys.

Insuring Our Primary Asset

וַיִּפְרֹץ הָאִישׁ מְאֹד מְאֹד וַיְהִי לוֹ צֹאן רַבּוֹת וגו': (בראשית ל, מג)

**[Jacob] became exceedingly prosperous.
He owned prolific flocks.**

Jacob worked primarily with sheep because sheep submit humbly to the direction of their shepherd. They are therefore a metaphor for the humble submission to G-d's will that we must cultivate in order to keep our spiritual bearings during our "sojourn with Laban," that is, when we are involved in the mundane world.

Nonetheless, selflessness alone is not enough to fulfill our Divine mission; we must also employ the more advanced aspects of our personality. These are alluded to by the "bondwomen, bondmen, camels, and donkeys" that Jacob later bought.[6]

Making use of these other aspects of ourselves involves acting with self-awareness and self-assertion. But cultivating self-assertion could undermine the self-negation that we need in order to succeed in our encounter with "Laban." Jacob therefore "purchased" each of these aspects with "sheep," meaning that his use of these aspects was based on and infused with the selflessness characteristic of sheep.

This is also why Jacob continued to maintain sheep as his primary asset, and likewise, we should value our sheep-attitude as our basic approach to life, so that our actions will always be permeated with selflessness.[7]

---

6. See *Torah Or* 24c; *Torat Chaim, Bereishit* 185d.
7. *Likutei Sichot*, vol. 15, pp. 252–257.

SIXTH READING
Genesis 31:17–42

Jacob fled Aram with his family and flock in secret, fearful that his possessive father-in-law would try to prevent him from leaving. Laban indeed pursued him, and when he overtook him, he accused Jacob of spiriting his daughters and grandchildren away before he could say goodbye properly. Jacob countered that based on Laban's previous mistreatment of him and his family – despite the fact that Jacob had worked for Laban beyond the call of duty – he was afraid that Laban would force his daughters to remain in Charan.

Enduring Pain for the Right Reasons

הָיִיתִי בַיּוֹם אֲכָלַנִי חֹרֶב וְקֶרַח בַּלָּיְלָה וַתִּדַּד שְׁנָתִי מֵעֵינָי: (בראשית לא, מ)

[Jacob told Laban,] "This is how I existed: I was consumed by day by scorching heat and at night by frost, and sleep deserted my eyes."

In general, we have no right to afflict our bodies or injure them, since in essence they belong to G-d.[8] Nevertheless, we learn from Jacob's behavior that if it is necessary in order to earn a living, we are permitted to engage in work that might tax or even afflict our bodies.[9]

Spiritually, this means that Jacob sacrificed his own comfort in order to redeem the sparks of holiness embedded in Laban's domain. Like Jacob, we should not hesitate to engage in our Divine mission even if doing so means that we might have to forego some form of personal comfort.[10]

8. Commentary of Rabbi David ben Zimra on *Mishneh Torah, Sanhedrin* 18:7.
9. *Shulchan Aruch HaRav, Choshen Mishpat, Nizkei Guf* 4; *Kuntres Acharon* (ad loc.) 2.
10. *Likutei Sichot*, vol. 1, pp. 77–78.

SEVENTH READING
Genesis 31:43–32:3

When Jacob rebuked Laban for mistreating him and his family, Laban relented, although he denied the very notion that he would harm his own grandchildren. Jacob and Laban then made a pact, and Jacob erected a stone mound as a monument to their agreement to pass it only to do business, not for hostile purposes.

Modernity in Perspective

הַבָּנוֹת בְּנֹתַי וְהַבָּנִים בָּנַי וְהַצֹּאן צֹאנִי וגו': (בראשית לא, מג)

[Laban said to Jacob,] "The children are my children and the flocks are my flocks."

Allegorically, Laban is the perennial voice within us and without us that seeks to oppose spiritual life. "You belong to the old generation," he says, "so it's okay for you to be old-fashioned and live life Jewishly. But why should the new generation adhere to your outdated rituals? These children live in the modern world and should be raised in the spirit of progress!

"And even you yourself should be spiritual and religiously observant only in your own personal domain. But when you are outside, pursuing your livelihood, you must leave behind the Torah's moral and ethical standards of behavior and conduct business in the 'normal,' unscrupulous manner. Otherwise, how do you expect to compete in our ruthless world?"[11]

Our proper response to Laban's claim is the same as Jacob's: to ignore it, denying its validity. Although materiality may appear to be the domain of Laban alone, it is in fact very much part of G-d's domain. Our mission is to elevate it and sanctify it by conducting our affairs in accordance with the Torah's lofty expectations of us.[12]

---

11. *Likutei Sichot*, vol. 3, p. 790.
12. *Hitva'aduyot 5742*, vol. 2, pp. 900–901.

Vayishlach

Jacob in the Land of Israel

Genesis 32:4–36:43

THE EIGHTH SECTION OF THE BOOK OF GENESIS CHRONICLES the patriarch Jacob's challenges as he returns to the Land of Israel after concluding his stay in Aram. It opens as he hears that his grudge-bearing brother Esau is on his way to attack him. Jacob sends (*Vayishlach*, "he sent," in Hebrew) an entourage of angels to conciliate Esau. After soothing Esau, Jacob must respond to his daughter Dinah's abduction and violation by the inhabitants of the city of Shechem. After this, Jacob's wife Rachel dies in childbirth. The narrative then concludes its account of Jacob's father Isaac and his brother Esau, preparing to focus on the chronicle of Jacob in the next section.

FIRST READING
Genesis 32:4–13

Jacob sent an entourage of angels as messengers to Esau – first, in order to inform Esau that Jacob wanted to make peace with him, and then, to relay Esau's response back to Jacob. The messengers returned to Jacob with the news that Esau was not seeking a peaceful rapprochement, but was preparing to confront Jacob with a battalion of warriors.

Objectivity

וַיִּשְׁלַח יַעֲקֹב מַלְאָכִים וגו': (בראשית לב, ד)

Jacob dispatched angels.

Divine providence is always presenting us with opportunities to engage in various mundane activities. This does not mean, however, that G-d wants us to *take* every such opportunity – even one that might appear to serve some holy purpose. G-d might want us instead to recognize the possibly harmful spiritual effects of a particular opportunity, and therefore to turn it down.[1] We must therefore carefully assess every opportunity presented to us before taking it.

Naturally, our partiality for certain activities can cause us to leap to harmful conclusions. We can remain unbiased, however, when, as Jacob did, we "dispatch a messenger" to assess the extent to which mundane opportunities – our personal "Esaus" – stand to be beneficial or detrimental. The "messenger" we dispatch is our imagination. Imagining ourselves engaging in an activity presented to us allows us to gauge its effect on us first.[2]

---

1. See *Tanya*, chapter 30.
2. *Likutei Sichot*, vol. 5, pp. 392–395.

SECOND READING

Genesis 32:14–30

During the night after Jacob's messenger angels returned with the report of Esau's evil intentions, Esau's guardian angel wrestled with Jacob. Jacob prevailed, but the angel succeeded in dislocating Jacob's hip joint. Jacob demanded that the angel bless him; the angel informed him that G-d Himself was going to bless Jacob by giving him the additional name of Israel, which means "He who has striven with [angels[3] of] G-d."

The Challenges of Nature and Men

כִּי שָׂרִיתָ עִם אֱלֹקִים וְעִם אֲנָשִׁים וַתּוּכָל: (בראשית לב, כט)

[The angel said,] "For you have striven with [angels of] G-d and with men, and you have prevailed."

The channels through which G-d funnels His energy into the world in order to continuously create it and sustain it – the spiritual forces that guide what we commonly refer to as "the forces of nature" – are His entourage of angels.[4]

Nature hides G-d's presence in the world. Seeing beyond nature's façade – acknowledging G-d's existence and His involvement in our lives – is already a great challenge. But a still greater challenge is the toxic cynicism of those who mock our spiritual path.

Esau's guardian angel told Jacob that he had "prevailed over angels and men," meaning over the angels of nature as well as the negativity of cynics. By giving us the name "Israel," G-d thus assured us that both the forces of nature and human scoffers will ultimately join our efforts to lead a spiritually moral life and reveal G-d's presence in the world – and bless us with success, as well.[5]

---

3. *Targum Yerushalmi* I; *Chulin* 92a.

4. See *Igeret HaKodesh* 25.

5. *Likutei Sichot*, vol. 3, pp. 796–797.

THIRD READING
Genesis 32:31–33:5

Since Esau's guardian angel dislocated Jacob's hip joint when they were wrestling, the Torah prohibits the Jewish people from eating the nerve of the hip joint, even of kosher animals.

Celebrating G-d's Protection

עַל כֵּן לֹא יֹאכְלוּ בְנֵי יִשְׂרָאֵל אֶת גִּיד הַנָּשֶׁה וְגו': (בראשית לב, לג)

Therefore, the Israelites do not eat the nerve of the hip joint.

The purpose of this prohibition is not just to commemorate the fact that Esau's guardian angel dislocated Jacob's hip joint, but to remember the entire story of the struggle with this angel and how G-d miraculously rescued Jacob from him.[6]

The reason we commemorate this miracle in particular is because it expresses G-d's promise of our survival throughout history. By rescuing Jacob from the power of Esau, G-d was telling Jacob's descendants, the Jewish people, that despite all the persecutions they would later suffer throughout their various exiles at the hands of oppressing nations, they would never be destroyed.[7]

It is significant that we commemorate this episode by recalling a seemingly minor detail of it – what happened to Jacob's hip. By doing so, we celebrate how G-d's love and commitment to Jewish survival extends to every detail of our existence, even seemingly minor ones.[8]

6. See Rashbam, et al.
7. *Sefer HaChinuch, mitzvah* 3. See also Nachmanides on v. 26 above, et al.
8. *Likutei Sichot*, vol. 30, pp. 148–154.

FOURTH READING

Genesis 33:6–20

As his brother Esau approached, Jacob presented his family to him. Esau was overcome by Jacob's display of brotherly sentiments, embracing and kissing him. After parting with Esau, Jacob camped for a year and a half at a place he would later name Sukkot ("huts") after the huts that he built there.

Furnishing Our True Home

וַיִּבֶן לוֹ בָּיִת וּלְמִקְנֵהוּ עָשָׂה סֻכֹּת וגו': (בראשית לג, יז)

[Jacob] built himself a house and made huts for his livestock.

Allegorically, this means that Jacob made a "home" for his true, inner self – his Divine soul and its spiritual needs – but only temporary "huts" for his possessions and physical needs (his "livestock"). In other words, he made sure that his Divine soul felt "at home" in his daily life, but kept his material concerns "outside" of his focus, lest they feel too much "at home" and start to take over his life.

Similarly, a visitor once asked Rabbi DovBer, the Maggid of Mezeritch, why his home was so poorly furnished. Rabbi DovBer answered by asking his visitor, "Well, why don't I see any of *your* furniture with *you*?" "Because I am now in transit," replied the visitor, "but my *home* is properly furnished!" Rabbi DovBer then told his visitor, "I, too, am just in transit through this world, and like you, I do take care to furnish my real *home* – the next world – properly."[9]

9. *Likutei Sichot*, vol. 1, p. 68.

FIFTH READING
Genesis 34:1–35:11

Jacob and his family proceeded to the city of Shechem, where Jacob bought a parcel of land from the local inhabitants. Jacob's daughter Dinah went out to meet the women of Shechem and was abducted and violated by the prince of Shechem. The king then brazenly suggested that his and Jacob's clans intermarry. In order to demonstrate that Jewish women must not be violated, Jacob's sons replied that the citizens of Shechem would first have to circumcise themselves, to which they readily agreed. When they were recovering from their circumcision, Jacob's sons Simeon and Levi executed all the males – who were guilty by complicity in Dinah's violation – and rescued Dinah.

Achieving Maturity

וַיִּקְחוּ שְׁנֵי בְנֵי יַעֲקֹב שִׁמְעוֹן וְלֵוִי ... אִישׁ חַרְבּוֹ וגו': (בראשית לד, כה)

**Jacob's two sons Simeon and Levi...
took up each man his sword.**

Simeon and Levi are referred to here as "men" even though they were only 13 years old at the time. For this reason, this verse is cited by some Talmudic sages as the source for the notion that a boy becomes bar mitzvah – that is, he matures sufficiently to be obligated to practice all of G-d's commandments – at the age of 13.[10]

But significantly, the Torah refers to Simeon and Levi as "men" specifically in the context of their selfless (and even self-endangering) defense of morality. This teaches us that our observance of G-d's commandments – and even our mature, rational appreciation for them – must be based upon a supra-rational and selfless commitment to morality.[11]

10. Rashi on *Nazir* 29b, *s.v. veRabbi Yosi*; Rashi, Bartenura, and *Machzor Vitri* on *Avot* 5:22.
11. *Likutei Sichot*, vol. 15, pp. 289–293; ibid., vol. 5, pp. 162, 421.

SIXTH READING

Genesis 35:12–36:19

Jacob rejoined his father Isaac in Hebron. The Torah then records the death of Isaac and lists the descendants of Esau.

The Benefits of Inspiring Others

וְאֶת בָּשְׂמַת וְגו': (בראשית לו, ג)

[Esau married] Basemat.

Esau's wife Basemat was nicknamed Machalat ("The Forgiven One") when they were married[12] as an expression of the fact that G-d forgives a couple's sins when they marry.[13] At marriage, we commence a new phase of life and, in that sense, are born anew and are granted a clean slate.[14]

One of the purposes of marriage is to bring new life into the world. Spiritually, positively influencing others imbues them with new spiritual life.[15] Thus, just as G-d forgives our shortcomings when we get married, He forgives our shortcomings when we take upon ourselves to influence others positively.

The Torah specifically teaches us this lesson in the context of the wicked Esau's marriage in order to impress upon us that we should never consider ourselves unworthy of teaching the Torah to others. When we devote ourselves sincerely to this goal, we are elevated to a new spiritual level, revealing our true essence, which is indeed free of sin, and we are granted a clean slate.[16]

---

12. Genesis 28:9.
13. See Rashi ad loc.; *Yerushalmi Bikurim* 3:3.
14. See *Gur Aryeh* on this verse.
15. See *Sanhedrin* 19b.
16. *Likutei Sichot*, vol. 30, p. 168.

SEVENTH READING
Genesis 36:20–43

The Torah then describes the Horites, the original inhabitants of
Mount Se'ir, and how they intermarried with Esau's family.

The Refinement of Civilization

אַלּוּף מַגְדִּיאֵל אַלּוּף עִירָם: (בראשית לו, מג)

[Esau's tribal chiefs included] the chief
of Magdi'eil and the chief of Iram.

These names – Magdi'eil and Iram – allude to Rome.[17]

    G-d told Abraham that the Jewish people would go into exile
four times, the fourth time under the Romans.[18] Our present
exile is an extension of the Roman exile, since the culture, legal
system, and even many of the languages of Western civilization
derive from those of the ancient Romans.

    At first, the Romans actively opposed G-dliness, destroying
the Second Temple and repudiating the Torah's values. Since
then, however, Western culture has become increasingly refined.
From a spiritual perspective, it has gradually shed its opposition
to G-dliness and has begun marshalling its material and cultural
resources to contribute to the spiritual refinement of the world.

    We can facilitate this process by studying the Torah and deep-
ening our observance of its commandments. This will enable us to
identify the differences between Jewish and "Roman" values, and
then elevate the latter by revealing their innate Divine potentials.
This will hasten the advent of the ultimate Redemption, when
all of mundane reality will express its inner spiritual essence.[19]

---

17. *Pirkei d'Rabbi Eliezer* 38; Rashi on this verse; *Bereishit Rabbah* 83:4; see
Nachmanides on this verse.
18. *Bereishit Rabbah* 44:20.
19. *Likutei Sichot*, vol. 5, pp. 411–412.

Vayeishev

Joseph in Egypt

Genesis 37:1–40:23

THE NINTH SECTION OF THE BOOK OF GENESIS BEGINS THE chronicle of Jacob's son Joseph, after Jacob settles (*Vayeishev*, "he settled," in Hebrew) in Hebron. Joseph shares his dreams with his brothers; in these dreams, he envisions himself as the future leader of Jacob's family. Joseph's seeming vanity and egoism convinces his brothers that he is a threat to the family's Divine mission, so they conclude that they must eliminate him. He is sold to Egypt as a slave, where he first rises to a position of responsibility in his master's household, but is later placed in prison as a result of slanderous accusations. Interrupting this narrative is the account of how Jacob's son Judah is ostracized by his family and is later deceived into fathering children by his widowed daughter-in-law, Tamar.

FIRST READING
Genesis 37:1–11

Jacob arrived safely at the family home in Hebron. His son Joseph shared his dreams with the family; in these dreams, he envisioned himself as the future leader of Jacob's family. Joseph's brothers took this display of seemingly brazen conceit as evidence that Joseph was more the spiritual heir of the self-centered Esau than of Jacob, and could not understand why Jacob envisioned Joseph as his successor and future leader of the family.

Engaging the World

וְיִשְׂרָאֵל אָהַב אֶת יוֹסֵף מִכָּל בָּנָיו וגו': (בראשית לז, ג)

Israel [i.e., Jacob] loved Joseph more than all his [other] sons.

Joseph's mother, Rachel, was the true spiritual complement to Jacob, for she was able to express Jacob's abstract spiritual inspiration in every aspect of daily life. Joseph inherited this ability from his mother, and even surpassed her, possessing the ability to spread Divine consciousness even in settings that were utterly antagonistic to it.

Jacob's aspiration in life was to fulfill the patriarchal vision of a world filled with Divine consciousness. He knew that his other sons could only imagine expressing holiness in settings that were already holy. It was inconceivable to them that holiness could survive and even subdue the realm of anti-holiness.

Jacob designated Joseph as his successor rather than one of his other sons, not as an act of favoritism, but as a lesson to his other sons. The same lesson applies to us as well: to value the ideal of applying spiritual inspiration to the material world and to develop our abilities to do so.[1]

---

1. *Bi'urei HaZohar* (Mitteler Rebbe) 29d–30d; *Bi'urei HaZohar* (Tzemach Tzedek), vol. 1, pp. 168–176; *Likutei Sichot*, vol. 3, p. 832.

SECOND READING
Genesis 37:12–22

Perceiving Joseph as a threat to the patriarchs' mission, his brothers plotted to eliminate him. At first they thought to kill him outright, but Reuben, the oldest brother, convinced them to leave him to die in a pit, intending to rescue him alone later.

The Need for Humility

וַיֹּאמֶר אֲלֵהֶם רְאוּבֵן אַל תִּשְׁפְּכוּ דָם הַשְׁלִיכוּ
אֹתוֹ אֶל הַבּוֹר הַזֶּה וְגוֹ': (בראשית לז, כב)

**Reuben said to them, "Do not shed
blood; throw him into this pit."**

Joseph's brothers studied the Torah and tried to live by it, but their righteous indignation caused them to distort the Torah's teachings. Since they studied the Torah with insufficient humility, they failed to absorb its wisdom properly. Therefore, when it came to their brother Joseph, they applied the Torah's teachings erroneously.[2] Unable to countenance any perspective other than their own, they arrogantly concluded that the Torah *required* them to kill Joseph.[3]

The brothers' lack of humility is alluded to in the phrase that describes the pit into which they chose to throw Joseph: "The pit was empty; there was no water in it." Water is a metaphor for the humility required in studying the Torah. As the Talmud states, the Torah is compared to water because "just as water seeks its lowest level, so does the Torah only endure within one who is humble."[4]

From this we see how crucial it is to cultivate humility. Without humility, we run the risk of distorting the Torah's teachings; with it, we are assured that we will interpret them properly.[5]

2. See *Berachot* 34b, beginning.
3. See *Or HaChayim*, et al.
4. *Ta'anit* 7a.
5. See *Bereshit Rabbah* 84:16. *Likutei Sichot*, vol. 15, pp. 324–328.

THIRD READING

Genesis 37:23–36

Joseph's brothers sold him as a slave to a caravan that brought him to Egypt.

We Cannot Be Enslaved

וַיִּמְכְּרוּ אֶת יוֹסֵף . . . בְּעֶשְׂרִים כָּסֶף וְגו': (בראשית לז, כח)

[The brothers] sold Joseph . . . for 20 pieces of silver.

The Torah considers our firstborn sons to "belong" to G-d, requiring us to "redeem" them from Him by paying 20 silver pieces (five Biblical shekels) to a descendant of Aaron, the first priest.[6] This rule, which is still practiced today, is meant to remind us that *everything* we possess really belongs to G-d, and that therefore we should use all our possessions for holy ends.[7]

In addition, the redemption price of 20 silver pieces is meant to remind us how Joseph – Rachel's firstborn – was sold as a slave for that price.[8] Yet despite the sale, Joseph was never truly enslaved – for, as G-d tells us, "The Israelites are *My* servants."[9] On account of our inviolable bond with G-d, we can never be truly enslaved to anyone else.[10]

The redemption price of the firstborn is thus fixed as the price for which Joseph was sold into slavery. This teaches us that both we and all we possess belong irrevocably to G-d, and can never be enslaved to any other master.[11]

---

6. Numbers 18:16.
7. See *Sefer HaChinuch, mitzvah* 18.
8. *Yerushalmi Shekalim* 2:3; *Bereishit Rabbah* 84:18, et al.
9. Leviticus 25:55.
10. Rashi ad loc.
11. *Likutei Sichot*, vol. 20, pp. 185–190.

FOURTH READING

Genesis 38:1–30

Judah left Hebron, married, and had three sons. He later had two additional sons by his widowed daughter-in-law Tamar. He named these sons Peretz and Zerach.

Breaking Through

וַיִּקְרָא שְׁמוֹ פָּרֶץ ... וַיִּקְרָא שְׁמוֹ זָרַח: (בראשית לח, כט-ל)

[Judah] named him Peretz.... he named him Zerach.

The name Zerach ("shining") alludes to the sun, which shines constantly, while the name Peretz ("breaking through") alludes to the moon, whose light periodically "breaks through" its diminishment and disappearance.[12]

Metaphorically, the sun represents consistently righteous people, whose Divine light shines without fluctuation. The moon represents people who have strayed from the proper path but mend their former ways and return to G-d, transforming their diminished light into increased light.

Because of their challenges, "returnees" reach a higher spiritual level than the consistently righteous.[13] Thus, Peretz, who is associated with the moon and is therefore the archetype of repentance, preceded Zerach and was the firstborn.

For the same reason, Peretz is the ancestor of King David, whose inspiring Psalms express the great yearning and poetry of repentance. Through King David, Peretz is the ancestor of the Messiah, who will "break through" the walls of exile, ushering in the Redemption by inspiring and teaching the whole world to repent.[14]

---

12. *Sefer HaBahir* 197, cited by Nachmanides and Rabbeinu Bachye.
13. *Berachot* 34b; *Mishneh Torah, Teshuvah* 7:4.
14. *Likutei Sichot* vol. 30, pp. 188–189.

FIFTH READING

Genesis 39:1–6

THURSDAY

Joseph had been sold as a slave to the Egyptian Potiphar, Pharaoh's chief butcher. Recognizing Joseph's intelligence, integrity, piety, and regal bearing, Potiphar appointed him to oversee his household affairs.

Transforming Tragedy

וְיוֹסֵף הוּרַד מִצְרָיְמָה וְגו': (בראשית לט, א)

Joseph had been taken down to Egypt.

Ancient Egypt was the world's foremost bastion of paganism, a land thoroughly steeped in sophisticated, virtually irresistible idolatry. The chances were nil that Jacob's small family of monotheists could spiritually survive there – let alone grow into an independent, monotheistic nation.

G-d therefore arranged for Joseph to descend to Egypt ahead of his brothers and rise to greatness there, when Pharaoh would eventually appoint him to be viceroy. As viceroy, Joseph took measures to weaken the influence that Egyptian culture would have on his family when they would arrive. As a result, even the Egyptians who lived after Joseph could not corrupt the Jewish people. On the contrary, the Jews flourished there both physically and spiritually, remaining separate from the Egyptian culture – even during their enslavement.[15]

We thus see that seemingly tragic events, such as Joseph's sale into Egyptian service, are meant to be catalysts for the larger process of physical and/or spiritual redemption. Recognizing this, we can then seize the opportunities for personal growth inherent within our challenges.[16]

---

15. See *Vayikra Rabbah* 32:5; *Midrash Lekach Tov* on Deuteronomy 26:5.
16. *Shir HaShirim Rabbah* 2:11. *Torat Moshe* on Genesis 45:4. *Ma'amarei Admor HaEmtza'i, Bereishit*, pp. 299–302; *Or HaTorah, Bereishit*, vol. 2, 343b; *Sefer HaMa'amarim 5654*, p. 107; *Sefer HaMa'amarim Melukat*, vol. 5, pp. 259–260.

SIXTH READING

Genesis 39:7–23

Potiphar's wife saw through astrological means that she was destined to be the ancestress of Joseph's descendants. Not knowing that this would happen through her daughter, she sought to seduce Joseph.

Seeing Beneath the Surface

וַתִּשָּׂא אֵשֶׁת אֲדֹנָיו אֶת עֵינֶיהָ אֶל יוֹסֵף: (בראשית לט, ז)

[Joseph's] master's wife cast her eyes on Joseph.

Joseph's master's wife had noble intentions in trying to seduce him. This incident demonstrates that beneath the surface even of circumstances that seem antagonistic to holiness there is a holy purpose.

Rabbi Shneur Zalman of Liadi offers the example of someone deliberately trying to disrupt us when we are immersed in prayer. In such a case, we should not allow the person to disrupt our prayers. On the contrary, we should recognize that G-d has sent this person as His messenger to stimulate us to pray with even greater concentration.[17] The disruptive person himself, like all of existence, is rooted ultimately in holiness, and is therefore motivated by a subconscious desire to serve G-d. It is only his conscious self that distorts this desire and expresses it in a form that outwardly opposes holiness.

The same principle is true with regard to all obstacles that we encounter. Rather than being discouraged by their antagonistic veneer, we should perceive their essence, i.e., that they are not obstacles to holiness but its servants.[18]

17. *Igeret HaKodesh* 25.
18. *Likutei Sichot*, vol. 1, pp. 79–81.

SEVENTH READING
Genesis 40:1–23

Having failed to seduce Joseph, the chief butcher's wife accused him of accosting her and had him imprisoned. In prison, Pharaoh's chief cupbearer and chief baker told Joseph their disturbing dreams, which Joseph interpreted correctly. Joseph asked the cupbearer to speak to Pharaoh on Joseph's behalf after his release, but the cupbearer forgot about Joseph.

Resisting Temptation

וַיִּקְצֹף פַּרְעֹה ... עַל שַׂר הַמַּשְׁקִים וְעַל שַׂר הָאוֹפִים: וַיִּתֵּן

אֹתָם בְּמִשְׁמַר בֵּית שַׂר הַטַּבָּחִים: (בראשית מ, ב-ג)

Pharaoh got angry at the chief cupbearer and the chief baker, and put them in jail under the care of the chief butcher.

When we understand the implications of some insight into the nature of G-d or His relation to the world, the natural result is for it to affect our heart, increasing our love and reverence for G-d. However, overindulgence in sensual, worldly pleasures can distract us from G-dliness, acting as a wedge between our minds and hearts. These worldly pleasures are allegorically represented by Pharaoh and his three assistants – the chief butcher, the chief cupbearer, and the chief baker.

In his interactions with these Egyptians, Joseph resisted the temptation to be drawn into the sensual indulgences that they represented. Instead, he focused on the Divine spark within these pleasures, thereby utilizing them as means for spiritual growth.

Joseph's example teaches us that we, too, can rise above the material distractions that threaten to stunt our spiritual growth. By so doing, we enable the ideals of our minds to reach and inspire our hearts.[19]

19. *Torah Or* 58b, 71d, 102c; *Ma'amarei Admor HaEmtza'i, Bereishit*, pp. 489–490.

Mikeitz

Joseph the Viceroy

Genesis 41:1–44:17

THE TENTH SECTION OF THE BOOK OF GENESIS CONTINUES the chronicle of Joseph. It opens at the end of (*Mikeitz*, in Hebrew) two years since Joseph had asked Pharaoh's cupbearer to intercede for him. This time it is Pharaoh who dreams – twice – and seeks a qualified interpreter. Joseph interprets Pharaoh's dreams convincingly as referring to seven coming years of plenty followed by seven years of famine, and this leads Pharaoh to appoint Joseph as viceroy of Egypt. The onset of famine – which also affects the Land of Israel – brings Joseph's brothers to Egypt to buy food that Joseph stored up during the years of plenty. Joseph devises a way to determine whether his brothers have abandoned their former hatred of him and are ready to join him in moving the family forward in its Divine mission.

FIRST READING

Genesis 41:1–14

In his first dream, Pharaoh saw seven robust cows emerge from the Nile River, followed by seven lean cows that devoured the seven robust ones. In his second dream, he saw seven healthy ears of grain devoured by seven scrawny ears of grain.

How to Neutralize Evil

וַיְהִי מִקֵּץ שְׁנָתַיִם יָמִים וּפַרְעֹה חֹלֵם וגו': (בראשית מא, א)

After two years had passed, Pharaoh had a dream.

Jacob was the central spiritual figure of his generation, and Joseph was the one who was able to channel Jacob's spiritual energy into the world. Therefore, the spiritual dimension of everyone's life took its cue from Joseph's. Since Joseph learned of his future through dreams, Pharaoh also learned about the future of his land through dreams.

The same is true in every generation. The spiritual dimension of the world at large takes its cue from the world's collective "Joseph" – the Jewish people. Even forces that oppose G-dliness derive power from us, either by capitalizing on the negative energy produced by our misdeeds or by challenging us to tap potentials that would otherwise remain dormant.

When we encounter evil, we are apt to assume that it possesses its own power, and therefore be intimidated by it, or even seduced by it. Instead, we should recognize that evil is nothing more than a reflection of our own shortcomings or simply a challenge designed to elicit our dormant spiritual powers. It will then neither intimidate nor tantalize us. By rectifying our own shortcomings and rising to life's challenges, we cut off evil's supply of power, thereby bringing spiritual sustenance to the entire world.[1]

1. *Likutei Sichot*, vol. 3, pp. 819–820.

Genesis 41:15–38

None of Pharaoh's advisors could explain how robust cows or grain could exist at the same time as scrawny ones. At that point, Pharaoh's cupbearer mentioned to Pharaoh how Joseph had correctly interpreted his dream in prison. Pharaoh immediately summoned Joseph. Joseph interpreted the simultaneous existence of robust and scrawny years to mean that grain should be stored away during the plentiful years for use during the famine years.

Feasting during Famine

וְנִשְׁכַּח כָּל הַשָּׂבָע בְּאֶרֶץ מִצְרָיִם וְגו': (בראשית מא, ל)

[Joseph told Pharaoh, "In the years of famine,] all the abundance in Egypt will be forgotten."

Metaphorically, the years of abundance in Pharaoh's dreams allude to the years of *spiritual* abundance that the Jewish people enjoyed when the holy Temples stood: G-d's presence was perceivable in the miracles that occurred in the Temples. The eras following the destruction of each Temple were spiritual "famines," when G-dliness became much less perceivable. The ravages of our long exile have made us forget how good it was when the Temples stood and when G-dliness was revealed.

But, as Joseph advised, our predecessors did store up "food," by preserving the wisdom and knowledge of the Torah during the "years of plenty." This inspiration has sustained us during our exile. As King David wrote, "[The Torah] is my comfort in my affliction, for Your word has given me life."[2] By studying the Torah, we can continue to thrive until the spiritual "famine" ends and G-dliness is once again revealed.[3]

2. Psalms 119:50.
3. *Or HaTorah, Bereishit*, vol. 5, 975b–976a.

THIRD READING
Genesis 41:39–52

Pharaoh was so impressed with Joseph's skillful interpretation of his dream that he appointed him viceroy of Egypt, instructing him to implement his plan. After he was made viceroy, Joseph's former master, Potiphar, gave him his daughter in marriage. During the seven years of plenty, Joseph had two sons: Manasseh and Ephraim.

True vs. False Humility

אֹכֶל שְׂדֵה הָעִיר אֲשֶׁר סְבִיבֹתֶיהָ נָתַן בְּתוֹכָהּ: (בראשית מא, מח)

[Joseph] placed the food of the fields surrounding the city in [the food].

In order to preserve the grain that he had gathered, Joseph stored it together with some of the soil in which it had grown.[4]

Spiritually, the "food" that nourishes us is our knowledge of the Torah. Humility is the lowly "soil" that we mix with our knowledge in order to preserve it. We can cultivate humility as we amass knowledge of the Torah by recalling that the Torah is the wisdom of the infinite G-d; therefore, no matter how much we learn, we have not even scratched the surface.[5]

---

4. Rashi on this verse.
5. *Likutei Sichot*, vol. 25, pp. 224–226.

FOURTH READING
Genesis 41:53–42:18

The Egyptians stored up grain during the seven years of plenty, as Joseph had directed them. But as soon as the seven years of famine began, everyone's grain except for Joseph's rotted. The entire populace of Egypt thus found themselves dependent upon Joseph for food. Joseph agreed to give them grain on the condition that they circumcise themselves first.

To Compromise or Not?

וַיֹּאמֶר פַּרְעֹה לְכָל מִצְרַיִם לְכוּ אֶל יוֹסֵף אֲשֶׁר
יֹאמַר לָכֶם תַּעֲשׂוּ: (בראשית מא, נה)

**Pharaoh said to all Egypt, "Go to Joseph;
do whatever he tells you."**

Although Joseph succeeded in refining Egypt somewhat by having the Egyptians circumcised, he was acting on his own initiative. Therefore, despite his good intentions, his plan backfired. By becoming more refined, Egypt was made worthier of receiving Divine beneficence, and receiving this beneficence strengthened it. Unfortunately, Egypt was not refined enough to use this power properly, eventually using it instead to persecute the Jewish people.[6]

Similarly, we too must be careful not to overreach or compromise the Torah's rules in our efforts to do good, because no lasting good can come out of compromising the Torah's laws. The same G-d who created the world gave us the Torah, His Divine instructions for how to live in it. Only by following the Torah's rules will our efforts to help others be crowned with ultimate success.[7]

6. *Peri Eitz Chayim, Sha'ar Chag HaMatzot* 7.
7. *Likutei Sichot*, vol. 1, pp. 98–102.

FIFTH READING
Genesis 42:19–43:15

Jacob sent his sons – except Benjamin – to Egypt to buy grain. Joseph's brothers did not recognize him. Joseph threatened not to receive them the next time without Benjamin; this way, he could invent an excuse to keep Benjamin in Egypt and thereby see if his brothers would be prepared to fight in order to free Benjamin. If they would be, it would prove that they had overcome their jealousy of Rachel's sons. When Joseph's brothers heard his threat, they assumed that it was G-d's punishment for having thrown him into a pit and having sold him as a slave.

Sensitivity to Our Soul

אֲשֶׁר רָאִינוּ צָרַת נַפְשׁוֹ בְּהִתְחַנְנוֹ אֵלֵינוּ וְלֹא שָׁמָעְנוּ וְגוֹ': (בראשית מב, כא)

[Joseph's brothers said to one another,] "We saw [our brother's] anguish when he pleaded with us, but we did not listen."

During its life in the body, the Divine soul's consciousness is constricted by the body's mundane perspective. The soul's mission in life is to refine both the body and the world at large. Fulfilling this mission enables the soul to ascend in the afterlife to a spiritual level higher than the one on which it existed prior to its life in this world. Consequently, as long as we remain true to the purpose of life, the soul is happy to endure the spiritual "pain" of existing inside a body. When, however, we ignore our Divine mission, the soul suffers needlessly.

Allegorically, our indifference to our soul's pain is comparable to Joseph's brothers ignoring his pleas to rescue him from the pit. Conversely, when we listen to our soul's plea, we alleviate its pain and hasten the advent of the final and ultimate Redemption.[8]

8. *Sefer HaMa'amarim Melukat*, vol. 5, pp. 261–262.

SIXTH READING
Genesis 43:16–29

Back in Egypt, Jacob's sons sensed that Joseph was planning to falsely incriminate them in order to keep them there, so they explained why they were innocent of any wrongdoing.

Double Descent and Double Ascent

יָרֹד יָרַדְנוּ בַּתְּחִלָּה לִשְׁבָּר אֹכֶל: (בראשית מג, כ)

[Joseph's brothers said,] "We originally came down – yes, we came down – to buy food."

These two expressions of descent prophetically allude to the two stages of the Jewish people's spiritual descent into Egypt.

The Land of Israel is watered by rain, which falls sporadically and inconsistently. Therefore, living in the Land of Israel is conducive to making its inhabitants pray for rain, recognizing that their sustenance depends upon G-d.[9] In contrast, Egypt is watered by the Nile's consistent, annual overflow. Living in Egypt therefore makes its inhabitants more likely to see the forces of nature as their provider, rather than G-d. Thus, leaving the Land of Israel to live in Egypt was Jacob's family's first spiritual descent. Nonetheless, since Joseph sustained Egypt miraculously – always ascribing his success to G-d – the Divine concealment that characterized Egypt was temporarily lessened during his lifetime.

After Joseph died, Egypt's true character reasserted itself. The Jewish people then underwent a second, further spiritual descent.

G-d promised Jacob that these two descents would be countered by two ascents, saying, "I will . . . *bring you up*, yes, *bring you up* from there."[10] The first ascent occurred with the Exodus from Egypt; the second will occur with the Messianic Redemption.[11]

9. *Bereishit Rabbah* 13:9.
10. Genesis 46:4.
11. *Likutei Sichot*, vol. 6, pp. 28–32. See *Torah Or* 49a ff.

SEVENTH READING
Genesis 43:30–44:17

Joseph sent his brothers off back to the Land of Israel, having secretly hidden his goblet in Benjamin's pack. When Joseph's servant accused the brothers of stealing the goblet, they protested that they would never disgrace themselves in this manner. But the goblet was discovered in Benjamin's pack. When brothers were returned to Joseph, he informed them that they were all free to return home except for Benjamin.

Inner Identity

חָלִילָה לַעֲבָדֶיךָ מֵעֲשׂוֹת כַּדָּבָר הַזֶּה: (בראשית מד, ז)

[Joseph's brothers said,] "It would be a disgrace
for us, your servants, to do such a thing."

Spiritually sensitive people regard their misdeeds as indications of what aspects of their spiritual life they need to work on. Aware that everything happens by Divine providence, they even regard being falsely accused of doing some misdeed as a Divine sign that there is some flaw in their spiritual life.[12]

Thus, the fact that Joseph's brothers were found with something that did not belong to them – even if it was deliberately planted – was meant to inform them that they were spiritually lacking in some way.

We see from this that the true, inner purpose of everything that happens to us is to refocus us properly. By developing our spiritual sensitivity this way, we can hasten the advent of our own redemption, along with the redemption of the whole world.[13]

---

12. See *Igeret HaKodesh* 28, end; *Likutei Sichot*, vol. 3, pp. 944 ff.
13. *Likutei Sichot*, vol. 15, pp. 359–363.

Vayigash

Jacob and Joseph Reunited

Genesis 44:18–47:27

IN THE ELEVENTH SECTION OF THE BOOK OF GENESIS, WE reach the dramatic climax of the chronicle of Joseph. It begins as Judah approaches (*Vayigash*, "and he approached," in Hebrew) Joseph in defense of Benjamin. Judah's willingness to save Benjamin convinces Joseph that his other brothers have repented and risen above their previous jealousy. Joseph therefore ends the masquerade, revealing his true identity to them. Joseph then immediately sends all the brothers to bring their father, Jacob, to Egypt, where the family will settle in order to live through the famine. The famine ends as soon as Jacob arrives, but the family stays in Egypt in fulfillment of G-d's plan as originally foretold to Abraham.

FIRST READING
Genesis 44:18–30

Hearing that Joseph intended to retain Benjamin as his slave, Judah approached Joseph to argue with him. Although Judah spoke respectfully, he told Joseph that he would not tolerate this injustice to his brother – as well as to his father, Jacob. Judah told Joseph that Jacob would not survive the loss of Benjamin, the only remaining son of his wife Rachel.

Self-Sacrifice for Our Children

וַיִּגַּשׁ אֵלָיו יְהוּדָה וְגוֹ': (בראשית מד, יח)

Judah then approached [Joseph].

Although he was begging Joseph for mercy, Judah was at the same time intimating to Joseph that he and his brothers were prepared, if necessary, to kill him – as well as Pharaoh and the rest of the Egyptians – in order to free their brother Benjamin.[1]

Judah and his brothers were extraordinarily strong, but obviously no match for all of Egypt. In fact, the Midrash relates that at one point during this face-off, Joseph demonstrated his own might to Judah, prompting Judah to remark to his brothers, "This one is stronger than me."[2] Furthermore, Benjamin's physical life was not in danger; Joseph was only threatening to separate him from Jacob's household. Yet, Judah realized that leaving Benjamin in Egypt would endanger him spiritually. Because Judah had assured Jacob that he would take personal responsibility for Benjamin's safe return, he was prepared to risk his life for him, notwithstanding any rational considerations.

We learn from Judah how to set aside rational caution when it comes to the spiritual safety and education of our children, for whom G-d has made us responsible.[3]

1. Rashi.
2. *Bereishit Rabbah* 93:7.
3. *Likutei Sichot*, vol. 1, pp. 94–95.

SECOND READING
Genesis 44:31–45:7

Judah's display of self-sacrifice for Benjamin convinced Joseph that his brothers had truly repented of their former attitude. He therefore revealed his true identity to them. The brothers were understandably afraid that Joseph would take revenge on them. Joseph, however, assured them that he viewed the entire episode as Divine providence and did not bear any personal grudge against them.

Influencing the Whole World

וַיִּשְׁלָחֵנִי אֱלֹקִים לִפְנֵיכֶם וגו': (בראשית מה, ז)

[Joseph said to his brothers,] "G-d sent me ahead of you."

When G-d arranged for Joseph to rule over Egypt, this included the mandate to positively influence it spiritually, as well. Therefore, when (in the following verse) Joseph alluded to his position and ability, he made it clear to his brothers that he was not acting as their emissaries, but as G-d's: "It was not *you* who sent me here, but G-d. *He* has made me...ruler over all Egypt."

Egypt is the archetype of all exiles, and Joseph is the archetype of all Jewish leaders. Thus, the ability to positively influence reality, even during exile, is vested in Joseph's heirs, the spiritual leaders of each generation. When we act as their emissaries – inspired, empowered, and guided by them – we too possess the ability to affect the entire world positively. We do this by encouraging our fellow Jews to embrace the teachings of the Torah, and by encouraging all humanity to embrace the Noahide laws – in order to create a world of justice, goodness, and kindness.[4]

4. See *Mishneh Torah, Melachim* 8:10–11. *Likutei Sichot*, vol. 30, pp. 224–228.

THIRD READING
Genesis 45:8–27

Joseph then told his brothers to return to the Land of Israel and bring their father, Jacob, to Egypt. He arranged for the family to settle in the lush province of Goshen, which was also distant from the negative spiritual influence of the rest of Egypt.

Minimizing Discipline

מַהֲרוּ וַעֲלוּ אֶל אָבִי וגו': (בראשית מה, ט)

[Joseph said to his brothers,] "Make
haste and go up to my father."

At this moment, Joseph realized that his father had been separated from him for exactly 22 years. He understood prophetically that this was Divine providence's way of rectifying Jacob's failure to honor *his* parents during the 22 years he was separated from them. Now that the 22 years were up, Joseph urged his brothers to hastily bring their father to Egypt so that his punishment of separation could end without even one moment of unnecessary delay.

This teaches us that although discipline and corrective punishment are at times necessary,[5] we must limit our use of such measures to the absolute minimum. The very *moment* that they become unnecessary, we must immediately and urgently revert to the ways of kindness and affection.[6]

---

5. See *Sotah* 47a, *Sanhedrin* 107b.
6. *Likutei Sichot*, vol. 15, pp. 389–390.

FOURTH READING
Genesis 45:28–46:7

Jacob was overjoyed to hear that his beloved son Joseph was still alive and had remained true to Jacob's ideals. Although he looked forward to joining Joseph, Jacob regretted having to leave the Land of Israel. G-d therefore appeared to him and assured him that his family would grow into a nation while in Egypt and that He would ultimately return them to the Land of Israel.

Celebrating Our Children's Achievements

וַיֹּאמֶר יִשְׂרָאֵל רַב עוֹד יוֹסֵף בְּנִי חָי וְגו': (בראשית מה, כח)

**Israel said, "[I am blessed with] much
[joy], for my son Joseph is still alive."**

Just as Jacob had managed to survive the spiritually antagonistic environment of his father-in-law Laban's house, Joseph remained unaffected by the spiritually antagonistic environment of Egypt. But whereas Jacob merely survived Laban, Joseph affected Egypt positively. Joseph's spiritual achievements thus surpassed those of his father Jacob.

The preceding section ends with Jacob's first realization – that Joseph had survived spiritually intact. In contrast, this section opens with Jacob's second realization – that Joseph had not only spiritually survived Egypt, but had spiritually affected it positively. "I am blessed with *much* joy – that is, joy for how my son Joseph's successes have exceeded my own."[7]

We can emulate the example of Jacob, who did not resent his son having surpassed his own achievements, but on the contrary, found great joy in his son's superior accomplishments.[8]

7. *Bereishit Rabbah* 94:3.
8. *Likutei Sichot*, vol. 30, pp. 222–228.

FIFTH READING
Genesis 46:8–27

The Torah then lists and counts Jacob's family. The 70th and youngest in this census was Levi's daughter Yocheved, whom we will meet later as the mother of Moses.

The Power of Belief

כָּל הַנֶּפֶשׁ לְבֵית יַעֲקֹב הַבָּאָה מִצְרַיְמָה שִׁבְעִים: (בראשית מו, כז)

**The total of Jacob's household who
came to Egypt was 70 persons.**

The mission of the Jewish people is to be a light to the 70 nations of the world,[9] and spiritually, they could not begin this mission until they themselves numbered 70 unique individuals.

The person who completed the number of 70 persons was Jacob's granddaughter Yocheved, who was born just as Jacob's family was entering Egypt.

It was no accident that Yocheved was the one who brought Jacob's family to this new level, for she and her children later emerged as living examples of the enormous power of faith. She and her daughter Miriam inspired the Jewish people to trust in G-d by defying Pharaoh's command to kill all newborn male Jewish babies.[10] Yocheved's sons, Moses and Aaron, revived the people's belief in redemption.[11] Thus, Yocheved's unwavering faith played a pivotal role in the Jewish people's redemption from Egypt.

The same holds true today: it is our faith in the ultimate Redemption – which we learn from Yocheved's example – that empowers us to fulfill our mission of spreading Divine consciousness to all humanity and thereby hastening the advent of the Redemption.[12]

9. Listed in Genesis 10.
10. Exodus 1:17.
11. Ibid. 4:29–31.
12. *Likutei Sichot*, vol. 20, pp. 218 ff.

SIXTH READING
Genesis 46:28–47:10

In advance of his arrival in Egypt, Jacob sent Judah to prepare a *yeshiva* – a place where he and his descendants could devote themselves to the constant study of the Torah. When Jacob arrived in Egypt, Joseph presented him to Pharaoh, and Jacob blessed Pharaoh.

Gratitude

וַיְבָרֶךְ יַעֲקֹב אֶת פַּרְעֹה וגו': (בראשית מז, י)

Jacob blessed Pharaoh.

We are taught that Jacob blessed Pharaoh that the Nile River would overflow and irrigate the country whenever he approached it. The Egyptians viewed the Nile as the source of their sustenance and therefore worshipped it as a deity. By blessing Pharaoh that the Nile would overflow only when he approached it, Jacob weakened the idolatrous reverence in which the Egyptians held the river by demonstrating that it was controlled by G-d.[13]

Pharaoh himself, however, proved to be the ultimate ingrate. Instead of thanking G-d for this blessing, he falsely attributed it to his own powers. This contrasts sharply with Jacob's own response to G-d's blessings: "I [– that is, my sense of worthiness] have been diminished due to all the acts of kindness and trustworthiness that You have done for me, Your servant."[14]

By learning from Jacob's example of humility, honesty, and gratitude – rather than from Pharaoh's example of arrogance, vanity, and ingratitude – we will receive, as did Jacob, G-d's supranatural assistance in all that we do.[15]

---

13. *Likutei Sichot*, vol. 6, pp. 31–32.
14. Genesis 32:11. See *Igeret HaKodesh* 2.
15. *Sefer HaMa'amarim 5710*, p. 121.

SEVENTH READING
Genesis 47:11–27

As a result of Jacob's blessing, the predicted seven years of famine ended after only two years. Seeing that the famine had ended, the Egyptians asked Joseph for seed in order to plant crops for the following year.

Sowing Spiritual Seeds

הֵא לָכֶם זֶרַע וּזְרַעְתֶּם אֶת הָאֲדָמָה: (בראשית מז, כג)

[Joseph said to the Egyptians,] "Here is seed grain for you so you can sow the ground."

Joseph gave the people seed, but they knew that it was not enough to simply eat the seed; they needed to plant it, tend it, and harvest it.

The "Josephs" of our generation are our spiritual guides and teachers. When we receive spiritual "sustenance" from them – that is, inspiration and knowledge – we must not be satisfied simply to receive it and use it for our own spiritual survival. Rather, we must plant these spiritual seeds and actualize their potential, both for our own spiritual growth and in order to inspire others.[16]

---

16. *Hitva'aduyot 5711*, vol. 1, p. 165.

Vaichi

The Close of the Patriarchal Era

Genesis 47:28–50:26

THE TWELFTH AND FINAL SECTION OF THE BOOK OF GENESIS chronicles the last period in the life of Jacob and the succession of his son Joseph. Jacob lived (*Vaichi*, "and he lived," in Hebrew) the last 17 years of his life in Egypt. Besides devoting himself to the ongoing spiritual and moral education of his descendants, Jacob organizes his family into tribes in order to prepare them for their destiny by bequeathing to each tribe its unique spiritual characteristics. After his death, Jacob's sons bury him in the family tomb in Hebron. The section closes with the final days of Joseph and his reminder that G-d would eventually return Jacob's descendants to the Promised Land.

FIRST READING

Genesis 47:28–48:9

Jacob's final years, spent in Egypt, were the best in his life. He was surrounded by his reunited family and free from worry or enemies.

The Antidote to Darkness

וַיְחִי יַעֲקֹב בְּאֶרֶץ מִצְרַיִם שְׁבַע עֶשְׂרֵה שָׁנָה וגו': (בראשית מז, כח)

Jacob lived 17 years in Egypt.

When Rabbi Menachem Mendel of Lubavitch (the *Tzemach Tzedek*) was a young boy, he asked the following of his grandfather, Rabbi Shneur Zalman of Liadi: "Granted, Jacob was happy to see how Joseph had remained faithful to Jewish values even in Egypt, the embodiment of decadence. But even so, how could the *best* years of Jacob's life be those that he lived in such a place?"

Rabbi Shneur Zalman's answer was that Jacob had sent Judah to set up a house of learning so the family could study the Torah in Egypt.[1] When we study the Torah, we become closer to G-d. Studying the Torah in an environment of spiritual darkness transforms that darkness into light. This explains why Jacob lived his *best* years in the decadent society of Egypt.[2]

This answer is especially relevant today. Our personal and collective world is limited and imperfect; we still live in "Egypt." But since G-d is beyond the limitations of our imperfect world, when we study the Torah and thereby connect with Him, we are not only immune to the negative effects of "Egypt" – we are empowered to transform the darkness of exile into light.[3]

1. Genesis 46:28; *Midrash Tanchuma* (ed. Buber) and Rashi ad loc.
2. *HaYom Yom*, 18 Tevet.
3. *Likutei Sichot*, vol. 10, pp. 160–162.

SECOND READING

Genesis 48:10–16

When Jacob sensed that he was about to die, he sent for Joseph. Jacob instructed Joseph not to bury him in Egypt, fearing that the Egyptians might turn his grave into an object of worship since it was his blessing that had ended the years of famine. Instead, Jacob instructed Joseph to bury him in the family tomb in Hebron. When Jacob later became ill, Joseph took his two sons, Manasseh and Ephraim, to Jacob in order for them to receive his final blessing. Jacob surprised Joseph by informing him that he was making Joseph's sons the heads of two separate tribes, on an equal footing with Jacob's own sons.

The Lesson of Fish

וַיִּדְגּוּ לָרֹב וגו': (בראשית מח, טז)

**[Jacob blessed Manasseh and Ephraim, saying,]
"May they propagate abundantly, like fish."**

Fish are completely submerged and concealed by their native environment – water – and are constantly dependent upon it for their survival. Fish therefore express the notion of selflessness (*bitul*) more than other creatures.

This selflessness is also the key to their great fertility. Selflessness ensures that our ego does not become an obstacle between ourselves and G-d; it thereby opens us up to receiving His limitless blessings.

The lesson we take from Jacob's blessing is thus to emulate the selflessness exhibited by fish, for by doing so we receive G-d's infinite blessings in our Divine mission to make the world into His ultimate home.[4]

4. *Likutei Sichot*, vol. 25, pp. 10–13.

THIRD READING

Genesis 48:17–22

Jacob then told Joseph that in consideration for taking the trouble to bury him in the Land of Israel, Jacob was awarding Joseph's descendants the city of Shechem.

Spiritual Weapons

אֲשֶׁר לָקַחְתִּי מִיַּד הָאֱמֹרִי בְּחַרְבִּי וּבְקַשְׁתִּי: (בראשית מח, כב)

[Jacob said to Joseph, "I bequeath you the
city of Shechem,] which I conquered from the
Amorites with my sword and my bow."

A sword is used to kill an enemy who is close by, whereas a bow and arrow are used to kill an enemy who is far away.

Spiritually, our "close enemies" are the flaws in our manner of thinking, speaking, or acting that we can recognize easily. Our "distant enemies" are our subtle imperfections, of which we are often unaware and can only identify by means of deep introspection.

Allegorically, Jacob was teaching Joseph how to conquer both types of spiritual flaws. We battle them both – and identify the more subtle ones – by following the inward path of meditative prayer.[5]

5. Rashi on this verse. *Sefer HaMa'amarim Melukat*, vol. 1, p. 321.

FOURTH READING

Genesis 49:1–18

Realizing prophetically that his family would be enslaved soon after his death, Jacob summoned all his sons in order to reveal to them when the final Redemption would occur. Jacob thought that this knowledge would inspire his descendants to do their utmost to hasten the advent of the Redemption. But G-d foresaw that this knowledge would dishearten Jacob's descendants who would be of weaker spiritual character. G-d therefore withdrew this prophetic knowledge from Jacob so he could not divulge it to his sons.

Staying Focused on Our Goal

וַיִּקְרָא יַעֲקֹב אֶל בָּנָיו וַיֹּאמֶר הֵאָסְפוּ וְאַגִּידָה לָכֶם אֵת
אֲשֶׁר יִקְרָא אֶתְכֶם בְּאַחֲרִית הַיָּמִים: (בראשית מט, א)

**Jacob summoned his sons, saying, "Gather together and
I will tell you what will befall you at the End of Days."**

Jacob, like all the patriarchs and matriarchs, had surrendered his own will to G-d's. His desires therefore always reflected G-d's desires. Thus, even though G-d did not allow Jacob to reveal the date of the Redemption, Jacob's desire to do so reflected a similar desire to do so on G-d's part.

We are taught that on account of G-d's deep desire, He did in fact reveal this knowledge to us on a subconscious level. This subconscious knowledge of the date of the Redemption enables us to "not take exile seriously," that is, to already live to some extent in the reality of Redemption – free from the physical and spiritual constraints of exile, free from servitude to foreign masters, and free from our own yet-unrectified selves.

By living this way, we hasten the advent of the true Redemption itself.[6]

6. *Likutei Sichot*, vol. 20, pp. 228–234.

FIFTH READING
Genesis 49:19–26

Jacob then blessed each of his 12 sons in accordance with their unique contribution to the overall Divine mission of the Jewish people. Jacob blessed his son Asher's territory with fruitful olive trees, whose oil would be used to prepare tasty food that would be served at the tables of kings.

The King's Delicacies

מֵאָשֵׁר שְׁמֵנָה לַחְמוֹ וְהוּא יִתֵּן מַעֲדַנֵּי מֶלֶךְ: (בראשית מט, כ)

[Jacob said,] "From Asher will come the richest foods, and he will provide the king's delicacies."

A delicacy is consumed not to satisfy hunger or nutritional needs but to provide delight. A king is used to having all his needs provided for amply and even having common delicacies readily available. Thus, a *king's delicacy* is something so rare and special that it can delight even royalty.

G-d has made us all "kings" over the part of reality that we can refine and elevate.[7] We are therefore worthy of being provided with the rarest delicacies. Indeed, in the Messianic Redemption, not only will our basic needs be provided for in abundance, but "all manner of delicacies will be as abundant as dust."[8] The purpose of this abundance will be to free us from the distractions of work and to enhance our appreciation of G-d's goodness, enabling us to devote our energies to heightening our Divine consciousness.[9]

Thus, by providing for the needs of our fellows – ensuring that none of them lack not only the necessities of life but even delicacies that befit a king – we can hasten the advent of the Messianic Era.[10]

---

7. *Tikunei Zohar,* Introduction (1b).
8. *Mishneh Torah, Melachim* 12:5.
9. Isaiah 11:9.
10. *Likutei Sichot,* vol. 32, pp. 186–191.

SIXTH READING
Genesis 49:27–50:20

Jacob blessed Benjamin with power to fight the Jewish people's enemies like a wolf, which fearlessly grabs its prey away from its owners.

Being a Wolf

בִּנְיָמִין זְאֵב יִטְרָף וגו': (בראשית מט, כז)

[Jacob said,] "Benjamin will be like a wolf that grabs."

Allegorically, our greatest enemy is our own evil inclination. Thus, Jacob blessed the tribe of Benjamin with the intense soul-powers that would enable them to "grab" hold of themselves and return to the path of holiness.

Through repentance, we "grab" the Divine sparks hidden in evil, since, as our sages teach, through repentance we transform sins into merits.[11] This power of Benjamin to transform darkness into light was demonstrated when, in the historical events leading up to the miracle of Purim, Mordechai and Esther – who were Benjaminites – foiled Haman's plot and were given his estate: the very house that King Ahasuerus had given to Haman, the embodiment of evil, was transferred to Esther, i.e., to the domain of holiness.

Inasmuch as all the tribes were blessed with each other's individual blessings,[12] we are all empowered with Benjamin's blessing to be able to transform darkness into light.[13]

11. *Yoma* 86b.
12. Genesis 49:28.
13. *Likutei Sichot*, vol. 25, pp. 275–284.

SHABBAT

SEVENTH READING
Genesis 50:21–26

After concluding his blessings to his family, Jacob passed away.
Joseph then led his brothers to the Land of Israel to bury their
father in the family tomb in Hebron, as Jacob had instructed. After
they returned to Egypt, Joseph continued to provide for his family
while serving as viceroy of Egypt. Before his own death, Joseph
reminded the family of G-d's promise to return their descendants
to the Land of Israel.

Investing in Our Future

וַיַּרְא יוֹסֵף לְאֶפְרַיִם בְּנֵי שִׁלֵּשִׁים גַּם בְּנֵי מָכִיר בֶּן
מְנַשֶּׁה יֻלְּדוּ עַל בִּרְכֵּי יוֹסֵף: (בראשית נ, כג)

**Joseph lived to see [his son] Ephraim's great-grandchildren.
Even the children of Machir son of [Joseph's son]
Manasseh were born between Joseph's knees.**

The Biblical idiom of "being born between someone's knees"
means to be educated and mentored by that person.

According to Jewish law, a father and a grandfather are obligated to educate their children and grandchildren in the ways
of the Torah.[14] But the sages differ regarding whether a *great*-
grandfather is obligated to educate his great-grandchild.[15]

Nevertheless, we see from Joseph's behavior that if we merit
living long enough to see our great-grandchildren, we should,
as Joseph did, study the Torah with them. If we are incapable of
doing so, we can follow Joseph's example by financially supporting
their Torah education. We will thereby be contributing to their
future and ensuring their greatest spiritual happiness.[16]

14. Deuteronomy 4:9; *Kidushin* 30a.
15. *Siftei Kohen* on *Yoreh Deah* 245:1. See *Shulchan Aruch HaRav, Talmud
Torah*, 1:8–9 and sources cited there.
16. *Likutei Sichot*, vol. 20, pp. 247–248.

EXODUS

Shemot

Slavery

Exodus 1:1–6:1

THE FIRST SECTION OF THE BOOK OF EXODUS OPENS BY LIST-
ing the names (*Shemot*, in Hebrew) of Jacob's sons, and then
chronicles the growth of their descendants into a nation and their
subsequent enslavement in Egypt. As the conditions of slavery
progressively worsen, the Jews cry out to G-d. G-d then charges
Moses with freeing the Jewish people from slavery in order to
receive the Torah. G-d informs them that the purpose of their
redemption is so they can assume their role as the moral guides
of humanity, steering the world toward its Divine fulfillment as
G-d's true home.

FIRST READING
Exodus 1:1–17

The Jews multiplied prolifically. In less than a century, their numbers increased so dramatically that Pharaoh feared that they could take over Egypt. He therefore began conscripting the Jews to labor in his building projects. Unfortunately, the Jews – except for the tribe of Levi – had begun to neglect their moral heritage, which left them susceptible to Pharaoh's artful appeal to their patriotic loyalty to Egypt. Thus, Pharaoh eventually succeeded in enslaving the Jews altogether, except for the Levites.

The Individual and the Community

וְאֵלֶּה שְׁמוֹת בְּנֵי יִשְׂרָאֵל ... וַיְהִי כָּל נֶפֶשׁ ... שִׁבְעִים נָפֶשׁ וגו': (שמות א, א-ה)

These are the names of the descendants
of Israel .... They numbered seventy.

The Torah first lists Jacob's descendants by name and then tells us how many there were. A name reflects an entity's unique identity in contrast to other entities in the same group. In contrast, when we count the entities in a group, we focus on their common denominator – the fact that they are all members of the same group. Their individual identities disappear.

Thus, by both listing the Jewish people by name and counting them, G-d indicated that He loves them both on account of each individual's unique personality and on account of their common Jewish identity – their shared, basic Jewish consciousness.

By stating His love both for every individual Jew and for the Jewish people as a whole before they descended into the bitter exile of spiritual and physical servitude, G-d indicated that when we suffer, it does not mean that He does not love us any less. Although hidden, His love for us is always present and will eventually be revealed as well.[1]

---

1. *Likutei Sichot*, vol. 6, pp. 7–8, vol. 3, p. 844.

SECOND READING
Exodus 1:18–2:10

Thirty years of conscripted labor neither broke the Jews' spirit nor curbed their fertility. So, when Pharaoh's astrologers discerned that the Jews' future redeemer would soon be born, Pharaoh attempted to prevent the redemption by decreeing that every newborn Jewish boy be killed. Amram, the leader of the Jews in Egypt, therefore concluded that there was no point in bringing more Jewish children into the world. He divorced his wife Yocheved – and the rest of the Jews followed his example, divorcing their wives. But Amram's daughter Miriam convinced him that they must continue their efforts toward the survival of the Jewish people. Amram therefore remarried Yocheved – and again, the rest of the Jews followed his example.

Women of Redemption

וַיֵּלֶךְ אִישׁ מִבֵּית לֵוִי וַיִּקַּח אֶת בַּת לֵוִי: (שמות ב, א)

A Levite man went and married a daughter of Levi.

Referring to the Jewish women's efforts to conceive and raise children despite Pharaoh's decree, our sages state that "in the merit of the righteous women of that generation our forefathers were redeemed from Egypt."[2]

In the present exile, too, we will hasten the advent of the Redemption by ignoring societal pressure to "drown" our children in materialistic culture, raising them instead to be a generation of Jews faithful to G-d's Torah. Once again, the efforts of the women of our generation in this regard will be decisive – as the sages also state,[3] "The future generations will be redeemed only in the merit of the righteous women of those generations."[4]

---

2. *Sotah* 11b.
3. *Yalkut Shim'oni*, Ruth, §606.
4. *Likutei Sichot*, vol. 1, pp. 112–113.

THIRD READING

Exodus 2:11–25

Moses was born to Amram and Yocheved. Informed by his astrologers that the Jews' redeemer had been born, Pharaoh ordered that all newborn boys be thrown into the Nile River to die. In order to save Moses' life, Yocheved placed him in a basket, which she hid among the reeds in the Nile River. He was discovered by Pharaoh's daughter, Bitya, who adopted him. Bitya employed Yocheved as Moses' wet nurse. Yocheved kept Moses at home, and thus Moses grew up in his family's household, joining Pharaoh's household only at about age 12. Pharaoh knew that Moses was a Jew, but he hoped that by raising him as an Egyptian, his exceptional intelligence and talents could be put to good use in Pharaoh's government. When Moses was about 18 years old, he killed an Egyptian taskmaster whom he saw beating a Jew mercilessly. As Moses feared, Pharaoh heard of this and sentenced him to death.

Taking Spiritual Risks

וַיַּךְ אֶת הַמִּצְרִי וגו': (שמות ב, יב)

[Moses] struck down the Egyptian.

At the time when he killed the taskmaster, Moses was being groomed for greatness in Pharaoh's household. He nonetheless risked his life and his comfortable and privileged royal lifestyle in order to help his kinsmen.

Similarly, we should not hesitate to risk our own spiritual, social, or material comfort in order to help rescue our fellows who are suffering under spiritual or material bondage.[5]

---

5. *Sichot Kodesh 5740*, vol. 1, pp. 784–788.

FOURTH READING

Exodus 3:1–15

Moses fled from Egypt, eventually arriving in Midian. At the age of 77, he married Tziporah, daughter of the local chieftain, Jethro. Jethro had denounced idolatry, and had therefore been ostracized by his fellow Midianites. Moses went to work shepherding Jethro's flocks.

Tending G-d's Flock

וּמֹשֶׁה הָיָה רֹעֶה אֶת צֹאן יִתְרוֹ וגו': (שמות ג, א)

Moses was tending Jethro's sheep.

Jethro was an intelligent person (having previously served as an advisor to Pharaoh and as the leader of Midian). He surely discerned Moses' intelligence and knew about his aristocratic status, both as the son of Amram and as a prince in Pharaoh's court. It seems strange, then, that Jethro should have put Moses to work as a shepherd.

But Jethro sensed – consciously or subconsciously – that Moses was destined to lead G-d's "flock" and therefore – intentionally or unintentionally – employed him in a way that would foster his innate leadership traits in preparation for his mission.

A lesson we can learn from this is that even those of us who feel that their social stature and intellectual training entitle them to advanced career positions should not consider it beneath their dignity to teach young children or those at the beginning of their quest for Jewish knowledge – G-d's "flock." Rather, like Moses, we should not be haughty about our qualifications. On the contrary, tending G-d's flock is the best preparation for an eventual position of leadership, should Divine providence lead us in this direction.[6]

6. *Likutei Sichot*, vol. 8, pp. 250–251.

FIFTH READING

Exodus 3:16–4:17

The Egyptians had intensified their slavery of the Jews, so G-d appeared to Moses on Mount Sinai, speaking to him from a bush that was burning but was miraculously not consumed. G-d informed Moses that He was now going to redeem the Jewish people from Egypt in order to give them the Torah and to bring them to the Land of Israel.

Milk and Honey

וָאֹמַר אַעֲלֶה אֶתְכֶם מֵעֳנִי מִצְרַיִם ... אֶל אֶרֶץ זָבַת חָלָב וּדְבָשׁ: (שמות ג, יז)

[G-d said to Moses,] "I am going to take [the
Jewish people] out from the affliction of Egypt ...
to a land flowing with milk and honey."

Spiritual "exile" means being deprived of the full use of all our abilities and potentials in cultivating our relationship with G-d – either by outside forces or by our own materialism. Conversely, "redemption" means the freedom to express the full gamut of our abilities and put them to use, blending and developing them to express our inherent Divinity. When our relationship with G-d is allowed to blossom and grow, it eventually taps the innermost longings of our heart.

Allegorically, the land represents our relationship with G-d. The sweetness of milk represents the delight we experience in comprehending as much of G-d's nature as we can; the even greater sweetness of honey represents the delight we experience in feeling so close to G-d that we become one with Him.

G-d therefore describes the type of "land" that He seeks to bring His people to as "flowing with milk and honey." He has blessed our relationship with Him to be infused with both these aspects of delight.[7]

7. *Sefer HaMa'amarim 5686*, pp. 246–248.

SIXTH READING
Exodus 4:18–31

G-d then told Moses that Pharaoh would refuse to release the Jewish people, and that only after suffering a series of miraculously harsh plagues would he do so. G-d therefore instructed Moses to warn Pharaoh about these plagues.

We Are G-d's Children

וְאָמַרְתָּ אֶל פַּרְעֹה כֹּה אָמַר ה' בְּנִי בְכֹרִי יִשְׂרָאֵל: (שמות ד, כב)

[G-d told Moses,] "Say to Pharaoh: 'Thus says G-d: Israel is My preeminent son.'"

By referring to the Jewish people as His "son," G-d implied two things: First, that He would be angry with anyone who harms them, just as any father would be angry with anyone who harms his child.[8] Second, that the love between G-d and His people is as essential as that between a father and a son.

From the second point we learn that no matter how depraved we may become, G-d's love for us always remains intact. And conversely, each of us should feel as close to G-d as a son or daughter feels to his or her parents. Just as a child's feelings of closeness to his or her parents may sometimes be dormant, so might our feelings of closeness to G-d sometimes seem dormant. But just like a child's feelings of closeness to his or her parents can always be awakened, so can our feelings of closeness to G-d always be awakened.[9]

---

8. *Sefer HaMa'amarim 5701*, p. 82; *Sefer HaMa'amarim 5684*, p. 236.
9. *Tanya*, chapter 2; *Sefer HaMa'amarim 5689*, p. 112.

SEVENTH READING
Exodus 5:1–6:1

Moses took leave of Jethro and set out for Egypt. As Levites, Moses and Aaron were exempt from Egyptian slavery and were able to visit Pharaoh as they pleased. But, as G-d had predicted, when Moses demanded that Pharaoh release the Jews, even for three days, Pharaoh refused. Instead, Pharaoh told Moses and Aaron to abandon their dreams of national liberation and go back to their personal affairs.

Not Just for the Elite

וַיֹּאמֶר אֲלֵהֶם מֶלֶךְ מִצְרַיִם ... לְכוּ לְסִבְלֹתֵיכֶם: (שמות ה, ד)

The king of Egypt said to [Moses and Aaron,] "Get back to your own chores."

Pharaoh realized that every nation needs its elite class devoted to preserving its cultural identity and heritage. He therefore did not object to Moses and Aaron studying the Torah and even teaching it to the other Jews. What he did object to was their proposal to upset the natural order by freeing the Jews. Pharaoh believed in nature, and since the Egyptians were more powerful than the Jews and nature decrees that the strong rule the weak, the Jews should be slaves to the Egyptians. The essence of the Exodus, however, was to demonstrate that the Jewish people are not bound by the laws of nature, and therefore Moses and Aaron did not accept Pharaoh's reasoning.

Similarly, we should never succumb to accepting Pharaoh's outlook – the notion that the Torah should be fully observed only by a spiritual elite – or even by the masses, but only on special occasions. On the contrary, we must seek to free everyone from the bonds of material slavery and allow the Torah to permeate all aspects of life.[10]

10. *Likutei Sichot*, vol. 16, pp. 29–32.

Va'eira

The First Seven Plagues
Exodus 6:2–9:35

IN THE SECOND SECTION OF THE BOOK OF EXODUS, G-D begins the process that will lead to the redemption of the Jews from Egyptian slavery. He first informs Moses that it is crucial that he and the Jewish people demonstrate the same faith in G-d that the patriarchs did when He appeared (*Va'eira*, in Hebrew) to them. After some additional preparations, G-d then begins to strike the Egyptians with plagues.

FIRST READING
Exodus 6:2–13

At the end of the previous section, Moses was troubled by the seeming contradiction between G-d's promise of redemption and His apparent mistreatment of the Jewish people. G-d therefore told Moses: "You must learn from the patriarchs and matriarchs. They believed in Me unquestioningly, even though I made promises to them that I did not fulfill during their lifetimes."

Freedom from Bondage

וַיְדַבֵּר אֱלֹקִים אֶל מֹשֶׁה וַיֹּאמֶר אֵלָיו אֲנִי ה': (שמות ו, ב)

G-d spoke to Moses, saying to him, "I am G-d."

In order to impress upon Moses that He is indeed trustworthy, G-d deliberately referred to Himself in this verse by His Name *Havayah*. This Name indicates that G-d is beyond time and space – that He is not subject to any of the limitations that operate in the physical world He created. Therefore, there is nothing that can prevent Him from keeping His word.

In fact, the reason why G-d exiled the Jewish people to Egypt altogether was in order to elevate our consciousness to the level signified by the Name *Havayah*. In Hebrew, the word "Egypt" (*Mitzrayim*) means "limitations." G-d placed us within a world of seemingly inescapable limitations and then elevated us beyond it.

The exile and redemption from Egypt thus contain a key lesson that the Jewish people had to learn in order to become G-d's chosen nation. This lesson enables us today to rise above the empty routine of mundane life: Our personal redemption is not complete until we realize that G-d is unlimited and we learn to rely on His promise to free us from the bondage of materiality.[1]

1. *Likutei Sichot*, vol. 31, pp. 23 ff.

SECOND READING

Exodus 6:14–28

The Torah then reviews the lineage of Moses and Aaron, for their lineage was an important factor contributing to the Jewish people's acceptance of them as their leaders.

The Importance of History

הוּא אַהֲרֹן וּמֹשֶׁה אֲשֶׁר אָמַר ה' לָהֶם הוֹצִיאוּ אֶת בְּנֵי יִשְׂרָאֵל מֵאֶרֶץ
מִצְרַיִם וְגוֹ': הֵם הַמְדַבְּרִים אֶל פַּרְעֹה ... הוּא מֹשֶׁה וְאַהֲרֹן: (שמות ו, כו-כז)

They were Aaron and Moses, to whom G-d said, "Take the Israelites out of Egypt...." They were the ones who spoke to Pharaoh ... they were Moses and Aaron.

Allegorically, Aaron signifies our intellectual bond with G-d, while Moses signifies our supra-intellectual bond with Him. Similarly, "the Israelites" signify our Divine nature, while "Pharaoh" signifies our human/animal nature.

Therefore, when discussing how to speak to the Israelites, Aaron is mentioned before Moses, since it is usually enough to use the intellect to rouse our inner Divinity and generate feelings of love for G-d. Our Divine side can respond to logic and philosophical explanations. But when discussing how to speak to Pharaoh, Moses is mentioned first, for in order to get the human/animal side of our personalities to answer G-d's calling, intellect and logic are usually not sufficient. We must emulate Moses, exciting our baser nature with supra-intellectual revelations of G-d.

It is therefore important to recount how G-d has performed miracles for us throughout our history, even up to the present time.[2]

2. *Or HaTorah, Shemot*, vol. 1, pp. 225–230; cf. *Sha'ar HaYichud VeHaEmunah*, chapter 5 (79b–80a).

THIRD READING

Exodus 6:29–7:7

G-d informed Moses that one of the purposes of the plagues would be to demonstrate to the Egyptians G-d's mastery over nature.

G-d's Miraculous Mercy

וְיָדְעוּ מִצְרַיִם כִּי אֲנִי ה' וגו': (שמות ז, ה)

The Egyptians will recognize that I am G-d.

G-d refers to Himself here by the Name *Havayah*, which indicates how He is not bound by any limitations. One of the implications of this Name, therefore, is that G-d can be *merciful*; that is, He can exercise kindness even when the laws of logic would demand corrective punishment or vengeance.

In this context, the purpose of the plagues was to introduce the Egyptians to the concept of G-d's *mercy*. As worshippers of nature, the Egyptians were fully acquainted with G-d's power of apparently blind judgment, by which survival belongs to the fittest. However, the Egyptians did not yet recognize that G-d is *greater* than nature, and can override the unforgiving laws of nature when He sees fit.

Thus, what later impressed Pharaoh the most was Moses' ability to *stop* the plagues, rather than to initiate them. The magicians of Pharaoh's court were indeed able to duplicate some of the plagues, for they knew how to manipulate nature to an extent, and were thus able to summon the forces of nature to wreak destruction. But the magicians could not *reverse* or *check* these forces. Only Moses could do so – by invoking G-d's mercy through prayer.

We, too, should never doubt G-d's ability or readiness to overrule the natural laws of strict justice, invoking His mercy through prayer.[3]

---

3. *Torat Chaim, Shemot* 396b–397a; *Sefer HaMa'amarim 5678*, p. 240; *Sefer HaMa'amarim 5705*, p. 139; *Sefer HaMa'amarim 5706*, p. 71.

FOURTH READING

Exodus 7:8–8:6

G-d told Moses to transform the Nile River's water into blood, as the first of the ten plagues. The plague of blood was followed by the plague of frogs.

Warmth and Coldness

וְשָׁרַץ הַיְאֹר צְפַרְדְּעִים וְעָלוּ . . . וּבְתַנּוּרֶיךָ וְגו': (שמות ז, כח)

[Moses told Pharaoh,] "The river will swarm with frogs, and they will go . . . into your ovens."

The lesson of the plague of blood was that Egypt's cold indifference toward G-d must be replaced with warm enthusiasm for Him. Once this has been accomplished, the second, complementary stage is to replace the Egyptian enthusiasm for materiality with cold indifference toward it. Although the Torah does require us to tend to our physical needs, we must be careful not to let this involvement divert our attention from the primary purpose of life – spiritual growth and accomplishing G-d's plan for us and for all reality.

Inasmuch as frogs are cold creatures, their invasion of the Egyptians' ovens allegorically signified how the oven-like Egyptian "heat" – the Egyptians' enthusiasm for materialism – should be replaced by cold apathy. This is a basic stage in our own, ongoing redemption from the bondage of our personal "Egypt."[4]

4. *Likutei Sichot*, vol. 1, p. 123.

FIFTH READING
Exodus 8:7–18

Pharaoh promised to send forth the Jewish people if Moses would stop the plague of frogs. Moses prayed to G-d, and most of the frogs died.

The Secret of Survival

וַיָּמֻתוּ הַצְפַרְדְעִים מִן הַבָּתִּים מִן הַחֲצֵרֹת וּמִן הַשָּׂדֹת: (שמות ח, ט)

The frogs in the houses, the courtyards, and the fields died.

The Torah previously mentioned that some of the frogs had gone into the ovens. What happened to them?[5]

A frog's natural habitat is water; for a frog to jump into a piping hot oven is an act of the ultimate self-sacrifice. G-d did not let this selfless act of obedience to His will go unrewarded: when it was time to end this plague, "the frogs in the houses, the courtyards, and the fields died" – but those in the ovens remained alive.

Similarly, our historical survival as a people is due to our willingness to comply with G-d's will no matter what the cost.[6]

5. Exodus 7:28. See insight for the preceding day.
6. *Yalkut Shim'oni* 182.

SIXTH READING
Exodus 8:19–9:16

The sixth plague was an inflammation that erupted into blisters that struck the Egyptians and their animals.

Healthy Distinctions

וְלֹא יָכְלוּ הַחַרְטֻמִּים לַעֲמֹד לִפְנֵי מֹשֶׁה מִפְּנֵי הַשְּׁחִין וְגו': (שמות ט, יא)

The magicians could not stand before Moses because of the inflammation.

Until this point, the Egyptian magicians had admitted that the plagues were "the finger of G-d" only when they were caused either by something that could not be manipulated by magic (because it was too small, as was the case with the plague of lice) or when they were not caused by means of any specific act of Moses' or Aaron's whatsoever (as was the case with the plagues of the mixed horde and the epidemic). They still believed, however, that G-d's power over the forces of nature that *are* susceptible to magic was no greater than their own wizardry.

After the plague of inflammation, however, they had to admit that G-d could manipulate the forces of nature that are susceptible to magic far beyond *their* ability to do so. Therefore, they were completely demoralized and "could not stand before Moses."

Similarly, we have our inner "Egyptian magicians" – the voices that try to demoralize us by minimizing G-d's involvement in the world, ascribing everything to the workings of nature. We can combat these inner voices by using natural means to serve G-d and then allowing G-d to crown our efforts with unexpected success, which cannot be explained away by the laws of nature. Our inner "Egyptian magicians" will then "not be able to stand before" us.[7]

7. *Likutei Sichot*, vol. 36, pp. 31–32.

SEVENTH READING
Exodus 9:17–35

The seventh plague was a rain of hail formed miraculously of ice together with fire. Pharaoh again agreed to send forth the Jewish people if Moses would stop the plague. Moses prayed to G-d, and the thunder and hail ceased and the rain stopped.

Combining Mercy and Severity

וּמָטָר לֹא נִתַּךְ אָרְצָה: (שמות ט, לג)

The rain stopped pouring down on the ground.

Pharaoh repented for his sin of not listening to G-d's word by agreeing at this point to follow His will and release the Jewish people from slavery. This act of repentance elevated Pharaoh to the status of a Righteous Gentile – until he changed his mind again.

A Righteous Gentile is a non-Jew who has chosen to root himself in the Divine source of goodness by accepting his obligations as defined by the Torah. (These are known as the Noahide laws.) Once a non-Jew attains this status, his repentance not only has the power to eliminate the harm caused by his sin, but its effects altogether.

Therefore, in Pharaoh's case, not only did the destructive hail cease, the raindrops evaporated in midair. His short-lived repentance caused whatever was produced by his sin to disappear altogether.

From here we see the great power of proper repentance, and its ability to wipe away the effects of past wrongdoing.[8]

---

8. *Likutei Sichot*, vol. 6, pp. 52–56.

Bo

The Last Three Plagues; The Exodus
Exodus 10:1–13:16

THE THIRD SECTION OF THE BOOK OF EXODUS OPENS AS G-D tells Moses to come (*Bo*, in Hebrew) to Pharaoh in order to announce the eighth plague. Two more plagues follow, after which the Jews are finally released from slavery and sent forth from Egypt. G-d tells the Jewish people to observe the anniversary of the Exodus as the holiday of Passover.

FIRST READING

Exodus 10:1–11

G-d told Moses to approach Pharaoh and warn him about the imminent eighth plague, a huge swarm of locusts that would decimate Egypt's extensive grain fields.

Coming Home

וַיֹּאמֶר ה' אֶל מֹשֶׁה בֹּא אֶל פַּרְעֹה: (שמות י, א)

G-d told Moses, "Come to Pharaoh."

We would expect G-d to tell Moses to "*go* to Pharaoh" rather than to "*come* to Pharaoh." By saying "*come* to Pharaoh," G-d is teaching us how we should understand the Exodus from a broader perspective, including our personal process of redemption from our own states of "bondage" and "exile."

Redemption can only happen if we are "coming" rather than "going." *Going* somewhere implies that our home base is where we already are; we are simply *visiting* the place we are headed toward. *Coming* somewhere, in contrast, implies that we are *moving* our home – that we are going where we are headed with our whole being.

Thus, when we free ourselves of the bondage of materiality by communing with G-d in Torah study or prayer, we should be sure to "come home," immersing ourselves in the words and ideas completely, rather than just "going" there for a visit. In this way, our study and prayer can affect us and change us; it can take us out of our personal Egypt.

Moreover, going out of our personal Egypt hastens the advent of the collective redemption of the Jewish people and all humanity, as well.[1]

---

1. *Sichot Kodesh 5740*, vol. 1, pp. 843–845.

SECOND READING

Exodus 10:12–23

The ninth plague was absolute darkness that descended upon Egypt for six uninterrupted days. Miraculously, the darkness only affected the Egyptians; the Jewish people experienced daylight as usual.

Light and Darkness

וּלְכָל בְּנֵי יִשְׂרָאֵל הָיָה אוֹר בְּמוֹשְׁבֹתָם: (שמות י, כג)

There was light for all the Israelites in their dwellings.

The Egyptians, like many ancient peoples, assumed that the opposing forces of day and night – light and darkness – were the manifestations of two opposing deities. G-d therefore caused darkness and light to occur simultaneously, so the Egyptians could see that nature is ruled by one supreme power.

We, too, should realize that both the "darkness" and the "light" in our lives originate in the one and only G-d. We can then realize that the darkness is really an opportunity for us to bring more Divine light into our lives. This hastens the advent of both our own personal redemption and the Redemption of the world at large.[2]

---

2. *Or HaTorah, Bo*, p. 250; *Sefer HaMa'amarim 5663*, pp. 83–84.

TUESDAY

THIRD READING
Exodus 10:24–11:3

In the tenth and final plague, all the Egyptian firstborn died instantaneously at midnight of the 15th of the month of Nisan.

Slaying the Intellect

וַיֹּאמֶר ה' אֶל מֹשֶׁה עוֹד נֶגַע אֶחָד אָבִיא עַל פַּרְעֹה וְעַל מִצְרַיִם: (שמות יא, א)

G-d said to Moses, "I will send one more plague upon Pharaoh and upon Egypt."

Allegorically, the term "firstborn" refers to the intellect, the first faculty of the soul that emerges in our conscious minds. The intellect is followed by the emotions and the faculties of expression.

It is self-evident that natural human intellect cannot grasp G-d's essence. None of us has the capability to fully understand the true nature or essence of G-d on our own. Nonetheless, we can still "grasp" G-d's essence non-intellectually, through the inner yearning of the heart.[3] In order to reveal this yearning, however, we have to temporarily suspend our intellect in order that it not obstruct our experience of our heart's inner dimension.

"Egypt" in Hebrew (*Mitzrayim*) means "limitations." In order to completely liberate ourselves from "Egypt" – that is, from all the limitations in our lives that keep us from relating directly to G-d – the first stage[4] is to "slay the Egyptian firstborn," which allegorically means to temporarily "neutralize" our limited, human intellect. This way, our hearts' inner yearning for G-d can assert itself and energize our lives.[5]

---

3. See *Zohar* 3:289b (in the *Idra Zuta*).
4. The second stage is the subject of the insight for Shabbat, below.
5. *Ma'amarei Admor HaZakein HaKetzarim*, pp. 33–34.

FOURTH READING

Exodus 11:4–12:20

In preparation for the Exodus, G-d instructed Moses and Aaron concerning the Jewish calendar, which is based primarily on the monthly lunar cycle. G-d then commanded Moses and Aaron to tell the Jewish people to offer up the Passover sacrifice on the fourteenth day of the first month, Nisan.

Study and Prayer

וַיֹּאמֶר ה' אֶל מֹשֶׁה וְאֶל אַהֲרֹן ... הַחֹדֶשׁ הַזֶּה
לָכֶם רֹאשׁ חֳדָשִׁים וגו': (שמות יב, א-ב)

**G-d said to Moses and Aaron…, "This month
will be the first of the months for you."**

The commandment to declare a new month whenever the moon begins anew its cycle of growth and decline is the first law that G-d gave to the Jewish people as a collective entity.

Moses personifies the "downward" revelation of the Torah from on high, which we re-experience whenever we study the Torah. In contrast, Aaron personifies the "upward" striving of the soul toward Divinity, which we experience primarily in prayer.

It was therefore appropriate that G-d addressed the very first, all-encompassing commandment to us through both Moses and Aaron, for the essence of the commandments is the connection between G-d and the people, the twin sides of which we experience through the study of the Torah and prayer.[6]

6. *Sefer HaMa'amarim 5626*, p. 41; *Sefer HaMa'amarim 5632*, vol. 1, pp. 263, 270; *Sefer HaMa'amarim 5716*, pp. 459–465.

FIFTH READING
Exodus 12:21–28

In preparation for the plague of slaying the firstborn, G-d told
the Jews to put some of the blood of the Passover animal sacrifice
on their doorways. This would be a sign for the Angel of Death
to skip over their homes, leaving their own firstborn unharmed.

Achieving Personal Redemption

וּפָסַח ה' עַל הַפֶּתַח וְלֹא יִתֵּן הַמַּשְׁחִית לָבֹא אֶל בָּתֵּיכֶם לִנְגֹּף: (שמות יב, כג)

**[Moses told the Jewish people,] "G-d will pass
over the entrance [to your homes] and not allow
the destructive plague to enter your houses."**

The purpose of the first nine plagues was to bring the Egyptians to
the knowledge of G-d.[7] The Jewish people already believed in G-d,
so there was no concern that these plagues would strike them.

The tenth plague, however, was meant to *slay* the firstborn of
the idolatrous Egyptians, not to *educate* them. Since many Jews
had lapsed in their loyalty to G-d during their Egyptian slavery –
some even serving idols – there was an acute need to counteract
their liability to the death penalty.

This was accomplished by the Passover sacrifice. The lamb was
one of the deities of Egypt, so by slaughtering a lamb, the Jews
were risking offending the Egyptians, thereby putting their lives
in jeopardy. The Jewish people's willingness to suffer martyrdom
in order to fulfill G-d's instructions expressed their essential bond
with Him. The merit of this act neutralized their culpability for
whatever sins they had committed during their slavery in Egypt.

Similarly, whenever we summon up our unconditional and
genuine devotion to G-d, it wipes our past, blemished record
clean, affording us a fresh start in our relationship with Him.[8]

7. Exodus 7:3–5.
8. *Likutei Sichot*, vol. 3, pp. 864–866.

SIXTH READING
Exodus 12:29–51

As Moses had said, all the firstborn Egyptian males died precisely at midnight. The Egyptians urged the Jews to leave, showering them with gifts of silver, gold, and clothing.

Yearning for Redemption

וַתֶּחֱזַק מִצְרַיִם עַל הָעָם: (שמות יב, לג)

The Egyptians urged the people on.

Despite the horrors of slavery, some Jews had second thoughts about leaving Egypt. G-d had to force these reluctant Jews out of Egypt by having the Egyptians urge them to depart.

Nowadays, as well, some might prefer to remain in exile rather than face what they incorrectly imagine to be the "oppression" of living constantly in G-d's presence – as we all will after the Messianic Redemption. Nonetheless, G-d will redeem these people, too – even against their will. Since G-d's mercy extends to all His creatures, He always does what is best for us on all levels, even if we do not presently realize or appreciate it.

On the other hand, if we study the Torah's teachings about the Redemption, we will truly yearn for it. Our increased, collective yearning for the Redemption will, in turn, hasten its arrival.[9]

9. *MiMa'ainei HaChasidut*, vol. 2, p. 61, quoting *Sichot Kodesh 5730*.

SEVENTH READING
Exodus 13:1–16

G-d then told the Jewish people to commemorate the Exodus by consecrating to Him every firstborn. The firstborn boys would be privileged to officiate as priests, and the firstborn bulls, goats, and sheep would be given to the priests and sacrificed.

Transcending the Intellect

קַדֶּשׁ לִי כָל בְּכוֹר וְגוֹ': (שמות יג, ב)

[G-d told Moses to instruct the Israelites,] "Consecrate to Me every firstborn."

As noted above,[10] our human intellect is allegorically referred to as the "firstborn." This "firstborn" has to be "slaughtered" in order to enable the inner yearnings of our heart to lead us where our human intellect cannot.

Besides our human intellect, we also possess a Divine intellect – the intellect of our Divine soul. In order to "grasp" G-d with the inner yearnings of our heart, the Divine intellect, too, has to be bypassed, but it does not have to be "slaughtered." Although it cannot grasp G-d (since G-d cannot be grasped by *any* form of intellect), it can still lead us far above the material world, to the point beyond which only the inner yearnings of the heart can tread.

Therefore, this "firstborn" need only be "consecrated," not "slaughtered." We "consecrate" it by employing it to delve intellectually as deeply as we can into the nature of G-d.[11]

---

10. In the insight for Tuesday.
11. *Ma'amarei Admor HaZakein HaKetzarim*, pp. 33–34.

Beshalach

The Splitting of the Sea
Exodus 13:17–17:16

THE FOURTH SECTION OF THE BOOK OF EXODUS BEGINS AS Pharaoh "sent forth" (*Beshalach*, in Hebrew) the Jewish people from Egypt. The Jews proceed toward Mount Sinai to receive the Torah, but are pursued by Pharaoh and the Egyptian army. G-d splits the Sea of Reeds, enabling the Jews to pass to safety and then drowning the Egyptians in it. The Jews then continue on toward Mount Sinai, with G-d miraculously providing them with food (manna) and water from a rock. Just as they approach their destination, the Jews are attacked by the nation of Amalek.

FIRST READING
Exodus 13:17–14:8

The Jewish people, released from slavery by Egypt, set out into
the desert.

Until the Final Redemption

וַחֲמֻשִׁים עָלוּ בְנֵי יִשְׂרָאֵל מֵאֶרֶץ מִצְרָיִם: (שמות יג, יח)

The Israelites left Egypt armed.

Although the Jews were leaving Egypt unchallenged, they took
weapons with them, for their redemption was not yet complete.
They would have to face other enemies in their journey to the
Promised Land and conquest of it. In contrast, after the Messianic
Redemption, no nations will oppose goodness and justice. Therefore, the whole world "will beat their swords into ploughshares"[1]
for there will be no more need for weaponry.

The same difference applies to the spiritual dynamics of the
Egyptian and Messianic redemptions, respectively. At the Exodus
from Egypt, evil was temporarily subjugated, but it continued
to exist. It was therefore necessary for the Jewish people to be
"armed" spiritually as well as physically – to be on guard against
evil and wary of it. This will continue to be the case until the final
Redemption. Goodness does sometimes gain the upper hand, but
caution against evil is always necessary. Only in the Messianic Era
will G-d "wipe the spirit of evil off the face of the earth,"[2] fully
refining the world and transforming it into good. There will then
no longer be any need for spiritual "weaponry" either.

In the meantime, as we continue to contend with evil, our
awareness that the battle will soon be won keeps us inspired and
properly directed.[3]

---

1. Isaiah 2:4.
2. Zechariah 13:2.
3. *Sefer HaMa'amarim 5716*, pp. 537, 542.

SECOND READING

Exodus 14:9–14

G-d inspired Pharaoh to pursue the Jews to the shore of the Sea of Reeds (the present-day Gulf of Suez). The Jews panicked, but Moses reassured them of G-d's assistance.

Elevating the Last Sparks

כִּי אֲשֶׁר רְאִיתֶם אֶת מִצְרַיִם הַיּוֹם לֹא תֹסִפוּ

לִרְאֹתָם עוֹד עַד עוֹלָם: (שמות יד, יג)

[Moses told the Jewish people, "Do not fear . . . ,] for the Egyptians whom you have seen today you will never see again."

We are taught that this statement is also to be understood as a commandment: We are not allowed to settle in Egypt but may only visit there for the sake of commerce.[4]

According to Kabbalah, the reason for this prohibition is that there are "sparks" of holiness scattered throughout the entire world; our mission is to return these sparks to their source by utilizing the physical world to fulfill G-d's plan. When the Jewish people left Egypt, they took all the sparks that could be elevated along with them. There is therefore no longer any reason for a Jew to live in Egypt.

Visiting Egypt for business, in contrast, *is* permitted. Although the sparks from Egypt itself were all elevated by the Exodus, objects continue to be brought into the country from elsewhere through trade, together with their inherent holy sparks. It is therefore necessary for us to conduct trade there, thereby liberating those elusive sparks as well.

But since there is no *intrinsic* mission left to be accomplished in Egypt, it is forbidden for Jews to live there, since every aspect of our lives must have a spiritual purpose.[5]

4. See *Mishneh Torah, Melachim* 5:7.
5. *Sichot Kodesh 5734*, vol. 2, pp. 432–433.

THIRD READING
Exodus 14:15–25

Moses started to pray to G-d for deliverance. But G-d told Moses that there was no need to pray; all that was necessary was that he lift his staff over the sea and it would split, enabling the Jews to pass through it to safety.

Jumping In

דַּבֵּר אֶל בְּנֵי יִשְׂרָאֵל וְיִסָּעוּ: (שמות יד, טו)

**[G-d told Moses,] "Speak to the Israelites
and let them journey forth."**

According to the Midrash,[6] the sea had not yet split when G-d told the Jews to enter it. The people hesitated until the prince of the tribe of Judah, Nachshon son of Aminadav, jumped in. Only then did G-d tell Moses to raise his hand and split the sea.

Nachshon knew that G-d had instructed the people to travel to Mount Sinai to receive the Torah. He was therefore unfazed by obstacles. If he had to jump into the sea in order to reach Mount Sinai, so be it. Thus, in his merit, the sea split.

Nowadays, as well, we have been informed that since we stand at the threshold of the Messianic Redemption, our sole task is to proceed forward toward that goal. If it appears to us that obstacles still remain, let us learn from Nachshon to proceed nonetheless; in this merit, the obstacles will disappear.[7]

---

6. *Mechilta, Beshalach* 5; *Sotah* 37a and *Chidushei Agadot* ad loc.
7. *Likutei Sichot*, vol. 1, pp. 135–136.

FOURTH READING

Exodus 14:26–15:26

As G-d promised, the sea split and the Jews passed through it to safety. The Egyptians, including Pharaoh, followed them onto the dry seabed, but G-d let the water return to its natural state, drowning them all. When the waves of the sea threw the dead Egyptians and their chariots upon the shore, Moses and Miriam led the Jewish men and women in praising G-d for rescuing them.

Upgrading Belief

וַיַּרְא יִשְׂרָאֵל ... וַיַּאֲמִינוּ בַּה' וגו': (שמות יד, לא)

Israel saw . . . and they believed in G-d.

Generally, after seeing something, we no longer need to accept it on "blind" faith. Why, then, after *seeing* G-d's deliverance, did the Jewish people still need to *believe* in G-d? The answer is that once they had seen the aspect of G-d that they had previously only believed in – His ability to rescue them – they could then "upgrade" their belief to believing in newer, higher aspects of G-d, which remained beyond what they had seen.

The potential to "upgrade" our faith is infinite. Through the process of spiritual growth, we eventually come to *know* what we currently only *believe* about G-d. We then realize that there is still more to believe about G-d. In this way we perpetually broaden the horizons of our faith and our capacity to relate to G-d on ever higher levels.[8]

8. *Derech Mitzvotecha*, pp. 44b–46b.

FIFTH READING
Exodus 15:27–16:10

Led by G-d's pillar of cloud, the people proceeded on their journey toward Mount Sinai. One month after the Exodus, on 15 Iyar, the Jews arrived at Alush, where they ran out of the matzo that they took with them when they left Egypt. G-d then began to feed them with manna, a type of bread that descended from heaven each morning.

Bread and Meat

וַיֹּאמֶר מֹשֶׁה בְּתֵת ה' לָכֶם בָּעֶרֶב בָּשָׂר לֶאֱכֹל
וְלֶחֶם בַּבֹּקֶר לִשְׂבֹּעַ וְגוֹ': (שמות טז, ח)

Moses said [to the Jewish people,] "G-d will give you meat to eat in the evening and bread to satiety in the morning."

Allegorically, bread signifies the *outer* dimension of the Torah – its laws and lessons for life; meat signifies the *inner* dimension of the Torah – its teachings regarding the inner workings of the universe and the spiritual life of the soul. Oil/fat is another metaphor for the inner dimension of the Torah; thus, quail meat – which is particularly fatty – represents the innermost secrets of the Torah.

This explains why every Jew received equal portions of manna, just as the laws and lessons of the Torah apply to every Jew equally. In contrast, there was no specific quantity of quails per person, for each of us plumbs the depths of the inner dimension of the Torah differently in accordance with our spiritual disposition.

But just as our daily diet of bread should be complemented by some protein, we must all delve at least somewhat into the inner dimension of the Torah in order to achieve optimal spiritual health.[9]

---

9. *Likutei Sichot*, vol. 16, pp. 168–171.

SIXTH READING
Exodus 16:11–36

The manna did not descend on the Sabbath. Instead, a double portion descended on Friday. This was the only exception to G-d's directive not to save manna from one day for use on the next day.

The Sabbath

רְאוּ כִּי ה' נָתַן לָכֶם הַשַּׁבָּת וגו': (שמות טז, כט)

**[Moses told the Jewish people,] "See that
G-d has given you the Sabbath."**

By saying that "G-d has given *you* the Sabbath," Moses was implying that G-d has given it "to each of you individually" – to every Jewish person. Although the external form of Sabbath observance is the same for every Jew, the nature of the inner, spiritual experience of the Sabbath differs from person to person.

The quality of spiritual inspiration we experience on the Sabbath is dependent largely on how much effort we expend preparing for it during the preceding workweek. Firstly, this includes physical preparation, ensuring ahead of time that everything is prepared so we are free from physical distractions. Secondly, devoting time during the week to spiritual growth enables us to reap the fruits of this effort on the coming Sabbath in the form of heightened spiritual consciousness.[10]

---

10. *Likutei Torah* 2:2c.

SEVENTH READING

Exodus 17:1–16

G-d led the people from Alush to Refidim, closer to Mount Sinai. There was no water to drink, but instead of trusting that G-d would provide for them, the people complained. G-d had Moses strike a rock with his staff, and this rock miraculously gave forth enough water for all the people's needs. This "well" accompanied the Jews during their trek through the desert. It was also at Refidim that the Jews were attacked by the nation of Amalek.

To Ignore or to Fight

וַיָּבֹא עֲמָלֵק וַיִּלָּחֶם עִם יִשְׂרָאֵל בִּרְפִידִם: (שמות יז, ח)

Amalek came and fought against Israel at Refidim.

Amalek was the second enemy the Jews encountered after they left Egypt. The first was the Egyptians, who pursued them into the Sea of Reeds. There, Moses said, "G-d will do battle for you and you shall remain silent." In contrast, G-d told the Israelites to fight the Amalekites themselves.

This is because the Egyptians stood *in back of* the Jews; they were not blocking their path to Mount Sinai. In contrast, the Amalekites were impeding their progress. Similarly, whenever we are confronted with adversity, we must determine the nature of its threat: does it stand as a barrier between us and the Torah or is it merely a spiritual nuisance? In the latter case, we can safely ignore it, trusting that G-d will take care of it if we press on toward our goal. If, on the other hand, it is a threat that, like Amalek, stands in the way of bringing spiritual light to the world, we must tackle it head on.[11]

11. *Likutei Sichot*, vol. 1, p. 144.

Yitro

The Giving of the Torah

Exodus 18:1–20:23

THE FIFTH SECTION OF THE BOOK OF EXODUS BEGINS WITH the account of how Moses' father-in-law, Jethro (*Yitro*, in Hebrew), joins the Jewish people at Mount Sinai. It continues with the culmination of all human history from the creation of the world up until that point: the Giving of the Torah. Sandwiched in between these two accounts is the narrative of how Jethro advised Moses – after Moses' descent from Mount Sinai – to set up a judicial system.

FIRST READING
Exodus 18:1–12

After hearing about the Exodus from Egypt, the Splitting of the Sea, and the war with Amalek, Jethro went to meet Moses and the Jewish people, who were camped at Refidim, a short distance from Mount Sinai. Although he had already renounced idolatry, Jethro now felt it was time to take the next step and become a Jew. When he arrived, Moses hosted a festival meal in his honor.

Serving Others

וַיָּבֹא אַהֲרֹן וְכֹל זִקְנֵי יִשְׂרָאֵל לֶאֱכָל לֶחֶם עִם חֹתֵן מֹשֶׁה וְגוֹ': (שמות יח, יב)

**Aaron and all the elders of Israel came to
eat bread with Moses' father-in-law.**

Moses himself, however, did not eat at this meal; he was busy hosting and serving his guests.[1]

The lesson here is that regardless of our social status (and who can claim a higher social status than Moses'?) we should consider it more important to take care of others' needs than to see to our own.

This applies both to other people's physical needs and to their spiritual advancement.[2]

---

1. Rashi.
2. *Sichot Kodesh 5741*, vol. 2, p. 519.

SECOND READING

Exodus 18:13–23

In order to complete the story of Jethro, the Torah now jumps four months ahead to 11 Tishrei 2449, the day after Moses descended Mount Sinai for the last time. Jethro urged Moses to establish a system of courts rather than judge all the people's cases solely by himself.

The Contributions of the Community

כִּי כָבֵד מִמְּךָ הַדָּבָר לֹא תוּכַל עֲשֹׂהוּ לְבַדֶּךָ: (שמות יח, יח)

[Jethro told Moses,] "For this matter is too much for you; you will not be able to do it alone."

Being a consummately righteous individual has both its advantages and its disadvantages. Someone who has never had to repent has never felt estranged from G-d, but neither has he tasted the sweetness of reconciliation. A penitent – precisely because he has experienced spiritual "darkness" and has successfully transformed that darkness into light – is able to serve G-d with more drive, and at times more insight, than someone who has never experienced spiritual darkness.

Jethro therefore told Moses to delegate aspects of his leadership to individuals of lesser spiritual stature than him. These people would then be able to contribute their talents and experiences – which Moses himself lacked – toward leading the people.

The lesson for us is that we must not let the established leadership assume sole responsibility for the material and spiritual welfare and the future of the world. Each of us has unique talents and experience to contribute, and therefore each of us has a unique role to play in guiding the Jewish people in particular and the world in general toward fulfilling its Divine mission.[3]

3. *Hitva'aduyot 5726*, vol. 1, pp. 359–361.

THIRD READING
Exodus 18:24–27

Moses set up a hierarchy of judges. He reserved for himself only those cases that were too difficult for the judges of the lower courts. After concluding this episode, the Torah returns to its account of the Exodus, recounting how the Jewish people arrived at Mount Sinai in preparation to receive the Torah.

The Role of the Intellect

וְשָׁפְטוּ אֶת הָעָם בְּכָל עֵת: (שמות יח, כו)

[Moses appointed judges] who would judge the people at all times.

The new insights that we constantly glean as we study the Torah constitute the ongoing revelation of G-d that began at Mount Sinai. Often, the depth of our insights is so powerful that we sense that they come from someplace far beyond us – which indeed they do. Because of this, we can easily fall into the trap of thinking that it is pointless to try to elicit these Divine revelations with our own effort.

To demonstrate that this is not the case, G-d prefaced the account of the Giving of the Torah with the account of the judiciary system, which functions largely on human logic and reasoning. This teaches us that Divine revelation is granted to us only after we have fully exercised our human intelligence to comprehend G-d's will as it is expressed in the Torah.[4]

---

4. *Sichot Kodesh 5719*, pp. 128–129.

FOURTH READING

Exodus 19:1–6

The Jews arrived at the foot of Mount Sinai on 1 Sivan 2448.

Relying on G-d

בַּיּוֹם הַזֶּה בָּאוּ מִדְבַּר סִינָי: (שמות יט, א)

On this day they came to the Sinai desert.

In order to receive the Torah, the Jewish people had to venture into the desolate desert, trusting that G-d would provide for them. To their credit, they did this without hesitation.

Just as our ancestors could easily have balked at the notion of following Moses into the desert, we too can easily find reasons to postpone, minimize, or even excuse ourselves altogether from studying ("receiving") the Torah. Sometimes we may feel that we are discharging our obligations to G-d in other ways; at other times we may feel that we are too distracted, hungry, tired, or so on to concentrate. In such cases, we can learn from our ancestors' example that the proper approach to studying the Torah is total immersion in it, abandoning all other considerations and worries.

When we rely on G-d, studying the Torah devotedly, He will provide for all our material and spiritual needs, just as He provided for our ancestors when they relied on Him by "following" Him out of Egypt and into the desert.[5]

5. *Likutei Sichot*, vol. 2, pp. 308–309.

FIFTH READING
Exodus 19:7–19

During the next six days, G-d had the Jewish people prepare for the Giving of the Torah.

The Power of Preparation

וְכִבְּסוּ שִׂמְלֹתָם: (שמות יט, י)

[G-d told Moses to tell the Jewish people,] "They must wash their clothes [in preparation for the Giving of the Torah]."

Our spiritual "clothes" are our thought, speech, and deed. These are the means by which the soul expresses and presents itself to the outside world, just as we clothe ourselves in accordance with the image of ourselves that we wish to convey to society.

G-d gave Moses the job of sanctifying the people, but it was the people's job to cleanse their clothing. Similarly, it is the role of our teachers and rabbis – the Moseses of our generation – to inspire us, direct us, and connect us to G-d. Ultimate success, however, depends upon our own efforts to cleanse our thoughts, our speech, and our actions, for only then can they serve as means of expression for Divine revelation.[6]

6. *HaYom Yom,* 5 *Sivan; Sefer HaSichot 5697,* p. 243.

SIXTH READING
Exodus 19:20–20:14

On the morning of 6 Sivan 2448, G-d gave the Jewish people the 613 commandments contained in the Torah. Of these, He gave 10 explicitly: (1) to believe in G-d, (2) not to serve idols, (3) to respect G-d's Name, (4) to observe the Sabbath, (5) to honor parents, (6) not to murder, (7) not to commit adultery, (8) not to kidnap, (9) not to lie when testifying, and (10) not to desire other people's homes, spouses, or possessions. The remaining 603 commandments were implicit within these 10.

Receiving the Torah Constantly

וַיְדַבֵּר אֱלֹקִים אֵת כָּל הַדְּבָרִים הָאֵלֶּה לֵאמֹר: (שמות כ, א)

**[At the Giving of the Torah,] G-d spoke
all these words, saying....**

Literally, this verse reads, "G-d spoke all these words *to say*." This implies that when G-d gave us the Torah, He gave it in such a way that – under the proper conditions – He would "say" it over and over again. The condition is that we open ourselves up to the Divine nature of the Torah; if we do this, we will re-experience G-d revealing Himself through the Torah whenever we study it.

G-d therefore refers to the Torah as "My word, which I have placed in your mouth."[7] Similarly, our sages encourage us to feel the same "awe, fear, trembling, and excitement"[8] when we study the Torah today that our ancestors felt when G-d revealed Himself and gave us the Torah on Mount Sinai.[9]

7. Isaiah 59:21.
8. *Berachot* 22a.
9. *Torah Or, Yitro* 67b.

SEVENTH READING

Exodus 20:15–23

After the Giving of the Ten Commandments, G-d told Moses to ascend Mount Sinai and remain there for 40 days in order to learn the rest of the Torah. The first laws that G-d taught Moses during these 40 days concerned how to worship G-d properly.

Passiveness vs. Activeness

לֹא תַעֲשׂוּן אִתִּי אֱלֹהֵי כֶסֶף וֵאלֹהֵי זָהָב לֹא תַעֲשׂוּ לָכֶם: (שמות כ, כ)

[G-d instructed Moses to tell the Jewish people,] "You must not make idols [to worship] along with Me."

The first commandment following the Giving of the Torah is passive ("you must *refrain from* making idols…"). This teaches us that the first step toward internalizing any new insight from the Torah that we have just learned – the first step in spiritual growth – is to be passive.

This momentary inactivity enables us to relinquish our previous self so that we are free to ascend to a new, higher way of thinking. Ascending to a higher way of thinking will then, in turn, remake us into a new, higher version of ourselves.

Thus, in order to ascend from one level of spirituality to another, we should always be ready to abandon our previous way of thinking, traversing an intermediary and temporary state of self-nullification on the way to greater spiritual heights.[10]

---

10. *Likutei Sichot*, vol. 36, pp. 96–101; ibid., vol. 2, p. 564.

Mishpatim

Laws

Exodus 21:1–24:18

AFTER GIVING THE TORAH TO THE JEWISH PEOPLE, G-D TOLD
Moses to ascend Mount Sinai again – this time for 40 days – in
order to teach him the details of the Torah's laws. The sixth sec-
tion of the Book of Exodus is primarily a selection of the laws
(*Mishpatim*, in Hebrew) that G-d taught Moses while he was on
Mount Sinai.

FIRST READING
Exodus 21:1–19

G-d prefaced His explanation of the Torah's laws by saying that the Jewish people are required to set up a system of courts in order to try all cases of criminal, civil, and ritual law. G-d then explained the laws pertaining to servants, marital obligations, murder, honoring parents, kidnapping, and compensation for injuries. The first law in this list pertains to a thief who is too poor to repay what he stole. The court is instructed to "sell" such a thief as a bondman for a period of time, in order to use the money of the sale for the repayment. Despite his status as a bondman, his temporary "owners" must still treat him with respect.

Care for the Criminal

כִּי תִקְנֶה עֶבֶד עִבְרִי וגו': (שמות כא, ב)

[G-d told Moses to tell the Jewish people,] "If you acquire a Jewish bondman...."

This case is quite rare, and moreover, it reflects negatively on the Jewish people, focusing our attention on the sinners among them. It is nevertheless chosen to open the Torah's presentation of civil law.

We might consider the criminal discussed in this case to be unworthy of our respect. After all, by stealing, he has clearly placed the materialistic desires of his body above the higher calling of his soul. Therefore, the Torah begins its laws specifically with this person's case, immediately informing us that even this blatant sinner must be treated with respect and compassion.

This compassionate approach to justice is the very heart of the system of Jewish civil law, whose goal is the refinement and elevation of our physical and material day-to-day lives.[1]

---

1. *Hitva'aduyot 5747*, vol. 2, pp. 481–482.

SECOND READING

Exodus 21:20–22:3

G-d also taught Moses the laws pertaining to damages caused by
a person's animals or property, including those caused by a pit in
the public domain. If an animal falls into such a pit, the person
who dug it or uncovered it is liable for damage to the animal. He
is not liable, however, for damages caused to utensils that the
animal is carrying when it falls, or damages suffered by people
who accidentally fall into the pit.

G-d's Inscrutable Will

וְכִי יִפְתַּח אִישׁ בּוֹר אוֹ כִּי יִכְרֶה אִישׁ בֹּר וגו': (שמות כא, לג)

**[G-d told Moses to tell the Jewish people,] "If
a person opens a pit or digs a pit...."**

The laws of damages are among the most comprehensible laws
in the Torah, since they are seemingly based on human logic.
However, G-d provides us with several reminders that this part of
the Torah, too, reflects G-d's often unfathomable will. This law is
one such reminder. Logically, there would seem to be no reason
to differentiate between different types of damage caused by the
same pit. Nevertheless, the person who dug or uncovered the pit
is only liable for certain damages and not for others.

This demonstrates that even the Torah's civil laws are not
just another man-made legal system that suffers from the imperfections of all such systems, even the most advanced. They are
G-d's will, which is by definition beyond our ability to fully
comprehend.

This awareness helps us see these laws in their true light – as
the means G-d provides us with to refine and elevate our physical
and material lives – and serves to inspire us to pursue these goals
enthusiastically.[2]

2. *Hitva'aduyot 5747*, vol. 1, pp. 487–488.

THIRD READING
Exodus 22:4–26

G-d continued with the laws governing damages; responsibilities of borrowers, guardians, and renters; seduction; sorcery; bestiality; idolatry; exploitation; and loans.

Irrevocable Good

כִּי תֵצֵא אֵשׁ וּמָצְאָה וְגוֹ': (שמות כב, ה)

[G-d told Moses to tell the Jewish people,] "If a fire breaks out and spreads...."

In the Talmud, lighting a fire is compared to shooting an arrow. Just as an archer is liable for damages even if his arrow lands outside his own domain, the person who ignites a fire is liable for damages even if his fire spreads outside his own domain.[3] This is because once the arrow or fire is out of the perpetrator's hands, it cannot be retrieved.

This is true, however, only of human beings. Nothing is ever out of G-d's hands. He can always reverse any punishment that He may unleash against us. Nevertheless, G-d has decreed that when He promises to do something good, it *must* occur.[4] In this sense, G-d has made Himself similar to humans: once the promise of goodness is made, it is "out of His hands" and cannot be rescinded.

Knowing that G-d's promise for good is irrevocable gives us the inspiration to endure the darkness of the last days of our exile. Our certainty of the final Redemption helps us see past the confusion and obstacles that we encounter in life, enabling us to perceive the dawning light of the future.[5]

---

3. *Bava Kama* 22a.
4. *Mishneh Torah, Yesodei HaTorah* 10:4.
5. *Likutei Sichot*, vol. 1, pp. 125–127.

FOURTH READING

Exodus 22:27–23:5

G-d continued with the laws governing respect for authority, donations to be given to the tribe of Levi, truth in the administration of justice, and behavior toward enemies.

Ignoring Slander

לֹא תִשָּׂא שֵׁמַע שָׁוְא אַל תָּשֶׁת יָדְךָ עִם רָשָׁע לִהְיֹת עֵד חָמָס: (שמות כג, א)

[G-d told Moses to tell the Jewish people,] "You must not accept a false report. You must not join forces with a wicked person to be a corrupt witness."

The Ba'al Shem Tov connected the two halves of this verse as follows:

Every soul is granted its particular, individual strength as it is dispatched to this world. Of course, we all have our shortcomings too, but our particular, individual strength – the arena in which we truly shine – normally compensates for our flaws.

However, if two witnesses testify that we have betrayed our mission, this unique asset is taken away from us. Therefore, the Torah warns us: "Do not listen to slander. If you do, your incrimination of your fellow will join forces with that of your evil inclination, and you will thus rob your fellow of his special Divine strength."[6]

---

6. *Sefer HaSichot 5701*, p. 65.

FIFTH READING
Exodus 23:6–19

G-d continued with the laws governing the sabbatical year, the yearly cycle of holidays, and mixtures of milk and meat.

Celebrating Spiritual Growth

שָׁלֹשׁ רְגָלִים תָּחֹג לִי בַּשָּׁנָה: (שמות כג, יד)

[**G-d told Moses to tell the Jewish people,**] **"You must celebrate a pilgrim festival for Me three times a year."**

The pilgrim festivals mark the three significant milestones in the agricultural cycle: *Pesach* (Passover) occurs in the spring, when the produce begins to ripen; *Shavu'ot* occurs in the early summer, when the wheat is harvested; and *Sukkot* occurs in the fall, when all of the produce is gathered in from the fields.[7]

Allegorically, the Jewish people are G-d's "produce."[8] Just as one sows grain in the hope of reaping a much greater return, G-d "plants" souls in the physical world in order for them to accomplish much more than they can in their native, heavenly abode.

When we plant a seed, it does not begin to grow immediately. Growth can begin only once the outer, protective coating of the seed disintegrates. Once the original seed per se no longer exists, the new growth is not restricted by the limitations of the original form of the seed.

The same is true of human growth: ego is its greatest hindrance. Only when we overcome and negate the ego can the soul reach its full potential.[9]

---

7. See Rabbeinu Bachye on Exodus 13:4.
8. See Jeremiah 2:3; Hosea 2:25.
9. *Likutei Sichot*, vol. 36, pp. 82–85. See also, in greater depth, *Sefer HaMa'amarim Melukat*, vol. 5, pp. 169–176.

SIXTH READING

Exodus 23:20–25

G-d continued with the laws governing the conquest of the Land of Israel and the eradication of idolatry.

Two Aspects of Spiritual Health

וַהֲסִרֹתִי מַחֲלָה מִקִּרְבֶּךָ: (שמות כג, כה)

[**G-d told Moses to tell the Jewish people,**] "**I will remove illness from your midst.**"

Shortly after the Exodus, G-d promised the Jewish people, "I will bring none of the sicknesses that I brought on Egypt upon you,"[10] meaning that no one would get sick in the first place. Why, then, did He promise us here that He will heal us whenever we do get sick?

There are two types of sicknesses: natural sicknesses, which we expect to occur when we do not take care of ourselves properly, and unnatural sicknesses that are obviously acts of G-d. Regarding unnatural sicknesses, G-d says, "I will bring none of these upon you" in the first place. Regarding natural sicknesses, G-d says, "I will remove these from you" when they do occur.

Similarly, there are two types of spiritual sicknesses. Succumbing to a lust for something that the Torah prohibits makes us spiritually sick, hampering our ability to function in full spiritual health. This is a "natural," expected result of transgressing the Torah's prohibitions. It is also true, however, that repeated overindulgence in things that the Torah *permits* also impairs our spiritual health. This is an "unnatural" effect, which we would not necessarily expect, since, after all, these indulgences are permitted.

Nonetheless, if we are sufficiently dedicated and devoted to G-d, He promises to cure us of the ill effects of both natural and unnatural temporary spiritual lapses.[11]

10. Exodus 15:26.
11. *Or HaTorah, Shemot*, vol. 4, p. 1218.

SEVENTH READING
Exodus 23:26–24:18

G-d concluded His presentation of the Torah's laws with the promise that if the Jewish people would observe them, He would bless them and drive out the nations occupying the Land of Israel, enabling them to settle it peacefully. The narrative then returns to its account of the Giving of the Torah, this time focusing on the covenant that G-d forged between Himself and the Jewish people by giving them the Torah.

Little by Little

מְעַט מְעַט אֲגָרְשֶׁנּוּ מִפָּנֶיךָ: (שמות כג, ל)

[G-d told Moses to tell the Jewish people,] "I will drive [the nations occupying Canaan] out before you little by little."

The strategy of "little by little" is a lesson for us in our spiritual battles, as well. In our struggle to banish our spiritual enemies from within, patience is the greatest virtue. Tackling all our obstacles at once will almost certainly end in failure; the methodical and gradual line of attack has much greater hope for success. We must begin with the easier steps, banishing first the most obvious forms of evil, and only then advance to subtler struggles.

Similarly, we should first attempt to avoid whatever is bad before striving for perfection in doing all that is good. First, we must subdue our animal soul; only after this should we begin boosting our G-dly soul to the spiritual pinnacles to which it aspires. Such is the method of attack in all battles of the spirit: through advancing little by little, we can indeed "conquer the land."[12]

---

12. *Sefer HaMa'amarim 5745*, p. 133; *Sefer HaMa'amarim 5746*, pp. 59–60. *Igrot Kodesh*, vol. 11, pp. 82, 116.

Terumah

The Tabernacle

Exodus 25:1–27:19

WHEN THE JEWS BECAME CONVINCED THAT MOSES WAS NOT going to come down from Mount Sinai, they committed the sin of making a golden calf. Some of the people worshipped this calf as an idol; as a result, G-d withdrew His presence from the people as a whole. In order to reinstate His presence among the Jewish people, G-d commanded them to construct a portable "housing" for His presence, consisting of a tent-sanctuary (the "Tabernacle"), a surrounding Courtyard, and various furnishings placed in specific positions within this sanctuary and its enclosure. The seventh portion of the Book of Exodus opens with G-d's command for the Jewish people to contribute (*Terumah*, in Hebrew) toward the construction of this Tabernacle.

FIRST READING
Exodus 25:1–16

G-d began His instructions regarding the Tabernacle by listing the materials needed for its construction, as well as defining its spiritual purpose.

The Advantage of the Commonplace

וְזֹאת הַתְּרוּמָה אֲשֶׁר תִּקְחוּ מֵאִתָּם זָהָב וָכֶסֶף וּנְחֹשֶׁת: (שמות כה, ג)

[G-d told Moses,] "This is the contribution that you must take from them: gold, silver, and copper."

Although gold surpasses silver in value, silver was the metal of choice for use as currency. The very fact that silver is not as rare as gold makes it more suited for daily purposes, and in this respect it is more important than gold.[1] Copper, on the other hand, is even more common than silver, but it is so common that it lacks the distinction possessed by silver. (In the Torah, copper is not used as currency at all, and in societies where it *is* used for currency, it is typically used for coins of smaller denominations.)

Spiritually, the rarity of gold alludes to the otherworldly, transcendent element of our personalities – our desire to rise above the natural and experience what is beyond the common. Conversely, the currency of silver alludes to our drive to draw otherworldly holiness into our common and mundane lives. The advantage of silver over gold reflects the fact that it is the "silver" aspect of our lives that achieves the Divine plan.[2]

1. See *Bava Metzia*, 44a–b, commentary of Rabbeinu Asher (the *Rosh*) ad loc.
2. *Likutei Sichot*, vol. 6, pp. 157–160.

SECOND READING

Exodus 25:17–30

The first furnishing of the Tabernacle that G-d instructed the Jews to make was the Ark of the Covenant, an open, gold-covered wooden box that housed the two tablets upon which G-d had engraved the Ten Commandments. This Ark was sealed by a golden Cover, upon which were two figurines of winged angels with infant faces, known as the cherubim.

G-d's Enveloping Love

וְעָשִׂיתָ כַפֹּרֶת: (שמות כה, יז)

[G-d told Moses,] "You must have them make a Cover [for the Ark]."

The tablets housed in the Ark signify the union with G-d that we achieve by studying the Torah. The Cover of the Ark signifies G-d's grace from above, which we require in order to maintain Divine consciousness at all times – even while uniting with Him through studying the Torah. G-d grants us this assistance in virtue of our intrinsic connection to Him, which exists independent of the connection that we forge with Him through studying the Torah and observing the commandments.

This intrinsic bond is alluded to by the fact that word for "Cover" (*kaporet*) is related to the word for "atonement" (*kaparah*). Atonement for sin is possible only when we invoke and evoke G-d's essential love for us, which overrides the deficiencies in our relationship to Him that we cause when we disobey the Torah's instructions.

Our constant opportunity to repair and renew our relationship with G-d (represented by the Cover of the Ark) transforms our study of the Torah (represented by the tablets within the Ark) from a purely intellectual pursuit to a springboard for spiritual growth.[3]

3. *Likutei Sichot*, vol. 26, pp. 180–182.

TUESDAY

<u>THIRD READING</u>
Exodus 25:31–26:14

Next, G-d commanded the people to make a golden Table specifically designed to hold twelve loaves of bread that would be placed
on it every Sabbath. After this, G-d commanded the people to
make an ornate, seven-branched golden Candelabrum.

Lighting Up the World

וְעָשִׂיתָ מְנֹרַת ... וְקָנָהּ גְּבִיעֶיהָ כַּפְתֹּרֶיהָ וּפְרָחֶיהָ מִמֶּנָּה יִהְיוּ: (שמות כה, לא)

**[G-d told Moses,] "You must have them make a
Candelabrum.... Its stem, its goblets, its spheres,
and its flowers must be an integral part [of it]."**

The stem of the Candelabrum alludes to the Written Torah, and
the six branches that extend from it allude to the six orders of the
Mishnah, the basic compendium of the Oral Torah.

In this context, the spheres and flowers on the Candelabrum's
branches allude to the extra-mishnaic teachings of the sages,
which were later recorded and discussed in the commentary on
the Mishnah known as the Gemara. The Mishnah and Gemara
together are known as the Talmud.

The goblets on the Candelabrum's branches allude to the
Torah's "wine" – its inner, mystical dimension.

The spiritual light of the Candelabrum – the Written Torah,
the Oral Torah, and the Torah's inner dimension – are the means
through which we acquire Divine consciousness and disseminate
it throughout the world.[4]

---

4. *Torah Or* 88b; *Or HaTorah, Shemot*, pp. 1491, 1486.

FOURTH READING

Exodus 26:15–30

G-d next instructed the Jews concerning how they were to construct the Tabernacle itself. The walls were to be made out of vertical planks of acacia wood inserted into silver bases.

The Foundation of Everything

וְאַרְבָּעִים אַדְנֵי כֶסֶף תַּעֲשֶׂה וְגו': (שמות כו, יט)

[G-d told Moses,] "You must have them make 40 silver bases [for the southern wall of the Tabernacle]."

The ten-cubit-high planks forming the walls of the Tabernacle allude to the three facets of our intellect[5] and our seven emotions.[6] The coverings forming the roof of the Tabernacle allude to our enveloping powers of will and delight. The bases, in contrast, allude to our ability to enforce the Torah's code of behavior upon ourselves. Raw self-discipline is the lowest rung on the ladder of self-refinement, since it is devoid of any feeling or intellect. Nonetheless, just as the bases were the foundation that kept the Tabernacle's structure standing firmly, self-discipline is the foundation of the character-structure in a well-built life.

Inasmuch as the norms of religious behavior ensured by self-discipline are the same for everyone, the bases were made out of the one contribution everyone gave equally. In contrast, since each of us relates to G-d differently via our delight, will, intellect, and emotions, the components of the Tabernacle alluding to these aspects of our personalities were made out of the contributions the people gave according to their individual means and desires.[7]

5. Wisdom, understanding, and knowledge.
6. Love, fear, compassion, confidence, sincerity, loyalty, and humility.
7. *Likutei Sichot*, vol. 1, pp. 162 ff.

FIFTH READING
Exodus 26:31–37

The inside of the Tabernacle was divided by a curtain into two sections. The first section as one entered was known as the outer chamber (which is described as being "holy"); the section beyond the curtain was known as the inner chamber (or "Holy of Holies").

Intellect vs. Emotion

וְהִבְדִּילָה הַפָּרֹכֶת לָכֶם בֵּין הַקֹּדֶשׁ וּבֵין קֹדֶשׁ הַקֳּדָשִׁים: (שמות כו, לג)

[G-d told Moses to tell the Jewish people,] "The Curtain will separate for you between the Holy and the Holy of Holies."

The outer and inner chambers of the Sanctuary correspond respectively to the emotions and intellect of the Divine soul. The Curtain dividing these two chambers corresponds to the quantum leap of consciousness that characterizes the difference between emotion and intellect.

Emotions require us to be quite aware of ourselves; otherwise, we cannot react emotionally to anything. In contrast, when we are absorbed in thought, we often lose all consciousness of ourselves. In fact, in order to fully grasp an idea, we practically *must* lose our self-awareness – if not, our preconceived notions will likely prevent us from experiencing and comprehending the new insight truthfully.

Thus, the Divine consciousness we experience when our intellect is absorbed in contemplating any given G-dly idea is entirely different than the Divine consciousness we experience when feeling some G-dly-oriented emotion. Realizing this difference can help us open ourselves up to new insights and thereby climb the ladder of spiritual growth.[8]

8. *Or HaTorah, Shemot,* vol. 6, p. 2121.

SIXTH READING
Exodus 27:1–8

G-d then gave the instructions for constructing the Altar used for sacrifices. This Altar was situated in the Courtyard, outside the Tabernacle itself. The Altar was a hollow structure that was filled with earth each time the Tabernacle was set up.

Returning to the Garden of Eden

נְבוּב לֻחֹת תַּעֲשֶׂה אֹתוֹ וְגוֹ': (שמות כז, ח)

[G-d told Moses,] "You must have them make [the Altar] a hollow structure."

We are taught that G-d created Adam out of the earth located at the future site of the Altar,[9] indicating that the possibility for atonement and repentance is an intrinsic aspect of our humanity. This notion is also alluded to by the fact that the Altar was filled with earth, for the name of the original human being, Adam, means "earth." Metaphorically, then, just as humanity was formed from Altar-earth, the Altar was constructed out of the very humanity for which it was built to atone.

Similarly, when Adam was banished from the Garden of Eden, the Torah says that he was sent "to work the *earth* from which he was taken."[10] We use the earth to cultivate the food that powers our lives, to produce the clothes that protect our bodies, and to build the homes that shelter us from harm. When we do all this in order to devote ourselves to our Divine mission, we elevate the earth. This is how we restore the world's lost harmony and return to the Garden of Eden.[11]

---

9. *Yerushalmi Nazir* 7:2; *Bereishit Rabbah* 14:8.
10. Genesis 3:23.
11. *Or HaTorah, Shemot*, vol. 3, pp. 1024–1025.

SEVENTH READING
Exodus 27:9–19

G-d then gave the instructions for demarcating the Courtyard with netted hangings suspended from copper-plated wooden pillars.

The Flax of Monotheism

וְעָשִׂיתָ אֵת חֲצַר הַמִּשְׁכָּן ... שֵׁשׁ מָשְׁזָר וְגוֹ': (שמות כז, ט)

[G-d told Moses,] "You must have them make the Courtyard of the Tabernacle... [by enclosing a space with] nettings made of twined linen."

These nettings were made of linen because flax, from which linen is made, differs from other plants in that only a single stalk grows from each seed.[12] One of the words for "linen" in biblical Hebrew (*bad*) reflects this attribute, since it also means "alone." Inasmuch as the Jewish people are distinguished from other nations by virtue of our absolute monotheism, it is appropriate that the curtain separating the Tabernacle from the surrounding world was made of linen.[13]

In addition, the flax plant alludes to our mission to spread of the knowledge of G-d's oneness to the world at large. Our sages tell us that "flax depletes the land," meaning that it drains the soil of its nutrients more than other crops do.[14] Allegorically, the "land" signifies the earthly, materialistic consciousness that opposes faith in one G-d. Thus, by "cultivating flax" – by spreading the knowledge of G-d's oneness throughout the world, we "deplete the land" – we help cure the world of its materialistic outlook.

Thus, while the linen nettings indeed functioned as the border between the holy and the mundane, they also expressed the ideal of refining the entire world with the perspective of holiness.[15]

---

12. *Zevachim* 18b; Rashi ad loc.
13. *Likutei Torah* 2:28b ff.
14. *Bava Metzia* 109a.
15. *Reshimot* 107; *Tanya, Igeret HaKodesh* 9, etc.

Tetzaveh

The Priests

Exodus 27:20–30:10

THE EIGHTH SECTION OF THE BOOK OF EXODUS BEGINS AS G-d tells Moses to command (*Tetzaveh*, in Hebrew) the Jewish people to provide the olive oil to be used to fuel the lamps of the Tabernacle's Candelabrum. G-d then described the special garments that the priests – Moses' brother Aaron and Aaron's present and future descendants – are to wear whenever they officiate in the Tabernacle. Aaron's sons became the first "ordinary" priests, who officiated in a uniform comprising four garments; Aaron became the first "high priest," who wore an eight-garment uniform and was entrusted with duties and privileges beyond those of ordinary priests. After describing the priests' garments, G-d instructed Moses to follow a week-long ritual in order to install his brother and nephews into their priestly office. This is followed by the description of the Altar for incense, which was positioned in the outer chamber of the Sanctuary, near the Candelabrum and the Table of twelve breads.

FIRST READING
Exodus 27:20–28:12

G-d taught Moses the procedure for kindling the lamps of the Candelabrum.

Moses and Aaron

וְאַתָּה תְּצַוֶּה אֶת בְּנֵי יִשְׂרָאֵל וְיִקְחוּ אֵלֶיךָ שֶׁמֶן זַיִת זָךְ גו': (שמות כז, כ)

[G-d told Moses,] "You will command the Israelites to bring you clear olive oil."

The priests were the ones who lit the Candelabrum. Allegorically, this means that it was their job to "light the fire" of Divine inspiration in the souls of the people. They were able to do this by virtue of Aaron's pure love for all Jews.

But what about people who seem disinterested in or incapable of being inspired? How can the priests "kindle" the flame of such people?

G-d therefore told the Jews to bring the oil for the Candelabrum's lamps to Moses. When Moses declared that he was willing to lay down his life even for those Jews who worshipped the Golden Calf, he demonstrated that all Jews possess an indestructible, intrinsic worth – specifically, the Divine essence of their souls. Therefore, Moses could enable Aaron to set aflame the souls of even those Jews who seem not to be fit to be "lamps."

We are all called upon to set our own souls and the souls of others aflame with love and awe of G-d. In order to succeed, we must approach the task with the same motivation as Aaron – pure love of our fellow – and with the perspective of Moses, in whose eyes all Jews are indeed capable of being ignited, of shining brightly, and of becoming a source of Divine illumination for the entire world.[1]

---

1. *Likutei Sichot*, vol. 21, pp. 177–178.

SECOND READING

Exodus 28:13–30

G-d then began to describe the high priest's garments, beginning with the Ephod and Breastplate. The Ephod was an apron-like garment tied around the waist, possessing two straps that rose in the back up to and over the priest's shoulders. A precious stone was attached to the upper end of each of these straps. The Breastplate was a square piece of material onto which were fastened twelve different precious stones inscribed with the names of the twelve tribes. The Breastplate was tied to the Ephod at the top with gold chains and at the bottom with wool cords. A parchment inscribed with G-d's Name was inserted into the Breastplate; this parchment was called the "*urim* and *tummim*," meaning "lights and sincere devotions."

The Duality of Spiritual Life

וְנָתַתָּ אֶל חֹשֶׁן הַמִּשְׁפָּט אֶת הָאוּרִים וְאֶת הַתֻּמִּים וְגוֹ': (שמות כח, ל)

[G-d told Moses,] "You must have them place the *urim* and *tummim* into the Breastplate of Judgment."

The double name of the single parchment inserted into the Breastplate indicates the dual nature of our relationship with G-d. The word *urim* ("fiery lights") denotes our soul's ardent yearning to return to its Divine source and dissolve in it. The word *tummim* ("sincere devotions") denotes our soul's humble submission to G-d's will and its commitment to fulfill His commandments. This devotion counterbalances the *urim*-aspect of the soul, pulling it down from its ecstatic rapture in order to engage the mundane aspects of life and elevate them to Divinity.

Balancing these two complementary drives is both the challenge and the exhilaration of our spiritual life.[2]

2. *Ma'amarei Admur HaZakein – Et'haleich Liyozhna*, p. 55.

THIRD READING

Exodus 28:31–43

The next garment that G-d described was the high priest's ankle-length Robe, over which the Ephod and Breastplate were worn. The bottom seam of this Robe was adorned all around with small golden bells and woolen pomegranates.

The Estranged Pomegranate

וְנִשְׁמַע קוֹלוֹ בְּבֹאוֹ אֶל הַקֹּדֶשׁ וגו': (שמות כח, לה)

[G-d told Moses,] "The sound [of the bells] must be heard as [the high priest] enters the sanctuary."

The pomegranate is the symbol of those Jews who seem to lack merits, yet upon closer examination are revealed to be as filled with merits as a pomegranate is filled with seeds.[3] The noise of the bells at the bottom of the high priest's robe reflects the clamor that characterizes such people's relationship with G-d. Acutely aware of their apparent spiritual shortcomings, they cry out from the depths of their heart to be shown how to return to full Jewish observance.

Hence the critical need for these bells. A high priest who fails to include these "pomegranate-Jews" as he approaches G-d's presence is unworthy of his title.

We see here firstly that no matter how estranged we may feel from G-d, He insists that the high priest take us with him inside the Sanctuary. On the other hand, no matter how close we may feel to G-d, we must always make the plight of our estranged fellows an essential part of our spiritual agenda.[4]

---

3. *Berachot* 57a.
4. *Likutei Sichot*, vol. 16, pp. 338–339.

FOURTH READING

Exodus 29:1–18

G-d then described the other garments of the priests. After this, G-d taught Moses the rituals through which he would install the priests in their office. These rituals included various sacrifices, among which was a bull offered up to atone for the sin of the Golden Calf.

Careful Innovations

וְאֶת בְּשַׂר הַפָּר ... תִּשְׂרֹף בָּאֵשׁ וגו': (שמות כט, יד)

[G-d told Moses,] "You must burn the flesh of the bull."

Normally, the meat of the sin-offerings was eaten by the priests. In the case of the installation sin-offering, however, the priests were commanded to burn the meat.

The reason for this is that it is human nature to take ongoing, regular practices more seriously. In contrast, we tend to take new or temporary practices that are instituted by the rabbinic authorities of our generation less seriously. After all – we tell ourselves – previous generations got along fine without these practices.

It is therefore necessary to turn the matter on its head by being *extra* careful regarding the new or temporary additions to Jewish practice. This is why the one-time-only installation sin-offering had to be treated exceptionally.

Nowadays, in the final moments of our exile, the call of the hour is to prepare ourselves and the world at large for the coming of the Messiah. Inasmuch as this directive was not emphasized in previous generations, it is easy to undervalue it. Therefore, we must be sure to take *extra* care to fulfill it, dedicating to it all our enthusiasm and all our latent potentials.[5]

5. *Likutei Sichot*, vol. 27, pp. 71–73.

THURSDAY

FIFTH READING

Exodus 29:19–37

G-d told Moses that he should repeat the installation rituals for the priests for a full week.

The Power of the Number Seven

שִׁבְעַת יָמִים תְּמַלֵּא יָדָם: (שמות כט, לה)

[G-d told Moses,] "You must consecrate [the priests] for seven days."

The number seven reflects natural perfection. In terms of time, seven days form a complete spiritual unit; after the passage of seven days, the spiritual nature of the first cycle repeats itself. This is because each day expresses one of the seven attributes of G-d alluded to in the verse, "G-d, Yours is [1] the greatness, [2] the power, [3] the glory, [4] the victory, and [5] the majesty, for [6] all in heaven and earth [is Yours]. G-d, Yours is [7] the kingship...."[6] This is why creation took precisely a seven-day week.

G-d therefore required the installation rites to be performed for seven consecutive days, in order that Aaron and his descendants become empowered to function as priests in all possible situations.

It follows that whenever we want to take on some additional or new spiritual practice, we should try to do so uninterruptedly throughout a full week (where applicable) in order to lend it the strength and solidity of having been performed in the context of all the seven hues of spirituality.[7]

6. 1 Chronicles 29:11.
7. *Hitva'aduyot 5745*, vol. 2, p. 1334.

SIXTH READING
Exodus 29:38–46

G-d concluded His description of the installation rites by nam-
ing the Tabernacle the "Tent of Meeting." This term implies that
once the Tabernacle would be erected, it would serve as the place
where G-d would "meet" with Moses in order to communicate
with him, and as the place where G-d would "meet" the Jewish
people whenever they would gather there to pray or listen to
what G-d told Moses.

A Home for G-d

וְשָׁכַנְתִּי בְּתוֹךְ בְּנֵי יִשְׂרָאֵל וְגוֹ': (שמות כט, מה)

[G-d told Moses,] "I will dwell among the Israelites."

We might think that only righteous and holy people can create a
physical sanctuary for the Divine presence. Yet the Torah makes
it clear that the Tabernacle was built by every man, woman, and
child, regardless of their spiritual status.[8]

This was possible only because of the Giving of the Torah,
when G-d made His essence – which transcends the limitations of
the natural order – the inner essence of every Jew. On account of
our inner Divine essence, we remain inwardly true to our Divine
nature even when we appear not to be focused on holiness. At
our core, our truest and purest desire is to be one with G-d and
fulfill His will.

Thus, even a Jew who appears to be self-oriented is capable
of building a dwelling for G-d. Every one of us has the capacity
to transform the world into a place about which G-d can say: "I
will dwell there, among you."[9]

8. *Avot d'Rabbi Nathan* 11:1.
9. *Sefer HaSichot 5752*, vol. 2, p. 384.

SEVENTH READING

Exodus 30:1–10

G-d then taught Moses how to construct the incense Altar. This Altar was placed inside the Tabernacle, and was therefore known as the "Inner Altar," in contrast to the "Outer Altar," which stood in the Tabernacle's Courtyard and was used for the animal sacrifices.

Inner and Outer Desires

קֹדֶשׁ קָדָשִׁים הוּא לַה': (שמות ל, י)

[G-d told Moses, "The Inner Altar] is holy of holies unto G-d."

The Inner Altar alludes to our "inner heart," our true desires, whereas the Outer Altar alludes to our "outer heart," our indirect desires – our desires for things that we want because they help us achieve our true desires.

The sacrifices offered up on the Outer Altar served to refine the mundane ("animal") aspects of our lives. In contrast, the incense offered up on the Inner Altar served to intensify and deepen our bond with G-d.[10] This teaches us that our mundane activities should be the focus only of our "outer hearts." Our "inner hearts," in contrast, should always be focused on purely holy pursuits. We should always aspire to maximize the time and energy we can devote to studying the Torah, fulfilling G-d's commandments, and prayer.

True, we must never shy away from the task of elevating the physical world, for this is an essential facet of making the world into G-d's home. But at the same time, we must remember that despite the sublime effect of elevating the material world, our real "home" is in the spiritual world, enveloped in walls of the Sanctuary and bound to G-d.[11]

---

10. *Sefer HaMa'amarim Melukat*, vol. 2, pp. 122–123.
11. *Likutei Sichot*, vol. 6, pp. 185–187.

Tisa

The Golden Calf

Exodus 30:11–34:35

THE NINTH SECTION OF THE BOOK OF EXODUS BEGINS WITH
G-d's final instructions regarding the Tabernacle. G-d tells Moses
to take (*Tisa*, in Hebrew) a census of the adult male Jews by
collecting a silver half-shekel coin from each one. The silver thus
collected was used to purchase those sacrifices offered up on
behalf of the people as a whole. G-d then proceeds to instruct
Moses how to construct the Laver (an urn used by the priests to
wash their hands and feet before officiating in the Tabernacle),
how to make and use the anointing oil and incense, and whom
he should appoint to oversee the construction of the Tabernacle
and the fashioning of its furnishings and utensils. All of this is
followed by the account of the incident of the Golden Calf and
its aftermath.

FIRST READING

Exodus 30:11–31:17

G-d instructed Moses to have the artisans produce a Laver, which was a large, water-filled urn with two spouts, from which the priests washed their hands and feet before officiating in the Tabernacle.

The First Step

וְעָשִׂיתָ כִּיּוֹר נְחֹשֶׁת וגו': (שמות ל, יח)

[G-d told Moses,] "You must have them make a copper Laver."

Spiritual refinement comprises various stages. Entering the Tabernacle and performing the rites associated with its furnishings reflects these stages, which we are bidden to follow as part of our ascent on the ladder of spiritual renewal and growth.

When entering the Tabernacle, a person first entered the Courtyard, in which the Laver stood. This teaches us that whenever we leave our mundane affairs in order to enter our personal, inner Tabernacle, we must first cleanse ourselves of any materialistic orientation that may be lingering in our consciousness as a result of our most recent encounters with the mundane world.

But if washing from the Laver is a prerequisite to entering the spiritual consciousness associated with the Tabernacle, we would expect the Laver to be located *outside* the Tabernacle (or at most at its threshold) rather than inside it.

The Laver's location inside the Tabernacle teaches us that the purification from materiality really begins when we are still outside the Tabernacle, involved in our mundane pursuits. If we approach our mundane affairs from the Torah's perspective, we can sanctify them. Thus, we can cleanse ourselves of materiality even while "outside" our inner Tabernacle. Washing from the Laver then serves to complete the process that we begin while still in the midst of our mundane existence.[1]

1. *Reshimot* 108.

SECOND READING
Exodus 31:18–33:11

Moses told the Jewish people that he would remain on Mount Sinai for 40 full days, but the people mistakenly counted the first half-day as one of the 40. When Moses failed to appear when expected, some people feared that he had died on Mount Sinai and wanted to arrange some substitute for him. Aware that there would be gold figurines (the cherubim) in the Tabernacle, they imagined that if Aaron – the holiest person available in Moses' absence – would make a similar gold figurine, G-d would consent to communicate with them through it. Aaron was opposed to this idea, so he worked slowly in order to gain time until Moses would arrive. But the people hurried Aaron in his work, and when the Golden Calf was finished, some people worshipped it as an idol.

Seeing People in Their Best Light

וַיִּתֵּן אֶל מֹשֶׁה כְּכַלֹּתוֹ לְדַבֵּר אִתּוֹ בְּהַר סִינַי שְׁנֵי לֻחֹת הָעֵדֻת וְגוֹ': (שמות לא, יח)

When G-d finished speaking with Moses on Mount Sinai, He gave him the two Tablets of the Testimony.

G-d gave Moses the tablets on the 40th day of his stay on the mountain. But the people had already made the Golden Calf on the 39th day! In other words, even after the people had committed this most heinous sin, G-d continued to teach the Torah to Moses, and even gave him the tablets in order to transmit the Torah to all the Jewish people.

Similarly, we should always see people in their best light, encouraging them to study the Torah and fulfill G-d's commandments even if their actions seem to contradict G-d's wishes.[2]

---

2. *Likutei Sichot*, vol. 11, pp. 179–180.

THIRD READING
Exodus 33:12–16

While Moses was still on Mount Sinai, G-d told him that He was going to destroy the Jewish people, holding the majority responsible for not preventing the minority from worshipping the Golden Calf. Moses pleaded with G-d to forgive the people, so G-d agreed only to punish the guilty minority, but still insisted that His presence could no longer accompany the people. When Moses descended the mountain and saw those who were worshipping the Golden Calf, he understood that the people were not yet ready to receive the Torah. So Moses threw down the tablets, breaking them. He then ascended Mount Sinai for another 40 days, during which He secured G-d's forgiveness even for those who had worshipped the Golden Calf. After descending from Mount Sinai again, Moses asked G-d to once more let His presence dwell among the people, and G-d agreed.

Denying the Illusion

וַיֹּאמַר פָּנַי יֵלֵכוּ וַגוֹ': (שמות לג, יד)

[G-d] told [Moses,] "My Presence will [again] go [with you]."

By virtue of our Divine soul, we are all inherently and irrevocably bound to G-d, and are incapable of denying that bond – or even *wanting* to deny it.[3] We can go against G-d's will only when our mind is overtaken by the illusion that ignoring this bond is somehow advantageous.[4]

But even then, deep down, we remain faithful to our intrinsic bond with G-d.[5] We know that the illusion is a ruse. We are always able and ready to renew and reinstate our relationship with G-d.[6]

---

3. *Sefer HaMa'amarim 5710*, p. 114–116; *HaYom Yom*, 25 Tamuz (from *Igrot Kodesh Admor MeHoRayatz*, vol. 4, p. 383).
4. *Sotah* 3a.
5. *Tanya*, chapter 24.
6. *Likutei Sichot*, vol. 15, p. 407.

FOURTH READING

Exodus 33:17–23

Moses asked G-d further to show Him how everything He does is out of kindness. G-d replied that it is only possible for the human mind to grasp this "from the back," i.e., after the fact.

The Connecting Knot

וְרָאִיתָ אֶת אֲחֹרָי וּפָנַי לֹא יֵרָאוּ: (שמות לג, כג)

**[G-d told Moses,] "You may see My 'back,'
but My 'face' may not be seen."**

By His "back," G-d meant, allegorically, the knot of His head-*tefillin*.

Our connection to G-d can be envisioned metaphorically as a multi-stranded cord tied to us on one end and to Him on the other. When we sin, we sever one of the strings that compose that cord. In order to repent, we have to strengthen our commitment to G-d's will specifically with regard to how we just went against it. We have to tie a knot precisely where the string was severed. Joining two pieces of a severed string with a knot creates a stronger connection between the two pieces than existed before they were severed.[7]

This is why, when describing the process of repentance, G-d showed Moses specifically the *knot* of the *tefillin*. *Tefillin* express our connection to G-d, and the knot teaches us that when it is necessary to repair that connection, we do so by strengthening our observance and our awareness that G-d is present in all facets of our lives.

By strengthening our connection to G-d, we hasten the advent of the messianic Redemption, when G-d's presence will be openly revealed – and it will no longer be necessary to remind ourselves of its reality.[8]

7. *Igeret HaTeshuvah*, chapter 9.
8. *Likutei Sichot*, vol. 21, pp. 236–237.

FIFTH READING

Exodus 34:1–9

G-d then summoned Moses to Mount Sinai for a third 40-day stay. During this stay, G-d revealed His thirteen attributes of mercy to Moses. By invoking these attributes, it would always be possible to secure G-d's forgiveness.

G-d's Kindness

נֹצֵר חֶסֶד לָאֲלָפִים ... פֹּקֵד עֲוֹן אָבוֹת וגו׳: (שמות לד, ז)

[G-d told Moses to say, "G-d] preserves kindness for 2000 generations.... He remembers the premeditated sins of the fathers."

G-d articulated these same two ideas in the Ten Commandments[9] but in reverse order: "I am G-d ... who remembers the premeditated sins of the fathers ... and who shows kindness for 2000 generations." Furthermore, in the Ten Commandments G-d says that He "*shows* kindness," while in this passage He says that He "*preserves* kindness."

We can explain these differences by noting that G-d demonstrates two types of kindness:

The first is the kindness that He shows toward someone who has done something wrong. Such a person needs G-d's kindness in order to rectify his misdeeds. This is the type of kindness referred to in the Ten Commandments, in which G-d describes Himself as "showing kindness" after the "sins of the fathers."

The kindness referred to here, in contrast, is that which G-d shows us simply because He loves us. This kindness is mentioned *before* any mention of sin. Therefore, G-d describes Himself here as "preserving," i.e., storing up His kindness for use at *all* times and under *all* circumstances.[10]

9. Exodus 20:5–6.
10. *Torah Or* 69c.

SIXTH READING

Exodus 34:10–26

G-d then renewed the covenant He forged with the Jewish people at Mount Sinai, which had been rendered null and void by the sin of the Golden Calf.

Purifying Thought, Speech, and Action

וַיֹּאמֶר הִנֵּה אָנֹכִי כֹּרֵת בְּרִית וגו': (שמות לד, י)

[**G-d told Moses,**] **"I hereby make a covenant."**

Once the Jewish people broke the promise they had made at Mount Sinai to serve G-d faithfully, a new covenant became necessary, which would make the original covenant apply even if the people were unfaithful. In order to establish this type of covenant, G-d had to reveal a much deeper level of His connection to the Jewish people, which would remain intact regardless of how well they would obey His commandments.

But Moses sensed that if G-d were to declare that it is possible to remain connected to Him regardless of how well we keep His commandments, this might negate the uniqueness of the Jewish people. All nations could claim, "If obeying G-d's will does not matter, then we should also be able to enjoy the same, close relationship with You that You have promised the Jews."

Moses therefore asked G-d that His presence rest uniquely on the Jewish people, despite the apparent logic of this argument, and G-d consented.[11]

The implications of this renewed covenant between G-d and the Jewish people should inspire all Jews to cherish their unique relationship with G-d, and motivate all non-Jews to both encourage their Jewish friends to appreciate and remain true to their heritage and to work with them to fulfill G-d's Divine plan for humanity.[12]

11. Exodus 33:16–17.
12. *Or HaTorah, Shemot*, pp. 1847–1848; *Sefer HaMa'amarim 5630*, pp. 102–108.

SEVENTH READING
Exodus 34:27–35

Moses remained on Mount Sinai for 40 days. During this period, his physical body assumed angelic qualities, and he did not need to eat or drink.

The Nourishing Torah

לֶחֶם לֹא אָכַל וּמַיִם לֹא שָׁתָה וגו': (שמות לד, כח)

[While Moses was on Mount Sinai] he ate no bread and drank no water.

Just as the physical food we eat nourishes our bodies, the Torah that we study and internalize nourishes our Divine soul. Thus, although Moses did not consume physical food during each of the 40-day periods that he was atop Mount Sinai, he most certainly consumed "spiritual" food, as he spent the entire time learning the Torah directly from G-d.

Referring to Moses on Mount Sinai, it is said in the Psalms, "A [mortal] man ate the bread of the angels."[13] The angels subsist off whatever G-d allows them to comprehend about Him; they internalize this comprehension and it fuels their existence. More-over, their delight in this comprehension inspires them to Divine ecstasy, which they express by constantly singing songs of praise to G-d. When Moses was on Mount Sinai, he too subsisted off his comprehension of Divinity and the delight accompanying this comprehension.

Similarly, we can taste something of this spiritual nourishment and delight whenever we study the Torah, provided that we approach it as did Moses, constantly aware that we are "hearing" it directly from G-d.[14]

13. Psalms 78:25.
14. *Or HaTorah, Shemot,* vol. 6, pp. 2159–2160.

Vayakheil

Constructing the Tabernacle
Exodus 35:1–38:20

THE TENTH SECTION OF THE BOOK OF EXODUS OPENS AS
Moses descends from Mount Sinai for the third and final time and
immediately assembles (*Vayakheil*, in Hebrew) the Jewish people.
Moses informs them that G-d has forgiven them for the sin of the
Golden Calf and has instructed them to build the Tabernacle as
a sign of this forgiveness.

FIRST READING

Exodus 35:1–20

Moses prefaced his instructions for the Tabernacle by reminding the Jewish people that they must keep the Sabbath. They must not let their enthusiasm for building the Tabernacle lead them to transgress the prohibition against working on the seventh day.

Making the Sabbath Holy

שֵׁשֶׁת יָמִים תֵּעָשֶׂה מְלָאכָה וּבַיּוֹם הַשְּׁבִיעִי יִהְיֶה לָכֶם קֹדֶשׁ וגו': (שמות לה, ב)

[Moses told the Jewish people,] "Work may be done for six days, but the seventh day must be holy for you."

Our weekday work is important – especially if we perform it in a manner that helps refine the world, transforming it into G-d's home. Nonetheless, we must not allow work to overwhelm us, claiming the exclusive attention of our minds and hearts. Work must not be allowed to encroach on our set times for prayer, Torah study, charitable deeds, educating our children, and so forth.

Devoting all our energies to work during the week can make it difficult to disengage from it on the Sabbath – thoughts and worries of work will continue to haunt us. But if we preserve a sense of balance throughout the week, we will be able to focus properly on the holiness of the Sabbath when it comes.

This is why weekday work is described in this verse in the passive voice ("work *may be done*"), as if we are allowing it to happen by itself, so to speak. We can then read the above-quoted verse as follows: "If, during the six-day workweek, you let your work 'happen by itself,' you will then be able to experience the seventh day as a day of pure, undistracted holiness."[1]

---

1. *Likutei Sichot*, vol. 1, p. 187–190.

SECOND READING

Exodus 35:20–29

The twelve tribal princes let the people donate materials for the Tabernacle first, intending to provide whatever was still necessary afterward. However, the people donated all the basic materials, leaving the princes to donate only the gems, spices, and oil.

Personal vs. Communal Responsibility

וְהַנְּשִׂאָם הֵבִיאוּ וגו': (שמות לה, כז)

The princes brought....

The princes' decision bespoke an exaggerated sense of self-importance. Instead of viewing themselves merely as G-d's agents in taking care of His people, they considered themselves independent agents, taking care of the people on their own. This led them to focus on the responsibilities of their public role at the expense of meeting the private, individual responsibilities that they shared in common with the rest of the people.

We, too, are "princes" over the charges for whom we are responsible – our bodies, our families, and our wider sphere of influence. In our zeal to assume responsibility for our charges, we must not make the mistake that the princes made. By recalling that we are G-d's agents, we will not think that we can fulfill our obligations to Him just by influencing others. We will fulfill our personal obligations to study His Torah and fulfill His commandments properly.

We can thereby succeed both in fulfilling our own Divine mission and in helping others fulfill theirs – to "construct G-d's Tabernacle" by making the world into His home. This will hasten the advent of the Messianic Redemption, when the world will be G-d's true home in the fullest sense.[2]

2. *Likutei Sichot*, vol. 16, pp. 432–433.

THIRD READING
Exodus 35:30–36:7

As G-d instructed him, Moses then appointed the artisans to oversee the work.

Unique Contributions

כָּל מְלֶאכֶת עֲבֹדַת הַקֹּדֶשׁ וְגוֹ': (שמות לו, א)

[The artisans did] all the work required for the Tabernacle.

The "tools" we use to construct our inner, personal "Tabernacle" are our study of the Torah and our observance of its commandments.

The furnishings inside the Tabernacle allude to the Torah, which is the soul's "food." Just as physical food sustains our bodies and enables us to grow physically, studying the Torah sustains our souls and allows us to grow and develop spiritually.

Specifically, the Ark housed the Tablets of the Covenant, on which were engraved the Ten Commandments, which represented the entire Torah. The Table displayed the showbread, alluding to the nourishing quality of the Torah.[3] The Candelabrum spread light, alluding to how the Torah is the source of enlightenment.[4]

The walls and coverings of the Tabernacle allude to the commandments, which are the soul's "garments." Just as our clothing allows us both to express ourselves and to accomplish the specific tasks that require special clothing, fulfilling G-d's commandments allows our souls to both express themselves and to creatively transform the world.

Studying the Torah and performing G-d's commandments in order to construct our inner, personal Tabernacle will hasten the final Redemption and the accompanying restoration of the holy Temple in Jerusalem.[5]

3. Proverbs 9:5.
4. Ibid. 6:23.
5. *Torah Or* 88bc.

FOURTH READING

Exodus 36:8–19

The first articles the artisans made were the tapestries that formed the first covering of the Tabernacle. They then made the sheets of goat hair that served as the Tabernacle's second covering. The women had spun the threads of goat yarn that was used to weave these sheets directly off the goats, in order to produce wool of exceptional softness and pliability.[6] This required special skill.

Talents and Skills

וַיַּעַשׂ יְרִיעֹת עִזִּים וגו': (שמות לו, יד)

[The artisan made] sheets of goat hair.

These women understood that G-d had endowed them with a unique skill in order that they utilize this skill for holy purposes, and this is exactly what they did.

Similarly, those among us who have been blessed with special talents or skills, or who have received some unexpected Divine gift (for example, a disproportionately high return on an investment or transaction) should understand that the purpose of this gift is not that we use it for selfish purposes. Rather, we should use it to construct the "Tabernacle," the home that we all construct for G-d out of our personal lives through the study of the Torah, prayer, and the observance of G-d's commandments.[7]

6. Exodus 35:26; Rashi ad loc.
7. *Likutei Sichot*, vol. 16, p. 456.

FIFTH READING

Exodus 36:20–37:16

After fashioning the coverings and walls of the Tabernacle, the artisans proceeded to fashion its furnishings, first of which was the Ark of the Covenant.

A Place for the Broken Tablets

וַיַּעַשׂ בְּצַלְאֵל אֶת הָאָרֹן וגו': (שמות לו, א)

[The artisan] Betzalel made the Ark.

According to the Talmud,[8] the Ark contained not only the second set of tablets, which G-d gave the Jewish people to replace the broken first set, but also the broken remains of the first set of tablets.

The first tablets (before they were broken) represent the Jew in his pristine state at Mount Sinai, prior to the sin of the Golden Calf.

The second tablets, which G-d gave the Jewish people on *Yom Kippur* – after He forgave them for this sin – represent the Jew that has strayed and then returned to the Ark of Torah.

There is also a third type of Jew: one who has strayed but has not yet returned to the path of the Torah sufficiently to deserve receiving the second tablets. He, too, is represented in the Ark – in the broken pieces of the first tablets.

This teaches us that even those of us who are shattered and broken are worthy of a place in the Ark. We must never let our awareness of our own or others' imperfections make us think that we or they are unworthy to participate fully in the lifestyle that G-d has prescribed for all of us in the Torah.[9]

8. *Bava Batra* 14a.
9. *Likutei Sichot*, vol. 6, p. 156.

SIXTH READING
Exodus 37:17–29

The artisans fashioned the Inner, incense Altar.

Oneness with G-d

אַמָּה אָרְכּוֹ וְאַמָּה רָחְבּוֹ רָבוּעַ וְאַמָּתַיִם קֹמָתוֹ וגו': (שמות לז, כה)

**[The Inner Altar] was square – one cubit long
and one cubit wide – and two cubits high.**

According to our sages, there are five levels of the soul:

level of the soul		experience
yechidah	"unique one"	unity with G-d
chayah	"living being"	awareness of G-d as continually creating the world
neshamah	"breath"	vitality of intelligence
ruach	"spirit"	vitality of emotion
nefesh	"creature"	physical vitality

The lowest level of the soul is the *nefesh*, our basic, normative consciousness of simply being alive. As we refine ourselves, we experience the higher levels of our soul. The highest level is the *yechidah*, our innermost experience of unity with G-d. At this level of consciousness, we have risen far beyond consciousness of ourselves as separate, self-aware individuals.

Whereas the dimensions of the other furnishings of the Tabernacle made use of the half-cubit, the dimensions of the Inner Altar were measured only in single cubits. This is because the incense offering expressed the *yechidah*, the inner point of the Jewish soul's oneness with G-d.

We can access our *yechidah* whenever we rise above our own self-centeredness and devote ourselves unreservedly to G-d's will.[10]

10. *Sefer HaSichot 5752*, vol. 2, p. 414.

SEVENTH READING
Exodus 38:1–20

The artisans then fashioned the Outer Altar. These were followed by the Laver and the pillars of the Courtyard.

Precautions

וַיַּעַשׂ אֵת הַכִּיּוֹר נְחֹשֶׁת וגו': (שמות לח, ח)

[The artisan] made the copper Laver.

The priests were required to wash their hands and feet before every service they performed on the Outer Altar and before each time they entered the Sanctuary (no matter how many different rituals they might perform there).

The spiritual reason why the priests had to wash their hands and feet was in order to cleanse their active faculties of any "dirt," i.e., of any materialistic orientation that could impede their effectiveness in raising and spreading Divine consciousness.

Similarly, whenever we are working on our "Outer Altar" – elevating the outside, material world – we need to "wash" before each separate foray into it. We need to take extra precautions in order to resist the constant draw of materiality.

On the other hand, once we have successfully passed this stage and have entered our "Sanctuary" – enhancing our inward connection to G-d – it is enough to "wash" once before each entry into this realm, no matter how many separate aspects of our inner lives we focus on while there.[11]

---

11. *Likutei Sichot*, vol. 21, pp. 221–222.

Pekudei

Erecting the Tabernacle
Exodus 38:21–40:38

THE ELEVENTH AND FINAL SECTION OF THE BOOK OF EXODUS opens by informing us whom Moses appointed (*Pekudei*, in Hebrew) over the functioning and transport of the Tabernacle. Having concluded the account of how the artisans fashioned the various components of the Tabernacle, the Torah proceeds to describe how these same artisans fashioned the priestly garments and how the Tabernacle was finally erected.

FIRST READING
Exodus 38:21–39:1

In order to demonstrate how Moses was in charge of the entire process of constructing the Tabernacle, the Torah gives some examples[1] of the quantities of raw materials that the people brought to him.

Warmth and Enthusiasm

וְכֶסֶף פְּקוּדֵי הָעֵדָה וגו': (שמות לח, כה)

The tally of silver from those of the community who had been counted was....

The materials that the people donated for the construction and operation of the Tabernacle atoned for their involvement in the incident of the Golden Calf. Moses was perplexed by the notion that the soul can be redeemed from such a severe sin by a mere donation of silver. After all, the soul is spiritual, and moreover, its focus and drives are spiritually oriented. Silver, in contrast, besides being itself material, represents our lust for materiality. Since the reason the soul needs to be redeemed is because it has succumbed to materiality, how can too much materiality (i.e., sin) be cured by even more materiality (i.e., donated coins)?

G-d answered Moses by showing him a coin of fire. Indeed, a "cold" coin, given without feeling, cannot redeem the soul. But a "fiery" coin, given with the Divine soul's warmth and enthusiasm for Divinity, can atone for even the gravest sin.

This lesson applies to all the commandments we perform. If we perform them with spiritual vitality and enthusiasm, they become coins of fire, atoning for our past misdeeds and binding us to G-d Himself.[2]

---

1. *Likutei Sichot*, vol. 26, pp. 276–278.
2. Ibid., vol. 3, p. 925; ibid., vol. 26, pp. 231–237.

SECOND READING

Exodus 39:2–21

The Torah then describes how the artisans fashioned the priestly garments. Among these was the high priest's Ephod, an apron-like garment tied around his waist.

Revealing the Source

וַיַּעַשׂ אֶת הָאֵפֹד זָהָב תְּכֵלֶת וְאַרְגָּמָן וְתוֹלַעַת שָׁנִי וְשֵׁשׁ מָשְׁזָר: (שמות לט, ב)

[The artisan] made the Ephod out of [threads composed of] gold, turquoise wool, purple wool, scarlet wool, and twined linen.

Flax (out of which linen is made) was the offering of Cain, Adam's wicked son, while wool was the offering of Abel, Adam's righteous son.[3] In this context, flax represents evil while wool represents good.[4] Normally, then, the Torah prohibits mixing linen into woolen garments,[5] for we are enjoined to distinguish between good and evil.

From a deeper perspective, however, evil is often the expression of some holy entity that has suffered a tragic fall. Even so, evil still has to be avoided, since what matters is how an entity is expressed in *this* world, regardless of its source. In the Tabernacle, however, everything manifested its spiritual source, so mixing wool and flax was permitted.

Similarly, by showing people who exhibit toxic behavior that their evil is really the fallen version of some deep drive for holiness, we enable them to express their true, holy selves. They will then cease to be our enemies, becoming instead our allies in spreading Divine consciousness.[6]

3. Genesis 4:3–7.
4. Rabbeinu Bachye on Leviticus 19:19; *Zohar* 3:86b.
5. Leviticus 19:19; Deuteronomy 22:11. Such mixtures are called *shatnez*. The other exception to this rule is ritual tassels (*tzitzit*, see Numbers 15:38–41).
6. *Or HaTorah, Nach*, vol. 1, p. 132; ibid., *Devarim*, vol. 2, pp. 961–962; *Likutei Sichot*, vol. 36, pp. 153–160.

THIRD READING
Exodus 39:22–32

The high priest's garments also included the Breastplate and the Robe. He wore the Breastplate over his chest and attached to the Ephod, both of which he wore over the Robe.

Our Intrinsic Relationship with G-d

וַיַּעַשׂ אֶת מְעִיל הָאֵפֹד וגו': (שמות לט, כב)

[The artisan] made the Robe of the Ephod.

Each of the rites that the priests performed in the Tabernacle reflects a particular way in which we maintain our relationship with G-d. This relationship normally depends upon our behavior: the better we behave, the closer we are to G-d and the more we earn His love.

From a deeper perspective, however, we deserve G-d's love on the simple merit of being His children. This is reflected by the fact that while the high priest performs his priestly duties he must be wearing three garments – the Ephod, the Breastplate, and the Robe – each of which emphasizes our intrinsic connection to G-d.[7] The names of the tribes were engraved on the stones affixed to the Ephod and to the Breastplate, expressing our intrinsic merit as descendants of our patriarchs and matriarchs. The bells and pomegranates of the Robe alluded to how even the least of the Jewish people are full of merits as a pomegranate is full of seeds.[8]

Similarly, whenever we meet other Jews, our first priority should be to remind them of their illustrious heritage and inherent worth. Once they are aware of their intrinsic relationship with G-d, they will be further inspired to maintain this relationship by living up to His expectations of them.[9]

7. Exodus 28:35.
8. See above, p. 160.
9. *Likutei Sichot*, vol. 21, pp. 184–189.

FOURTH READING
Exodus 39:33–43

After all the components of the Tabernacle were fashioned, the people brought them to Moses. Among these components was the Ark, which housed the tablets upon which G-d had engraved the Ten Commandments and was kept in the Holy of Holies, the innermost chamber of the Tabernacle. Rods were attached to the sides of the Ark for carrying it.

Keeping Others in Mind

אֶת אֲרוֹן הָעֵדֻת וְאֶת בַּדָּיו וגו': (שמות לט, לה)

[The people presented] the Ark of Testimony and its rods [to Moses].

The rods had to remain attached to the Ark even after it was placed in the Holy of Holies.[10] One reason for this is because it might be necessary at some point to take the Ark out of the Tabernacle hurriedly. If there were no permanently attached rods, there might not be time to check if the available rods were strong enough to bear the Ark's weight. Permanently installed rods preclude this concern.[11]

The Ark housed the tablets, which represent the Torah. When we immerse ourselves in the study of the Torah, we have figuratively "entered the Ark." We might think that while we are studying the Torah, we must focus on it entirely, totally detached from any other concerns – particularly the spiritual or material needs of others.

The message of the permanent rods is that an Ark must always be ready to travel. Even when we are in the Holy of Holies, the holiest place in the world, we must always be ready to quickly bring the Torah wherever its inspiration and instruction are needed.[12]

10. Exodus 25:15.
11. *Sefer HaChinuch* 96.
12. *Likutei Sichot*, vol. 16, p. 334.

FIFTH READING

Exodus 40:1–16

G-d then instructed Moses how to erect the Tabernacle and install the priests in their office.

Joining the Ranks of the Priests

וְהִקְרַבְתָּ אֶת אַהֲרֹן וְאֶת בָּנָיו אֶל פֶּתַח אֹהֶל מוֹעֵד וגו': (שמות מ, יב)

[G-d told Moses,] "You must bring Aaron and his sons to the entrance of the Tent of Meeting."

In order to install Aaron and his sons as priests, G-d instructed Moses to draw them to himself, because Moses had already served as a priest and was therefore able to endow them with that spiritual power.

So, too, in every generation, G-d commissions the spiritual leaders of the generation to gather to themselves those who have committed themselves to follow their guidance. The leaders then grant their followers some of their own strengths so these followers can serve the spiritual needs of the rest of humanity.

Although only some of us are members of the priestly family – descendants of Aaron – all of us can choose to become "spiritual priests" by dedicating ourselves to the mission outlined for us by the spiritual leaders of our generation.[13]

SIXTH READING
Exodus 40:17–27

On 1 Nisan 2449, Moses erected the Tabernacle according to G-d's instructions. As mentioned previously, one of the Tabernacle's furnishings was the Ark, which housed the tablets upon which G-d had engraved the Ten Commandments.

Engraved Consciousness

וַיִּקַּח וַיִּתֵּן אֶת הָעֵדֻת אֶל הָאָרֹן וגו': (שמות מ, כ)

[Moses] took the [Tablets of] Testimony and placed them in the Ark.

The Holy of Holies was the innermost chamber of the Tabernacle and thus embodied the highest level of Divine consciousness, that of total unity with G-d. The only article in the Holy of Holies was the Ark housing the tablets upon which were engraved the Ten Commandments, which encapsulated the entire Torah. Eventually, a Torah scroll was placed inside the Ark as well.[14] All this teaches us that we can achieve the greatest unity with G-d through studying the Torah.

Specifically, it is the study of the inner dimension of the Torah – Kabbalah and Chasidic teachings – that enables a person to reach this unity with G-d. This unity is alluded to by the *engraved* tablets, for engraved words become one with their medium. In contrast, when words are written *on* a certain material – parchment, for example – the ink and parchment remain two separate entities; the ink can be scraped off.

Once we are engaged in the study of the Torah's inner dimension, our study of the rest of Torah can also enhance our union with G-d.[15] This is alluded to by the presence of the Torah scroll (which was written with ink on parchment) in the Ark as well.[16]

---

14. Deuteronomy 31:26.
15. See at length *Kuntereis Eitz HaChayim*, chapters 11 ff.
16. *Reshimot* 108.

SEVENTH READING
Exodus 40:28–38

Moses then performed all the rites that inaugurated the Tabernacle and the priests. As a sign that all was done properly and the Tabernacle was indeed ready to serve as a place where G-d's presence could be felt, a cloud materialized and hovered above the Tabernacle.

Our Inner Moses

וַיָּקֶם אֶת הֶחָצֵר וגו': (שמות מ, לג)

[Moses] set up the Courtyard.

Although the people fashioned the components of the Tabernacle, it was Moses who actually erected it.[17]

Similarly, with regard to the spiritual Tabernacle that we each build for G-d out of our own lives, it is our inner Moses that actually erects it. Our inner Moses is our innate capacity to know G-d directly, despite the limitations of our human intellect.[18] It is only by tapping this aspect of our souls and coming to know G-d in this way that we can construct a "sanctuary" for Him – a realm within our consciousness that we can enter whenever we need to renew our awareness of Him and our oneness with Him.[19]

17. Exodus 40:2.
18. *Tanya*, chapter 42; *Likutei Torah* 2:2a.
19. *Reshimot* 107.

LEVITICUS

Vayikra

Offerings
Leviticus 1:1–5:26

LEVITICUS, THE THIRD BOOK OF THE TORAH, IS PRIMARILY devoted to the rules governing the relationship of G-d with the Jewish nation collectively as well as His relationship with each person individually. The first two-and-a-half sections describe the procedures for the offerings to be made in the Tabernacle. The first section of the Book of Leviticus opens as G-d calls out (*Vayikra*, in Hebrew) to Moses, bidding him to enter the Tabernacle so He can teach him these procedures.

FIRST READING
Leviticus 1:1–13

After Moses erected the Tabernacle on 1 Nisan 2449, G-d called him into the Tabernacle and began instructing him regarding the procedures for the sacrifices.

Balancing Self-Esteem and Humility

וַיִּקְרָא אֶל מֹשֶׁה וְגוֹ': (ויקרא א, א)

[G-d] called to Moses.

The first word of the Book of Chronicles is the name of the first human being, Adam. The *alef* in Adam's name is written larger than usual (אדם), alluding to Adam's exaggerated sense of self-esteem over being the pinnacle of G-d's creation. Adam allowed what should have been healthy self-esteem to degenerate into conceit, and this caused his downfall.

Moses rectified Adam's mistake. Despite being aware of his own greatness – and of the fact that G-d Himself selected him for his exalted role in human history – Moses remained humble. Thus, the *alef* of the first word in the Book of Leviticus, "[G-d] called [to Moses]," is written smaller than usual (ויקרא), alluding to Moses' humility.

Moses remained humble by reasoning as follows: "I cannot take credit for any of my gifts or accomplishments, since they are all G-d-given. Indeed, were another person to have been given my potential, he would have accomplished much more."

We are all the spiritual heirs of both Adam and Moses. When we feel inadequate, we must remember that we are Adam, formed by G-d's own hands and fully capable of caring for His garden. But if we start to feel vain, we must recall that we are also Moses, thereby ensuring that our self-assurance does not develop into conceit.[1]

---

1. *Likutei Sichot*, vol. 17, pp. 7–8.

SECOND READING
Leviticus 1:14–2:6

Five types of animals were brought as sacrifices: cattle, goats, sheep, pigeons, and doves. Whereas cows, sheep, and goats had to undergo ritual slaughter (just like animals intended for our own consumption), fowl-sacrifices had to have their necks "nipped."

Advancing in Spirituality

וּמָלַק אֶת רֹאשׁוֹ וגו': (ויקרא א, טו)

[G-d instructed Moses to tell the Jewish people, "The priest] must nip off its head."

Ritual slaughter and nipping differ both with regard to who may perform them and how they are performed. Whereas ritual slaughter may be performed by a layperson, nipping may only be performed by a priest. Whereas ritual slaughter must be performed with a properly prepared knife, nipping is performed with the priest's thumbnail.

Allegorically, this is because a ritual slaughterer is considered G-d's agent, killing the animal "indirectly," by means of a tool (the knife). In nipping, however, the priest is acting as his own agent, killing the fowl directly with his own hand.

These differences allude to the distinctions between the initial and advanced stages of our relationship with G-d. Initially, our emphasis is on correct behavior – avoiding what is forbidden and performing what is prescribed. We are imposing Divine discipline on ourselves externally, so to speak. Although we ourselves are dictating our behavior, we are doing so only as G-d's agents.

Once we have aligned our behavior with G-d's will, however, we can shift our focus onto our inner selves – our intellect and emotions. At this stage, we are our own agents, actively pursuing Divine wisdom and developing our love and fear of G-d.[2]

2. *Igrot Kodesh*, vol. 1, pp. 46–47, 130–131.

THIRD READING

Leviticus 2:7–16

If someone wanted to offer up an ascent-offering but could not afford an animal, he could offer up an offering of grain.

Humble Sincerity

וְאִם מִנְחַת . . . קָרְבָּנֶךָ וְגו': (ויקרא ב, ז)

**[G-d instructed Moses to tell the Jewish people,]
"If your sacrifice is a grain-offering...."**

When someone brought a beautiful animal as an offering to G-d, he was liable to take pride in his generosity and in the fact that he fulfilled G-d's will in the best and most beautiful manner. In contrast, when all a person could afford to bring G-d was a grain-offering, such feelings of pride were most likely absent. As such, the sole reason he was bringing his sacrifice was to subjugate himself to G-d. It was therefore specifically the grain-offering that most eloquently expressed the essence of the sacrifices – the offering up of *ourselves* to G-d.

When we truly negate our sense of self, serving G-d with simple faith devoid of any ulterior motives or personal ambitions, we are assured that G-d will accept our efforts, atoning for our past misbehavior and drawing us closer to Him.[3]

3. *Likutei Sichot*, vol. 27, p. 15.

FOURTH READING

Leviticus 3:1–17

Someone wishing to draw close to G-d by praising Him can elect to bring a "peace-offering," so called because it promotes peace in the world.

The Importance of Intention

וְאִם זֶבַח שְׁלָמִים קָרְבָּנוֹ וגו': (ויקרא ג, א)

[G-d instructed Moses to tell the Jewish people,]
"If his sacrifice is a peace-offering...."

All the sacrifices that the Torah has discussed from the beginning of the Book of Leviticus to this point – including peace-offerings – are voluntary offerings. The Torah begins to discuss obligatory offerings only after it has discussed all the voluntary offerings.

By discussing voluntary offerings first, the Torah implies that all offerings, even obligatory ones, should be voluntary in essence. People were inspired to bring voluntary offerings because they appreciated the spiritual significance of these offerings. They knew that such offerings must express an inner process occurring within themselves, not within the animal. They also knew that what matters most is not the size or impressiveness of the animal but the intention of the heart.[4]

Like all aspects of the sacrifices, this insight applies to our spiritual lives today, as well. By studying the inner meaning and significance of the commandments that G-d obligates us to perform, we can fulfill them with the same inspiration and enthusiasm that usually characterize only voluntary practices.[5]

4. Rashi on Leviticus 1:17; *Menachot* 110a.
5. *Likutei Sichot*, vol. 32, p. 15, note 23.

FIFTH READING

Leviticus 4:1–26

G-d then taught Moses the procedures for sin-offerings. These sacrifices atoned principally for unintentional misdeeds. Special sin-offerings are prescribed when such sins are committed by the community's leaders – the high priest, the Sanhedrin (high court), or the king.

Inspiring Leaders

אֲשֶׁר נָשִׂיא יֶחֱטָא וגו׳: (ויקרא ד, כב)

[G-d instructed Moses to tell the Jewish people,] "If a leader sins...."

In terms of their respective roles in the spiritual life of the people, the function of the high priest is to imbue the people with the love of G-d, whereas the function of the king is to imbue them with the fear of G-d – a sense of awe before His presence.

Loving G-d does not necessarily shrink our ego. In fact, it can even enhance our ego by reminding us how spiritually advanced we are for loving G-d more than we love the material delights of this world. Therefore, loving G-d does not prevent our egos from causing us to inadvertently commit some offense. It can only guarantee that we will try to repair the damage.

Fear, in contrast, focuses us on the immensity of the thing before us, shriveling our sense of self into a sliver of what it was previously. Therefore, the experience of fear or awe of G-d can indeed assure us of not sinning even inadvertently.

Thus, by prescribing special sacrifices for the high priest and the king, the Torah seeks to inspire us both to atone for our inadvertent misdeeds and to deflate our egos so we not commit offenses, even inadvertently.[6]

6. *Likutei Sichot*, vol. 17, pp. 39–40.

SIXTH READING
Leviticus 4:27–5:10

After G-d taught Moses about sin-offerings for the high priest, the Sanhedrin (high court), and the king, He taught him about sin-offerings for common people.

Remaining Faithful to G-d

וְאִם נֶפֶשׁ אַחַת תֶּחֱטָא בִשְׁגָגָה וגו': (ויקרא ד, כז)

[G-d instructed Moses to tell the Jewish people,] "If a person unintentionally transgresses...."

The soul is intrinsically connected with G-d, and any deviation from this connection is unnatural. In the words of Rabbi Shneur Zalman of Liadi, "A Jew is by nature neither capable of sinning, nor does he desire to do so."[7]

How, then, do we sin? The Talmud states: "A person does not commit a sin unless he has been overcome by a spirit of folly,"[8] meaning that the person convinces himself that sinning will not disconnect him from G-d. This misconception allows the individual to stray.

This being the case, there are two antidotes to sin: First, thinking carefully and rationally about what we are doing, exposing the foolishness of our rationalizations. Second – if the first strategy fails – calling upon our intrinsic connection to G-d, which will empower us to resist our rationalizations no matter what.[9]

7. *HaYom Yom*, 25 Tamuz; *Igrot Kodesh Admor Mehorayatz*, vol. 4, p. 384.
8. *Sotah* 3a.
9. *Tanya*, chapter 14 (19b); *Sefer HaMa'amarim Melukat*, vol. 1, pp. 29–35.

SEVENTH READING
Leviticus 5:11–26

G-d then taught Moses about guilt-offerings. One type of guilt-offering was prescribed for someone who had falsely denied (1) having taken something as collateral, or (2) having received money from someone, or (3) having committed robbery, or (4) having withheld an employee's wages, or (5) having found a lost article – and then wishes to repent for having falsely denied these claims.

Offering Assistance

נֶפֶשׁ כִּי תֶחֱטָא וּמָעֲלָה מַעַל בַּה' וְכִחֵשׁ בַּעֲמִיתוֹ וְגוֹ': (ויקרא ה, כא)

[G-d instructed Moses to tell the Jewish people,] "If a person sins, acting unfaithfully to G-d by denying his fellow.... "

A sin committed against a fellow human being is also a sin committed against G-d.[10]

However, the word for "sin" in Hebrew can also be understood to mean "a failing." This teaches us that even if one merely fails to offer assistance to his fellow, this too is a wrong committed against G-d.[11]

---

10. See p. 201.
11. *Likutei Sichot* vol. 7, pp. 7–8.

Tzav

Details of the Sacrifices; The Installation Rites

Leviticus 6:1–8:36

THE SECOND SECTION OF THE BOOK OF LEVITICUS IS THE continuation and completion of the preceding section, opening as G-d tells Moses to command (*Tzav*, in Hebrew) Aaron and his sons to follow the procedures for offering up sacrifices. The second half of the section describes the weeklong installation rites by which the priests and the Tabernacle were inaugurated.

FIRST READING
Leviticus 6:1–11

Every morning, one of the priests would be appointed to remove the innermost ashes left from the previous day's sacrifices, depositing them at the foot of the Altar. In addition, whenever the remaining ashes accumulated to the point that they prevented the fire from consuming the sacrifices, the priest appointed that day to remove the innermost ashes removed these accumulated ashes as well, depositing them outside the camp.

The Importance of Preparations

וְהוֹצִיא אֶת הַדֶּשֶׁן אֶל מִחוּץ לַמַּחֲנֶה וגו': (ויקרא ו, ד)

[G-d told Moses, "The priest appointed to remove the accumulated ashes] must take the ashes outside the camp."

Removing the innermost ashes was an integral part of the daily Tabernacle ritual, whereas removing the accumulated ashes was done solely to make it possible to offer up more sacrifices. Nonetheless, both deeds had to be performed by the same priest. This teaches us that preparing to fulfill a Divine commandment – in this case, clearing ashes in order to offer up additional sacrifices – is a bona fide part of our spiritual life, no less than fulfilling the commandment itself.

In our desire to connect to G-d through performing His commandments, we may consider fulfilling the commandments much more important than preparing for them. From G-d's perspective, however, both the commandment and its prerequisite preparation are expressions of His will. Therefore, when we are focused on G-d's will (as opposed to our own spiritual advancement), we can prepare for the commandment with the same joy and enthusiasm that we experience while performing it.[1]

---

1. *Likutei Sichot*, vol. 37, pp. 5–6.

SECOND READING
Leviticus 6:12–7:10

G-d instructed Moses regarding the procedures for a guilt-offering. One of the cases in which a person had to bring a guilt-offering was when he admitted that he falsely denied owing someone something.

Positive Relations

וְזֹאת תּוֹרַת הָאָשָׁם וגו': (ויקרא ז, א)

[G-d told Moses,] "The following is the regulation of the guilt-offering."

The Torah describes the situations requiring a guilt-offering as "acting unfaithfully to G-d."[2]

Certainly committing *any* sin can be considered "acting unfaithfully to G-d," yet the Torah makes this point specifically in the case of someone who seeks to harm his fellow human being financially.

It is easy to understand that transgressing a "religious" commandment is committing a sin against G-d. In contrast, it is easy to think that transgressing a "social" commandment is between us and the other person, and does not reflect upon our relationship with G-d – even if we acknowledge that it was G-d who gave us these laws. The Torah therefore specifies clearly that wronging our fellow human being is equally an affront to G-d. The ritual of the guilt-offering assures us that G-d holds open the door for repentance, allowing all our sins to be completely forgiven.

The awareness that our good standing with our fellow human beings is essential to our good standing with G-d helps us aspire to the highest standards of social behavior.[3]

2. Leviticus 5:21.
3. *Likutei Sichot* vol. 7, pp. 1–8.

THIRD READING
Leviticus 7:11–38

A person was required to offer up a thanksgiving-offering when-ever he or she experienced some open example of G-d's protec-tion or help.

Reasons to Be Thankful

אִם עַל תּוֹדָה יַקְרִיבֶנּוּ וגו': (ויקרא ז, יב)

[G-d told Moses,] "If [a person] brings
[a sacrifice] in order to give thanks...."

In general, the sacrifices served to disentangle us from our mate-riality, drawing us nearer to G-d. Prayer, which in the absence of the Temple substitutes for the sacrifices, largely serves the same purpose.

Inasmuch as the physical realm is the lowest rung of existence, we need to rise above it in order to cleave to our Divine source. In the Messianic Era, however, the physical realm will be saturated with G-dliness even more than the loftiest spiritual realms. We will therefore not need to rise above our milieu, and both sacri-fices and prayers will become obsolete.

The exception will be thanksgiving sacrifices and prayers. This is because rather than the effort to *reach* higher consciousness, thanksgiving is *the experience* of that consciousness – our recog-nition and awe of G-d's presence in our lives. Since our Divine awareness will perpetually ascend in the Messianic Era, our joy in experiencing it will also perpetually intensify. We will therefore continue to offer sacrifices and prayers of thanksgiving.

By focusing our prayers nowadays on being thankful for feeling close to G-d, we can hasten the advent of the Messianic Redemp-tion, when this will indeed be the sole focus of our prayers.[4]

---

4. *Torah Or* 97a; *Or HaTorah, Vayikra,* vol. 1, p. 23; ibid., *Nach,* vol. 2, pp. 963–964; *Yaheil Or,* p. 369.

FOURTH READING

Leviticus 8:1–13

Having completed the instructions regarding the procedures for the sacrifices, the Torah describes how Moses installed Aaron and his four sons into the priesthood.

Entering the Priesthood

וַיִּתֵּן עָלָיו אֶת הַכֻּתֹּנֶת וגו': (ויקרא ח, ז)

[Moses] placed the Tunic upon [Aaron].

Aaron and his sons were elevated to their office by wearing the sacred priestly garments. Since G-d instructed Moses to install Aaron and his sons as priests, it was he who had to dress them.

The priesthood was a holy occupation, but its purpose was to affect all people, even those who were not openly interested in holiness.

Moses was uniquely qualified to empower the priests to affect everyone because he had previously demonstrated his self-sacrifice for even the least worthy among the Jewish people.

There is a "Moses" in each generation: the Torah authorities who selflessly guide us in our Divine mission. In addition, every Jew possesses an inner "Moses," an inner point of consciousness that fully identifies with G-d and His concern for every individual. These "Moseses" enable us to act as "priests," connecting ourselves and others to G-d.[5]

5. *Likutei Sichot*, vol. 21, pp. 178–179.

FIFTH READING
Leviticus 8:14–21

The sacrifices that Moses offered up in order to install Aaron and his sons included ascent-offerings, sin-offerings, and peace-offerings.

The Soul is Aware
─────────────────

וַיַּגֵּשׁ אֵת פַּר הַחַטָּאת וגו': (ויקרא ח, יד)

[Moses] brought the sin-offering bull....

The minds and hearts of the people who offered up sacrifices were spiritually elevated, even if the people themselves were not consciously aware of it. This is because our Divine soul is always aware of the true state of our relationship with G-d.

Thus, the Torah does not need to explicitly state that the physical offering must be accompanied by a spiritual, inner offering – because this is always the case, from the soul's perspective. Instead, the Torah begins its discussion of offerings with voluntary offerings, since these clearly involve the offerer's mind and heart. This indicates that all offerings, even obligatory ones, are essentially voluntary offerings, stemming from the soul's innate desire to come close to G-d.[6]

The same is true of our prayers, which correspond to the daily sacrifices. Our minds and hearts are always involved in our prayers, even when we do not consciously sense this involvement. Thus, we need never feel that when our minds or hearts "wander" during our prayers that nothing was accomplished.

This awareness can inspire us firstly to cultivate the habit of praying regularly (no matter how well we succeed in concentrating), and secondly to invest more effort in involving our conscious minds and hearts when we pray.[7]

6. See p. 195.
7. *Likutei Sichot*, vol. 17, pp. 12–13.

SIXTH READING
Leviticus 8:22–29

Inasmuch as Moses offered up the sacrifices of the installation ritual, he was acting in the capacity of a "temporary" priest.

Emulating Moses

וַיִּקַּח מֹשֶׁה אֹתָם מֵעַל כַּפֵּיהֶם וַיַּקְטֵר הַמִּזְבֵּחָה וגו': (ויקרא ח, כח)

**Moses took [the designated parts of the
animal] from [Aaron and his sons'] hands
and burned them up on the Altar.**

During the seven days of installation, Moses officiated in the Tabernacle in a simple, white tunic. Although he *acted* temporarily as a priest, he never *became* a priest. He never wore either the garments of a regular priest or of a high priest. This is because his priestly function was subordinate to his main role as the conveyor of G-d's teachings to the Jewish people.

Similarly, each of us has an "inner Moses,"[8] an ability to devote ourselves fully and exclusively to hearing and understanding G-d's message to us by studying His Torah. When our inner Moses is active, even the thought of serving G-d in any other way should seem foreign to us.

This occasional ascent into "Moses consciousness" hastens the advent of the Messianic Redemption, for at that time, as Maimonides writes,[9] "the occupation of the entire world will be solely to enhance its knowledge of G-d. The Jewish people will therefore be [the world's] great sages, possessing esoteric knowledge and comprehending their Creator's consciousness as far as is humanly possible, as it written,[10] 'For the earth will be full of the knowledge of G-d as water covers the seabed.'"[11]

---

8. *Tanya*, chapter 42.
9. *Mishneh Torah, Melachim* 12:5.
10. Isaiah 11:9.
11. *Likutei Sichot*, vol. 32, pp. 34–35.

SEVENTH READING
Leviticus 8:30–36

The installation rituals were repeated every day for a full week.

Bringing Creation to its Fulfillment

וַיַּעַשׂ אַהֲרֹן וּבָנָיו אֵת כָּל הַדְּבָרִים אֲשֶׁר צִוָּה ה' בְּיַד מֹשֶׁה: (ויקרא ח, לו)

Aaron and his sons did all the things that G-d commanded through Moses.

This verse implies that Aaron and his sons did not deviate from the procedure that G-d prescribed. Even if Aaron and his sons thought that a specific situation warranted additional effort or precautionary stringencies, they fulfilled everything exactly as they heard it from Moses, without regard to their own appraisal of the situation.

The first, obvious lesson that we learn from this is that we should trust G-d, fulfilling His directions precisely, regardless of our own appraisal of the situation – even if we mean well.

The second, subtler lesson is that it is specifically Aaron and his sons who were correct in not changing anything, for they were then in a setting of sublime spirituality, in which extra caution was unnecessary. In our times, however, there is a need for both types of deviation: to go beyond the letter of the law and to avoid those permissible activities that might lead to dangerous consequences.

Learning how to balance these two lessons and when to apply each is part of the process of spiritual growth.[12]

---

12. *Hitva'aduyot 5748*, vol. 1, pp. 523–524.

Shemini

The Conclusion of the Installation Rites; Kashrut

Leviticus 9:1–11:47

THE THIRD SECTION OF THE BOOK OF LEVITICUS OPENS WITH
the description of the eighth (*Shemini*, in Hebrew) and final day
of the installation rituals for the Tabernacle. After this, it records
which animals are permitted for Jewish consumption.

FIRST READING
Leviticus 9:1–16

During the week of 23–29 Adar 2449, Moses performed the sacrificial rites designed to install Aaron and his sons as priests. On the eighth day, 1 Nisan, it was time for Aaron to officiate for the first time as high priest and his sons as regular priests. But on account of the role he played in the incident of the Golden Calf, Aaron hesitated to step forward.

When Not to be Bashful

וַיֹּאמֶר מֹשֶׁה אֶל אַהֲרֹן קְרַב אֶל הַמִּזְבֵּחַ וגו': (ויקרא ט, ז)

[Moses told Aaron,] "Approach the Altar."

We are taught that there are three inherent traits of the Jewish people: bashfulness, mercifulness, and kindness.[1] Therefore, although Aaron knew that G-d chose him for his role as high priest – and indeed, had been preparing for it for a full week before this – he was naturally reluctant to assume a position of greatness.

Moses therefore reminded Aaron that as praiseworthy as bashfulness is, we must overcome it when it is at odds with performing our Divine mission.

We, too, while cherishing our innate shyness, must not let it interfere with fulfilling our Divine mission. Our innate mercifulness and kindness toward those that need us to help them should in such cases override our innate bashfulness.[2]

1. *Yevamot* 79a.
2. *Hitva'aduyot 5747*, vol. 3, pp. 62–64.

SECOND READING

Leviticus 9:17–23

Aaron finished performing his sacrificial rites, but there was no miraculous manifestation of G-d's presence. So Moses and Aaron prayed to G-d to consume the sacrifices with heavenly fire, blessing the Jewish people that G-d should favorably accept the Tabernacle that they built and Aaron's offerings on their behalf. Divine fire then descended and consumed the sacrifices.

Consummate Humility

וַיֵּצְאוּ וַיְבָרֲכוּ אֶת הָעָם וגו': (ויקרא ט, כג)

[Moses and Aaron] came out [of the Sanctuary] and blessed the people.

It was only as a result of the combined efforts of Moses and Aaron that the Divine presence descended upon the Tabernacle – and thereby upon the Jewish people in general. Aaron performed all the sacrificial rites, but Moses instructed Aaron how to perform them.

Aaron embodied the trait of brotherly love. As the Talmudic sage Hillel instructs us, "Be of the disciples of Aaron, loving peace and pursuing peace, loving your fellow creatures and drawing them close to the Torah."[3] Moses' role was to convey G-d's teachings to the people, which included teaching Aaron how to love others.

From this we learn that the key to constructing our own Tabernacle – i.e., to making our own lives into a home for G-d, wherein G-d's presence can be revealed – is loving our fellow Jews as G-d instructs us in His Torah.[4]

3. *Avot* 1:12.
4. *Hitva'aduyot 5742*, vol. 3, pp. 1125–1126.

THIRD READING
Leviticus 9:24–10:11

When the Jewish people saw fire descend from heaven, consuming the parts of the sacrifices that had been placed on the Altar, they were ecstatic that G-d's presence appeared to them again openly. But then, Aaron's sons Nadav and Avihu, motivated by a misplaced desire to experience Divine ecstasy, offered up some incense on their own. To everyone's horror, Divine fire again descended, but this time as two pairs of flames that entered Nadav's and Avihu's nostrils, killing them instantly.

Managing Ecstasy

וַיַּקְרִיבוּ לִפְנֵי ה' אֵשׁ זָרָה אֲשֶׁר לֹא צִוָּה אֹתָם: (ויקרא י, א)

**[Nadav and Avihu] brought before G-d a
fire that was foreign – inasmuch as He had
not commanded them [to offer it up].**

In his mystical vision, the prophet Ezekiel saw "the living [angels] running and returning,"[5] which allegorically means that "being alive entails alternately running and returning." Physically, this oscillation is manifest in our breathing and our heartbeat. Spiritually, it is manifest as our periodic alternation between world-forsaking flights of inspiration ("runs") and world-affirming involvement in our Divine mission ("return").

Inasmuch as the purpose of creation is to make the physical world into G-d's home, all our "runs" should be for the purpose of enhancing our "returns." In this context, Nadav and Avihu's mistake was pursuing the "run" for its own sake rather than as a prelude to the subsequent "return."

Learning from their error enables us to "run" for the sake of improving our "return," thereby fulfilling the purpose of creation and hastening the advent of the Redemption.[6]

5. Ezekiel 1:14.
6. *Likutei Sichot*, vol. 3, pp. 987–991.

FOURTH READING

Leviticus 10:12–15

Even though it is normally forbidden for a priest in mourning to officiate, Moses instructed Aaron and his two surviving sons, Eleazar and Itamar, to continue with the sacrificial service – including eating their designated portions of the sacrifices – as an exceptional case.

Ascent and Descent

וְאֵת חֲזֵה הַתְּנוּפָה וְאֵת שׁוֹק הַתְּרוּמָה וּגו': (ויקרא י, יד)

[Moses told Aaron and his sons, "You must eat] the breast used as the wave-offering and the thigh used as the raised-offering."

The installation offerings were a type of peace-offering. All peace-offerings require "raising" and "waving": the priest and the offerer must together hold specific parts of the animal and lift them, lower them, and then move them back and forth.

The vertical movements allude to our relationship with G-d: sometimes we ascend to great heights, and sometimes we suffer temporary descents or setbacks. The horizontal movements allude to our relationship with our fellow human beings: sometimes we need to draw them close to us, and sometimes we need to push them away, encouraging them to assert their independence.

The fact that both the raising and lowering movements are part of the sacrifice indicates that we can remain conscious of G-d's presence in our lives both when we are on the spiritual ascent and when we are suffering a setback.

The fact that both the back and forth movements are part of the sacrifice indicates that we must both teach this lesson to others and encourage them to develop their appreciation of it on their own.[7]

7. *Hitva'aduyot 5746*, vol. 2, pp. 784, 787–790.

FIFTH READING
Leviticus 10:16–20

G-d instructed Aaron and his two surviving sons to eat their designated portions of the day's sacrifices as an exception to the rule that priests in mourning may not eat sacrificial meat. Moses assumed that this exception applied to all the sacrifices of the day, while Aaron assumed that it applied only to the special sacrifices that were offered up exclusively on this unique day. When Aaron explained his perspective, Moses agreed that he was right.

Respect for the Truth

וַיִּשְׁמַע מֹשֶׁה וַיִּיטַב בְּעֵינָיו: (ויקרא י, כ)

Moses heard [Aaron's explanation] and it pleased him.

When Moses heard Aaron's reasoning, he acknowledged that it made more sense than his own, admitting that he had not received any direct instructions from G-d in the matter.

The obvious lesson for us in this episode is never to be afraid to admit the truth, even if doing so may prove to be embarrassing. Moreover, we should admit the truth even if we might think that our social or religious standing obligates us not to. G-d Himself had appointed Moses as the transmitter of the Torah, and it was therefore paramount that the people trust his integrity. Moses was fully aware of this, and could have thought that admitting his own fallibility might compromise his authority as G-d's messenger. But he correctly realized that, on the contrary, demonstrating his readiness to bow before the truth would only enhance the people's respect for his message.

We, too, can be effective messengers of truth when we demonstrate that it means more to us than our esteem in the eyes of others.[8]

---

8. *Sichot Kodesh 5739*, vol. 2, pp. 571–573.

SIXTH READING
Leviticus 11:1–32

G-d then instructed Moses to inform the Jewish people that because of their unique Divine mission, G-d has endowed them with unique souls. In order to maintain the health of these unique souls, they are required to follow a special diet: the laws of kashrut. These laws govern, first of all, which animals we may eat and may not eat.

Being Kosher

כֹּל מַפְרֶסֶת פַּרְסָה וְשֹׁסַעַת שֶׁסַע פְּרָסֹת מַעֲלַת
גֵּרָה בַּבְּהֵמָה אֹתָהּ תֹּאכֵלוּ: (ויקרא יא, ג)

[G-d instructed Moses to tell the Jewish people,] "You must [only] eat an animal whose feet are cloven, completely split into two feet, and who regurgitates its cud."

Feet, touching the ground, signify the primary way that we contact and elevate the material world: by harnessing it for holy purposes. Rumination, in contrast, signifies the secondary, subtler way that we refine the material world: by revealing its inherent holiness and thereby absorbing it ("digesting it") into our Divine consciousness.

Both of these phases should be double – just as a kosher animal's feet are split *into two* and it digests its food *twice*. Every step we take in elevating the physical world should be taken with a mind toward our next step in elevating the physical world, indicating that our goals in this regard are unlimited. Similarly, every morsel of the physical world that we "digest," i.e., refine into spirituality, should be subsequently refined on a still higher level. Since G-d is infinite, the ascent into Divine consciousness is likewise infinite.[9]

9. *Sefer HaSichot 5751*, vol. 1, pp. 160, 163.

SEVENTH READING
Leviticus 11:33–47

Among the animals prohibited for Jewish consumption is the snake.

Outsmarting Evil

כֹּל הוֹלֵךְ עַל גָּחוֹן ... לֹא תֹאכְלוּם וגו': (ויקרא יא, מב)

**[G-d instructed Moses to tell the Jewish people,]
"You may not eat [the snake], who moves about
bent over [and only then falls on its belly]."**

The *Zohar* compares the snake to the evil inclination (the *yetzer hara*).[10] The evil inclination is smart: it does not immediately suggest that we "crawl on our belly" and bury ourselves in earthliness. It begins by suggesting that we walk with a "lowered head," that we forget G-d who is above us, neglecting as well the higher purposes of life. This eventually leads us to forget our purpose altogether.

The antidote to the snake's schemes is to immerse ourselves in the study of the Torah, especially the inner dimension of Torah, which lifts us into a realm that the snake cannot reach.[11]

10. *Zohar* 1:35b.
11. *Likutei Sichot*, vol. 17, p. 122.

Tazri'a

Tzara'at

Leviticus 12:1–13:59

IN THIS SECTION OF THE BOOK OF LEVITICUS, THE TORAH discusses ritual defilement, which prevents a person from entering the Tabernacle or consuming the parts of the sacrifices that are meant to be eaten. The Torah first discusses the type of ritual defilement that automatically rests upon any Jewish woman who gives birth (*Tazri'a*, in Hebrew). The justified pride that a woman is likely to feel after the miracle of giving birth prevents her from feeling the absolute humility before G-d required in order to enter His Tabernacle. She is therefore obligated to undergo a fixed period of recuperation and a purification process, after which she can again visit the Tabernacle and participate in its rituals. The second type of defilement discussed in this section is a now-extinct disease known as *tzara'at*, which appeared on a Jewish man or woman's skin, garments, or home as a reflection of some subtle spiritual imperfection in the person.

FIRST READING
Leviticus 12:1–13:5

Giving birth to a baby boy renders a Jewish woman ritually defiled for one week. After immersing herself in a *mikveh* (ritual pool) at the end of this week, she is technically undefiled, but she must wait 33 days before entering the Tabernacle or consuming sacrifices. During this waiting period, however, uterine bleeding does not ritually defile her as it normally would. The periods of one week and 33 days are each doubled for a baby girl, inasmuch as[1] a baby girl is herself a future birth-giver.

Healing Subconscious Flaws

וּשְׁלֹשִׁים יוֹם וּשְׁלֹשֶׁת יָמִים תֵּשֵׁב בִּדְמֵי טָהֳרָה וְגוֹ': (ויקרא יב, ד)

[G-d instructed Moses to tell the Jewish people, "A woman who gives birth] remains [in a transitional state] for 33 days, [during which] blood is not a source of defilement."

Comparable to a woman who has immersed herself in a *mikveh* after giving birth, the Jewish people have been purified by their exile. We are now waiting for the Divinely-determined waiting period to pass until our redemption.

During this period, we need to behave as the new mother does regarding her post-immersion bleeding. We may indeed see "blood," i.e., aspects of the world that would normally "defile" us, i.e., weaken our Divine consciousness. But we must remain unaffected by these enticements by staying true to our authentic selves and to our Divine mission.

We will then be able to proceed to the next stage: revealing that the "blood" itself is undefiled, i.e., transforming the material world into an expression of Divinity. The required period of waiting will then be over and the final Redemption will be ushered in.[2]

---

1. Commentary of Rabbi Shimshon Raphael Hirsch on Leviticus 12:5.
2. *Likutei Sichot*, vol. 7, pp. 90–91.

SECOND READING

Leviticus 13:6–17

Tzara'at afflicted only people who had risen to the extremely high levels of Divine consciousness that are attainable only when the Tabernacle – or its successor, the holy Temple – is standing. Whenever such a person suffered the specific type of dermal lesion that could have been *tzara'at*, he was brought to a priest for examination. If the priest determined that the person was indeed suffering from *tzara'at* and pronounced him ritually defiled, the sufferer had to go through a period of separation from the community followed by a process of ritual purification.

The Value of Joy

וּבְיוֹם הֵרָאוֹת בּוֹ בָּשָׂר חַי יִטְמָא: (ויקרא יג, יד)

[G-d instructed Moses to tell the Jewish people,] "On the day that live flesh appears in [the lesion], he will be declared defiled."

A priest may examine someone suspected of suffering from *tzara'at* and declare him defiled only on certain days. During the festivals, or in the case of a bridegroom during the seven days of rejoicing following his wedding, the priest may not inspect the suspected sufferer.[3]

We see from this how greatly G-d prizes the joy even of someone guilty of whatever misconduct caused him to break out with *tzara'at*. G-d insists that this person's process of repentance be delayed so as not to mitigate his joyful observance of the festivals or his wedding.

From this we can learn to value fulfilling G-d's commandments specifically with joy – both with regard to ourselves and with regard to others.[4]

---

3. *Nega'im* 3:2.
4. *Likutei Sichot*, vol. 37, pp. 37–41.

THIRD READING

Leviticus 13:18–23

Tzara'at of the skin can develop out of a lesion, an inflammation, or a burn.

Positive Speech

נֶגַע צָרַעַת הִוא וגו': (ויקרא יג, כ)

[G-d instructed Moses to tell the Jewish people,] "It is a *tzara'at*-lesion."

The Talmud[5] states that someone afflicted with *tzara'at* is similar in certain ways to a dead person.

Allegorically, we can understand "death" to mean any lack of vitality. Someone afflicted with *tzara'at* is typically guilty of slander, indicating that his Divine consciousness has not affected his faculty of speech as it should have. There is an unhealthy disconnect between the inspired knowledge of G-d that he has worked hard to attain, on the one hand, and the way he relates to others and treats them, on the other. Instead of looking at others from G-d's perspective, seeing his fellows' positive and infinite worth and potential, he perceives them from the perspective of human shortsightedness. Cut off from the positive, life-affirming vitality of Divine consciousness, his power of speech is a "deadened" force of negativity.

Keeping this insight of our sages in mind enables us to ensure that the way we speak to and about others (and this includes other means of communication, as well) is always infused with the positive, optimistic attitude that characterizes true Divine consciousness.[6]

---

5. *Nedarim* 64b; *Avodah Zarah* 5a.
6. *Reshimot* 40.

FOURTH READING

Leviticus 13:24–28

The first symptom of *tzara'at* of the skin is a white spot on the flesh.

Seclusion

נֶגַע צָרַעַת הוּא: (ויקרא יג, כז)

[G-d instructed Moses to tell the Jewish people,] "It is a *tzara'at*-lesion."

We noted previously[7] that the Talmud[8] states that someone afflicted with *tzara'at* is similar in certain ways to a dead person. We interpreted this statement allegorically to refer to this person's lack of spiritual vitality and optimism as reflected in his speech.

The Talmud's statement may also be interpreted positively. In this sense, "death" refers not to a lack of vitality but to the process that occurs when one has completed one's task of self-refinement in this world and is ready to progress to the next level, in the next world.

In this context, the fact that a person suffering from *tzara'at* must be ostracized from the community makes him similar to someone who is leaving this world behind. His being denied of participating in Jewish life alludes to the negation of most of the commandments in the Messianic future.

In this positive sense, we can indeed occasionally aspire to be "afflicted with *tzara'at*," separating ourselves from the world in order to temporarily seclude ourselves in Divine meditation. These periodic retreats into the spiritual world will then renew our inspiration to fulfill our Divine purpose in the world as we work to transform it into G-d's true home.[9]

7. In the previous insight.
8. *Nedarim* 64b; *Avodah Zarah* 5a.
9. *Reshimot* 40.

FIFTH READING
Leviticus 13:29–39

Special laws apply to *tzara'at* that appears on the head.

The Power of Words

וְאִישׁ אוֹ אִשָּׁה כִּי יִהְיֶה בוֹ נָגַע וגו': (ויקרא יג, כט)

[G-d instructed Moses to tell the Jewish people,]
"If a man or a woman has a lesion...."

The condition of *tzara'at* no longer afflicts people, but people unfortunately still commit the sins that used to cause it. Studying the laws of *tzara'at*, as they are described both in the written and the oral Torah, is meant to encourage us to avoid the types of behavior that gave rise to this condition.

The surest way to avoid the improper use of speech – which was the most common cause of *tzara'at* – is by taking care to use the power of speech only for good and holy purposes. In the words of Maimonides, at the conclusion of his description of the laws regarding *tzara'at*:[10] "The conversation of virtuous Jews revolves solely around the teachings of the Torah and wisdom in general. G-d therefore assists them, purifying them through [their speech], as it is written,[11] 'Then those who fear G-d spoke to one another, and G-d listened and heard, and a book of remembrance was written before Him for those who fear G-d and those who give thought to His Name.'"[12]

10. *Mishneh Torah, Tum'at Tzara'at* 16:10.
11. *Malachi* 3:16.
12. *Likutei Sichot*, vol. 27, p. 100.

SIXTH READING
Leviticus 13:40–54

When a person has been declared by the examining priest to have contracted *tzara'at* on his skin, he must dwell outside the city until the *tzara'at* disappears.

Purging Negativity

בָּדָד יֵשֵׁב מִחוּץ לַמַּחֲנֶה מוֹשָׁבוֹ: (ויקרא יג, מו)

[G-d instructed Moses to tell the Jewish people, "The person afflicted with *tzara'at*] must dwell isolated; his dwelling must be outside the camp."

The simple reason why someone afflicted with *tzara'at* must reside outside the camp is so he can experience firsthand the alienation that results from slanderous speech. This will motivate him to repent.

On a somewhat deeper level, the reason for his banishment is because the defining characteristic of holiness is unity. Holiness rests on individuals or a group when they renounce their egocentricity in favor of being focused on G-d and performing His will. Those who have submitted to G-d's higher authority and have ascended to His higher perspective get along with each other easily and willingly. Thus, those who promote dissension are by that very fact excluded from even the outermost "camp" of holiness.

Nonetheless, G-d assures us that no matter how far we may stray from holiness, He will bring us back. The next section of the Torah therefore discusses how a person afflicted with *tzara'at* is to be purified of his ritual defilement in order to resume his life with the community.[13]

---

13. *Likutei Sichot*, vol. 7, pp. 101–102.

SEVENTH READING
Leviticus 13:55–59

Tzara'at can also affect clothing and houses. The final stage in the purification process of an article of clothing is immersing it in a *mikveh* (ritual pool).

Total Immersion

וְהַבֶּ֫גֶד ... וְסָ֣ר מֵהֶ֔ם הַנֶּ֑גַע וְכֻבַּ֖ס ... וְטָהֵֽר: (ויקרא יג, נח)

[G-d instructed Moses to tell the Jewish people,] "Any garment...from which the lesion disappears must be immersed...and then it will be rid of defilement."

From the fact that a garment needs to be immersed in a *mikveh* (ritual pool) even after it has been physically rid of all trace of *tzara'at* teaches us that there are two stages of repentance:

The first stage – corresponding to the disappearance of *tzara'at* from the garment – is to admit having sinned, acknowledge that we regret having done so, and resolve not to do so again. This rids us of the effect of the sin and procures G-d's forgiveness.

However, it is not enough that G-d simply forgives us; we want to be restored to His favor, as well. The second stage, therefore – corresponding to the immersion of the garment in a *mikveh* – is to re-commit ourselves to G-dly living, this time with greater dedication than before. We do this by vigorously immersing ourselves in the study of the Torah. This restores us to G-d's favor. Ideally, we should intensify our love of G-d, for if our re-commitment is motivated by love, we will merit G-d's favor even greater than before.[14]

---

14. *Likutei Sichot*, vol. 7, p. 99.

Metzora

Purification from *Tzara'at*

Leviticus 14:1–15:33

THE FIFTH SECTION OF THE BOOK OF LEVITICUS CONTINUES
the preceding section's discussion of *tzara'at*, a now-extinct disease that appeared on a Jewish man or woman's skin, garments,
or home as a reflection of some subtle spiritual imperfection in
the person. This section opens with the rituals that someone who
was afflicted with *tzara'at* (*Metzora*, in Hebrew) must undergo
in order to be allowed to enter the Tabernacle precincts again.
It then describes how *tzara'at* can appear on buildings and how
affected buildings are purified from this condition. Finally, it
discusses the various forms of ritual defilement that result from
certain bodily discharges.

FIRST READING
Leviticus 14:1–12

Once *tzara'at* has disappeared from the body, the formerly afflicted person has to be brought to a priest, who will then begin the rituals that will purify the person of his ritual defilement.

Seeing Holy Potential in Others

וְהוּבָא אֶל הַכֹּהֵן: (ויקרא יד, ב)

[G-d instructed Moses to tell the Jewish people, "The afflicted person] must be brought to the priest."

Tzara'at was usually caused by the sin of slander or by exhibiting haughtiness. Someone afflicted with *tzara'at* was banished from society altogether, even from the outermost domains of the camp (or – after the Jewish people settled in the Land of Israel – the person's city or town). This banishment was meant to teach the person that the behavior that brought on his affliction is the very antithesis of holiness.

Such a person, having fallen so low on the ladder of spirituality, might lose the motivation to re-enter the domain of holiness. For this reason, the Torah instructs us that the person afflicted with *tzara'at* is to be brought to the priest to begin his purification process even against the afflicted person's will.[1] G-d decreed that we must extricate him from his situation even when he is too despondent to take the initiative to do so himself.

Thus, we see that G-d promises us that He will not give up even on such individuals. Taking this cue, we too should never give up on our fellows – even if they have given up on themselves – persisting in our efforts to awaken their dormant spirituality, optimism, and desire for holiness and joy.[2]

---

1. See *Siftei Cohen* and *Keli Yekar* on this verse.
2. *Likutei Sichot*, vol. 7, pp. 101–102; ibid., vol. 18, pp. 139–140.

SECOND READING

Leviticus 14:13–20

When the priest concludes all the rituals designed to rid the person formerly suffering from *tzara'at* of his ritual defilement, the individual may again take part in society and enter the Tabernacle precincts.

Rebuke with Love

וְכִפֶּר עָלָיו הַכֹּהֵן וגו': (ויקרא יד, כ)

[G-d instructed Moses to tell the Jewish people,]
"The priest will thus effect atonement for him."

Just as only a priest can release a person from *tzara'at*, only a priest can pronounce the verdict that someone is afflicted with this condition. This is because the priest personifies the attribute of loving-kindness (*chesed*), and therefore, he will seek every possible legal loophole to avoid ostracizing the individual from society. By the same token, if the priest has no choice but to pronounce the dreaded sentence against the individual, the person will feel in the priest's words that the treatment he is about to undergo is an expression of G-d's loving-kindness, a way to bring him back to the proper path in life.

So too, whenever we must criticize or censure the behavior of others, we must be sure to make them feel that we are doing this only for the ultimate good that will come out of it, and that we have only their best interests at heart.[3]

3. *Hitva'aduyot 5714*, vol. 2, pp. 179–180.

THIRD READING
Leviticus 14:21–32

If the person formerly afflicted with *tzara'at* could not afford to purchase the lambs required for the sacrifices of his purification rites, he could substitute fowl.

According to Our Capabilities

וְאִם דַּל הוּא וְאֵין יָדוֹ מַשֶּׂגֶת וגו': (ויקרא יד, כא)

[G-d instructed Moses to tell the Jewish people,] "If [the afflicted person] is poor and cannot afford...."

The offerings that someone afflicted with *tzara'at* has to offer up as part of his purification process are subject to his financial means. This is an example of the principle that G-d asks of us only what we are capable of.[4] This holds true both regarding what He requires of us materially and what He requires of us spiritually.

The spiritual dimension of sacrifices is our G-d-given mission to elevate the physical world by sanctifying it, thereby bringing it "closer" to G-d. (The word for "sacrifice," *korban*, means "something brought close.") G-d requires us to fulfill this mission only to the maximum extent possible. If it sometimes seems as if He is asking more from us that we are capable of, it only means that He is more aware of our strengths than we are ourselves, and is prodding us to live up to our fullest spiritual potential.[5]

4. *Midrash Tanchuma, Naso* 11; *Bemidbar Rabbah* 12:3.
5. *Hitva'aduyot 5756*, vol. 1, p. 420.

FOURTH READING
Leviticus 14:33–53

Tzara'at could also break out on a person's home. Whereas the purification process from *tzara'at* that appears on garments is relatively simple, the purification process from *tzara'at* that appears on homes, like the purification process from *tzara'at* that appears on the skin, is more elaborate.

Challenges as Tools for Spiritual Growth

וְנָתַתִּי נֶגַע צָרַעַת בְּבֵית וגו': (ויקרא יד, לד)

[G-d instructed Moses to tell the Jewish people,]
"When I place a *tzara'at*-lesion upon a house...."

In the Torah's text, the rules for the diagnosis and purification of *tzara'at* on the skin are given separately, and are even spread over two sections of the Torah. In contrast, the rules for the diagnosis and purification of *tzara'at* on *homes* are given in one continuous sequence, which appears entirely within one section of the Torah.

The reason for this is that the home is the most external of the three possible "venues" for *tzara'at* – skin, clothing, and home. As such, the home is the physical correlate of the most sublime aspect of our soul, which is most removed from our normative consciousness.[6] It is specifically from the exalted perspective of this level of our soul that *tzara'at* is clearly seen as a tool for spiritual refinement. From this perspective, therefore, the experience of *tzara'at* and the awareness of its potential as a tool for spiritual refinement are united as one whole.

This teaches us that enhancing our higher, spiritual perspective on life can help us view any challenge in life as an opportunity for spiritual growth.[7]

---

6. Known as the *yechidah*.
7. *Likutei Sichot*, vol. 27, pp. 107–114.

FIFTH READING
Leviticus 14:54–15:15

The Torah now turns to the laws regarding ritual defilement caused by bodily discharges. The first of these that it discusses is urethral discharges in men.

Overcoming Self-Awareness

אִישׁ אִישׁ כִּי יִהְיֶה זָב מִבְּשָׂרוֹ וגו': (ויקרא טו, ב)

[G-d told Moses,] "If a man has a discharge from his reproductive organ...."

No human activity can produce pleasure comparable to that produced by carnal intimacy. It is therefore important that we experience this pleasure only in the course of making our spouses the *subject* of the experience (by striving to please them) rather than the *object* (by using them as means to please ourselves).[8] Objectifying others is antithetical to the essence of redemption.

Still, no matter how altruistic their motivation, men are rendered ritually defiled by marital relations, since it is impossible to conduct them without experiencing at least some pleasure. Indeed, in order to please his wife, the husband *has* to enjoy marital relations, for only by doing so does he show her that he desires her company. But since even the smallest bit of self-awareness separates us from G-d[9] – even if subtly – this pleasure renders the husband ritually defiled.

In the Messianic future, however, G-d will free us from the limitations of self-awareness, and we will be able to feel totally selfless love for one another. Striving toward this ideal to the best of our ability now will hasten the advent of the Redemption.[10]

8. See Rabbi Avraham ben David (c. 1125–1198), *Ba'alei HaNefesh*, etc.
9. Cf. *Sotah* 5a.
10. Based on *Igrot Kodesh*, vol. 9, pp. 252–253, etc.

SIXTH READING
Leviticus 15:16–28

The Torah then discusses the laws regarding ritual defilement caused by discharges from women's reproductive organs. It first discusses the laws of normal menstrual bleeding.

Celebrating Femininity

וְאִשָּׁה כִּי תִהְיֶה זָבָה וגו': (ויקרא טו, יט)

[G-d instructed Moses to tell the Jewish people,] "If a woman has a discharge...."

The menstrual cycle was introduced into human physiology on account of the incident with the Tree of Knowledge.[11] It follows that the Torah's laws surrounding the menstrual cycle are meant to rectify the effects of this incident, restoring us to the idyllic innocence we lived in prior to it, in the Garden of Eden.

The root of negativity within us is our sense of self and self-importance, and nothing can exaggerate our intoxication with ourselves like being G-d's partner in creation by producing another human being. It is therefore crucial that a means of humbling ourselves be built into the reproductive process. Thus, each new menstrual cycle renders the woman ritually defiled, meaning that she is temporarily barred from entering the Tabernacle precincts and she and her husband are forbidden to engage in marital relations until her period is over and she immerses herself in a *mikveh* (ritual pool). These restrictions serve to remind us of our human limitations, preventing us from becoming egotistical as a result of our G-dlike ability to perform the miracle of having children.

Appreciating the educational value of these laws will help us usher in the Redemption, when we will all achieve true selflessness, and there will therefore be no more need for the menstrual cycle.[12]

11. Genesis 3:16.
12. Based on *Likutei Sichot*, vol. 14, pp. 26–28, etc.

SEVENTH READING

Leviticus 15:29–33

The Torah then discusses the laws regarding ritual defilement brought about by abnormal, non-menstrual bleeding.

Eternal Hope

מְזוֹב טֻמְאָתָהּ: (ויקרא טו, ל)

[**G-d instructed Moses to tell the Jewish people, "By following this procedure, a woman will be rid**] **of the defilement of her discharge."**

As mentioned in the preceding day's insight, the regular menstrual cycle became a feature of human life after Adam and Eve partook of the fruit of the Tree of Knowledge. It is meant to check our normal tendency to become conceited over our G-dlike ability to produce another human being.

Non-menstrual bleeding, in contrast, is the symptom of an abnormally inflated ego, in which the self-centeredness that should have been humbled by the menstrual cycle is instead fed by repeatedly overstepping the bounds of G-d's will. In order to check this sinful egocentricity, uterine bleeding occurs before its scheduled resumption. The resulting ritual defilement is more serious, requiring a much more extensive purification process than does normal menstruation.

We see here yet another instance of how G-d has provided the means by which even someone who has become excessively self-centered can return to the proper path. Our knowledge of how much G-d loves us, providing ways for us to come closer to Him, can inspire us to love Him in return and make use of the methods He has provided us in the Torah for coming ever closer to Him.[13]

13. *Likutei Sichot,* vol. 14, pp. 26–28.

Acharei

Yom Kippur

Leviticus 16:1–18:30

THE SIXTH SECTION OF THE BOOK OF LEVITICUS OPENS AS G-d addresses Moses after (*Acharei*, in Hebrew) the death of Aaron's two oldest sons (which was recounted in the third section, *Shemini*). G-d gives Moses the laws regarding the Day of Atonement (*Yom Kippur*). This is followed by a list of various types of behavior that G-d has forbidden to the Jewish people as a result of having made them into "a kingdom of priests and a holy nation" at the Giving of the Torah.

FIRST READING

Leviticus 16:1–17

When the Tabernacle (or its successor, the holy Temple) stood, the Jewish people's most severe misdeeds were atoned for through the rituals of the annual Day of Atonement (*Yom Kippur*). These rituals were performed by the high priest, who was required to wear special linen garments while performing them.

Renewing Our Faith

כְּתֹנֶת בַּד קֹדֶשׁ יִלְבָּשׁ וּמִכְנְסֵי בַד ... וּבְאַבְנֵט
בַּד ... וּבְמִצְנֶפֶת בַּד וגו': (ויקרא טז, ד)

**[G-d told Moses, "Aaron] must wear a linen tunic ...
linen trousers ... a linen sash ... a linen turban."**

Flax plants yield one stalk per seed. Thus, flax (and linen, the fabric made from it) alludes to G-d's simple oneness. The requirement that the *Yom Kippur* garments be made out of linen indicates that we are meant to focus throughout *Yom Kippur* on our simple faith in G-d's oneness. Practically, this means to renew our faith that G-d exclusively controls all reality.

This awareness is meant to permeate all our faculties, which are alluded to by the high priest's four garments:

- the turban, situated on the head, alludes to our faculties of delight, will, and insight;
- the sash, near the heart, alludes to our faculty of understanding;
- the tunic, covering the body, alludes to our emotions;
- the trousers, covering our procreative organs, allude to our powers of expression.

Bringing the awareness of G-d's oneness into all our faculties ensures that we will be able to fulfill our creative potential to the greatest extent possible.[1]

1. *Sefer HaMa'amarim 5736*, pp. 188–192.

SECOND READING

Leviticus 16:18–24

One of the *Yom Kippur* rituals that the high priest performs is offering up incense in the innermost chamber of the Tabernacle, the "Holy of Holies." *Yom Kippur* is the only time anyone enters this most sacred domain.

Becoming a New Person

וּבָא אַהֲרֹן אֶל אֹהֶל מוֹעֵד וגו': (ויקרא טז, כג)

[G-d told Moses,] "Aaron must enter the Tent of Meeting."

According to the Talmud,[2] even angels are not allowed to be present in the Holy of Holies when the high priest offers up the incense. Inasmuch as angels are personifications of Divine energies, their identities are fixed and unchangeable. Repentance, in contrast, is change; it involves a reversal of the supposedly fixed laws of nature, including the laws normally governing spirituality. Thus, it is possible through repentance for a person to ascend – instantaneously! – from the lowest spiritual depths to the most exalted spiritual heights. Therefore, angels have no right to be present when the high priest is enabling the Jewish people to overcome nature through repentance.

Thus, although on *Yom Kippur* we are in many ways like angels,[3] this is true only with regard to our ascent beyond our physical natures (in particular, the need to eat). With regard to our *spiritual* growth, we surpass the capability of the angels whenever we renew ourselves, transforming ourselves into new people through repentance.[4]

2. *Yerushalmi Yoma* 1:5.
3. *Shulchan Aruch, Orach Chayim* 610:4 (in *Rema*); *Shulchan Aruch HaRav, Orach Chayim* 18:3, 610:9, 619:9.
4. *Sefer HaMa'amarim* 5737, pp. 28–29.

THIRD READING
Leviticus 16:25–34

One of the special rituals of *Yom Kippur* was that of the scapegoat. The high priest placed his hands on the head of this goat and confessed certain sins of which the Jewish people might be guilty. The goat was then taken to the desert and pushed off Mount Azazel to its death.

Rising above Logic

וְהַמְשַׁלֵּחַ אֶת הַשָּׂעִיר לַעֲזָאזֵל וגו': (ויקרא טז, כו)

**[G-d told Moses,] "The person who
sends the he-goat off Azazel.... "**

The scapegoat was selected by lot from two identical goats. The requirement to select this goat randomly, by lot, indicates that repentance itself – the essence of *Yom Kippur* – transcends logic.

Repentance transcends logic both from our perspective and from G-d's perspective:

- From our perspective: In order to truly repent, we must intensify our relationship with G-d beyond the extent that our logic previously decreed necessary. It is clear that our previous, logical relationship with G-d was not intense enough, for otherwise we would not have sinned.
- From G-d's perspective: In order to accept our repentance, He must override the logical system of reward and punishment according to which He designed the world.

By overriding logic from our perspective, intensifying our relationship with G-d beyond all logic, we elicit the concomitant response from G-d: He defies His own logical system of punishment, forgiving us lovingly, completely, and wholeheartedly.[5]

5. *Sefer HaMa'amarim Melukat*, vol. 5, pp. 190–191.

FOURTH READING

Leviticus 17:1–7

After concluding the laws regarding the rituals of *Yom Kippur*, G-d gave Moses further instructions regarding sacrifices in general. Specifically, He stipulated that sacrifices may be offered up only in the Tabernacle (or in its successor, the holy Temple).

Delight and Enthusiasm

אִישׁ אִישׁ ... אֲשֶׁר יִשְׁחַט שׁוֹר אוֹ כֶשֶׂב אוֹ עֵז בַּמַּחֲנֶה
אוֹ אֲשֶׁר יִשְׁחָט מִחוּץ לַמַּחֲנֶה: (ויקרא יז, ג)

[G-d instructed Moses to tell the Jewish people,]
"Anyone ... who slaughters an ox, lamb, or goat
inside the camp or outside the camp...."

The blood and fat of animal sacrifices are burnt on the Altar. Since the word for "sacrifice" in Hebrew (*korban*) means "a means to draw close," this signifies that in order to come close to G-d, we must orient our delight (signified by the fat) and enthusiasm (signified by the blood) toward Him.

Practically, this means focusing our delight and enthusiasm on studying the Torah and fulfilling G-d's commandments. The natural consequence of this is that we will engage the material world *without* delight and enthusiasm.

This is the allegorical meaning of the Torah's insistence that we not offer up sacrifices "outside the camp" or even "inside the camp" but only at the Altar. Focusing our delight and enthusiasm "outside the camp" – i.e., on unholy pursuits – is obviously forbidden. But focusing them "inside the camp" – i.e., on permitted pursuits but not "on the Altar," i.e., on holy endeavors – is likewise forbidden. We may engage in permitted pursuits as much as necessary, but our true excitement and enjoyment should be in furthering G-d's purpose in creation, making the world into His true home.[6]

6. *Sichot Kodesh 5741*, vol. 3, pp. 134–137.

FIFTH READING

Leviticus 17:8–18:5

G-d explained to the Jewish people why placing some of the blood of an animal offering on the Altar was an integral part of the sacrificial ritual.

Holy Thoughts

כִּי הַדָּם הוּא בַּנֶּפֶשׁ יְכַפֵּר: (ויקרא יז, יא)

[G-d instructed Moses to tell the Jewish people, "The blood must be placed on the Altar,] for the blood atones for the soul."

Part of the atonement process was placing some of the sin-offering's blood (which signifies our vitality and enthusiasm) on the Altar (which signifies our aspiration toward holiness).

There were two Altars in the Tabernacle: one located outside, in the Courtyard, and one inside, in the Sanctuary. The blood of sin-offerings that atoned for "outer" sins – improper speech and deeds – was applied to the Outer Altar,[7] whereas the blood of sin-offerings that atoned for "inner" sins – improper thoughts – was applied to the Inner Altar.[8]

This dispels the misconception that it does not matter what we think as long as our words and actions are faultless. Improper thoughts strike deeper in the soul. Therefore, in order to atone for them, we have to re-orient our innermost selves.

By the same token, we should never underestimate the great power of positive, holy thought. Optimistic and idealistic thinking can change reality at times as effectively as positive speech or action – and sometimes even more effectively.[9]

---

7. These include all sin-offerings other than those mentioned in the following footnote.

8. These are the sin-offerings of the high priest (Leviticus 4:3–12), of the Sanhedrin (ibid. 4:13–21; Numbers 15:22–31), and for *Yom Kippur* (Leviticus 16:3, 5).

9. *Reshimot* 144.

SIXTH READING
Leviticus 18:6–21

G-d then instructed Moses regarding the laws governing forbidden relations.

The Reward of the Challenge

אִישׁ אִישׁ אֶל כָּל שְׁאֵר בְּשָׂרוֹ לֹא תִקְרְבוּ לְגַלּוֹת עֶרְוָה אֲנִי ה': (ויקרא יח, ו)

[G-d instructed Moses to tell the Jewish people,]
"No one may approach any of his close relatives
to 'uncover [their] nakedness.' I am G-d."

G-d forbids us to have relations both with those that are too *similar* to us (e.g., incest, homosexuality) and with those who are too *dissimilar* to us (e.g., intermarriage, bestiality).

Although G-d has forbidden such relationships, He nevertheless created us with the ability to become attracted to them. He therefore added to these rules the emphatic statement, "I am G-d." This means two things:

Firstly, should we consider following such attractions, we should recall that G-d created the world to function in accordance with His will. Therefore, our ultimate personal and collective happiness can only be assured by following His rules.

Secondly, should we wonder why G-d implanted in us the potential to become so strongly attracted to others that it might compel us to defy Him, we should recall that He can be relied upon to reward us amply when we overcome this challenge.[10]

---

10. *Likutei Sichot*, vol. 12, pp. 83–90; ibid., vol. 22, pp. 97–99.

SEVENTH READING
Leviticus 18:22–30

G-d also closed the laws of forbidden relationships by saying "I am G-d, your G-d."

Divine Morality

וּשְׁמַרְתֶּם אֶת מִשְׁמַרְתִּי ... אֲנִי ה' אֱלֹקֵיכֶם: (ויקרא יח, ל)

[G-d instructed Moses to tell the Jewish people,] "You must safeguard My charge…for I am G-d, your G-d."

G-d closed the laws of forbidden relationships by saying "I am G-d, your G-d" in order to emphasize their importance. By observing these laws, we cause a triple positive spiritual reaction:

- We figuratively give G-d pleasure from seeing creation run according to His plan, thereby becoming a "home" for Him. This pleasure is alluded to by the word "I," since G-d's desire to have a "home" in the world is rooted in His very essence.
- We justify the continued existence of all creation. This is alluded to in the (first) word for "G-d" (the Name *Havayah*), which signifies the Divine power that brings creation into being and constantly re-creates it.
- We enhance the Divine power that pulsates through creation in order to enliven it. This power is alluded to in the word for "your G-d" (the Name *Elokim*), which denotes the contraction of G-d's infinite power necessary to grant vitality to each element of creation individually.[11]

---

11. *Likutei Sichot*, vol. 22, pp. 101–102.

Kedoshim

Holiness

Leviticus 19:1–20:27

THE SEVENTH SECTION OF THE BOOK OF LEVITICUS FOCUSES on how the Jewish people, having been made into "a kingdom of priests and a holy nation" at the Giving of the Torah, must adhere to a specific code of conduct in order to fulfill this role properly. Thus, this section opens as G-d instructs Moses to tell the Jewish people that they must be "holy" (*Kedoshim*, in Hebrew), i.e., that they must hold themselves to exceptional standards of conduct.

FIRST READING

Leviticus 19:1–14

G-d began to instruct Moses regarding the code of conduct the Jewish people are called upon to follow in order to be holy. G-d had already told the Jewish people not to worship idols; to this He now added that we must not even contemplate how idols are worshipped.

Elevating the Forbidden

אַל תִּפְנוּ אֶל הָאֱלִילִם וגו': (ויקרא יט, ד)

[G-d instructed Moses to tell the Jewish people,] "You must not turn to idols."

The Hebrew word for "permitted" (מותר) literally means "untied." Permitted things are "free" to be elevated by our direct involvement. In contrast, the word for "forbidden" (אסור) means "tied down." Forbidden things cannot be elevated by our direct involvement with them.

Nevertheless, we can elevate even these "tied down," forbidden aspects of reality (of which idolatry is one example) indirectly – by studying the Torah's discussion of them. In the Torah, these forbidden entities are not independent subjects of study, but form an intrinsic part of G-d's plan. In the context of the Torah's discussion of how they clash with holiness, they assume the holiness of the Divine wisdom of which they are a part.

We see here how by giving us the Torah, G-d has enabled us to bring all aspects of reality – even the lowest, non-holy aspects – to their ultimate purpose and fulfillment, absorbing them all into the realm of holiness.[1]

1. *Sefer HaMa'amarim 5743*, pp. 85–87.

SECOND READING

Leviticus 19:15–22

One aspect of being holy is being fair in judgment.

The Benefit of the Doubt

בְּצֶדֶק תִּשְׁפֹּט עֲמִיתֶךָ: (ויקרא יט, טו)

[G-d instructed Moses to tell the Jewish people,] "You must judge your fellow with righteousness."

Our sages exhort us to "be extremely humble in relation to every person,"[2] i.e., to consider ourselves less worthy than anyone else. Yet, objectively speaking, how can we consider ourselves less meritorious than those who appear to be unworthy of our respect?

The answer is by keeping in mind the sages' teaching: "Do not judge your fellow until you reach his place."[3] In other words, we all our challenges; the fact that we do not succumb to a particular temptation while another person does, does not make us superior to him. Who can measure the effect of his upbringing, environment, or inborn character weaknesses against the temptations he faces?

By judging our fellows favorably – or better yet, by not judging them at all – we can both cultivate our own humility more effectively and allow our fellows' positive traits to manifest themselves unhindered. Both of these effects help hasten the advent of the Redemption.[4]

2. *Avot* 4:10.
3. Ibid. 2:4.
4. *Tanya*, chapter 30.

THIRD READING

Leviticus 19:23–32

G-d told the Jewish people that when they would enter the Land of Israel and plant fruit trees, they must not eat the fruit that any newly-planted tree produces during the first three years of its growth.

Spiritual Agriculture

וְכִי תָבֹאוּ אֶל הָאָרֶץ וּנְטַעְתֶּם כָּל עֵץ מַאֲכָל וְגו': (ויקרא יט, כג)

[G-d instructed Moses to tell the Jewish people,] "When you enter the land and plant there any food-tree...."

The Midrash notes that G-d's first act after creating the world was to plant the Garden of Eden,[5] and that this verse implies that the same is expected of the Jewish people. Upon arriving in the Land of Israel, agricultural planting was to be their first endeavor.[6]

The importance given to planting stresses the central position of cultivation both in civilization in general and in one's personal, spiritual life. Just as trees and plants constantly bear fruit, so too, we must fulfill our Divine mission in a manner that "bears fruit" – i.e., that affects ourselves and others in a lasting and meaningful way.[7]

5. See Genesis 2:8.
6. *Vayikra Rabbah* 25:3.
7. *Igrot Kodesh*, vol. 22, p. 378.

FOURTH READING

Leviticus 19:33–37

Another form of prohibited behavior is possessing inaccurate weights and measures.

The Power of Intention

מֹאזְנֵי צֶדֶק ... יִהְיֶה לָכֶם וגו': (ויקרא יט, לו)

[**G-d instructed Moses to tell the Jewish people,**] **"You must have accurate scales."**

The Midrash[8] states that whoever denies that G-d commanded us to possess only accurate measures is considered as having denied the Exodus from Egypt.

Although G-d had already decreed that the Egyptians would oppress the Jewish people, each individual Egyptian was still guilty for doing so, because each one could have individually chosen not to oppress us. Thus, they were punished not for the evil they did but for their desire to do it.

Similarly, G-d forbids us to possess false measures because of the inner evil intent displayed by possessing them. Someone who asserts that G-d does not prohibit the possession of inaccurate measures denies that harboring evil intentions is wrong. Thus, he is denying the justice of G-d's punishment of the Egyptians.

We see here that G-d attaches great importance to our intentions. This is because intentions have more power to influence reality than we typically realize. Having this fact brought to our awareness can inspire us to direct our power of thought positively.[9]

8. *Sifra* on this verse. See *Mishneh Torah, Geneivah* 7:12.
9. *Likutei Sichot*, vol. 27, pp. 149–157.

FIFTH READING
Leviticus 20:1–7

In the course of teaching Moses the laws of holiness, G-d promised the Jewish people that it is indeed possible for them to hold themselves to these standards of behavior.

Sanctifying the Mundane

וְהִתְקַדִּשְׁתֶּם וִהְיִיתֶם קְדֹשִׁים וְגוֹ': (ויקרא כ, ז)

**[G-d instructed Moses to tell the Jewish people,]
"You must sanctify yourselves and be holy."**

According to many authorities,[10] this verse enjoins us to sanctify ourselves not only through inherently holy pursuits, but through any pursuit that is permitted to us.[11] This means that we must endeavor to remain conscious of G-d even when we are involved in what would otherwise be everyday, mundane activities.

This is important because the inherently holy acts of studying the Torah and fulfilling G-d's explicit active and passive commandments are not enough to hasten the advent of the Messianic Redemption. The Redemption will signify a quantum leap in the revelation of Divinity – both within our own consciousness and in the world in general. In order to elicit such a sublime revelation, we need to go beyond our normal, "contractual" commitment to G-d that is defined by what He explicitly requires of us. We must infuse Divine consciousness even where it is not "normally" found – in the mundane.[12]

---

10. *Sefer Chareidim, Mitzvot Aseih min HaTorah* 7:13, citing Nachmanides, Rabbi Saadia Gaon, and Rabbi Shelomo ibn Gabirol; *Tanya*, chapters 27 (34b) and 30 (39a).

11. Rashi mentions this imperative in his commentary to Deuteronomy 14:21.

12. *Likutei Sichot*, vol. 1, pp. 256–257.

SIXTH READING
Leviticus 20:8–22

One type of behavior that is antithetical to holiness is incest.

The Love of G-d

וְאִישׁ אֲשֶׁר יִקַּח אֶת אֲחֹתוֹ ... חֶסֶד הוּא וגו': (ויקרא כ, יז)

[G-d instructed Moses to tell the Jewish people,] "A man who takes his sister ... it is a disgraceful act."

If G-d considers incest so disgraceful, why did he allow Adam and Eve's sons and daughters to marry each other? The answer, say the sages,[13] is that since these brothers and sisters had no one else to marry, G-d in His kindness made an exception to the rule in order to enable the human race to survive.

Similarly, in the Song of Songs, G-d addresses the Jewish people as, "My sister, My bride"[14] in order to make the same point. We join with G-d in "marital union" by studying the Torah, performing His commandments, and reaching out to Him in prayer. Our mutual "offspring" are the positive effects – on ourselves and on the world – that result from these holy acts.

But since G-d is infinitely beyond us, logically He should hardly even notice us. How can such insignificant creatures as ourselves propagate Divine consciousness throughout the world – let alone have the power to transform reality, making the world into G-d's true home?

The answer is that just as the union of the world's first siblings was made possible only through G-d's kindness, it is similarly only on account of G-d's kindness that our union with Him can bear fruit. Our efforts are indeed important and effective, but we must always remember that it is G-d who makes them so.[15]

---

13. *Sanhedrin* 58b.
14. Song of Songs 4:9, 10, 12, 5:1. See *Zohar* 3:7b.
15. *Sefer HaMa'amarim 5714–5716*, pp. 549–550.

SEVENTH READING

Leviticus 20:23–27

As part of His plan for making the Jewish people holy, G-d allowed them to eat even permitted animals only after slaughtering them according to His precise instructions.

Whom to Love

וְהִבְדַּלְתֶּם בֵּין הַבְּהֵמָה הַטְּהֹרָה לַטְּמֵאָה וְגוֹ': (ויקרא כ, כה)

[G-d instructed Moses to tell the Jewish people,]
"You must distinguish between a [spiritually]
undefiled and a [spiritually] defiled animal."

In other words, G-d wants us to be proficient in recognizing the often fine line between proper and improper ritual slaughter.

Many of the Torah's laws governing our actions are complex, and it is therefore sometimes tempting to play it safe by acting stringently. Taking this easier path avoids having to determine conclusively whether or not a particular case or situation is permitted according to Jewish law.

There are two reasons why we should not get into this habit:

Firstly, G-d Himself enjoins us not to deny ourselves things that He does not expressly prohibit.[16] This is not because G-d is anxious for us to indulge ourselves in the world's pleasures, but because by permitting them to us, He wants us to refine and elevate both ourselves and them by using them to enhance Divine consciousness in the world.

Secondly, these laws are part and parcel of G-d's wisdom, which He has shared with us in the Torah. Therefore, G-d wants us to study these cases (and even cases that will never apply to us personally) simply in order to imbibe His wisdom, thereby sharing in His vision of how He wishes His world to be run.[17]

16. *Yerushalmi Nedarim* 9:1; *Mishneh Torah, Dei'ot* 3:1.
17. *Hitva'aduyot 5747*, vol. 4, pp. 352–353.

Emor

The Priesthood; The Festivals

Leviticus 21:1–24:23

THE EIGHTH SECTION OF THE BOOK OF LEVITICUS BEGINS AS G-d directs Moses to tell (*Emor,* in Hebrew) the elder priests to educate the younger priests regarding the laws of the priesthood. G-d then teaches Moses these laws as well as the laws regarding the cycle of festivals in the Jewish year.

FIRST READING
Leviticus 21:1–15

G-d instructed Moses to tell the elder priests to educate the younger priests regarding the laws of the priesthood.

Children who Shine

וַיֹּאמֶר ה' אֶל מֹשֶׁה אֱמֹר אֶל הַכֹּהֲנִים . . . וְאָמַרְתָּ אֲלֵהֶם וְגוֹ': (ויקרא כא, א)

G-d told Moses, "Say to the priests . . . say to them. . . ."

The sages teach us that the verb "to say" is repeated in this verse in order to indicate that it is the priests' duty to "caution" their children regarding their priestly duties.[1] The Hebrew word for "to caution" (להזהיר) also means "to make shine,"[2] implying that we should not be content with training our youth to observe G-d's commandments minimally and perfunctorily. Rather, we should teach them to perform the commandments in the best way possible, even going beyond the letter of the law. By imparting this enthusiasm to our children, we will enable them – and the commandments they perform – to sparkle and "shine."

This lesson is emphasized by the fact that the Torah conveys it in the context of its instruction to the priests. The priests' task is to help others rise spiritually and become close to G-d. So too, we should strive to educate our youth not merely to be well-versed in the Torah and punctilious in observing its commandments, but to see their study and observance as ways to draw close to G-d.[3]

1. *Yevamot* 114a ff.
2. *Likutei Torah* 2:35b.
3. *Sefer HaMa'amarim* 5743, pp. 85–87.

SECOND READING
Leviticus 21:16–22:16

Priests are forbidden to render themselves ritually defiled by touching a human corpse. They are not allowed to marry certain women, and they are disqualified from officiating in the Tabernacle by certain bodily blemishes.

Helping People Succeed

וַיְדַבֵּר ה' אֶל מֹשֶׁה לֵּאמֹר: דַּבֵּר אֶל אַהֲרֹן לֵאמֹר וגו': (ויקרא כא, טז-יז)

G-d spoke to Moses, saying, "Speak to Aaron, saying...."

This section of the Torah discusses our responsibility to educate others. Since we are all responsible to educate those who need our edification or correction, the lessons in this section are relevant to all of us – not only to professional educators.

Throughout this section, the Torah uses the idiom of "soft speech" (אמירה) more than that of "hard speech" (דיבור). Educating through "soft speech" means praising the student. Praising the good in others draws out their infinite, latent positive qualities, allowing them to actualize their potential to a far greater extent than they could have on their own.

Of course, we must also assess other people's failings honestly. But G-d only places people in difficult situations if He has given them the strength necessary to overcome such situations. If they fail to do so, it is because their strengths have not been allowed to become manifest – and that is because we, who are responsible for educating them, have not praised them enough! Had we used our "soft speech" as much as we should have, we would have elicited our charges' latent potential and inner strengths.

Thus, we should all assume personal responsibility for the moral success of all those over whom we have influence.[4]

---

4. *Likutei Sichot*, vol. 27, pp. 158 ff; *Hitva'aduyot 5742*, pp. 1421 ff.

THIRD READING
Leviticus 22:17–33

G-d told Moses to instruct the priests regarding which bodily blemishes disqualify animals from being offered up as sacrifices. After this, G-d instructed Moses regarding the laws pertaining to the treatment of young animals, the thanksgiving-offering, and martyrdom. The Hebrew idiom for martyrdom – "sanctifying G-d's Name" – means "increasing respect for G-d among humanity," since our willingness to suffer martyrdom demonstrates to the world that G-d and His plan for humanity are our paramount values. Decreasing respect for G-d is termed "desecrating G-d's Name."

Sanctifying G-d's Name

וְנִקְדַּשְׁתִּי בְּתוֹךְ בְּנֵי יִשְׂרָאֵל וְגו': (ויקרא כב, לב)

**[Moses told the Jewish people,] "I must be
sanctified among the Israelites."**

The most flagrant desecration of G-d's Name is the Jewish people's exile. The true meaning of exile is the condition in which G-d's presence is hidden behind the façade of nature – the laws of mindless cause and effect. Exile thus gives the world the impression that G-d is powerless to overcome the forces of nature and history. In this context, the grandest sanctification of G-d's Name will be the miraculous advent of the Messianic Era.[5] This is why the Torah obligates us to do our utmost to bring the exile to a quick and final end.

We must therefore constantly urge G-d to redeem us immediately, and, in addition, reorient our own consciousness away from the mentality of exile and toward the mentality of redemption. By cultivating our awareness of G-d's presently hidden miracles, we hasten the time when His miracles will become openly revealed to all.[6]

---

5. Ezekiel 36:23.
6. *Likutei Sichot*, vol. 27, p. 175; *Hitva'aduyot 5745*, vol. 2, pp. 1265–1267.

FOURTH READING

Leviticus 23:1–22

G-d then instructed Moses regarding the laws of the festivals of the Jewish year. These comprise the three "pilgrim festivals" and the two High Holidays. On the three pilgrim festivals – Passover, *Shavu'ot*, and *Sukkot* – the Jewish people are required to make a pilgrimage to the holy Temple in Jerusalem. The two High Holidays are *Rosh HaShanah* (the day of judgment on the first day of the Jewish year) and *Yom Kippur* (the Day of Atonement).

Celebrating Spiritual Growth

אֵלֶּה הֵם מוֹעֲדָי: (ויקרא כג, ב)

**[G-d instructed Moses to tell the Jewish people,]
"The following are My appointed days."**

The three pilgrim festivals mark the key points of the agricultural cycle: Passover occurs when barley is harvested, *Shavu'ot* when wheat is harvested, and *Sukkot* when the produce is gathered in from the fields.[7]

Allegorically, G-d refers to the Jewish people as His "produce."[8] Just as a farmer sows grain in the earth in order to reap a much greater return, G-d "sows" Jewish souls in the physical world in order to enable them to accomplish much more than they can in their spiritual abode.

Furthermore, just as a seed's outer coating must disintegrate before the seed can grow, our coarse, outer husk – our ego – must be negated in order for us to grow spiritually.

Thus, in this context, the three pilgrim festivals celebrate our ongoing spiritual growth and the spiritual effect on the world (the "produce") that this growth yields.[9]

7. See Rabbeinu Bachye on Exodus 13:4.
8. See Jeremiah 2:3; Hosea 2:25.
9. *Likutei Sichot*, vol. 36, pp. 82–85. See also *Sefer HaMa'amarim Melukat*, vol. 5, pp. 169–176.

FIFTH READING
Leviticus 23:23–32

Although the months of the Jewish year are numbered from Nisan, the years are counted as beginning on the first day of Tishrei, the seventh month. The first of Tishrei is thus *Rosh HaShanah,* "the Beginning of the Year."

The Power of One

בַּחֹדֶשׁ הַשְּׁבִיעִי וְגו': (ויקרא כג, כד)

[**G‑d instructed Moses to tell the Jewish people,**] **"In the seventh month...."**

Tishrei, the seventh month of the Jewish year, can be divided into two contrasting yet complementary halves: The first half, containing the holidays of *Rosh HaShanah* and *Yom Kippur,* focuses us on *teshuvah* ("repentance"; "returning" to G‑d). During this half of the month, our attention is directed inward, toward personal spiritual growth and development.

In contrast, the second half of *Tishrei,* containing the holidays of *Sukkot* and *Shemini Atzeret,* focuses us on bringing Divine consciousness into the world through the performance of G‑d's commandments. This infusion of Divine consciousness into reality evokes the joyousness that characterizes this half of the month.

The common denominator of both halves is their emphasis on Jewish unity. It is our shared source in G‑d that enables us to re‑root ourselves during the first half of the month. It is our shared commonality that makes the joy we express in the second half of the month unlimited.

Thus, in order to optimally internalize the Divine revelations available to us in this month, it is important to demonstrate loving kindness throughout it. This will enable both the innerness and the joyousness of its holidays to last throughout the coming year.[10]

10. Encyclical letter of 13 *Tishrei* 5737, printed in *Likutei Sichot,* vol. 14, pp. 469–472 and *Igrot Melech,* vol. 1, pp. 157–161.

SIXTH READING
Leviticus 23:33–44

The week beginning with 15 Tishrei is *Sukkot* ("Huts"), during which we are commanded to dwell in temporary huts and also to hold together and wave four plant-parts: a citron, a palm stalk, myrtle branches, and willow branches.

FRIDAY

Uniting the People

וּלְקַחְתֶּם לָכֶם וגו': (ויקרא כג, מ)

[Moses told the Jewish people,] "You must take hold [of these four plant-parts]."

Study chiefly benefits the student; it is therefore represented by a fruit's taste, which can only be savored by the person eating it. Good deeds, in contrast, benefit the public; they are therefore represented by fragrance, which can be smelled by anyone within a reasonable distance from the fruit.

Therefore, the citron (*etrog*), which possesses both taste and fragrance, represents those who are rich both in knowledge of the Torah and in good deeds.

The palm stalk (*lulav*), whose fruit (the date) has taste but no smell, represents those who are rich in the knowledge of the Torah but deficient in good deeds.

The myrtle (*hadas*), which has fragrance but no taste, represents those who are rich in good deeds but deficient in the knowledge of the Torah.

The willow (*aravah*), which possesses neither taste nor fragrance, represents those who are deficient both in knowledge of the Torah and in good deeds.[11]

By bringing these four plants together, we express the intrinsic unity of the Jewish people.[12]

---

11. *Vayikra Rabbah* 30:12.
12. *Likutei Sichot*, vol. 4, pp. 1159–1160; ibid., vol. 29, pp. 223–224.

SEVENTH READING
Leviticus 24:1–23

Only one Jewish woman had been violated by an Egyptian task-master. When the Jewish people were organized into tribal camps one month after the Tabernacle was erected, her son, fathered by this Egyptian, attempted to camp together with his mother's tribe. He was refused on the grounds that tribal membership follows the father's tribal lineage, not the mother's. The case was taken to the court, which ruled against this son, who then cursed G-d. Not knowing what the punishment for blasphemy is, the court temporarily imprisoned the offender until G-d informed Moses that blasphemy is a capital crime.

We Are Born to Act

וַיַּנִּיחֻהוּ בַּמִּשְׁמָר וְגוֹ': (ויקרא כד, יב)

They placed him in the guardhouse.

The Torah never prescribes imprisonment as a final punishment. This is because the Torah seeks to rectify the damage that occurred, enabling the criminal to proceed with his life. The Torah therefore considers imprisonment counterproductive, for it denies the criminal the opportunity to act.[13] Every person has a purpose, and every moment has potential that must be fulfilled.

Nevertheless, if the country in which we live punishes criminals with imprisonment, we are enjoined to follow the law of the land.[14] Based upon the above insight, however, recent moves toward rehabilitative as opposed to purely punitive incarceration are worthy and welcome. Prisoners should be provided with opportunities for education and religious instruction, and furlough and parole programs should be available for those who have proven themselves ready to turn over a new leaf.[15]

13. *Hitva'aduyot 5710*, pp. 195–196.
14. *Nedarim 28a*, etc.
15. *Hitva'aduyot 5745*, vol. 4, pp. 2274–2275.

Behar

The Sabbatical and Jubilee Years
Leviticus 25:1–26:2

THE NINTH SECTION OF THE BOOK OF LEVITICUS OPENS AS Moses hears G-d's voice in the Tabernacle at the foot of the mountain (*Behar*, in Hebrew), commanding him to convey to the Jewish people the laws of the sabbatical and Jubilee years.

FIRST READING
Leviticus 25:1–13

G-d told Moses that the Jewish people must let their fields in the Land of Israel lie fallow for a full year once every seven years.

The Freedom of the Sabbath

כִּי תָבֹאוּ אֶל הָאָרֶץ . . . וְשָׁבְתָה הָאָרֶץ שַׁבָּת לַה': (ויקרא כה, ב)

[G-d instructed Moses to tell the Jewish people,] "When you enter the land...the land must observe a [year of] rest for G-d."

Just as the weekly Sabbath is intended to allow us the freedom to pursue spiritual growth, the same is true of the sabbatical year. G-d therefore instructs us to envision the sabbatical year as the goal of the work we do during the six preceding years, keeping it constantly in mind throughout as we work toward it. In this way, the inspiration of the sabbatical year will sanctify, energize, and focus the work we perform during the "mundane" years, bringing them Divinely-blessed success and infusing them with the joy of optimism and purpose.

The same holds true for the weekly Sabbath. Keeping the goal of the Sabbath in mind during the workweek sanctifies, energizes, and focuses our work, bringing success, joy, and optimism to the entire week.

"Entering our land" is also a metaphor for setting up our homes, whether at the beginning of our married lives or whenever we seek to revitalize our home life. We should set up our homes with the goal of the Sabbath in mind, creating an atmosphere conducive to spiritual growth and harmony. This way, every Sabbath will be imbued with spiritual content, thereby being a source of renewal and hope for ourselves, our families, and our guests.[1]

---

1. *Likutei Sichot*, vol. 1, pp. 245–249.

SECOND READING
Leviticus 25:14–18

Special laws regarding commerce apply during the sabbatical and
Jubilee years, beyond normal laws regarding equitable business
conduct.

Commitment to Holiness

אוֹ קָנֹה מִיַּד עֲמִיתֶךָ וגו': (ויקרא כה, יד)

**[G-d instructed Moses to tell the Jewish people,] "When
you acquire something from your fellow Jew...."**

Most of us cannot honestly promise that all our future ideas and
emotions will be holy and positive, since we cannot control which
ideas will occur to us and how we will emotionally react to what
happens to us. What we *can* promise is that we will try to think,
talk, and act in accordance with these ideals.

This is similar to how, according to Jewish law, a person can
only give someone else something the giver truly possesses. One
cannot, for example, give someone the fruit that an existing tree
will produce in the future, since this fruit does not yet exist. One
can, however, "give" someone the fruit-producing aspect of the
tree, since this does presently exist. By the force of that gift, the
other person will indeed receive whatever fruit the tree produces
in the future.

In this analogy, the tree corresponds to our intellect and
emotions, whereas its fruit corresponds to the thoughts, words,
and deeds that our intellect and emotions produce. Although we
cannot promise that every future thought, word, and deed will
be holy and positive, we *can* promise to refine our intellect and
emotions as best we can – through prayer, study, and meditation.
With G-d's help, this will ensure that our thoughts, words, and
deeds will indeed be holy and positive.[2]

2. *Likutei Sichot*, vol. 27, pp. 176–179.

THIRD READING

Leviticus 25:19–24

G-d promised that the produce of the sixth year would miraculously suffice for the sixth year, the sabbatical year, and the following year, until new crops could be harvested.

The Promise of Redemption

וְצִוִּיתִי אֶת בִּרְכָתִי לָכֶם בַּשָּׁנָה הַשִּׁשִּׁית וְעָשָׂת אֶת
הַתְּבוּאָה לִשְׁלֹשׁ הַשָּׁנִים: (ויקרא כה, כא)

**[G-d instructed Moses to tell the Jewish people,] "I
will command My blessing for you in the sixth
year, so it will yield produce for three years."**

Allegorically, the six years preceding the sabbatical year are compared to the six millennia that have transpired since Creation. The sabbatical year corresponds to the seventh millennium, that of redemption. We are now in the latter part of the sixth millennium, i.e., toward the end of the sixth "year."

The future Redemption will occur in three stages:

• The first stage is the period before the advent of the Messiah, in which we experience a foretaste of the Redemption.

• The second stage is the period immediately after the coming of the Messiah, in which we will be able to fulfill G-d's will without hindrance, but the world will still function within the limitations of nature.

• In the third stage, which begins with the Resurrection of the Dead, what we presently consider miraculous will become natural.[3]

In this context, G-d's promise for the sixth year means that by dedicating ourselves to our Divine mission, we will usher in all three stages of the final Redemption.[4]

---

3. *Or HaTorah, Nach,* vol. 1, pp. 433–434.
4. *Likutei Sichot,* vol. 27, p. 190.

FOURTH READING
Leviticus 25:25–28

After seven sabbatical cycles have passed, the fiftieth year, known as the Jubilee year, is observed. In this year, land that was sold during the previous 49 years is returned to its original owners.

Self-Refinement

וְיָצָא בַּיֹּבֵל וְשָׁב לַאֲחֻזָּתוֹ: (ויקרא כה, כח)

[**G-d instructed Moses to tell the Jewish people, "Land that has been sold**] **must go out** [**of the purchaser's possession**] **in the Jubilee year and revert to** [**the original owner's**] **estate."**

The Jubilee year is observed only after seven full sabbatical cycles. It is observed as a sabbatical year but with its own, additional laws. Thus, the Jubilee year seems to be both the culmination of the seven preceding sabbatical years and a "super-sabbatical" year, surpassing the regular sabbatical years and therefore expressing a higher, more sublime type of spirituality.

Yet, the provision that land must return to its original owner in the Jubilee year stands in stark contrast to the cancellation of loans in the sabbatical year. Cancelling loans forces the lender to relinquish part of his material wealth, which in turn serves to deflate his ego. Having our land restored to us, in contrast, increases our wealth and might inflate our sense of self.

The explanation is that observing seven consecutive sabbatical cycles has a cumulative effect on us, deflating our egos successively each time. By the end of this process, we are indeed sufficiently refined to acquire material wealth without fear that doing so will swell our sense of self-worth.

Rather than renouncing the physical world, we are meant to enjoy and utilize it for holy purposes, thereby transforming it into G-d's home.[5]

5. *Ma'amarei Admor HaZakein HaKetzarim*, pp. 75–76.

THURSDAY

FIFTH READING
Leviticus 25:29–38

G-d then taught Moses the laws of giving charity and the prohibition of charging interest on loans.

G-d's Investment in Us

אַל תִּקַּח מֵאִתּוֹ נֶשֶׁךְ וְתַרְבִּית וגו': (ויקרא כה, לו)

[G-d instructed Moses to tell the Jewish people,] "You must not charge interest."

The crucial difference between interest-bearing loans (which are forbidden) and investments (which are permitted) is that interest is a reward for a past deed: the one-time act of giving the loan. In contrast, a return on an investment is a reward for the ongoing involvement that continues throughout the life of the investment.

In this sense, charging interest is fundamentally opposed to how G-d is involved in our lives. G-d does not "loan" us the powers that He grants us, as a one-time act; He "invests" them in us, remaining constantly and intimately involved in helping us reap the rewards of our efforts.

G-d behaves toward us in the same way that we behave toward our fellows.[6] Thus, when someone charges interest, G-d responds in kind: He grants him the initial potential but refrains from extending him ongoing supernatural assistance. When we forego interest on our loans, G-d also responds in kind: He not only grants us the initial potential to be successful both materially and spiritually but continues to assist us throughout our labors.[7]

6. *Keter Shem Tov* (ed. Kehot, 2004), addendum 78 (= addendum 60 in 1998 and prior editions).
7. *Likutei Sichot*, vol. 3, pp. 1007–1012.

SIXTH READING
Leviticus 25:39–46

If a Jewish thief cannot pay back the value of what he has stolen, the court can hire him out as a servant, using the proceeds of this "sale" to pay off his debts. Also, if a Jewish man has no other way of supporting himself, he can hire himself out as a servant. In either case, the "master" is required to provide for the servant's children.

We are Free

וְיָצָא מֵעִמָּךְ הוּא וּבָנָיו עִמּוֹ וגו': (ויקרא כה, מא)

**[G-d instructed Moses to tell the Jewish people,
"When a bondman's term of service is up,] he
must leave you – both him and his children."**

Being provided for by the "owner" is the sole extent to which the servant's children are affected by their father's service. They themselves do not become servants along with their father when he is "sold."

The same is true allegorically: Exile can be seen as G-d's presence, so to speak, having been sold into slavery.[8] The degree to which G-d can be revealed in the world through the Jewish people observing His commandments is largely subject to the whims of the ruling nation. But although G-d can decree exile upon Himself, we – His children – cannot be exiled along with Him. The material aspects of our lives may be determined by others, but our souls can never be subject to a foreign power. We need never feel pressured to conform to the world's materialistic culture, for all aspects of our spiritual life remain forever unencumbered and free.[9]

8. *Megilah* 29a; Rashi on Deuteronomy 30:3.
9. *Likutei Sichot*, vol. 22, pp. 157–158.

SHABBAT

Although servants are required to respect their "masters," this requirement does not override every Jew's obligation to respect the Torah's laws. This includes respect for the Tabernacle and its successor, the holy Temple in Jerusalem.

Respecting Our Ideals

וּמִקְדָּשִׁי תִּירָאוּ וְגוֹ': (ויקרא כו, ב)

[**G-d instructed Moses to tell the Jewish
people,**] "**You must fear My sanctuary.**"

The essence both of the Tabernacle that accompanied the Jewish people through the desert and of its successor, the holy Temple in Jerusalem, is the notion that G-d's presence should be felt in our physical world. The "fear of the sanctuary" that G-d requires of us is the respect that we should give to this ideal.

The Torah is G-d's plan and dream for the world, describing how we can indeed come to feel His presence in our lives. Thus, it is by studying the Torah that this notion becomes important to us and we begin to respect it. This is why the innermost chamber of the Tabernacle (and subsequently, of the Temple) housed the Tablets of the Covenant, which embodied the entire Torah.

Respect for the ideal represented by the Sanctuary inspires us to conduct our personal lives in accordance with the Torah's instructions, as well as to influence society, as best we can, to adopt this ideal as its own.[10]

10. *Likutei Sichot*, vol. 16, pp. 307–308.

Bechukotai

Reward and Corrective Punishment; Donations

Leviticus 26:3–27:34

THE 10TH AND FINAL SECTION OF THE BOOK OF LEVITICUS opens as G-d promises the Jewish people that if they follow His rules (*Bechukotai*, in Hebrew) they will be rewarded with material wealth and well-being. The opposite is also true: By neglecting G-d's laws, they will forfeit His blessings. G-d then instructs the Jewish people regarding what, how, and under which circumstances they may donate to the Temple or to the priests.

FIRST READING
Leviticus 26:3–5

G-d promised the Jewish people material wealth and prosperity in reward for keeping His commandments.

Tangible Results

וְנָתַתִּי גִשְׁמֵיכֶם בְּעִתָּם וְגו': (ויקרא כו, ד)

[G-d instructed Moses to tell the Jewish people,] "I will give your rains in their time."

The rewards that the Torah promises in this passage are almost entirely material ones. Why is there almost no mention of spiritual reward?

Let us note that when people are profoundly affected by some occurrence, they express themselves physically – by smiling, clapping, dancing, crying, and the like. This is because when the core of our being has been touched, the effect is felt throughout our entire self, including our physical bodies.

Similarly, rather than superficial or rote performance, G-d wants us ideally to observe His commandments in a way that touches our very core, affecting us profoundly and making us into better people. When we achieve this deep unity with G-d and His Torah, our entire being is affected, even the physical aspects of our lives. In order to indicate that this is the case, the results must also be physical. Thus, the material rewards spoken of in this passage are not only an incentive to keep G-d's commandments, but are meant to teach us *how* we should keep them, namely, allowing them to touch us so profoundly that our observance produces tangible results.[1]

---

1. *Likutei Sichot*, vol. 37, pp. 79–84.

SECOND READING

Leviticus 26:6–9

The rewards that G-d promises for observing His commandments with true dedication are miraculous.

A Taste of the Future

וְהִשְׁבַּתִּי חַיָּה רָעָה מִן הָאָרֶץ וְגו': (ויקרא כו, ו)

[G-d instructed Moses to tell the Jewish people,]
"I will remove wild beasts from the land."

As was noted in the previous day's insight, the promises listed in this passage not only serve as incentives but as physical expressions of the extent to which Divine consciousness has permeated our very being.

Besides describing the material rewards that G-d promises us nowadays, the blessings in this passage allude to the even more miraculous material bounty that will characterize the Messianic future. Our sages tell us that in the Messianic Era, plants will yield their produce on the same day they are sown; entire trees will be edible, not only their fruit; even non-fruit-bearing trees will bear fruit,[2] and so on.[3]

The reason why our reward nowadays can "only" be miraculous, whereas the rewards of the Messianic future will be "super-miraculous," is because only in the future will we be able to infuse our *entire* beings with Divine consciousness. The results of this process will therefore be concomitantly all-pervasive. Just as there will be no disconnect between us and our Divine source, the physical world will be able to express G-d's infinite beneficence perfectly.

With this in mind, the blessings we currently receive from G-d can serve to inspire us to do whatever we can to hasten the advent of the Messianic Redemption.[4]

2. *Sifra* on this passage.
3. See *Ketubot* 111b.
4. *Likutei Sichot*, vol. 37, pp. 79–84.

THIRD READING

Leviticus 26:10–46

After describing the rewards for fulfilling G-d's will, the Torah describes the consequences of neglecting to fulfill His will.

Blessings in Disguise

וְאִם לֹא תִשְׁמְעוּ לִי וְגו': (ויקרא כו, יד)

[G-d instructed Moses to tell the Jewish people,] "If you do not obey Me...."

In the Talmud,[5] we are told that Rabbi Shimon bar Yochai sent his son, Rabbi Eleazar, to be blessed by some of the sages. They bestowed upon him what sounded like a string of curses. Only when he returned to his father did his father explain to him how all these "curses" were really blessings in disguise.

We, too, can learn how to decipher what we experience in our own lives as G-d's curses, seeing them for what they truly are – sublime but hidden blessings. Rabbi Shimon bar Yochai, who deciphered his colleagues' "curses," is the author of the *Zohar,* the basic text of the inner dimension of the Torah. This teaches us that the study of the Torah's inner dimension trains us to perceive the inner dimension of reality in general, including the inner dimension of G-d's apparent curses.

Once we are aware that G-d's curses are really blessings, we can instinctively fulfill the sages' counsel to "rejoice in suffering."[6] By framing these "curses" positively, removing them from the negative light in which we originally saw them, we allow their inner goodness to be fully revealed. This, in turn, will transform them from apparent evil into revealed goodness.[7]

5. *Mo'ed Katan* 9b.
6. *Shabbat* 88b, etc.
7. *Tanya,* chapter 26; *Igeret HaKodesh* 11, 22; *Likutei Sichot,* vol. 7, p. 233, vol. 19, pp. 136–139.

FOURTH READING
Leviticus 27:1–15

G-d then instructed Moses regarding the various forms of donations that individuals may make to the Temple or to the priests. One type of donation is when someone pledges the monetary "endowment-value" of a person or article. These values are fixed, varying only with regard to the age and gender of the individuals, without regard to their pedigree, achievements, or abilities.

Equality

אִישׁ כִּי יַפְלִא נֶדֶר בְּעֶרְכְּךָ נְפָשֹׁת וגו': (ויקרא כז, ב)

[G-d instructed Moses to tell the Jewish people,] "When a person articulates a vow of endowment of lives...."

The laws of endowments (*arachim*) is one of those areas in which the Torah emphasizes the class equality of the Jewish people. There are indeed many times when tribal affiliation, inborn talents, or hard-earned achievements serve to differentiate us and qualify or disqualify us for certain roles. But at the same time, our differences must not be allowed to overshadow our basic equality, which is ultimately based on the fact that we all possess a Divine soul, which endows us all with infinite worth.[8]

8. *Sichot Kodesh 5738*, vol. 2, pp. 359–360.

FIFTH READING

Leviticus 27:16–21

There are several ways that the Torah specifies for donating possessions to the Tabernacle (or its successor, the holy Temple). Donating one's possessions through "segregation" (*cherem*) is more absolute than "consecrating" (*hekdesh*) them. Consecrated possessions can generally be redeemed, whereas segregated possessions cannot.

Merging with G-d

וְהָיָה הַשָּׂדֶה בְּצֵאתוֹ בַיֹּבֵל קֹדֶשׁ לַה' כִּשְׂדֵה הַחֵרֶם וגו': (ויקרא כז, כא)

**[G-d instructed Moses to tell the Jewish people, "A
field that has been consecrated to the Temple
and not redeemed by the Jubilee year] will
remain holy to G-d like a segregated field."**

Allegorically, the fact that we can "segregate" our possessions to G-d, irrevocably transforming them into His property, teaches us that we are capable of uniting with G-d so completely that there is no longer any difference between what is ours and what is His.

This applies not only to our physical wealth, but to our spiritual wealth – our talents, our faculties, and sensibilities – as well. When we have accomplished so total a transformation, it is simply no longer *possible* for us to do something unholy.[9]

Our total identification with G-dliness, goodness, and positivity elicits G-d's goodness upon us, bringing His abundant blessings of children, health, and wealth.[10]

---

9. See *Mishneh Torah, Shemitah veYoveil* 13:13.
10. *Likutei Sichot*, vol. 22, pp. 170–172.

SIXTH READING
Leviticus 27:22–28

The Torah allows us to donate only *some* of our wealth to charity, but not all of it.

Spiritual Charity

מִכָּל אֲשֶׁר לוֹ וגו': (ויקרא כז, כח)

[G-d instructed Moses to tell the Jewish people, "When someone donates something] from any of his property...."

The limit that the sages put on how much we should give to charity is one fifth of our wealth. Giving more than this limit is considered disrespectful to G-d's gift of prosperity. The exception is if we are approached by a destitute person who needs more than a fifth of our wealth. In such a case, although we are not *required* to go beyond the usual limit, it is considered extra pious to do so. In cases of danger to life, however, there are no limits; we should give as much as we can.[11]

G-d responds to our actions in accordance with their degree and motivation. G-d routinely "donates" His normal, limited beneficence to the world; this is His response to our normal, limited charity. When we entreat Him in prayer, begging for His assistance, He "allows" Himself to give us in excess of the amount that He normally "budgets" for our continued existence. If we would only approach Him as captives pleading to be redeemed from our life-threatening exile, He would respond by sparing no "expense" to save us![12]

11. *Arachin* 28a; *Mishneh Torah, Arachin veCharamim* 8:3.
12. *Likutei Sichot*, vol. 27, pp. 217–223.

SHABBAT

SEVENTH READING
Leviticus 27:29–34

G-d then instructed Moses regarding the special laws that apply
to firstborn animals and to every tenth animal that is born.

Consecrating Reality

הָעֲשִׂירִי יִהְיֶה קֹּדֶשׁ לַה': (ויקרא כז, לב)

[G-d instructed Moses to tell the Jewish people,]
"Every tenth [animal] will be holy to G-d."

According to Jewish mysticism, every component of creation
is composed of ten facets. In virtually all cases, these ten facets
can be subdivided into three groups of three, all of which exist
within one specific context – which is the entity's tenth facet.
For example, our creative potential can be divided into intellect,
emotions, and behavioral patterns. Each of these three groups
comprises three facets, and all nine facets exist in the context of
the tenth facet, self-expression.

By consecrating one tenth of our wealth to G-d (seen here in
the Torah's requirement that we consecrate every tenth animal
born in our herds and flocks), we are consecrating the context
within which the other nine portions of our possessions exist.
This serves to consecrate the other nine facets of our existence. In
turn, consecrating our own personal existence helps consecrate
creation as a whole.[13]

13. *Sefer HaSichot 5750*, vol. 2, p. 471.

NUMBERS

Bemidbar

The Jewish Army

Numbers 1:1–4:20

NUMBERS, THE FOURTH BOOK OF THE TORAH, DESCRIBES THE
journey of the Jewish people from the foot of Mount Sinai to the
threshold of the Land of Israel. The first section begins as G-d
tells Moses to take a census of the adult Jewish males in the desert
(*Bemidbar*, in Hebrew). The purpose of the census is to form an
army from the adult males, should it be necessary to fight the
non-Jewish occupants of the Land of Israel.

FIRST READING

Numbers 1:1–19

On 1 Iyar 2449 – exactly one month after the Tabernacle was erected, while the Jewish people were still encamped at Mount Sinai – G-d told Moses to take a census of the Jewish men in preparation for their conscription into the Jewish army. This census excluded the tribe of Levi, who were exempt from military service in order to serve in the Tabernacle.

Making the Desert Speak

וַיְדַבֵּר ה' אֶל מֹשֶׁה בְּמִדְבַּר וגו': (במדבר א, א)

G-d spoke to Moses in the desert....

The silent desolation of the desert is a metaphor for the lack of Divine revelation in creation.

The fact that the Jewish people were organized into an army while still in the desert alludes to the notion that despite the world's spiritual silence, it can indeed be taught to express the Divinity hidden within it.[1] In this context, the enemies opposing the Jewish people's trek through the desert are the forces of negativity that we must battle in order to enable the world to reveal its inherent Divinity. The "weapons" we use to fight this battle are the study of the Torah and the observance of G-d's commandments.

When we "cultivate" the barren "desert," we help the world recognize its Divine source and the purpose of its creation. This, in turn, prepares it for the Messianic Redemption, when the world's innate Divinity will be clearly and fully revealed.[2]

---

1. This is alluded to by the fact that the word for "desert" in Hebrew (מדבר) is related to the word for "speaks" (מדבר).
2. *Sefer HaSichot 5749*, vol. 2, p. 477.

SECOND READING

Numbers 1:20–54

The conscription census included only men between the ages of 20 and 60.

Spiritual Conscription

מִבֶּן עֶשְׂרִים שָׁנָה וָמַעְלָה כֹּל יֹצֵא צָבָא: (במדבר א, כ)

[The tally of] all those twenty years old and over who were fit to serve in the army....

The Jewish army, like all armies, was the representative of its nation. As its soldiers went out into the world, they were expected to act as a living example of the high moral caliber of the Jewish people.

The same is true of all of us, since we are all G-d's "soldiers." G-d expects us to wear our "uniforms" proudly, acting in a manner that befits the soldiers of His army. Any observer should easily recognize that G-d has charged us with His mission to conquer the world with goodness and holiness.

This is why only mature Jews, age 20 and over, were conscripted into the army. We are counted only when we have sufficiently matured spiritually to identify with our Divine soul and this Divine consciousness has prompted us to "enlist" in G-d's "army."

As long as we exhibit this readiness, no distinction is made regarding our level of spirituality or achievements in the study of the Torah. No matter what, each of us counts as one, and has an equally important role to play in bringing the world to its spiritual fulfillment.[3]

3. *Likutei Sichot*, vol. 8, pp. 219–220.

THIRD READING
Numbers 2:1–34

G-d then instructed Moses to organize the 12 tribes into a specific army formation. The Tabernacle was in the middle, surrounded by three tribes on each side.

Guarding our Inner Sanctuary

כַּאֲשֶׁר יַחֲנוּ כֵּן יִסָּעוּ וגו': (במדבר ב, יז)

[G-d instructed Moses to tell the Jewish people,]
"Exactly as they camp, so must they travel."

Both when they camped and when they journeyed, the tribes kept their positions around the Tabernacle, protecting it on all sides.

This teaches us to protect our inner sanctuary and the Torah within it at all times and under all circumstances. Whether we are relaxed or restless, tranquil or unsettled, even when we are engaged in our struggle against the wilderness of the spiritual desert in which we find ourselves, we can remain centered and focused by preserving our inner connection to G-d and our consciousness of our purpose and goal in life.[4]

---

4. *Hitva'aduyot 5745*, vol. 4, pp. 2103–2104.

FOURTH READING
Numbers 3:1–13

G-d then instructed Moses to count the Levites. The Levites were exempt from military service because they were conscripted to serve in the Tabernacle. They guarded the Tabernacle, dismantled it whenever the Jewish people broke camp, reconstructed it whenever they camped, and assisted the priests in the Tabernacle rituals.

Spiritual Priorities

וְשָׁמְרוּ אֶת ... מִשְׁמֶרֶת בְּנֵי יִשְׂרָאֵל וגו': (במדבר ג, ח)

[**G-d instructed Moses to tell the Jewish people, "The Levites**] must keep ... the charge of the Israelites."

There are two types of righteous people:[5] One type is those who study the Torah and fulfill G-d's commandments perfectly, but do not share their spiritual wealth with others. A second type is those who devote some of the time and energy that they could have spent on striving for self-perfection to helping others.

Both paths are legitimate ways of serving G-d. However, as the Ba'al Shem Tov taught,[6] G-d prefers that we follow the second example, sparing neither time nor energy to ensure that we bring benefit to others.

This was the path of the tribe of Levi.[7] They did not serve G-d on their own behalf, but as representatives of the entire Jewish people. In this way, they showed us how we can illuminate the entire world.[8]

---

5. These two types are exemplified by the palm tree and the cedar tree. See Psalms 92:13.
6. *Tzava'at HaRibash* 125.
7. *Tanchuma, Bemidbar* 15.
8. *Likutei Sichot*, vol. 2, pp. 557–558.

FIFTH READING
Numbers 3:14–39

The Levites were subdivided into four groups: three Levite clans, each descended from one of the sons of Levi, and the priests – the direct descendants of Aaron.

Structure, Emotion, and Intellect

וַיִּהְיוּ אֵלֶּה בְנֵי לֵוִי בִּשְׁמֹתָם גֵּרְשׁוֹן וּקְהָת וּמְרָרִי: (במדבר ג, יז)

**These were the sons of Levi, by name:
Gershon, Kehat, and Merari.**

The three Levite clans were charged with transporting the three components of the Tabernacle. These three components of the physical Tabernacle reflect the three spiritual components of the personal, inner "Tabernacle" each of us constructs for G-d in our own lives:

• The clan of Merari was in charge of the walls of the Tabernacle and pillars of the Courtyard. The basic, rigid structural foundation of our inner Tabernacle is our uncompromising devotion to G-d's will.

• The clan of Gershon was in charge of the nettings of the Tabernacle and veils of the Courtyard. The fluid component of our inner Tabernacle is our emotional involvement with G-d and our loving expression of this emotional relationship in performing His commandments.

• The clan of Kehat was in charge of the furnishings inside the Tabernacle. The furnishings of our inner Tabernacle are the particular ways in which our relationship with G-d changes our lives and enables us to infuse the world with Divine consciousness. The central feature of this component of the Tabernacle was the Ark, which housed the Torah, which is our guide for transforming both ourselves and the world.[9]

9. *Likutei Torah* 3:20b–21a.

SIXTH READING
Numbers 3:40–51

G-d then told Moses to count all the firstborn male non-Levites who were at least one month old. The Levites were replacing the firstborn for service in the Tabernacle, since the firstborn had forfeited this privilege by participating in the incident of the Golden Calf.

Spiritual Meritocracy

וַיֹּאמֶר ה' אֶל מֹשֶׁה פְּקֹד כָּל בְּכֹר וגו': (במדבר ג, מ)

G-d told Moses, "Tally all the firstborn...."

G-d originally intended that the firstborn of each family perform the priestly service. He selected the tribe of Levi for this service only because the tribe of Levi – unlike the firstborn – refused to participate in the sin of the Golden Calf.

From this we see that a person who was not born into the spiritual elite and was therefore not originally destined for the highest levels of spiritual attainment can ascend to these levels by virtue of his or her merits. Businesspeople, manual workers, parents, students – none of us need think that we cannot engage in the in-depth study of the Torah, pray with intense fervor, or spread Divine consciousness throughout the world.

As Maimonides says, anyone "whose spirit has motivated him and whose perception has enlightened him to set himself apart to stand before G-d, serving Him... has [by this fact] been hallowed as the holiest of the holy."[10]

---

10. *Hitva'aduyot 5745*, vol. 4, pp. 2115–2116.

SEVENTH READING
Numbers 4:1–20

After Moses counted the tribe of Levi as a whole, G-d told him to count each of the three Levite clans (Kehat, Gershon, and Merari) separately, appointing each clan to carry specific components of the Tabernacle when the Jewish people would travel.

The Power of Peace

נָשׂא אֶת רֹאשׁ בְּנֵי קְהָת וגו': (במדבר ד, ב)

[G-d told Moses,] "Take a census of the clan of Kehat."

G-d uses the idiom of "take a census" (literally, "raise the head") only here, in the case of the clan of Kehat, and later, in the case of the clan of Gershon.[11] When G-d tells Moses to count the clan of Merari, He simply says, "count them."[12]

Allegorically, this is because the clan of Kehat personified the way our relationship with G-d enables us to transform reality, and the clan of Gershon personified our emotional involvement with G-d, while the clan of Merari personified the selflessness that serves as the foundation of our spiritual life.[13] Thus, the idiom of "raising up" is not used for the clan of Merari not because of any shortcoming on their part, but because they expressed pure selflessness. In this aspect, they exceeded the other two clans, who personified more the active, self-assertive facets of spiritual life.

Both self-assertion and selflessness are necessary and complementary components of the process of spiritual growth. But selflessness is the foundation upon which all of our spiritual progress and the fulfillment of our Divine mission is built.[14]

11. Numbers 4:22.
12. Ibid. 4:29.
13. See the insight for Thursday of this week.
14. *Sefer HaSichot 5748*, vol. 2, pp. 466–468.

Naso

Preparations for the Journey
Numbers 4:21–7:89

THE SECOND SECTION OF THE BOOK OF NUMBERS BEGINS AS
G-d instructs Moses to complete his count (*Naso*, in Hebrew) of
the Levite clans. The Torah then records certain laws pertaining to
the purification process that the Jews needed to undergo before
setting out from Mount Sinai toward the Land of Israel. Finally,
the Torah records the offerings that the tribal princes donated on
the day that the Tabernacle was erected and began to function.
Their offerings emphasized how the Jewish people's upcoming
journey through the desert – as well as each individual's journey
through life to fulfill his or her Divine mission – must be both an
individual and collective experience.

FIRST READING

Numbers 4:21–28

After having told Moses to count the Levite clan of Kehot, G-d instructed Moses to count the Levite clan of Gershon.

Avoiding the Negative; Pursuing the Positive

נָשֹׂא אֶת רֹאשׁ בְּנֵי גֵרְשׁוֹן וְגוֹ': (במדבר ד, כב)

[G-d told Moses,] "Take a census of the clan of Gershon."

Ever since the Giving of the Torah, each of us possesses an innate, subconscious love of G-d. This love of G-d is far more intense than any love of G-d that we can achieve on our own, by using our conscious intellect to focus on some *reason* to love G-d. When this innate love of G-d is revealed, it can "sanctify" us, i.e., re-orient us toward fulfilling G-d's positive, wholesome desires for us rather than satisfying our self-serving, negative material drives.

These two effects of the Giving of the Torah are alluded to in the name "Gershon." This name is derived from the Hebrew verb *le-garesh*, which means both "to drive out" and "to bring out" (i.e., "to reveal").[1] By revealing our innate love of G-d, we drive out our former negative, self-serving orientation.[2]

---

1. As in Deuteronomy 33:14.
2. *Likutei Sichot*, vol. 8, pp. 57–60.

SECOND READING
Numbers 4:29–49

G-d then instructed Moses to count the clan of Merari.

The Components of Spiritual Growth

בְּנֵי מְרָרִי ... תִּפְקֹד אֹתָם: (במדבר ד, כט)

[G-d told Moses,] "You must count the clan of Merari."

The Hebrew idiom for "taking a census" is "raising the head,"
which allegorically means "elevating our consciousness."

Studying the Torah, prayer, and performing G-d's commandments elevate our consciousness to varying degrees. These three
activities are personified by the three Levite clans. G-d therefore
used three different expressions for these clans:[3]

- G-d said: "*Take a census* of the clan of Kehat...,"[4] for they
  personified the study of the Torah – through which we meld
  our consciousness with G-d's, so to speak.
- G-d said: "*Take a census* of the clan of Gershon, *too*...,"[5] for
  they personified prayer. The word "too" indicates that prayer
  is an adjunct to the study of the Torah, purifying our motives
  so we can meld our consciousness with G-d's fully.
- Finally, G-d said: "*You must count* the clan of Merari...,"[6]
  not using the idiom of "raising the head" at all, for this clan
  personified the performance of the commandments, which
  is based on our simple devotion to G-d.

All three components working together enable us to achieve
our Divine purpose and promote our spiritual development.[7]

---

3. See also the insights for Thursday and Shabbat of *Bemidbar*.
4. Numbers 4:2.
5. Ibid., v. 22.
6. Ibid., v. 29.
7. *Sefer HaMa'amarim 5747–5751*, pp. 407–410.

THIRD READING
Numbers 5:1–10

G-d told Moses to teach the Jewish people some of the laws concerning the priesthood, including the law that every year the farmers must give the first fruits of their harvest to the priests.

Giving Our First Fruits

וְכָל תְּרוּמָה . . . לוֹ יִהְיֶה: (במדבר ה, ט)

[G-d instructed Moses to tell the Jewish people,] "Every first fruit offering ... must be given to [the priest]."

This principle applies to each of us, at all times, and in all locations. When needy people require our assistance, we should give them the "first fruits" – the first and best of our earnings, even before we take for ourselves.

Admittedly, this is not always easy. The first fruits to ripen are the pride and joy of every farmer, the first return for all the effort he invested. Similarly, we naturally feel the same about our hard-won wages or the returns on our investments. We may therefore be tempted to argue, "I have no problem donating to *public* charitable causes from which everyone benefits – myself included. But why should the first fruits of *my* hard work become some other *individual's* personal property?"

The Torah therefore instructs us to bring our first fruits "to the house of G-d,"[8] meaning to acknowledge that they are not ours in the first place. Once we realize that our first fruits belong to G-d, we can give them away without seeking ways to benefit from them personally.

The Torah then promises us, in the very next verse,[9] that if we indeed give our "first fruits" willingly, G-d will reward us with ample wealth.[10]

8. Exodus 23:19.
9. See Rashi on that verse.
10. *Likutei Sichot*, vol. 8, pp. 39–40.

FOURTH READING
Numbers 5:11–6:27

G-d then taught Moses the laws regarding a suspected adulteress. If a husband suspects his wife of adultery, he should first raise the issue with her privately; if her actions continue to arouse his suspicions, he may subject her to a test by which G-d would indicate whether she was innocent or guilty. As part of this test, the priest had to write a curse on parchment and then erase it by inserting the parchment into a container of water.

Putting Others First

וְכָתַב אֶת הָאָלֹת הָאֵלֶּה הַכֹּהֵן בַּסֵּפֶר וּמָחָה אֶל מֵי הַמָּרִים: (במדבר ה, כג)

[G-d instructed Moses to tell the Jewish
people,] "The priest must write these curses
on a scroll and erase it in the bitter water."

The text of these curses contained G-d's holy Name, which it is ordinarily forbidden to erase.[11] However, G-d was willing to have His Name erased in order to clear the name of the suspected adulteress and thereby restore peaceful relations between her and her husband.[12]

Similarly, we should also be prepared to act selflessly on another's behalf, not only when doing so comes easily or when the other person deserves our efforts. Even when it is for a person of questionable morality and it involves personal physical or spiritual sacrifice, we should be prepared to follow G-d's example.[13]

---

11. *Mishneh Torah, Yesodei HaTorah* 6:1–2.
12. *Shabbat* 116a; *Mishneh Torah, Chanukah* 4:14; *Yerushalmi Sotah* 1:4.
13. *Likutei Sichot*, vol. 25, p. 83.

FIFTH READING
Numbers 7:1–41

1 Nisan 2449 was the first day that the Tabernacle began functioning officially. On this special day, the tribal princes donated six wagons for the use of the Levites in transporting the components of the Tabernacle.

Maximizing Our Potential

עֲגָלָה עַל שְׁנֵי הַנְּשִׂאִים וְשׁוֹר לְאֶחָד וגו': (במדבר ז, ג)

[The tribal princes' donation was] a wagon from each two princes and an ox from each.

The princes donated the minimum number of wagons that was needed to carry the designated load, although more wagons would have made the Levites' job easier.[14] The princes understood that providing "extra" wagons would clash with the Tabernacle's essence – which was to express G-d's approach to creation, namely, that everything has a purpose. Since it was possible to carry the Tabernacle with six wagons, a seventh one would have meant that the other six would be partially wasted.

This concept is also true in the personal Tabernacle that we make for G-d out of our lives. Since G-d created everything for a purpose, if we are not using (or are under-using) some aspect of our lives for holy purposes, its purpose is not being fulfilled.

By fully utilizing everything at our disposal and fully living up to our own potential, we can indeed fashion our lives in particular and the world in general into the "Tabernacle" that G-d wants them to be. In this way, we fulfill G-d's plan, spreading Divine consciousness throughout the world and hastening the advent of the Messianic Redemption, when the whole world will be transformed into G-d's true home.[15]

---

14. See *Shabbat* 99a.
15. *Likutei Sichot*, vol. 28, pp. 40–48, p. 54 ff.

SIXTH READING

Numbers 7:42–83

The princes of each tribe also pledged a set of sacrifices to inaugurate the Altar. All 12 sets of sacrifices were identical, but the Torah nonetheless enumerates each one separately.

Forging a Spiritual Path

קָרְבָּנוֹ וגו': (במדבר ז, מג)

His offering was....

The purpose of the sacrifices was to bring the offerer closer to G-d and to elicit spiritual and material beneficence from heaven. The Altar's inauguration was thus its "initiation" into bringing the Jewish people closer to G-d and eliciting the spiritual and material nourishment they would require.

In particular, however, the twelve tribes represent the twelve general approaches to approaching G-d. It was therefore not sufficient for Moses and Aaron to inaugurate the Altar by themselves. The princes of each of the twelve tribes had to do this, so the Altar could then elevate all twelve approaches and elicit the spiritual and material beneficence necessary for each.

Nowadays, when the description of the princes' offerings is read from the Torah in the synagogue, each of us ascends via our unique tribal path to heaven and receives the spiritual nourishment that pertains to us.[16]

---

16. *Torah Or* 8b; *Likutei Torah* 4:98c; *Likutei Sichot*, vol. 23, p. 54.

SEVENTH READING
Numbers 7:84–89

After concluding its account of each prince's offerings, the Torah summarizes all the princes' offerings, giving the grand totals of each component.

Connecting to G-d

זֹאת חֲנֻכַּת הַמִּזְבֵּחַ וגו': (במדבר ז, פד)

This was the dedication offering of the Altar.

Unlike the rest of the tribes, Levi did not participate in the installation offerings for the Altar. This is because the Levites were G-d's employees, the servants of the Divine King in His Tabernacle. Just as an earthly king does not bring presents to himself for the inauguration of his own palace, so the Levites did not bring presents to the Tabernacle. On the contrary, the gifts that the other tribes brought to the Tabernacle were in order to enable the Levites to perform *their* service.

In another sense, however, the Levites are alluded to by the total given after the detailed account of each prince's offering. Whereas each prince, the representative of his tribe, personified a different aspect of our relationship with G-d, the tribe of Levi personifies our overall, total connection with G-d.[17]

This teaches us that spiritual growth requires developing both our particular, personal spiritual path as well as the general path we share in common with the rest of the Jewish people.[18]

---

17. The name *Levi* means "to connect" or "to accompany." See Genesis 29:34.
18. *Hitva'aduyot 5747*, vol. 3, pp. 459–460; 463–464; *Hitva'aduyot 5745*, vol. 3, pp. 1760–1762.

Beha'alotecha

The Journey Begins
Numbers 8:1–12:16

THE THIRD SECTION OF THE BOOK OF NUMBERS BEGINS AS
G-d tells Moses to instruct Aaron how to kindle (*Beha'alotecha*, in
Hebrew) the lamps of the Tabernacle's Candelabrum. It continues
with the final preparations for the Jewish people's departure from
Mount Sinai and the events that occurred at their first stops in
the desert.

FIRST READING
Numbers 8:1–14

The tribal princes did not include Aaron when they brought their offerings for the inauguration of the Altar. G-d reassured Aaron by noting that he had inaugurated the Candelabrum, which was just as important – if not more so – than inaugurating the Altar.

Setting the Soul on Fire

דַּבֵּר אֶל אַהֲרֹן וְאָמַרְתָּ אֵלָיו בְּהַעֲלֹתְךָ אֶת הַנֵּרֹת וגו': (במדבר ח, ב)

[G-d told Moses,] "Speak to Aaron, telling him, 'When you kindle the lamps.... '"

As King Solomon says, "The lamp of G-d is the human soul."[1] The flame of a candle constantly flickers upward, as if yearning to leave the wick behind and ascend heavenward. The soul shares this nature, constantly striving to reconnect with its spiritual source by breaking out of the boundaries of time and space imposed on it by the body and the physical world.

At times, however, this nature becomes dormant. The soul is so blinded by its surroundings that it forgets its natural thirst for Divinity. This is why every morning – after every period of spiritual darkness – our soul-lamps must be re-kindled. They must be reminded of their innate desire to ascend. Whether it is our own soul or that of someone with whom we come in contact – or even the soul of someone we have never met but have only heard about – if we see that it is not aflame, it is our privilege and challenge to re-kindle it.[2]

---

1. Proverbs 20:27.
2. *Sefer HaMa'amarim Melukat*, vol. 3, pp. 185–190.

SECOND READING
Numbers 8:15–26

The Torah previously recorded how the priests were installed into office; it now records how the Levites were installed.

Spiritual Qualifications

כִּי נְתֻנִים נְתֻנִים הֵמָּה לִי מִתּוֹךְ בְּנֵי יִשְׂרָאֵל וגו': (במדבר ח, טז)

**[G-d told Moses, "The Levites] are given
to Me from among the Israelites."**

Maimonides teaches us that anyone "whose spirit has motivated him and whose perception has enlightened him to set himself apart [from mundane life] in order to stand before G-d and serve Him...has [by this fact] been hallowed as the holiest of the holy."[3]

We might conclude from Maimonides' words that in order to lead a G-dly life, we have spiritually matured to the point at which our "spirit has motivated us and our perception has enlightened us" to dedicate ourselves to this lofty goal. But we see from the installation of the Levites that this is not true. The Talmud tells us that an agent cannot be empowered to accomplish more than his dispatcher can by himself.[4] Thus, if the Levites are our agents, it means that we have the spiritual power to do all that they do. All of us, even those who feel that they have not yet progressed to this point, can be a spiritual Levite, "setting ourselves apart from mundane life in order to stand before G-d and serve Him" by fulfilling our Divine mission in making the world into G-d's true home.[5]

---

3. *Mishneh Torah, Shemitah v'Yovel* 13:13.
4. *Kidushin* 23b.
5. *Likutei Sichot*, vol. 13, p. 15.

THIRD READING
Numbers 9:1–14

On 14 Nisan 2449 – two weeks after the inauguration of the Tabernacle – G-d commanded the Jewish people to observe the holiday of Passover. However, some people were ritually defiled and therefore unable to participate in the festival. They complained about being left out, and in response, G-d informed Moses that whoever was unable to perform the Passover rituals on the date of the holiday should perform them a month later, on 14 Iyar.

Our Lives Depend on It

וַיֹּאמְרוּ הָאֲנָשִׁים הָהֵמָּה אֵלָיו . . . לָמָּה נִגָּרַע וגו': (במדבר ט, ז)

Those men said to [Moses,] "Why should we be left out?"

These Jews fully understood why they could not offer up the Passover sacrifice along with everyone else, but they still complained, saying, "Why should we be left out?" They not only felt excluded from the community's positive experience; they felt as if their very lives depended on it.[6] Their heartfelt cry caused G-d to grant us the holiday of the second Passover, a second opportunity for redemption.

We can learn from their example. Because we are living in exile, we, too, cannot offer up the Passover sacrifices. But we can cry out to G-d, demanding the opportunity to connect with Him fully, feeling that the missed opportunity to do so jeopardizes our very lives. If we truly complain and fervently demand this of G-d, He will surely redeem us from exile and rebuild our Temple, affording us the opportunity to connect with Him in the fullest way possible.[7]

---

6. This is implied in the literal meaning of the words translated as "why should we be left out" (למה נגרע), which is "why should we be *diminished*."
7. *Likutei Sichot*, vol. 22, pp. 215–216.

FOURTH READING

Numbers 9:15–10:10

G-d instructed Moses to make two silver trumpets. Moses was to use these trumpets to summon the people when he wanted to speak with them, as well as to signal that it was time to travel. In addition, the people were to blow the trumpets in times of battle and when offering up communal sacrifices on the festivals.

Relying on G-d

וְכִי תָבֹאוּ מִלְחָמָה וגו': (במדבר י, ט)

[G-d told Moses,] "If you go to war...."

We are constantly fighting against our inborn materially-oriented passions. This fight is particularly intense during prayer, when these passions can distract us, keeping us from concentrating on G-d and deepening our relationship with Him.

The inner "trumpet" that we sound in order to enlist G-d's help is our acknowledgment of how dependent we are upon His assistance in this struggle. When we beseech G-d to come to our aid, He rescues us from our enemy.

But we see here that we must blow the trumpets not only while in the thick of battle, but also when we have overcome the enemy – and even on joyous festivals. Blowing the trumpets on these occasions reminds us that even if we have made great strides in spiritual growth, and no longer feel the downward pull of material passion, we are still dependent upon G-d's assistance in order to maintain and properly utilize our spirituality.[8]

8. *Likutei Sichot*, vol. 13, pp. 28–29, based on *Shenei Luchot HaBerit* on this passage.

FIFTH READING

Numbers 10:11–34

On 20 Iyar 2449, G-d gave the signal and the people set out from Mount Sinai. Moses asked his father-in-law Jethro to accompany them, but Jethro first went back to his homeland, Midian, to convert his family to Judaism.

The Pursuit of Secular Knowledge

וַיֹּאמֶר מֹשֶׁה לְחֹבָב בֶּן רְעוּאֵל וְגוֹ': (במדבר י, כט)

Moses said to Chovav son of Re'u'eil....

These alternate names for Jethro mean that he was "the cherisher" (*chovav*) of the Torah whose love of the Torah "was derived from" (*the son of*) his "love of G-d" (*re'u'eil*).

In searching for truth, Jethro had amassed expert knowledge of all the philosophical, spiritual, and scientific lore of his age. He eventually declared that all this knowledge must lead ultimately to the acceptance of G-d's Torah.

Because of the Giving of the Torah, G-d is not relegated to the "religious" facets of our existence, but can be sought and found in all life's aspects, even the most mundane. Jethro revealed this essential power of the Torah by declaring that all the world's wisdom – even what we normally consider "secular" – must be seen as part of G-d's wisdom.

We too, by studying the Torah, can reveal how G-d's essence encompasses all reality, even "secular" or "mundane" reality. This brings G-d into all aspects of life, making the world into His true home.[9]

9. *Sefer HaMa'amarim 5647*, p. 72 ff; *BeSha'ah SheHikdimu 5672*, vol. 2, pp. 861–862; *Sefer HaMa'amarim 5679*, pp. 289 ff; *Sefer HaMa'amarim 5709*, pp. 52 ff; *Sefer HaMa'amarim 5737*, pp. 157–162; *Sefer HaMa'amarim 5745*, pp. 102–106; *Sefer HaMa'amarim Melukat*, vol. 3, pp. 58 ff.

SIXTH READING
Numbers 10:35–11:29

The Jewish people miraculously covered a three-day journey on the first day of their trek through the desert, for G-d was anxious to bring them into the Land of Israel. But once the Jewish people were on their way, some of the former non-Jews who had accompanied them when they left Egypt and had converted to Judaism began to have second thoughts about submitting to G-d's laws. Seeking an excuse for their attitude, these recent converts complained about having to travel so far on the first day.

True Complaints

וַיְהִי הָעָם כְּמִתְאֹנְנִים וגו': (במדבר יא, א)

The people sought a pretext [to rebel against G-d].

These words read literally in the Hebrew, "The people were *like* complainers," implying that they were only *like* complainers, but not real complainers. This is so because a Jew, whose essence is one with G-d's essence, can never really complain against G-d. Even though they in fact complained, their complaint was only an expression of their deep yearning to become closer to G-d; their dissatisfaction with their present understanding of His ways.

This is how we should view all complaints against G-d. For this same reason, we should not shy away from complaining to G-d either, for we know that our complaints are really just expressions of our deep, unfulfilled yearning for Him.[10]

10. *Sefer HaSichot 5751*, vol. 2, p. 609.

SEVENTH READING
Numbers 11:30–12:16

Some of the Jews then began to complain about not having enough meat, even though they had taken many animals with them when they left Egypt. G-d answered the people's complaints by providing them with an abundance of quails. This demonstration of G-d's concern inspired many to regret their previous ingratitude. But others, who remained stubborn and defiant, greedily gathered the quails and started eating them. Aware of each individual's spiritual state, G-d killed off the incurable offenders. G-d named the place where this incident occurred "Graves of the Craving."

Spiritual Potential

וַיִּקְרָא אֶת שֵׁם הַמָּקוֹם הַהוּא קִבְרוֹת הַתַּאֲוָה וגו': (במדבר יא, לד)

[G-d] named that place "Graves of the Craving."

According to the Ba'al Shem Tov, each of the 42 stops along the Jewish people's journey from Egypt to the Land of Israel was an ascending step toward their spiritual redemption. Furthermore, these 42 stops are allegorically the stepping stones that every Jew must experience during his passage from the constraints of materialism to the apex of holiness.

In this context, the name "the Graves of Craving" refers to the stage in our spiritual growth at which we have completely vanquished and "buried" our improper cravings. Our experience of spirituality is so intense that the possibility for material cravings no longer exists.[11]

We see here that every stop in the journey of life has the potential to be a positive step in our spiritual development. It is our choice whether or not to actualize this positive spiritual potential.[12]

11. *Degel Machaneih Ephraim, Mas'ei* (80a) citing *Berit Menuchah*.
12. *Likutei Sichot*, vol. 4, pp. 1083–1084; *Or HaTorah, Bemidbar*, vol. 4, p. 1352; *Sefer HaSichot 5749*, vol. 2, p. 528.

Shelach

Scouting Out the Land

Numbers 13:1–15:41

THE FOURTH SECTION OF THE BOOK OF NUMBERS RECOUNTS how G-d told Moses to send (*Shelach*, in Hebrew) scouts to spy out the Land of Israel in preparation for the Jewish people's conquest of it.

FIRST READING
Numbers 13:1–20

By 29 Sivan 2449, the Jewish people had reached the border of the Land of Israel. Some of the people asked Moses to send spies into the land to scout it out in advance of the people's entry into it. Moses consulted with G-d, and G-d agreed to this plan. Moses chose 12 men, one from each tribe, for this mission. These men were among the most distinguished leaders of the Jewish people.

Unity and Plurality

אִישׁ אֶחָד אִישׁ אֶחָד לְמַטֵּה אֲבֹתָיו תִּשְׁלָחוּ וגו': (במדבר יג, ב)

[G-d told Moses,] "Send one man from each tribe."

The intrinsic unity of the Jewish people derives from the common Divine mission we all share: to make the world into G-d's home. The Jewish people is divided into twelve tribes because there are different ways in which this one goal must be accomplished. G-d gives each of us, as individuals, specific powers and characteristics that suit the part of reality that Divine providence has charged us to transform. At the same time, however, we should pursue our individual goals in the context of our general goal as a nation.

It was in order to express our common Divine mission that G-d instructed all twelve tribal representatives to walk the length and breadth of the *entire* land, rather than having each representative only scout out his tribe's specific territory. At the same time, the fact that all twelve tribes were represented signified that this overall unity of purpose should permeate daily reality, in which we must emphasize our individual identities and their accompanying differences in purpose and approach.[1]

1. *Sefer HaSichot 5751*, vol. 2, pp. 626–627.

<u>SECOND READING</u>
Numbers 13:21–14:7

After 40 days, the spies returned to the Jewish people's camp and reported their findings to Moses and the people. But then, instead of letting Moses interpret their evidence, the spies – with the exception of Caleb and Joshua – drew their own conclusion, namely, that the land could not be conquered.

Asceticism vs. Engagement

וַיֹּאמְרוּ ... טוֹבָה הָאָרֶץ מְאֹד מְאֹד: אִם חָפֵץ בָּנוּ ה׳
וְהֵבִיא אֹתָנוּ אֶל הָאָרֶץ הַזֹּאת וְגו׳: (במדבר יד, ז–ח)

[Joshua and Caleb] said, "... The land is very, very good. If G-d desires us, He will bring us to this land."

In the desert, all the physical needs of the Jewish people were provided, enabling the people to study the Torah unencumbered by the distractions of mundane life. The spies feared that even if the land *could* be conquered, it would still "conquer" the people, forcing them to work the land in order to wrest their livelihood from it.

Joshua and Caleb gave the spies a twofold answer:

• *The land is very, very good.* Studying the Torah is indeed very good, but elevating mundane reality by performing G-d's commandments is "very, *very* good," for this brings us to even higher spiritual levels. Thus, even from a "selfish" perspective, it pays to enter the land.

• *If G-d desires*: Moreover, entering the land is G-d's desire, and we should fulfill it with no second thoughts.

We, too, should not hesitate to engage the physical world, for doing so properly is both to our own advantage and G-d's true will.[2]

---

2. *Hitva'aduyot 5746*, vol. 3, pp. 653–654.

THIRD READING
Numbers 14:8–25

Joshua and Caleb insisted that since G-d had promised the Land of Israel to the Jewish people, there was no reason to fear that the people who were presently occupying it could not be overcome.

Misplaced Fear

וְאַתֶּם אַל תִּירְאוּ וְגוֹ': (במדבר יד, ט)

[Joshua and Caleb said to the people,] "Do not fear."

Since time immemorial, those who aspire to do what is right have faced opposition and even ridicule. Yet, the Code of Jewish Law begins with the instruction: Do not be embarrassed by the mockers. When G-d is with us, there is no reason for fear.

The same response applies not only to fear of others, but to fear for our spiritual well-being. Other than Joshua and Caleb, the spies were afraid that engaging in material life in the Promised Land would undermine the people's ability to lead holy lives. Since G-d is with us, aiding us in our mission to transform the physical world into His home, there is no reason to fear. We can indeed infuse Divine consciousness into all aspects of life, down to the most mundane.[3]

3. *Likutei Sichot*, vol. 33, p. 272.

FOURTH READING
Numbers 14:26–15:7

The overwhelming majority of the Jewish people accepted the other spies' conclusions, threatening to kill Caleb and Joshua for daring to differ. Since the people demonstrated that they lacked the faith in G-d necessary to enable them to conquer and live in the Land of Israel, G-d informed Moses that this generation would have to die out in the desert over the ensuing 39 years. Only the next generation would enter the Promised Land.

Understanding G-d's Message

וּבְנֵיכֶם יִהְיוּ רֹעִים בַּמִּדְבָּר אַרְבָּעִים שָׁנָה וגו': (במדבר יד, לג)

[G-d instructed Moses to tell the Jewish people,] "Your children will wander in the desert with you for 40 years."

Although the spies' sin added only 39 years to the Israelites' stay in the desert – the incident took place in the second year of their journey – the Torah refers to the decree as being for 40 years.

This is because the number 40 is associated with our ability to understand. The Talmud states[4] that we only reach our full capacity to understand at the age of 40, and that students can only fully understand their master's teachings after 40 years.[5] The incident of the spies demonstrated that the generation of Jews who left Egypt did not truly understand the Torah's message. Their children, after spending 40 years absorbed in studying G-d's teachings, achieved this level of understanding. They were therefore able to accomplish their Divine mission in the land.

Similarly, by setting aside periods for intense and concentrated study of the Torah, we can prepare ourselves spiritually to properly engage the material world, reveal its Divine potential, and transform it into G-d's true home.[6]

4. *Avot* 5:22.
5. *Avodah Zarah* 5b.
6. *Hitva'aduyot 5747*, vol. 3, p. 528.

FIFTH READING
Numbers 15:8–16

After the incident of the spies, G-d comforted the Jewish people
by focusing their attention on the fact that their children would
eventually enter and possess the Land of Israel. He did this by
giving them some laws that would apply only once they would
enter the land. The first of these laws was that in the Land of Israel,
their animal sacrifices would have to be accompanied by offerings
of grain, oil, and wine.

Complementary Directions

וְיַיִן תַּקְרִיב לַנֶּסֶךְ וגו': (במדבר טו, י)

**[G-d instructed Moses to tell the Jewish
people,] "You must offer up a wine-libation."**

The Talmud states that someone who recites the *Shema* while
not wearing *tefillin* is like someone who offers sacrifices without
libations.[7]

The main theme of the *Shema* is that our awareness that G-d
pervades and controls all reality should be so real to us that we
are willing to give up our life for G-d because of it. This is why the
Shema has always been on the lips of Jewish martyrs throughout
history. Thus, the *Shema*, like sacrifices that ascend in flame on
the Altar, represents our readiness to rise above the world.

Tefillin, on the other hand, draw Divine awareness into our
mind (via the head *tefillin*), our heart (via the hand *tefillin*), and
our actions (via the straps of the head *tefillin*[8]). Thus, *tefillin*, like
the libations that are poured onto the Altar, represent our dedication to our goal of bringing Divinity into the world.[9]

---

7. *Berachot* 14b.
8. The straps of the head-*tefillin* are required to extend past the navel. See
Tur, Orach Chayim 27.
9. *Hitva'aduyot* 5747, vol. 3, p. 525 ff; *Likutei Torah* 3:40a ff.

SIXTH READING
Numbers 15:17–26

The next law that G-d taught the Jewish people was the requirement to separate a portion of their dough and give it to the priests.

Collecting the Crumbs

רֵאשִׁית עֲרֹסֹתֵכֶם חַלָּה תָּרִימוּ תְרוּמָה וְגו': (במדבר טו, כ)

**[G-d instructed Moses to tell the Jewish people, "Of]
the first of your dough, donate a loaf [to a priest]."**

Flour consists of thousands of small and independent pieces
of grain, but when water is added, these pieces become a solid
mass of dough. Just as water makes a unified entity out of the
unconnected particles of flour, so does the Torah allow us to see
the underlying unity and harmony of all existence. Everything
serves a unique purpose, but these purposes can often seem at
odds with one another. The Torah reveals to us both the overall
purpose of creation as a whole and each entity's specific contribution toward this overall purpose.

According to Jewish Law, after we remove the required portion
of the dough, the flour that remains in the bowl after the dough
is made is still under the obligation to have its required portion
removed from it. This teaches us that even if we have illuminated
certain aspects of reality with the light and holiness of Torah, we
must not forget about the areas we have not yet touched.[10]

10. *Sichot Kodesh 5718*, pp. 266–267.

SEVENTH READING

Numbers 15:27–41

G-d then instructed Moses regarding three commandments that are deemed equivalent to observing the entire Torah: not worshipping idols, observing the Sabbath, and wearing tassels (*tzitzit*) on the corners of four-cornered garments. The numerical value of the Hebrew word *tzitzit* is 600; when this number is added to the number of half-threads (8) and knots (5) in each tassel, the sum is 613, the number of commandments in the Torah.

Common Purpose

דַּבֵּר אֶל בְּנֵי יִשְׂרָאֵל וְאָמַרְתָּ אֲלֵהֶם וְעָשׂוּ לָהֶם צִיצִת וגו': (במדבר טו, לח)

[G-d told Moses,] "Speak to the Israelites and tell them that they must make for themselves a tassel...."

A commandment whose observance is equivalent to observing the entire Torah expresses the common, overall effect of the commandments – as opposed to the particular effect that any specific commandment has on us. What distinguishes *tzitzit* from other all-encompassing commandments is that it also alludes to each of the 613 commandments individually. Thus, *tzitzit* alludes both to the general Divine mission common to all of us as well as the individual ways in which each of us accomplishes our specific part of this mission.

Tzitzit is thus a fitting conclusion to this section of the Torah, which opened by describing how the twelve spies scouted out the Land of Israel in accordance with this same ideal.[11] The spies scouted out the entire land together, rather than each scouting out only his tribe's specific territory, indicating that our common unity of purpose should inspire and direct the specific roles we play in helping the world fulfill its purpose.[12]

11. See the insight for Sunday of this section.
12. *Sefer HaSichot 5751*, vol. 2, pp. 625–627.

Korach

Mutiny

Numbers 16:1–18:32

THE FIFTH SECTION OF THE BOOK OF NUMBERS RECOUNTS the rebellion of Korach, Moses' first cousin, and its repercussions.

FIRST READING
Numbers 16:1–13

The incident of the spies, recounted in the previous section, underscored the importance of fulfilling G-d's commandments in the physical world. Moses' cousin Korach, noting that everyone can perform G-d's commandments equally, concluded that there is no justification for an elite class of leaders. He staged a rebellion against Moses' authority and Aaron's appointment as high priest. One of Korach's co-conspirators was On son of Pelet.

The Power of Women

וַיִּקַּח קֹרַח ... וְאוֹן בֶּן פֶּלֶת וְגו': (במדבר טז, א)

Korach took... and On son of Pelet.

Korach was a member of one of the Jewish people's most distinguished families, and also learned, wise, wealthy, and among the inner circle of Moses' and Aaron's closest confidants. In contrast, his fellow conspirator On son of Pelet was quite ordinary, both in terms of his intellectual capabilities and his lineage. Yet Korach came to a tragic end, dragging hundreds of other people down with him, whereas On was the only one of Korach's entire assembly who emerged completely unscathed.

The difference in the fates of these two conspirators was due to the behavior of their wives. Whereas Korach's wife encouraged him to rebel, On's wife prevented him from participating in Korach's mutiny.[1]

This demonstrates the great responsibility of women – particularly those who are wives, and especially those who are also mothers. Women should never underestimate their ability to influence their own destinies as well as those of their community, their husbands, and their families.[2]

---

1. *Sanhedrin* 109b; *Bemidbar Rabbah* 18:20.
2. *Likutei Sichot*, vol. 2, pp. 689–690.

SECOND READING

Numbers 16:14–19

Korach and his accomplices assembled a crowd of mutineers to back his rebellion.

Holy vs. Unholy Conflict

וַיַּקְהֵל עֲלֵיהֶם קֹרַח אֶת כָּל הָעֵדָה וגו': (במדבר טז, יט)

Korach assembled all the congregation against them.

There is positive, holy conflict and negative, unholy conflict. Holy conflict is the spirited and sincere debate over the proper interpretation of the Torah. Since all parties are humbly seeking the truth, their conflict leads to greater friendship and mutual love.[3] In contrast, unholy conflict results from selfish concerns and the search for personal gratification. Since everyone's selfish concerns are different, any confederation based on selfishness will be rife with conflicting interests.

Korach and his faction were the prime example of unholy strife and conflict.[4] Moses and his supporters did not quarrel with them; we are only told how "*they* gathered together against Moses and Aaron."[5] Rather, Korach's controversy raged between himself and the members of his own faction.

Thus, we need not shun differences of opinion or arguments per se; it is only unholy conflict, stemming from self-interest, that we should seek to avoid. On the contrary, healthy and respectful conflict, motivated out of a sincere, humble search for truth, is a positive force toward individual and communal spiritual growth.[6]

3. See *Kidushin* 30b.
4. *Avot* 5:17.
5. Numbers 16:3.
6. *Likutei Sichot*, vol. 4, pp. 1316–1318; ibid., vol. 13, pp. 203–204.

THIRD READING
Numbers 16:20–17:8

G-d told Moses to conduct a test that would demonstrate Korach's error. Offering up incense was part of the Tabernacle service that only priests were allowed to perform. G-d had Moses instruct both Aaron and Korach's company of 250 princes and judges to offer up incense. Whoever's incense was not accepted by G-d would perish. Besides these leaders, there was a large crowd of people whom Korach had drawn to his side. Moses tried to convince these other rebels to abandon Korach's mutiny, but despite Moses' efforts at reconciliation, Korach and his followers refused to back down. G-d therefore sent forth fire to consume the 250 people who had offered up incense; the rest of the rebels were swallowed up in a pit that opened up in the ground.

Never Despair of Anyone

וַתִּבָּקַע הָאֲדָמָה אֲשֶׁר תַּחְתֵּיהֶם: (במדבר טז, לא)

The earth beneath them split open.

G-d did not punish Korach and his supporters until they had acted on their beliefs. Even when Korach convinced the rest of the people to side with him, G-d did not punish the offenders until He had duly warned them not to commit their crime and they nonetheless did so.

We must learn from G-d's example here, and wherever possible give those who offend us or disobey G-d's laws the benefit of the doubt, patiently and lovingly encouraging them to better themselves.[7]

---

7. *Likutei Sichot,* vol. 28, p. 6.

FOURTH READING
Numbers 17:9–15

The day following the mutiny, the Jewish people complained about the fate that befell the rebels. This indicated that they also ascribed to their views. G-d therefore informed Moses of His intent to kill off the rest of the people, who began to die of an epidemic.

The Purpose of Divisions

הֵרֹמוּ מִתּוֹךְ הָעֵדָה הַזֹּאת וגו': (במדבר יז, י)

[G-d told Moses,] "Remove yourselves
from this congregation."

Korach called for abolishing the distinctions between different groups of Jews. Ironically, he became the classic example of argument and division.

Just as it is damaging to create arbitrary or artificial divisions, it is equally damaging to ignore the divisions that G-d has established in nature or legislated in the Torah. True unity is possible only when each component of a group is fulfilling its designated role. Only then can all the components combine to constitute a well-functioning unit.

Abolishing boundaries does not always produce unity; in fact, it can produce exactly the opposite. It is possible to unite fire and water (by heating the water with the fire) only if they are separated by a pot. So, too, respecting the Torah's divisions between different groups of people allows for the truest expression of unity and harmony among them.[8]

8. *Likutei Sichot*, vol. 18, pp. 204–211.

FIFTH READING
Numbers 17:16–24

In order to demonstrate conclusively that He Himself had set apart the tribe of Levi (the priests and the Levites) from the rest of the Jewish people for their respective tasks, G-d commanded Moses to take the staffs of the princes of each of the 12 tribes and place them next to the Ark in the Holy of Holies, the inner chamber of the Tabernacle. Moses did so, and Aaron's staff miraculously sprouted almonds overnight, whereas the other staffs remained unchanged.

Making Lifeless Wood Blossom

וַיֹּצֵא מֹשֶׁה אֶת כָּל הַמַּטֹּת מִלִּפְנֵי ה' וגו': (במדבר יז, כד)

Moses took out all the staffs from before G-d....

Allegorically, we are all given a "staff" taken from G-d's Tabernacle, i.e., Divine support that we can rely upon as we fulfill our Divine mission. We receive this "staff" from Moses, i.e., by studying the Torah that Moses gave us and by following its teachings.

The fact that Aaron's staff blossomed and bore fruit teaches us that G-d assists us in making everything in the world flower into a beautiful component of His earthly home. This is true even of "dead wood" – elements of creation that are seemingly deadened to spirituality.

The fact that Aaron's staff blossomed *quickly* teaches us that G-d also assists us in making these beautiful things bear fruit quickly, quickly increasing Divine consciousness in the world.[9]

9. *Hitva'aduyot 5743*, vol. 3, pp. 1671–1673.

SIXTH READING
Numbers 17:25–18:20

The Jewish people finally accepted the Divinely ordained distinction between the tribe of Levi and the lay people (as well as the division of the tribe of Levi itself into priests and Levites). However, the people then complained that since entering designated areas of the Tabernacle compound was a capital offense for non-Levites, they were constantly exposed to the danger of death. G-d therefore made the priests and Levites responsible for keeping non-Levites from entering off-limits areas.

Humility and Closeness

וְגַם אֶת אַחֶיךָ מַטֵּה לֵוִי שֵׁבֶט אָבִיךָ הַקְרֵב אִתָּךְ וְגוֹ': (במדבר יח, ב)

[**G-d instructed Moses to tell Aaron,**] **"Enlist also your brethren, the tribe of Levi...."**

The name *Levi* means "to accompany" or "to be attached." We would think, then, that the Levites enjoyed a direct connection with G-d.

In fact, however, the role of the Levites in the Tabernacle (and later, in the holy Temple) was only to assist the priests in *their* G-dly service. Moreover, whereas the entire tribe of Levi is denied a portion of the Land of Israel,[10] G-d only "appeases" the *priests* – telling them that He "is their portion and inheritance"[11] – but offers no such comfort to the regular Levites. Thus, the Levites are left out of both the physical inheritance of the land and the spiritual inheritance promised specifically to the priests.

It is precisely this subservience that propels the tribe of Levi to such great spiritual heights. Their secondary role keeps them humble and unimpressed with their own station in life, and it is specifically this humility that brings them so close to G-d.[12]

10. Numbers 26:62.
11. Ibid. 18:20.
12. *Likutei Sichot*, vol. 28, p. 122.

SEVENTH READING
Numbers 18:21–32

Finally, in order to certify the selection of the priests from the rest of the people, G-d enumerated the entitlements that they were to receive from the Jewish people. These included specific portions of their sacrifices, of their crops, and of their herds and flocks. The Levites also received specified portions of the Jewish people's crops, part of which they, in turn, were to give to the priests.

Following Moses

וְעָבַד הַלֵּוִי הוּא אֶת עֲבֹדַת אֹהֶל מוֹעֵד וְגוֹ': (במדבר יח, כג)

[G-d told Moses,] "The Levites must perform the service of the Tent of Meeting."

Korach had argued that inasmuch as all Jews are holy, there is no need to recognize any differences between them. This outlook leads to the mistaken notion that there is no need to encourage others to enhance their spiritual wellbeing or their connection to G-d, and that doing so is an insult to their intrinsic holiness.

The truth, of course, is the exact opposite: Our love for others leads us to devote ourselves to bettering their spiritual life and lot.

Our inner Korach is the temptation to ignore Moses' call to care for the spiritual needs of others in order to focus on our own spiritual self-fulfillment. Rather than listen to our inner Korach, let us respond to our inner Moses wholeheartedly. As for our own spiritual well-being, G-d assures us that if we champion His cause, devoting ourselves to our fellow human beings, He will treat us like spiritual Levites, drawing us close to Him and providing for all our needs, spiritual and material.[13]

13. *Mishneh Torah, Shemitah veYovel* 13:13. *Hitva'aduyot 5744*, vol. 3, pp. 2025–2029.

Chukat

Final Journeys in the Desert

Numbers 19:1–22:1

THE SIXTH SECTION OF THE BOOK OF NUMBERS OPENS WITH the law (or "rule," *chukat*, in Hebrew) governing the process of purification from the state of ritual defilement that a person contracts through contact with a human corpse. After this, the Torah's narrative advances to the final years of the Jewish people's wanderings in the desert until they arrived at the threshold of the Land of Israel.

FIRST READING
Numbers 19:1–17

On the day the Tabernacle was inaugurated, 1 Nisan 2449, G-d instructed Moses how to purify the Jewish people from ritual defilement contracted by contact with a human corpse.

Conquering Death

זֹאת חֻקַּת הַתּוֹרָה וְגוֹ': (במדבר יט, ב)

[G-d instructed Moses to tell the Jewish people,] "This is the rule of the Torah.…"

From the fact that everything eventually dies, it is tempting to conclude that life is futile and meaningless. This depressing world-view leads to spiritual paralysis – an unwillingness or inability to act positively – that is diametrically opposed to our Divine mission, which asserts that there is indeed a purpose to life and that we can fulfill it.

Therefore, the Torah declares everyone who comes in contact with death to be "ritually defiled," meaning that they are not allowed into the arena of life – the Tabernacle (or its successor, the holy Temple) – until they are cured of the depression (or potential for depression) that results from an encounter with death.

The logic of nature decrees that sooner or later everything and everyone dies; to defy this law is to defy logic. For this reason, the rite of purification from death must likewise defy logic. The Torah therefore states that although the rite purifies someone who has contracted ritual impurity, the priests who prepare the ingredients for the rite become – illogically – ritually defiled themselves[1] by doing so.

Similarly, by studying the Torah and fulfilling G-d's commandments with an eye toward connecting to G-d beyond the limits of logic, we can live our lives free of the paralysis of all forms of depression.[2]

1. Albeit to a lesser degree.
2. *Likutei Sichot,* vol. 4, p. 1058.

SECOND READING
Numbers 19:18–20:6

The priests who prepared the materials used for the purification rite were rendered ritually defiled themselves by doing so.

Pure Altruism

וּמַזֵּה מֵי הַנִּדָּה וגו': (במדבר יט, כא)

**[G-d instructed Moses to tell the Jewish people,]
"Anyone who [carries enough of] the sprinkling
water [to] sprinkle [with becomes defiled]."**

Although the rite purifies the defiled, it also defiles the pure. Thus, the priests who prepared the materials used for the purification rite had to be prepared to become temporarily ritually defiled – and thus excluded from all things holy – in order to purify their fellow Jews. It was the priests' willingness to overlook their personal interest that "inspired" G-d to "overlook" the bounds of nature and logic in order to wipe away the negativity and depression that threatened the person in need of ritual purification.

To be sure, the priests knew that G-d would reward them for putting aside their own purity and troubling themselves to purify their ritually defiled brethren. But in order for the ritual to work, they could not have this in mind; their motives had to be pure and selfless.

From this example, we can learn first of all how willing we should be to help another person reenter the dominion of purity and holiness, even if doing so requires us to become temporarily sullied ourselves. Secondly, we can learn how much care we must take to ensure that our motives are pure.[3]

THIRD READING
Numbers 20:7–13

At G-d's direction, the Jewish people remained encamped at the southern border of the Land of Israel for 19 years after Korach staged his rebellion against Moses. They then wandered in the desert for another 19 years. On 10 Nisan 2487, Moses' sister Miriam died. As soon as she died, the Jewish people's source of water – the miraculous well that had followed them in the desert – disappeared, for it had existed in her merit. G-d instructed Moses to restore the well by speaking to the rock from which the water had previously flowed.

Tending to the Needs of Others

וְהַקְהֵל אֶת הָעֵדָה . . . וְדִבַּרְתֶּם אֶל הַסֶּלַע לְעֵינֵיהֶם וְגוֹ': (במדבר כ, ח)

**[G-d told Moses,] "Assemble the congregation...
and speak to the rock in their presence...."**

When G-d restored the well that had existed in Miriam's merit, He did so through Moses, for the leaders of the Jewish people are responsible not only for guiding them spiritually and leading them politically but for providing for their physical needs as well.

We are all leaders, or potential leaders. The lesson of Miriam's well teaches us to assume responsibility for both the spiritual and material needs of our charges – or prepare to do so when our turn as leaders comes.[4]

---

4. *Likutei Sichot*, vol. 18, p. 260.

WEDNESDAY

FOURTH READING

Numbers 20:14–21

Moses then asked the king of Edom to allow the Jewish people to pass through his land on the way to the Land of Israel. The Edomites refused, so Moses led the people southward, detouring around their territory.

Emulating Esau

וַיִּשְׁלַח מֹשֶׁה מַלְאָכִים ... אֶל מֶלֶךְ אֱדוֹם כֹּה
אָמַר אָחִיךָ יִשְׂרָאֵל וְגוֹ': (במדבר כ, יד)

**Moses sent messengers...to the king of Edom,
[saying,] "So says Israel, your brother...."**

The Jewish people are descended from Jacob; the kingdom of Edom descended from Jacob's brother Esau.

There are two general paths to spiritual self-refinement: that of the naturally pious, who are not tempted by evil, and that of those who behave righteously despite their attraction to materiality. Jacob personified the naturally pious type, while Esau personified the type challenged by an inborn attraction to materiality. Esau's Divine mission was to demonstrate that even a person strongly drawn toward material indulgence can overcome temptation, using the physical world for holy purposes and thereby transforming it into G-d's home.

We, too, are given Esau's task of making the physical world into a home for G-d. But before we emulate Esau, we must first emulate Jacob, immersing ourselves in the study of the Torah and the fulfillment of G-d's commandments. The spiritual strength we thereby garner enables us to go on to transform material reality.[5]

5. *Likutei Sichot*, vol. 20, pp. 108–114.

FIFTH READING
Numbers 20:22–21:9

Moses then asked the kingdom of Moab, which was situated to the east of Edom, for permission to pass through their land, but they too refused. After this, Moses' brother Aaron died, and the nation of Amalek attacked the Jewish people.

Overcoming Amalek

וַיִּשְׁמַע . . . כִּי בָּא יִשְׂרָאֵל דֶּרֶךְ הָאֲתָרִים וַיִּלָּחֶם בְּיִשְׂרָאֵל וגו': (במדבר כא, א)

[The Amalekites] heard that Israel was coming by the route that the spies had taken ... and waged war against Israel.

The word "spies" in this verse refers both to the scouts whom Moses had sent to spy out the land[6] and to the Ark of the Covenant, which went before the Jewish people during their trek through the desert.[7]

Our inner Amalek attacks us in two ways. Sometimes he attacks via the intellect, explaining why we should ignore our commitments both to G-d and to our better selves. In such cases, it is enough to contemplate how unprofitable it is to follow his lead and how wise it is to remain true to our higher callings. This is "the route the spies had taken," seeking out the natural means of conquering the enemy and using these means.

At other times, our inner Amalek brazenly defies logic, insisting on our obedience to our worst instincts without any regard to rhyme or reason. In such cases, logic is of no help. If, however, we recall our intrinsic bond with G-d, Amalek is powerless against us. This is relying on "the Ark of the Covenant," which scatters all our enemies before us.[8]

6. Numbers 13.
7. Ibid. 10:33–36.
8. *Likutei Sichot*, vol. 38, pp. 83–84.

SIXTH READING
Numbers 21:10–20

The Jewish people traveled all around the kingdom of Moab and then turned northward. The Amorites, who lived north of Moab, planned to ambush the Jews as they crossed the border into their territory, but G-d caused an earthquake, killing the Amorites in their hideouts. The Jewish people only knew of this miraculous deliverance because the well that accompanied them detoured through the Amorite's ravine and carried the Amorite corpses within sight of the Jewish people.

From Salt Water to Fresh Water

אָז יָשִׁיר יִשְׂרָאֵל אֶת הַשִּׁירָה הַזֹּאת עֲלִי בְאֵר וגו': (במדבר כא, יז)

Then Israel recited this poem, "Ascend, well...."

Allegorically, rising well-water signifies our aspiration for Divine consciousness. Just as salty seawater is purified and made drinkable by passing through subterranean channels, our focus and desires in life are purified by our souls' descent from heaven into the materialism of this world. Acutely aware of our distance from G-d, our yearning for Divine closeness intensifies, purging all foreign desires from our consciousness.

The intensity of this yearning elicits an equal Divine reaction: G-d answers our yearning for Him by revealing His presence to us as we study His Torah.[9]

9. *Or HaTorah, Bemidbar*, vol. 3, pp. 844–848.

SHABBAT

SEVENTH READING
Numbers 21:21–22:1

The Jewish people then conquered the land that Sichon, king of the Amorites, had taken from the Ammonites and the Moabites. Sichon had been able to overcome these nations only by hiring the sorcerer Balaam to curse them.

Keys to Success

עַל כֵּן יֹאמְרוּ הַמֹּשְׁלִים וְגוֹ': (במדבר כא, כז)

Concerning this [victory], those who speak in parables said....

Allegorically, this and the following verse can be read:

Those who rule over their material desires –

Will say, "We have made an accounting concerning the descent of our soul into our bodies, and have realized that we must generate Divine consciousness in order to dispel the spiritual darkness." This awareness will –

Let the "city of speech" ["Sichon" is related to the word for "speech"] *be built*, i.e., bolster their prayer (which is recited aloud) and the study of the Torah (which is studied aloud), enabling them to thereby elicit Divine consciousness.

For fire, the flames of their all-consuming love of G-d –

Has issued from this accounting. This devotion to G-d –

Has consumed Ar of Moab: i.e., it will enable us to overcome both the illusions[10] that make us think that our own inventive scheming can lead us to greater wealth –

And the masters of the high places of Arnon: i.e., the haughtiness that comes along with material success.[11]

---

10. "Moab" is here interpreted as *Mei-Av*, meaning "from father," "father" being the Kabbalistic appellation for the *sefirah* of *chochmah*, in this context, the *chochmah* ("insight") of the animating soul.
11. *Likutei Torah* 3:64d–66d.

Balak

Curses into Blessings

Numbers 22:2–25:9

THE SEVENTH SECTION OF THE BOOK OF NUMBERS DESCRIBES the plot of King Balak of Moab and his hired sorcerer Balaam to curse the Jewish people in order to prevent them from attacking Moab. G-d frustrates their plan and forces Balaam to bless the Jewish people instead.

SUNDAY

FIRST READING
Numbers 22:2–12

King Balak of Moab became terrified that the Jewish people would attack his country, even though it was common knowledge that G-d had not promised them the territory of Moab. Balak sent for the sorcerer Balaam, proposing that he curse the Jews.

The Antidote to Evil

וַיִּשְׁלַח מַלְאָכִים אֶל בִּלְעָם וגו': (במדבר כב, ה)

[Balak] sent messengers to Balaam.

Two enemies opposed us on our journey from Egypt to the Land of Israel: Amalek and Balaam.[1]

What emboldened these two personalities to oppose G-d's plan was their common ancestry with the Jewish people: Amalek was a grandson of Jacob's brother Esau,[2] and Balaam was another name for Jacob's father-in-law Laban.[3] This common ancestry made them think that they had a say in the Jewish people's destiny.

Similarly, the evils represented by Amalek and Balaam oppose our journey from spiritual slavery to spiritual freedom.[4] Their common denominator is their haughty claim that they should have a say regarding what should be the proper Jewish attitude toward life.

We can resist their claims by asserting that the sole arbiter of Jewish life is the Torah. By cultivating humility – the opposite of the haughtiness demonstrated by Amalek and Balaam – we can summon the Divine strength to ensure that our attitudes remain holy and positive, free from unholy, negative influences.[5]

---

1. Regarding Amalek, see Exodus 17:8–16 and Numbers 21:1 (and Rashi ad loc.).
2. Genesis 36:12.
3. *Sanhedrin* 105a.
4. Regarding Amalek, see pp. 132, 318, and 402.
5. *Likutei Sichot*, vol. 3, pp. 338–340.

SECOND READING

Numbers 22:13–20

The sorcerer-prophet Balaam agreed to curse the Jews.

Exceeding the Bounds of Logic

וּלְכָה נָּא קָבָה לִּי אֵת הָעָם הַזֶּה: (במדבר כב, יז)

**[Balak said to Balaam,] "Please come
and curse this people for me."**

Balaam knew through prophecy that G-d had forbidden the
Israelites to attack Moab, and that therefore Balak had nothing to
fear. Nonetheless, Balaam did not reveal this fact to Balak, because
Balaam hated the Israelites fanatically and relished the opportunity to curse them. But G-d not only prevented Balaam from
cursing the Jews; He forced him to bless them by transforming
Balaam's curses into blessings.

Just as Balaam's anti-Semitism and the curses inspired by it
exceeded the bounds of logic, G-d's love for the Jews and the
blessings inspired by it exceed the bounds of logic.

It is therefore no surprise that the chief reference to the Messianic Redemption is found in Balaam's curses-turned-blessings.
The essence of the Redemption will be the revelation of the inner
dimension of our Divine soul, which connects us with G-d in a
manner that goes beyond the boundaries of logic.

Accordingly, the surest way to hasten the advent of the
Redemption is by demonstrating our devotion to the Torah's
principles of goodness and holiness even when – and especially
when – doing so defies logic.[6]

6. *Igeret HaKodesh* 4 (105b); *Likutei Sichot*, vol. 38, p. 89.

THIRD READING
Numbers 22:21–38

Anxious to curse the Jews, Balaam arose early in the morning, saddling his donkey in order to meet Balak. G-d told Balaam that his evil enthusiasm was counter-weighed by the holy enthusiasm that the patriarch Abraham had demonstrated by saddling his donkey early in the morning in order to selflessly obey G-d's command to sacrifice his son Isaac.[7]

Materiality

וַיָּקָם בִּלְעָם בַּבֹּקֶר וַיַּחֲבֹשׁ אֶת אֲתֹנוֹ וגו': (במדבר כב, כא)

Balaam arose in the morning and saddled his donkey.

The word for "donkey" (*chamor*) is phonetically related to the word for "materiality" (*chomer*). Thus, when the Torah informs us that both Abraham and Balaam saddled their donkeys, it is allegorically telling us how they related to the materiality of this world.

The Torah portrays Balaam saddling his donkey in a negative light, for Balaam used his donkey for forbidden purposes and harnessed it in order to rebel against G-d's will. Therefore, we learn from him that we should not attempt to make use of what is forbidden to us.

In contrast, the Torah portrays Abraham saddling his donkey in a positive light, for Abraham used his donkey to fulfill G-d's will. Thus, from Abraham we learn that we should harness materiality for the service of G-d, and that we should do so enthusiastically.[8]

---

7. See Genesis 22:3.
8. *Hitva'aduyot 5742*, vol. 4, pp. 1807–1808.

FOURTH READING

Numbers 22:39–23:12

Balaam arrived in Moab. Balak proceeded to take Balaam to a place he thought would be conducive to cursing the Jews. But G-d forced Balaam to praise and bless the Jews rather than curse them.

Hidden Treasure

כִּי מֵרֹאשׁ צֻרִים אֶרְאֶנּוּ וּמִגְּבָעוֹת אֲשׁוּרֶנּוּ וְגוֹ': (במדבר כג, ט)

[Balaam said,] "For from their beginning, I see [the Jews] as [sturdy as] mountain peaks, and I behold them as [sturdy as] hills."

The "sturdiness" referred to here is our unwavering, selfless devotion to G-d, including our willingness to lay down our lives, if necessary, rather than betray this devotion. We inherit this quality from the patriarchs and matriarchs, who internalized their devotion to G-d so intensely that it became part of their very being, enabling them to pass it on to us.

This intensity of devotion is an expression of our Divine soul, for the natural soul is not capable of sacrificing its own existence for a higher purpose that contradicts its own, material interests. The *persistence* of this trait in the Jewish people is a further expression of our Divine soul, for nature dictates that cultural ideals get weaker as the generations progress.

Our innate willingness to lay down our lives for G-d is a gift that we can access at any time, using it as a tool to keep us focused on our goals in life, particularly our Divine mission to refine and elevate the world.[9]

9. *Tanya*, chapter 25, etc.

FIFTH READING
Numbers 23:13–26

Balak then took Balaam to a second location, thinking that per-haps it would be easier for Balaam to curse the Jewish people from there. But once again, G-d forced Balaam to bless the Jews rather than curse them.

The Sabbath and the Workweek

לֹא הִבִּיט אָוֶן בְּיַעֲקֹב וְלֹא רָאָה עָמָל בְּיִשְׂרָאֵל
ה' אֱלֹקָיו עִמּוֹ וְגוֹ': (במדבר כג, כא)

**[Balaam said, "G-d] does not look at the evil in
[the descendants of] Jacob, and sees no perversity
in Israel. G-d, their G-d, is with them."**

Our patriarch Jacob faced many struggles during his life. G-d gave him his additional name, Israel, in acknowledgment of how he overcame these struggles.

Accordingly, the name "Jacob" applies to us as we struggle with mundane reality during the workweek, whereas "Israel" refers to us as we rise above mundane reality on the Sabbath.

When we attempt to pray during the week, we must strive to overcome the many confusing and distracting thoughts that intrude from our involvement in worldly affairs. We are only able to succeed in this struggle because "G-d, their G-d, is with them."

On the Sabbath, however, we do not have to expend any effort to rise above the distractions of the mundane world; all we need to do is be sensitive to the special illumination of our soul that accompanies the Sabbath. Thus, on the Sabbath, the same phrase "G-d, their G-d, is with them" takes on a new meaning – that we attain a higher consciousness of G-d than we possess during the workweek.[10]

10. *Likutei Torah* 3:70c.

SIXTH READING
Numbers 23:27–24:13

Balak then took Balaam to a third location, thinking that perhaps it would be easier for Balaam to curse the Jewish people from there. Balaam was about to curse them, but then he saw how the Jewish people had been faithful in their marriages and had camped such that no one could accidentally look inside someone else's tent. The Jewish people's modest conduct so impressed Balaam that he decided on his own to bless them rather than curse them.

Tents and Sanctuaries

מַה טֹּבוּ אֹהָלֶיךָ יַעֲקֹב מִשְׁכְּנֹתֶיךָ יִשְׂרָאֵל: (במדבר כד, ה)

**[Balaam said,] "How good are your tents,
Jacob; your sanctuaries, Israel."**

"Jacob" refers to us in our role as G-d's faithful servants, while "Israel" refers to us in our role as G-d's loving children. We all play both roles – sometimes one at a time, sometimes simultaneously while emphasizing one or the other.

When we serve G-d as "Jacob" – as His disciplined, faithful servants – we make protective "tents" that shield the spiritual lives that we have built for ourselves from the intrusion of negative, materialistic consciousness. When we serve G-d as "Israel" – as His loving, devoted children – we make our lives into a "sanctuary" for G-d, enhancing our Divine consciousness and identifying with G-d's values and dreams for His world.[11]

---

11. *Sefer HaMa'amarim Yiddish*, p. 122.

SHABBAT

SEVENTH READING
Numbers 24:14–25:9

Having blessed the Jewish people three times, Balaam prophesied the fate of Balak's people, as well as that of other nations, in the future. In these prophecies, he also mentioned how the Jewish people's future king – the Messiah – would bring all humanity to serve G-d.

Transforming Adversaries into Advocates

וְיֵרְדְּ מִיַּעֲקֹב וְהֶאֱבִיד שָׂרִיד מֵעִיר: (במדבר כד, יט)

[Balaam said,] "A ruler will come out of [the descendants of] Jacob and destroy the remnant of the city."

One of the defining characteristics of the Messianic Era, as described by the prophet Isaiah, is that "[foreign] kings will tutor your children, and their princesses will be your wet nurses."[12]

The members of a royal family are normally the national figures most steeped in the cultural values of their society – and who most proudly and loyally identify with it, as well. As such, it would seem that these would be the last people to whom we should entrust the care and education of our tiny, impressionable children! But in the Messianic Era, the nations of the world will be awakened to the values of the Torah and thereby transformed from its adversaries into its supporters.

Balaam himself presages this transformation, inasmuch as G-d transformed his attempted curses into great blessings and praise.

Certainly, then, working to transform our adversaries into friends and advocates will help hasten the advent of the final Redemption.[13]

12. Isaiah 49:23.
13. *Likutei Sichot*, vol. 23, p. 171.

Pinechas

Preparing for Conquest
Numbers 25:10–30:1

THE EIGHTH SECTION OF THE BOOK OF NUMBERS OPENS with the account of how G-d installed Moses' great-nephew Pinechas into the priesthood. The sorcerer Balaam, having failed to curse the Jewish people, devised a scheme to entice the Jewish people into the sins of immorality and idolatry. Balaam believed that this would anger G-d so much that He would wipe out the Jews Himself. In the course of this incident, Aaron's grandson Pinechas risked his life to slay two of the most brazen offenders. In reward for Pinechas' zealousness, G-d bestowed the priesthood on him. The Torah's narrative then continues with the final census of the Jewish people in the desert, the laws of inheritance, the transfer of leadership from Moses to Joshua, and the laws of the daily and festival sacrifices.

FIRST READING

Numbers 25:10–26:4

When G-d made Aaron and his sons priests, the priesthood could only be passed on to sons born to them from then on. Aaron's grandson Pinechas, however, had been born before this, so he had not been eligible for the priesthood. Nevertheless, as a reward for his zealousness, G-d made Pinechas a priest.

Attaining the Unattainable

הִנְנִי נֹתֵן לוֹ ... בְּרִית כְּהֻנַּת עוֹלָם וגו': (במדבר כה, יב-יג)

[G-d said regarding Pinechas,] "I hereby give him ... the eternal covenant of priesthood."

When we elicit a Divine revelation, its intensity depends upon the intensity of our initiative. Such a revelation is therefore limited, since as finite beings, we can only produce finite initiatives. An unsolicited Divine revelation, in contrast, can be infinite. But since it is infinite, we finite recipients cannot fully absorb it. The advantage of limited, elicited revelations is that we have laid the groundwork for them, so we can integrate them into our lives.

The Divine revelations of the Messianic future will have both advantages. They will convey all the infinity of unsolicited revelations, but – paradoxically – we will be able to fully absorb them. The finite will be able to absorb the infinite.

Priesthood, being hereditary, is similar to an unsolicited Divine revelation: no amount of human initiative can procure it. The one exception was Pinechas. His self-sacrifice elevated him above his finitude, enabling him to attain the unattainable.

Similarly, when we emulate Pinechas' self-sacrifice, we can experience infinite Divine revelations even while still in our pre-Messianic, finite world. This, in turn, serves to hasten the advent of the Messianic Redemption.[1]

1. *Likutei Sichot*, vol. 4, pp. 1070, 1074.

SECOND READING
Numbers 26:5–51

G-d then instructed Moses to take a census of the Jewish people.

The Keys of Redemption

וּבְנֵי אֱלִיאָב נְמוּאֵל וְדָתָן וַאֲבִירָם וְגוֹ': (במדבר כו, ט)

The sons of Eli'av were Nemu'eil, Dathan, and Aviram.

It would seem unnecessary for the Torah to mention Dathan and Aviram in a census whose purpose was to number those living at the time, since these individuals were already long dead.[2] The same is true of Eir and Onan, who are also mentioned[3] despite having died long before.[4]

The reason the Torah does count these individuals in this census, taken in preparation for the Jewish people's entry into the Land of Israel, is to teach us that negating the faults that these people personified was necessary in order for us to enter the Promised Land – and remains necessary even today.

Eir and Onan did not honor the holiness of their procreative power. We are taught that this lack of respect delays the Redemption.[5] Dathan and Aviram rebelled against Moses' leadership. Since contesting Moses' leadership was tantamount to contesting G-d's leadership,[6] they were not worthy of entering the Land of Israel.

From this we learn that by honoring the sanctity of our procreative energies and submitting ourselves both to G-d's will and to the leadership of His representatives on earth, we can hasten both our personal redemptions and the collective Redemption of the world in general.[7]

2. Numbers 16:1–14, 23–33.
3. Ibid. 26:19.
4. Genesis 38:1–10.
5. *Likutei Torah* (Arizal) on Isaiah 59:20; *Derech Mitzvotecha* 2b–3a.
6. As stated in this verse.
7. *Hitva'aduyot 5710*, pp. 143–145.

THIRD READING
Numbers 26:52–27:5

After the census was completed, G-d instructed Moses how to divide up the Land of Israel among the Jewish people. After hearing these laws, the five daughters of a deceased Jew named Tzelofchad argued that they should be collectively given a portion of land. Moses brought their case before G-d, and G-d informed him that Tzelofchad's daughters were correct.

Feminine Influence

וַתִּקְרַבְנָה בְּנוֹת צְלָפְחָד וגו': (במדבר כז, א)

The daughters of Tzelofchad came forward [to present their case to Moses].

Tzelofchad's daughters' desire for a portion of the Land of Israel was characteristic of all the Jewish women of their generation. Due to their love of the land, none of these women sympathized with the spies' counsel against entering it.[8]

The purpose of creation is to reveal G-d's presence in the world, which the Jewish people were meant to accomplish by entering the Land of Israel and engaging in mundane life in a holy way. This is why the Jewish women cherished the Land of Israel. They knew that "the eyes of G-d are always upon it,"[9] meaning that it is uniquely suited to revealing the Divine dimension within all mundane acts.

By cherishing this ideal, Jewish women in all places can positively influence not only their own conduct but that of their husbands, both within and outside the home. This, in turn, ensures Divine blessing in all aspects of their physical lives, as well as those of their families.[10]

---

8. Rashi on Numbers 26:64.
9. Deuteronomy 11:12.
10. *Hitva'aduyot 5717*, vol. 3, pp. 133–137.

FOURTH READING
Numbers 27:6–23

In preparation for his imminent death, Moses asked G-d to appoint a leader for the Jewish people in his stead. G-d instructed him to appoint Joshua as his successor.

The Power of Prayer

יִפְקֹד ה' ... אִישׁ עַל הָעֵדָה: (במדבר כז, טז)

[Moses said to G-d,] "Let G-d ... appoint a man over the congregation."

Moses knew full well that G-d would provide a leader for the Jewish people after his death. However, he was concerned that on account of the incident of the Golden Calf, G-d would decide that the people did not deserve a leader similar to him, that is, one uniquely blessed with the same qualities that he himself possessed.

Moses had also learned from the incident of the Golden Calf that G-d allows Himself to be influenced by our prayers, even altering His plans on their account. He therefore now, as then, asked G-d to deal with the Jewish people beyond the strict measure of the law. Now, as then, G-d assented to Moses' pleas.

From this, we see both how necessary our prayers are and how powerful they are. G-d wants us to ask Him to alter His plans for our better interests.[11]

11. *Hitva'aduyot 5745*, vol. 5, pp. 2642–2643, 2655–2657.

FIFTH READING
Numbers 28:1–15

G-d then instructed Moses regarding the daily and holiday communal sacrifices that were to be regularly offered up in the Tabernacle.

Awareness and Purpose

אֶת קָרְבָּנִי . . . תִּשְׁמְרוּ לְהַקְרִיב לִי בְּמוֹעֲדוֹ: (במדבר כח, ב)

[G-d instructed Moses to tell the Jewish people,] "You must watch over My offering, offering it up to Me at its appointed time."

G-d had responded to Moses' request for a successor by telling him to appoint Joshua for this position. G-d's subsequent instructions regarding the daily and holiday communal sacrifices were a further response to Moses' request.

This is because the need for a physical, human leader is part of our need to recognize that our lives – and indeed, the world in general – are not undirected and purposeless. Therefore, after providing them with a human leader, G-d ensured that the people always recognize that they are subject to Him, their Divine leader – that He runs the world and that all aspects of life occur through Divine providence. G-d accomplished this by instituting the daily and holiday communal sacrifices, which served to remind us that G-d is constantly present in our daily lives.

Our daily and holiday prayers correspond to the daily and holiday sacrifices, and substitute for them in their absence. Their purpose, too, is to enhance our awareness and recognition that the world is not subject merely to the blind laws of nature, but that there is also a G-d in the world, directing it toward its goal and giving it purpose.[12]

12. *Likutei Sichot*, vol. 12, p. 18.

SIXTH READING
Numbers 28:16–29:11

After detailing the procedures for the daily sacrifices, G-d instructed Moses regarding the weekly Sabbath sacrifices, the sacrifices offered up on the first day of every Jewish month, and the sacrifices offered up on the holidays. In the course of these instructions, G-d referred to *Rosh HaShanah*, the Jewish New Year, as a day for sounding the shofar, or ram's horn.

Renewal

וּבַחֹדֶשׁ הַשְּׁבִיעִי בְּאֶחָד לַחֹדֶשׁ ... יוֹם תְּרוּעָה יִהְיֶה לָכֶם: (במדבר כט, א)

[**G-d instructed Moses to tell the Jewish
people,**] **"The first day of the seventh month…
must be a day of shofar-sounding for you."**

G-d sent our Divine soul into the foreign environment of this material world for its own edification, which we accomplish by studying the Torah and fulfilling its commandments. But by indulging in the delights of this world, we become increasingly estranged from our Divine soul's native environment. We are drawn further and further into a world that is not concerned with Divinity, and we eventually all but forget about holiness and purity.

But at some point, we remember who we are and we cry out to G-d. This is the wordless blast of the shofar, which utters the innermost voice of our soul in our remorse over its failings, our longing for its Divine home, and our desire to rededicate ourselves to our higher purpose. When G-d hears this cry, it arouses His mercy, and He forgives us, restoring us to our former intimacy with Him.

Rosh HaShanah is thus a time of renewal, of returning to our source and drawing new levels of connection from the inexhaustible wellsprings of our relationship with G-d.[13]

13. *Torat Shmuel 5637 (Vechachah)* 80.

SEVENTH READING
Numbers 29:12–30:1

Special communal offerings were sacrificed every day of the
seven-day holiday of *Sukkot* and on the following day, the holiday
of *Shemini Atzeret.*

Absorbing Divine Revelation

בַּיּוֹם הַשְּׁמִינִי עֲצֶרֶת תִּהְיֶה לָכֶם וְגוֹ': (במדבר כט, לה)

**[G-d instructed Moses to tell the Jewish people,] "The
eighth day [of *Sukkot*] is a time of restriction for you."**

The Hebrew word for "restriction" (*atzeret*) also means "absorption" or "retention," preventing something from escaping one's
grasp. The Torah describes the seventh day of Passover, which
celebrates the Exodus from Egypt, as "a time of restriction *for
G-d, your G-d.*"[14] In contrast, it describes the eighth day of *Sukkot,*
which celebrates G-d's protection of us during our trek in the
desert, as "a time of restriction *for you.*"

When the Jewish people left Egypt, they were not spiritually
mature enough to absorb the great Divine revelations that they
had witnessed. Therefore, these revelations remained "for G-d,"
kept in safekeeping, so to speak, until they were ready for them.

By the time the Torah was given at Mount Sinai, the Jewish
people had matured spiritually, and could absorb Divine revelation. Therefore, from then on, throughout the bulk of their trek
through the desert, these revelations were "for you."

On the personal level, we are all reborn into a higher relationship with G-d every year on Passover, but we are not yet mature
enough to appreciate this new relationship. Six months later, at
the end of *Sukkot,* we have matured enough to absorb our new
Divine consciousness, and it becomes truly ours.[15]

14. Deuteronomy 16:8.
15. *Likutei Torah* 2:13; 4:76; *Sefer HaMa'amarim 5702,* p. 35.

Matot

Facing Challenges
Numbers 30:2–32:42

THE NINTH SECTION OF THE BOOK OF NUMBERS BEGINS AS Moses addresses the heads of the tribes (*Matot*, in Hebrew), teaching them the laws of vows and oaths. It then resumes the historical narrative, recounting the events during the last year of the Jewish people's trek in the desert as they prepare to cross the Jordan River into the Land of Israel, particularly G-d's instruction to attack the evil nation of Midian and wipe out its adult population.

FIRST READING

Numbers 30:2–17

G-d instructed Moses regarding the laws governing how a person can make vows and oaths to G-d.

Indulging in Permitted Pleasures

אִישׁ כִּי יִדֹּר נֶדֶר וְגוֹ': (במדבר ל, ג)

[G-d instructed Moses to tell the Jewish people,] "If a person makes a vow...."

The Torah generally allows us to indulge in pleasures that G-d has put in this world for our enjoyment, as long as doing so does not compromise our Divine consciousness.[1]

But when we notice that a particular indulgence affects us negatively, we should renounce it – at least temporarily. If we find ourselves incapable of resisting the urge to overindulge, we can make a formal vow, which forbids the indulgence just as if it had been forbidden by the Torah.[2] If, on the other hand, we feel that we are capable of controlling ourselves, it is better to abstain from the indulgence without taking a vow.

In either case, we must all be honest with ourselves about which aspects of life we are ready to elevate and which we are not, and to what lengths we must go in order to curb our appetites.[3] By guarding ourselves from things that would be detrimental to our Divine consciousness, we both weaken materialism's power over us and increase the power of holiness within us. This itself gives us more power to resist negative influences and focus on the spiritual aspects of life's permitted pleasures.[4]

---

1. *Yerushalmi Kidushin* 4:12; *Yerushalmi Nedarim* 9:5.
2. *Avot* 3:13.
3. *Likutei Torah* 3:83b, 84b; *Reshimot* 51; *Likutei Sichot*, vol. 33, pp. 186 ff.
4. *Likutei Sichot*, vol. 4, p. 1077.

SECOND READING

Numbers 31:1–12

Even though the Midianites had no reason to oppose the Jews, they nonetheless joined the Moabites in enticing the Jewish people into sinning in order that G-d punish the Jewish people. In recompense for their consummately evil behavior, G-d told Moses to send the Jewish army to attack the Midianites.

Reciprocal Love

וַיְדַבֵּר מֹשֶׁה אֶל הָעָם לֵאמֹר הֵחָלְצוּ מֵאִתְּכֶם אֲנָשִׁים לַצָּבָא
וְיִהְיוּ עַל מִדְיָן לָתֵת נִקְמַת ה' בְּמִדְיָן: (במדבר לא, ג)

[Moses told the Jewish people,] "Carry out G-d's revenge against Midian."

G-d sought vengeance against the Midianites because they had caused the death of thousands of Jews. But these Jews died because the Midianite women enticed them into idol worship and immoral transgressions. In other words, these Jews died because they had sinned!

We see here how much G-d loves His people. He cherishes even those among us who lack the moral fortitude to resist temptation, holding accountable those who take advantage of these people. This intense love can only inspire us to love Him with a reciprocal intensity, devoting ourselves to accomplishing His purposes in the world.[5]

5. *Sichot Kodesh 5734*, vol. 2, p. 323.

THIRD READING

Numbers 31:13–24

The Jews took the Midianite women and children captive. Since the adult women were those who had enticed the Jewish people into sinning, Moses instructed the Jewish soldiers to kill them.

Environmental Influences

וְכָל אִשָּׁה יֹדַעַת אִישׁ לְמִשְׁכַּב זָכָר הֲרֹגוּ: (במדבר לא, יז)

[Moses told the Jewish people,] "You must kill every [Midianite] woman who can have carnal intercourse with a man."

Those Midianite women who had seduced Israelite men clearly deserved the death penalty. By causing the Israelites to sin, they had proven themselves to be either outright malicious or incapable of standing up to their evil leaders.

Those Midianite women who had not seduced any Israelites but who were carnally experienced had to be killed because their attitudes toward carnality had been corrupted by the depraved Midianite society of which they were a part. Their attitudes not only rendered them unfit to join the ranks of the Jewish people, but made them a dangerous influence that could not be allowed to seep into the society of holiness and corrupt it.

The mature but inexperienced Midianite women had to be killed because the fact that they were ready at any time to join the ranks of their experienced compatriots meant that they already considered themselves part of the depraved Midianite culture and had absorbed its values.

From here we see how important it is to ensure that our youth grow up in a proper moral environment.[6]

---

6. *Likutei Sichot*, vol. 18, p. 368.

FOURTH READING

Numbers 31:25–41

The soldiers were allowed to keep half of the spoils of war and the other half was to be distributed to the rest of the Jewish people. The soldiers had to give ⅟₅₀₀th of their half to the priests, and the people had to give ⅟₅₀th of their half to the Levites.

Eradicating Hatred

וּמִמַּחֲצִת בְּנֵי יִשְׂרָאֵל תִּקַּח אֶחָד אָחֻז מִן הַחֲמִשִּׁים

... וְנָתַתָּה אֹתָם לַלְוִיִּם וְגוֹ': (במדבר לא, ל)

Take one fiftieth from the Israelite's half...and give it to the Levites.

The tribe of Levi was usually exempt from military service and received none of the spoils. In the war against Midian, however, the Levites were conscripted and received a portion of the spoils.

This is because whereas the purpose of other wars was to take possession of the Land of Israel, the attack against Midian was solely for the purpose of eradicating the evil that Midian represented. Midian had not had any reason to oppose the Jewish people; they did so only out of pure, senseless hatred.

With regard to our spiritual lives, we are all like Levites – dedicated to furthering G-d's goals in this world. The more dedicated we become to this cause, the less concerned we become with the passing matters of mundane life. This does not mean, however, that we should ignore our surroundings altogether. Like the Levites of Moses' day, when it comes to fighting "Midian" – to eradicating baseless hatred between people – we need to take our stand on the front lines along with everyone else.[7]

7. *Likutei Sichot,* vol. 23, pp. 206–213.

FIFTH READING
Numbers 31:42–54

The officers of the army counted the soldiers in their charge, and found that miraculously, not even one was missing.

The Proper Response to Miracles

וַיֹּאמְרוּ אֶל מֹשֶׁה ... וְלֹא נִפְקַד מִמֶּנּוּ אִישׁ: (במדבר לא, מט)

**[The officers] said to Moses, "...Not
one man is missing from us."**

Even when a battle is won, it is only natural that there will be casualties. The fact that after the battle with Midian not one of the 12,000 soldiers had been lost was a clear indication that their victory had been miraculous.

The proper response to an open demonstration of G-d's miraculous protection or favor is to acknowledge it – not to try to rationalize it. Thus, the returning Jewish army responded exactly as they should have, as is recounted in the next verse: "We therefore wish to bring an offering for G-d." They donated the jewelry found among the spoils of battle to the Tabernacle, acknowledging that they owed their victory to G-d alone.

We are taught to give a portion of our earnings to charity in any case, in order to express our awareness that it is G-d's blessing that enables us to accrue wealth[8] and that all that we possess is truly His.[9] But when wealth comes our way miraculously – such that it makes no sense to think that our own efforts earned it – it should be immediately obvious that this wealth belongs to G-d even before we "give" it to Him.

By taking care to acknowledge G-d's miracles, we strengthen our ability to sense His no less miraculous involvement in our daily, "non-miraculous" lives, as well.[10]

---

8. Proverbs 10:22.
9. 1 Chronicles 29:14.
10. *Likutei Sichot*, vol. 5, pp. 68–76.

SIXTH READING

Numbers 32:1–19

Noticing that the territory of Kings Sichon and Og – which the Jewish people had just conquered – were suited to grazing cattle and flocks, the tribes of Reuben and Gad asked Moses if they could take possession of these territories and not cross the Jordan River into the Land of Israel. Moses agreed, but made them promise to help the other tribes conquer their territories west of the Jordan before settling themselves on the river's east bank.

Moderating Asceticism

וַיֹּאמְרוּ אִם מָצָאנוּ חֵן בְּעֵינֶיךָ וְגו': (במדבר לב, ה)

[The tribes of Reuben and Gad] said [to Moses,] "If it pleases you...."

The tribes of Reuben and Gad preferred to be shepherds (outside the Land of Israel) rather than farmers (within its borders) because the lifestyle of the shepherd affords more opportunity for meditation and communion with G-d than does that of the farmer.

Praiseworthy as this motivation was, it was too escapist. The very purpose of life is to elevate the mundane aspects of life, infusing Divinity into them rather than renouncing them.

Moses therefore turned the tables on these tribes, stipulating that they be the vanguard of the invading force. He did this in order to train them in self-sacrifice, enabling them to face the challenge of elevating the world even while being shepherds.

From all this we learn that we must not shy away from the challenges of our Divine mission to disseminate Divine consciousness throughout the world – even in its most far-flung corners – but face them head-on. Only thus do we fulfill our task and make the world into G-d's home.[11]

---

11. *Sefer HaMa'amarim 5720–5721*, pp. 379–380.

SEVENTH READING
Numbers 32:20–42

Moses agreed to the proposal of the tribes of Reuben and Gad, and also settled half of the tribe of Manasseh on the east bank of the Jordan River. The tribes of Reuben and Gad fortified certain cities that were now in their possession, changing their names in order to emphasize the fact that these strongholds had become Jewish cities.

The Power in a Name

וּבְנֵי רְאוּבֵן בָּנוּ ... וַיִּקְרְאוּ בְשֵׁמֹת אֶת שְׁמוֹת
הֶעָרִים אֲשֶׁר בָּנוּ: (במדבר לב, לז–לח)

**The descendants of Reuben built ... and
changed the names of the cities they built.**

The original names of these cities were associated with the idolatries that were practiced by their original occupants. Changing their names was an act of conquest, of taking something formerly associated with idolatry and appropriating it for holy purposes. In this sense, the tribes of Reuben and Gad were continuing the task that began with Moses' stipulation that they cross the Jordan with their brothers: that of elevating the lowest ends of the spiritual continuum to holiness.

We see here that by referring to something in a positive, holy way, we can firstly dissociate it from whatever former, negative stigma it might have had, and secondly, ensure that it serve a positive moral and spiritual purpose from now on.[12]

12. *Likutei Sichot,* vol. 33, p. 198.

Mas'ei

Journeys
Numbers 33:1–36:13

THE TENTH AND LAST SECTION OF THE BOOK OF NUMBERS begins by reviewing the journeys (*Mas'ei*, in Hebrew) of the Jewish people from Egypt until the threshold of the Land of Israel. It continues with G-d's instructions regarding the Jews' imminent entry into the land and conquest of it.

FIRST READING
Numbers 33:1–49

Having concluded its account of the Jewish people's conquests on the east bank of the Jordan River, the Torah reviews all the stops the people made from when they left Egypt until their final camp in the desert.

Making the Desert Bloom

אֵלֶּה מַסְעֵי בְנֵי יִשְׂרָאֵל וְגו': (במדבר לג, א)

These are the journeys of the Israelites....

Because the Jews who left Egypt proved unready to enter the Land of Israel, G-d decreed that they wander in the desert until the next generation would be ready to take their place. Yet, if G-d's intent was only to keep the original generation from entering the Land of Israel, He could have had them live in some other, hospitable area outside the Holy Land. Even if it was necessary for them to remain in the desert, G-d could have let them remain in one location. Yet He had them spend at least half of the 40 years wandering in the desert.

The reason for this was because their wanderings served to transform the inhospitable, dangerous desert into a habitable, even hospitable place. Wherever the Jews traveled with the Tabernacle, the desert was transformed temporarily into a luxurious oasis.[1]

Similarly, our environment or our personal lives can sometimes seem like a spiritual "desert," devoid of spiritual life and hostile to the civilizing effects of a holy, optimistic lifestyle. Rather than let this glum situation depress us, we can recall that G-d has placed us in this spiritual desert in order to transform it into a spiritual paradise. And He has given us all the power that we need to accomplish this task.[2]

1. *Bemidbar Rabbah* 19:26.
2. *Likutei Sichot*, vol. 13, pp. 16–18.

SECOND READING

Numbers 33:50–53

G-d then informed the Jewish people that in order to conquer the Land of Israel successfully, they must cross the Jordan River with the intention to drive out the idolatrous nations from the land.

Eliciting G-d's Assistance

וְהוֹרַשְׁתֶּם אֶת הָאָרֶץ וִישַׁבְתֶּם בָּהּ כִּי לָכֶם נָתַתִּי

אֶת הָאָרֶץ לָרֶשֶׁת אֹתָהּ: (במדבר לג, נג)

[G-d instructed Moses to tell the Jewish people,]
"If you drive out [the present occupants of] the
land, you will settle it, for I have given you the
land in order to take possession of it."

G-d commanded the Jewish people to divide up the Promised Land among those entering it according to a specific process. Part of this process was logical, allocating the land according to the population of the various tribes. But part of the process was seemingly arbitrary, assigning the various parts of the land to the tribes by lot.[3]

The division of the land by lot was meant to remind us that the laws of nature and logic do not operate in the Land of Israel to the same extent that they do in the rest of the world. G-d's presence is more openly revealed in the Holy Land.

On the other hand, the division of the land according to population was meant to remind us that Divine revelation occurs only after we have paved the way for it, utilizing our natural powers and talents to the best of our abilities to accomplish our Divine mission. We thereby elicit His supernatural assistance, crowning our efforts with success beyond that which we could have achieved by ourselves.[4]

---

3. Numbers 26:54–55, 33:54.
4. *Likutei Sichot*, vol. 13, pp. 114–121.

THIRD READING
Numbers 33:54–34:15

Since there are many commandments that are to be observed only within the Land of Israel, G-d then described its exact boundaries.

Judging by Smell

מֵעֵבֶר לְיַרְדֵּן יְרֵחוֹ קֵדְמָה מִזְרָחָה: (במדבר לד, טו)

[Moses told the Jewish people, "The Land of Israel will not include the territory] on the east side of the Jordan opposite Jericho."

This location was the final stop in the Jewish people's trek from Egypt to the threshold of the Promised Land.[5] Inasmuch as this trek allegorically alludes to our collective journey until the Redemption, its final stop alludes to the advent of the Messiah, who will usher in the Redemption.

Similarly, this trek alludes to our individual journeys from any state of limitation to any subsequent state of redemption, its final stop alluding to our inner "Messiah," our power to redeem ourselves.

In this context, our sages point out that the name "Jordan" (*Yardein*) is related to the word for "judgment" (*din*) and the name "Jericho" (*Yericho*) is related to the word for "scent" (*rei'ach*). This means that the Messiah will be able to judge whether someone is innocent or guilty through his sense of smell.[6]

Framed in this context, we see that through our ongoing endeavors to refine ourselves and grow spiritually through studying the Torah and performing G-d's commandments, we can become so sensitive to ethical and moral quality that we are able to "smell" whether any aspect of creation is to our (or the world's) spiritual benefit or otherwise.[7]

---

5. Numbers 22:1, 33:48–49.
6. *Sanhedrin* 93b, based on Isaiah 11:3.
7. *Sefer HaMa'amarim 5746*, p. 230; *Likutei Torah* 3:94a–95a, etc.

FOURTH READING

Numbers 34:16–29

G-d then told Moses to appoint his successor, Joshua, and Aaron's successor, Eleazar, over the division of the Land of Israel.

Contemporary Leadership

אֵלֶּה שְׁמוֹת הָאֲנָשִׁים אֲשֶׁר יִנְחֲלוּ לָכֶם אֶת הָאָרֶץ
אֶלְעָזָר הַכֹּהֵן וִיהוֹשֻׁעַ בִּן נוּן: (במדבר לד, יז)

**[G-d instructed Moses to tell the Jewish people,]
"These are the names of the men who will inherit
the land on your behalf [under the leadership of]
Eleazar the priest and Joshua son of Nun."**

Moses assumed that Joshua would only assume the political and military leadership. Spiritual leadership would remain in the hands of the elders whom Moses had appointed during his own lifetime.

G-d, however, made it clear that Joshua's leadership would be all-inclusive, and moreover that his opinion should prevail over that of the elders who would survive from Moses' generation.

True, it was due to Joshua's selfless devotion to Moses that G-d chose Joshua as Moses' successor. The needs of Joshua's genera-tion, however, were different than those of Moses'. Joshua's leader-ship had to be based on Moses', but tailored to the generation that would enter the Promised Land. Allowing the elders appointed by Moses a continued say would be tantamount to having two clashing styles of leadership competing with one another.

Similarly, the spiritual tasks of our generation, which will undergo the transition from exile to Redemption, are different than those of previous generations. We should therefore look to our contemporary sages and spiritual leaders in order to ensure that we are fulfilling our Divine mission in the manner most suitable for our unique generation.[8]

8. *Likutei Sichot*, vol. 19, pp. 307–314.

THURSDAY

FIFTH READING
Numbers 35:1–8

G-d then instructed Moses and the Jewish people to set aside 48 cities for the Levites, since the tribe of Levi was not to receive any of their own agricultural territory in the Land of Israel. The Levite cities served also as "cities of refuge." When someone committed an unintentional act of murder, the relatives of the victim were allowed to kill the murderer unless he had fled to one of these specially designated cities.

Ambassadors of Love

אֶת שֵׁשׁ עָרֵי הַמִּקְלָט ... לָנֻס שָׁמָּה הָרֹצֵחַ וְגוֹ': (במדבר לה, ו)

[G-d instructed Moses to tell the Jewish people,] "The six cities of refuge ... to which a murderer can flee...."

Allegorically, the Torah itself is the "city of refuge," for when we are immersed in its study, internalizing the Divine consciousness it gives us, we are protected both from our own unholy passions and from the negative influence of our materialistic environment.[9] Besides helping us not to commit any misdeeds, studying the Torah also protects us from the ill effects of past misdeeds. It inspires us to regret our past failings and to make amends for them. And when we repent properly, our sins are transformed into merits. This is true even if we are guilty of intentional sins, just as the cities of refuge also provided asylum[10] for intentional murderers.[11]

9. *Makot* 9b–10a.
10. Until their case could be brought to court.
11. *Likutei Sichot*, vol. 2, pp. 363 ff.

SIXTH READING

Numbers 35:9–34

The unintentional murderer must remain in the city of refuge until the death of the current high priest. The death of the righteous atones for the sins of the generation; the death of the righteous high priest will atone for this tragedy of unintentional murder.

We Are One

וְיָשַׁב בָּהּ עַד מוֹת הַכֹּהֵן הַגָּדֹל וגו': (במדבר לה, כה)

[G-d instructed Moses to tell the Jewish people, "The murderer] must remain there until the high priest ... dies."

In linking the inadvertent killer specifically to the high priest, the Torah has effectively adopted the attitude of the Jewish people's very first high priest, Aaron. Aaron loved all Jews and drew them to the Torah; the Torah institutionalized this love as an integral aspect of the high priesthood.

This teaches us a great lesson in brotherly love and Jewish unity: No matter what heights we have reached on the ladder of spiritual or social status, we must remain concerned with all elements of society, even criminals. And even if we think that we, like the inadvertent killer, are on the lower rungs of humanity, we must remember that we are still connected with those on the highest levels, for we are all one people.[12]

---

12. *Likutei Sichot,* vol. 33, pp. 211–212.

<u>SEVENTH READING</u>
Numbers 36:1–13

G-d then concluded giving the laws of land inheritance, including the stipulation that Tzelofchad's daughters marry within their tribe.[13]

Two Types of Wisdom

וַתִּהְיֶינָה מַחְלָה תִרְצָה וְחָגְלָה וּמִלְכָּה וְנֹעָה בְּנוֹת
צְלָפְחָד לִבְנֵי דֹדֵיהֶן לְנָשִׁים: (במדבר לו, יא)

Tzelofchad's daughters – Machlah, Tirtzah, Choglah, Milkah, and No'ah – married their cousins.

In this verse, Tzelofchad's daughters are listed in the order of their birth, which was also the order in which they married. When they are mentioned elsewhere in the Torah,[14] No'ah and Tirtzah's positions in the list are reversed.

This is because in those contexts, the Torah is describing how they presented their claim to their inheritance. In this incident, they demonstrated not only that they were all wise, but that they were all *equally* wise – despite the fact that normally, older siblings have had more chance to acquire worldly wisdom than their younger siblings. The Torah therefore lists them *out* of their birth order.

True, in those other listings, the Torah always places No'ah, the youngest sister, second. This is because by exerting herself in her studies, No'ah indeed acquired more knowledge than her sisters. But the weight of wisdom gained through experiencing more of life balanced this out, so in the larger picture, all five sisters were equally wise.

We can learn from this to value both wisdom gained from experience and wisdom gained from the acquisition of knowledge.[15]

13. See insight for Tuesday of *Pinechas*.
14. Numbers 26:33 and 27:1. See also Joshua 17:3.
15. *Likutei Sichot*, vol. 8, pp. 200–206.

DEUTERONOMY

DEUTERONOMY

Devarim

Constructive Rebuke

Deuteronomy 1:1–3:22

THE BOOK OF DEUTERONOMY, THE FIFTH AND FINAL BOOK
of the Torah, is devoted chiefly to Moses' farewell addresses,
which he delivered to the Jewish people shortly before his death
and their entry into the Land of Israel. The first section of the
book records Moses' words (*Devarim*, in Hebrew) of rebuke to
the Jewish people over various incidents that took place during
their 40 years of wandering in the desert, and the lessons they
must learn from their mistakes.

FIRST READING

Deuteronomy 1:1–11

Moses began by recounting G-d's instructions 40 years earlier to leave Mount Sinai (also known as Mount Horeb) and to proceed toward the Land of Israel.

Overcoming Stagnation

ה' אֱלֹקֵינוּ דִּבֶּר אֵלֵינוּ בְּחֹרֵב לֵאמֹר רַב לָכֶם שֶׁבֶת בָּהָר הַזֶּה: (דברים א, ו)

[Moses told the Jewish people,] "G-d, our G-d, spoke to us at Horeb saying, 'You have dwelt too long at this mountain.'"

G-d here is alluding to the lesson that we should never remain too long on the same level in our relationship with Him, without advancing and ascending.

This idea is also articulated in the Prophets, where the human potential to progress in Divine consciousness is contrasted with the angels' lack of this potential: "If you go in My ways...I will make you into those who walk [i.e., constantly move forward] in contrast to these [angels], who [merely] stand here."[1]

Angels, being personified emotional states of involvement with G-d, are static, whereas human beings can progress from one level to another in their emotional involvement with G-d. In fact, we should strive to reach the next level of spirituality as soon as we become aware of its existence.[2]

Furthermore, this verse teaches us not to cloister ourselves in the study hall, devoting ourselves exclusively to our own self-refinement. Rather, G-d challenges us to leave this pristine and holy environment, traveling to a place far from "His mountain," to illuminate even these distant places with the Divine light of the Torah.[3]

---

1. Zechariah 3:7.
2. *Likutei Sichot*, vol. 24, p. 18.
3. Ibid., vol. 2, p. 695.

SECOND READING

Deuteronomy 1:12–21

Moses reminded the Jewish people that when they were at Mount Sinai, G-d instructed him to share the responsibility of resolving their lawsuits with a system of judges.

Appreciating Others

וָאֲצַוֶּה אֶת שֹׁפְטֵיכֶם בָּעֵת הַהִוא לֵאמֹר שָׁמֹעַ בֵּין אֲחֵיכֶם וגו': (דברים א, טז)

**[Moses told the Jewish people,] "I commanded
your judges at that time, saying, 'Hear
[disputes] between your brothers....'"**

The Hebrew word for "between" (*bein*) is related to the word for "understanding" (*binah*). Based on this, the Ba'al Shem Tov interpreted this phrase allegorically:

If you have refined spiritual senses, then you can *"hear"* G-d articulate His great love for every Jew. You will then be *"between" your brothers*, i.e., you will *understand* the true, great worth of every Jew.

Thus, if you can *"hear,"* you will delight in the company of any Jew, and you will make it a point to be *between your brothers* – to associate with them and socialize with them.

The reverse is also true:

If you want to *"hear,"* i.e., to develop your spiritual sensitivity so that you can "hear" G-d articulating His love for every Jew, then be *between your brothers*, i.e., make it a point to associate with them and socialize with them, even the simplest among them.[4]

4. *Igrot Kodesh Admor Mehorayatz*, vol. 4, pp. 96 ff.

THIRD READING
Deuteronomy 1:22–38

Moses then reminded the Jewish people how the scouts that were sent to spy out the Land of Israel spread their ill-founded fear among the people when they returned. As a result, that generation forfeited the privilege of entering the Land of Israel.

Charging Our Spiritual Batteries

אִם יִרְאֶה אִישׁ בָּאֲנָשִׁים הָאֵלֶּה ... אֵת הָאָרֶץ הַטּוֹבָה

אֲשֶׁר נִשְׁבַּעְתִּי לָתֵת לַאֲבֹתֵיכֶם: (דברים א, לה)

[G-d told Moses,] "None of these men ... will see the good land that I swore to give your forefathers."

Punishments are administered in order to correct the wrong committed. So why did G-d give the generation of the desert exactly what they wanted – to stay in the Divine atmosphere of the desert, protected by the clouds of glory and provided for by the manna and the well of Miriam?

The answer is that their request was not really evil. It was merely based on a mistaken premise. By expressing their preference for the spiritual life of the desert, they demonstrated that they were not yet ready to deal with the physical world. Only the next generation, who would benefit from growing up in an environment of spiritual sustenance and nurturing, would be able to safely settle in the real world.

We see from this that we can gather the strength necessary to elevate and refine the world in two ways: First, by periodically devoting time to re-charging our spiritual batteries in the spiritually conducive environments of houses of prayer and study, and secondly, by renewing our faith in G-d's supernatural assistance, which enables us to succeed even if our natural strengths are insufficient.[5]

5. *Likutei Sichot*, vol. 33, p. 87.

FOURTH READING

Deuteronomy 1:39–2:1

G-d decreed that the generation of the spies should die out in the desert, and only their children should enter the Land of Israel.

Joy from Children

וְטַפְּכֶם אֲשֶׁר אֲמַרְתֶּם לָבַז יִהְיֶה . . . הֵמָּה יָבֹאוּ שָׁמָּה
וְלָהֶם אֶתְּנֶנָּה וְהֵם יִירָשׁוּהָ: (דברים א, לט)

[**Moses told the people that G-d said,**] "**Your little ones, whom you said would be prey . . . will go there; I will give** [**the land**] **to them, and they will possess it.**"

Both the spies (in their complaint) and G-d (in His response) referred specifically to the "young ones." One of the ways the Torah characterizes young children is that they "crumble more bread than they eat."[6]

Spiritually, our "bread," our staple, is the Torah. It is "consumed" differently by different people: The spiritually mature among us (the "adults") devote the majority of their time and effort to studying the Torah for its own sake, therefore absorbing whatever they learn. In contrast, the less spiritually mature among us (the "children") devote the majority of their time and energy on mundane matters, therefore absorbing very little of what they learn.

The spies were concerned that the Jewish people would become "children" when faced with the realities of the physical world, thereby becoming "prey" to its negative influences.

G-d, however, replied that His primary satisfaction is seeing the "children" resist the pull of materiality. He values whatever focus they can muster for their Divine mission more than the accomplishments of the spiritually mature.[7]

6. *Lekach Tov* on Genesis 47:12; cf. *Pesachim* 10b.
7. *Likutei Sichot*, vol. 2, pp. 581–582; Ibid., vol. 13, pp. 195–197.

FIFTH READING
Deuteronomy 2:2–30

When the Jewish people were approaching the Land of Israel, G-d specified exactly which nations they were allowed to attack and which they were not.

Seeing the Future

כִּי יְרֻשָּׁה לְעֵשָׂו נָתַתִּי אֶת הַר שֵׂעִיר: (דברים ב, ה)

[G-d instructed Moses to tell the Jewish people,] "I have given Mount Sei'ir to Esau as an inheritance."

G-d states here that Esau is an heir of his father, Isaac. In contrast, the Torah states that Ishmael is *not* an heir of *his* father, Abraham.[8]

This difference between Ishmael and Esau stems from the difference between Abraham and Isaac. Abraham imposed Divine consciousness on his audience, regardless of whether they were ready for it. Isaac, in contrast, inspired others to refine themselves in order to attain Divine consciousness on their own. The advantage of Abraham's method over Isaac's was that he could reach a wider audience; the advantage of Isaac's method over Abraham's was that he could effect a lasting change in his disciples.

For the same reason, Abraham did not transfer his holiness to Ishmael sufficiently for Ishmael to be considered his heir, whereas Isaac did transfer his holiness to Esau sufficiently for Esau to be considered *his* heir. This is why Isaac wanted to bless Esau, whereas Abraham did not bless Ishmael.

From this we learn that we must encourage all Jews to participate fully in their Jewish heritage – even if they appear to be as estranged from Jewish values as was Esau. Just as Isaac sought to bless Esau, we must inspire our fellows to enhance their spiritual lives, thereby opening themselves up to G-d's blessings.[9]

8. Genesis 21:10–12.
9. *Likutei Sichot*, vol. 15, pp. 191–199.

SIXTH READING

Deuteronomy 2:31–3:14

Moses then encouraged the Jewish people by reminding them how they delivered a devastating defeat to the two Amorite kings whom they were allowed to attack, Sichon and Og.

Spreading Divine Consciousness

וַנִּלְכֹּד אֶת ... כָּל חֶבֶל אַרְגֹּב וגו': (דברים ג, ד)

**[Moses told the Jewish people,] "We conquered...
all of the territory of [Og's] royal palace...."**

The Land of Israel, relative to the rest of the world, is "the royal palace," i.e., G-d's home on earth. This means that the Land of Israel is more conducive to cultivating Divine consciousness than is anywhere else.

Whenever Divine providence leads us to "conquer" some place outside the borders of the Land of Israel – whether through military conquest, purchasing real estate, or even simply living there – it is in order that we spread Divine consciousness there. We thereby transform that part of the world into a spiritual extension of the Land of Israel.

Thus, when the Jewish people conquered King Og's royal palace, they transformed it from "the territory of the non-Jewish king's palace" into part of the true "royal palace," the Land of Israel.

Only with the final Redemption will "the [whole] world be filled with the knowledge of G-d as water covers the seabed."[10] Until then, the Divine consciousness we can achieve outside the Land of Israel cannot compare to what we can reach within its borders. Nonetheless, if we are sufficiently devoted to our Divine mission, we can indeed achieve an "extension" of the Divine consciousness available to us in the Holy Land. This, in turn, will pave the way for the final Redemption and hasten its advent.[11]

10. Isaiah 11:9.
11. *Likutei Sichot*, vol. 24, pp. 20–27.

SEVENTH READING
Deuteronomy 3:15–22

Moses then reminded the Jewish people how the tribes of Reuben and Gad had requested the territory that had been conquered on the east bank of the Jordan River.

Spiritual Indulgence

יָדַעְתִּי כִּי מִקְנֶה רַב לָכֶם וגו׳: (דברים ג, יט)

[Moses told the tribes of Reuben and Gad,]
"I know that you have much livestock."

The tribes of Reuben and Gad wanted to remain on the east side of the Jordan River because they had an abundance of cattle, sheep, and goats, and this territory was well-suited for pasture. The reason why these tribes had more animals than the others is because they appreciated the spiritual value of the manna, and therefore made it the chief staple of their diet. The other tribes, in contrast, also ate animals from their herds and flocks.

Their appreciation of spirituality was also a direct reason why the tribes of Reuben and Gad wished to remain on the east side of the Jordan River. By opting for the shepherd's life rather than the farmer's, they hoped to have more time to commune with G-d.

Praiseworthy as their appreciation seems, these tribes missed the point. The purpose of spirituality is to refine and elevate the material world; it is our ability to make spirituality affect materiality that we should appreciate, not the abstract experience of spirituality itself.[12]

12. *Likutei Sichot*, vol. 9, pp. 14–23.

Va'etchanan

The Foundations of Judaism
Deuteronomy 3:23–7:11

THE SECOND SECTION OF THE BOOK OF DEUTERONOMY opens as Moses recalls how he pleaded (*Va'etchanan*, in Hebrew) with G-d to allow him to enter the Land of Israel. Moses tells the rest of the Jewish people that they will soon enter the land without him. Moses then continues to review the Jewish people's 40 years in the desert, focusing on G-d's giving of the Torah at Mount Sinai.

FIRST READING
Deuteronomy 3:23–4:4

Moses described G-d's forgiveness of the Jewish people, contrasting how G-d had forgiven them for their wrongdoings, whereas He had not forgiven Moses for his own wrongdoings.

Confronting Life's Challenges

כִּי לֹא תַעֲבֹר אֶת הַיַּרְדֵּן הַזֶּה: (דברים ג, כז)

[G-d told Moses, "Observe the Land of Israel from Mount Nebo,] for you will not cross this Jordan River."

Had Moses accompanied the people into the Promised Land, their entry would have been miraculous: they would have been led by the Clouds of Glory and the Pillar of Fire, and the nations occupying the land would have offered no resistance. But since Moses did not accompany them into the land, the Israelites had to battle the Canaanite nations without relying on open miracles. Therefore, they had to be prepared for self-sacrifice.

This is the inner reason why G-d did not allow Moses to cross the Jordan River along with the Jewish people. Our purpose is to bring Divinity into the world, which we accomplish first and foremost by bringing Divine consciousness into ourselves. In order to make ourselves capable of self-sacrifice, we have to internalize G-d's message and mission so deeply that they mean more to us than anything else, even our own lives.

Similarly, when confronted with life's challenges, we can more successfully overcome them when we recall that G-d presents them to us in order for us to test our inner strength and dedication to our ideals.[1]

---

1. *Likutei Sichot*, vol. 9, pp. 57–58, 82; *Sefer HaSichot 5751*, pp. 741–743.

SECOND READING

Deuteronomy 4:5–40

Moses then proceeded to describe the revelation of G-d at the Giving of the Torah at Mount Sinai.

Seeing G-d

אַתָּה הָרְאֵתָ לָדַעַת כִּי ה' הוּא הָאֱלֹקִים אֵין עוֹד מִלְּבַדּוֹ: (דברים ד, לה)

[Moses told the Jewish people, "At Mount Sinai,] you were shown [the spiritual realm] in order to know that G-d is the only deity. There is nothing other than Him."

Sight is considered a higher level of perception than hearing because it evokes a much more intense emotional response, indicating that it touches the soul more deeply. Nonetheless, hearing does have an advantage over seeing: Rather than perceiving the event or object, hearing perceives the sound of its description, which is invisible and thus detached from the physical objects and events perceived by sight. In this sense, although the people had "seen" G-d's presence in the world, they had "heard" about how G-d is infinite – outside and beyond the finite universe.

Moses, on the other hand, experienced G-d's infinity with the same intensity that he experienced G-d's presence; he "saw" what we can only "hear" about. He asked G-d to enable the people, too, to "see" His infinity, and not just "hear" about it.

However, G-d did not grant Moses' request, because the world at large was not yet ripe for this level of Divine consciousness. Moses could therefore only enjoin the people to "hear" G-d's message. In the Messianic future, however, we will be granted this level of Divine consciousness. We can prepare for it nowadays by doing our best to fathom G-d's infinity intellectually. By developing our ability to "hear," we pave the way for being able to "see."[2]

2. *Or HaTorah, Devarim*, pp. 62–64.

THIRD READING
Deuteronomy 4:41–49

Moses concluded his first address by reminding the Jewish people that their entry into the Land of Israel and continued residence in it will depend on their loyalty to G-d and His Torah. Moses then designated three cities to the east of the Jordan River as "cities of refuge" for unintentional murderers.

The Torah is Our Refuge

אָז יַבְדִּיל מֹשֶׁה שָׁלֹשׁ עָרִים וְגוֹ': (דברים ד, מא)

Moses then designated three cities....

Allegorically, the study of the Torah is our "city of refuge." This is alluded to by the fact that in order for a city to be considered a city with regard to certain aspects of Jewish law, there must be at least ten people living in it who study the Torah all day long.[3]

The required number ten alludes to the ten powers of the soul (three intellectual, three emotional, three behavioral, and one of expression), indicating that in order for the Torah to function as a "city of refuge" for us, we must immerse ourselves in it fully, with all ten powers of our soul. Furthermore, the word for "refuge" (*miklat*) literally means "absorption." Thus, we must not only immerse ourselves in the Torah; we must fully absorb and internalize its message.

This is how we protect ourselves from the negative spiritual influences of our materialistic environment, thereby remaining spiritually strong enough to influence the world positively.[4]

---

3. *Megilah* 3b.
4. *Sefer HaMa'amarim 5717–5719*, p. 230.

FOURTH READING

Deuteronomy 5:1–18

Moses then reviewed the laws that the Jewish people had received from G-d at Mount Sinai. He began by repeating and reviewing the Ten Commandments.

Repeating the Ten Commandments

אָנֹכִי ה' אֱלֹקֶיךָ וגו': (דברים ה, ו)

[Moses told the Jewish people, "The Ten Commandments began,] 'I am G-d, your G-d.... '"

In its original description of the Ten Commandments, the Torah emphasized how the revelation shook both nature and the Jewish people. When the people expressed their fear of dying on account of the intensity of this revelation, Moses replied that although they would not die physically, G-d did intend for this experience to "kill" each person's sense of self.[5]

Here, in contrast, Moses is speaking to the next generation, who will enter the Land of Israel and will be subject to all the distractions of earning a livelihood and tending to their own needs. This generation will not be able to afford the spiritual "luxury" of annihilating their sense of self.

Therefore, in recounting the Giving of the Torah, Moses describes how G-d told the people that they were correct to be afraid, and that they should strive to retain this fear even when retaining their own sense of self. Although they may not be able to achieve the previous generation's self-nullification, they should remember it, nurturing a vision of that spiritual perfection.

Today, as well, the memory of how our ancestors' selfhood was dissolved in G-d's revelation at Mount Sinai inspires us when facing life's challenges, empowering us to successfully overcome them.[6]

5. Exodus 20:17.
6. *Likutei Sichot*, vol. 9, p. 69; *Sefer HaSichot 5751*, volume 2, p. 740.

FIFTH READING
Deuteronomy 5:19–6:3

Moses then described receiving the Torah on Mount Sinai.

Eternal Revelation

קוֹל גָּדוֹל וְלֹא יָסָף וְגו': (דברים ה, יט)

[**Moses told the Jewish people, "At Mount Sinai,
G-d spoke with**] **a great voice, not pausing."**

G-d's voice produced no echo when He pronounced the Ten Commandments.[7] G-d's voice was absorbed by the mountains themselves.

Inasmuch as the spiritual and material are two distinct aspects of reality, we normally would not expect the spirituality of the Torah to be absorbed into physical reality. But since G-d revealed His *essence* at Mount Sinai, and His essence transcends the normal dichotomy between spirituality and physicality, this revelation was indeed able to permeate the physical dimension of existence.

As the Jewish people were about to pass from their spiritual existence in the desert to their material existence in the land, they needed to be reminded that the voice of G-d and the Torah permeate all existence. As such, everything, even the inanimate kingdom, is saturated with latent Divine consciousness. Nothing about reality can truly be an obstacle to fulfilling G-d's will; if it appears to be so, this is only a façade, a test of our determination and devotion to our Divine destiny.

By approaching the Torah and its lifestyle as an encounter with G-d Himself, we continue to cause His voice to permeate all reality, thereby making the world a home for Him and fulfilling the purpose of creation.[8]

---

7. *Shemot Rabbah* 28:6.
8. *Likutei Sichot*, vol. 4, pp. 1092–1098.

SIXTH READING
Deuteronomy 6:4–25

Moses then told the Jewish people that the proper response to
G-d's self-revelation through the Torah is to fulfill His commandments out of love.

Encounters with G-d

שְׁמַע יִשְׂרָאֵל ה' אֱלֹקֵינוּ ה' אֶחָד: (דברים ו, ד)

**[Moses told the Jewish people,] "Hear,
Israel, G-d is our G-d; G-d is one."**

When we say "G-d is one," we mean that the creation of the world
did not change G-d in any way. He is the same after creation as
He was before creation – filling every moment of time and every
iota of space. When we look at the world from this perspective,
we no longer see trees and tables; we see only G-d.[9]

The implications of such a worldview are sweeping. If G-d
is everything, then there is no longer any possibility of self-
centeredness or even self-awareness. The importance and significance we normally grant the world and the attention and devotion
we normally let it command dissolve into nothingness. We can no
longer be fazed by any seeming obstacle that the world seems to
pose to the observance of the Torah, because we know that when
we look at trees and tables, we may be seeing trees and tables, but
we are really looking at G-d in the guise of trees and tables.[10]

This awareness enables us to truly "know G-d in all our ways,"[11]
to transform every aspect of our lives – whether sublime or mundane – into an encounter with G-d.[12]

---

9. *Tanya*, chapter 20; *Sha'ar HaYichud vehaEmunah*, chapters 6–8.
10. *Likutei Torah* 4:4ab.
11. Paraphrasing Proverbs 3:6. *Yom Tov shel Rosh HaShanah 5666*, pp.
153–154, 242; *Sefer HaSichot Torat Shalom*, pp. 51, 184–185.
12. *Sefer HaSichot 5690*, p. 86.

SEVENTH READING

Deuteronomy 7:1–11

Moses then encouraged the Jewish people to remain loyal to G-d, not imitating the ways of other nations, even though these nations are more numerous and powerful than the Jewish people.

Total Absorption

לֹא מֵרֻבְּכֶם מִכָּל הָעַמִּים חָשַׁק ה' בָּכֶם וַיִּבְחַר בָּכֶם,

כִּי אַתֶּם הַמְעַט מִכָּל הָעַמִּים: (דברים ז, ז)

[Moses told the Jewish people,] "G-d did not delight in you and choose you because you are more numerous than any other people, for you are the least [populous] of all nations."

An additional meaning of this verse is that G-d chose us because we do not aggrandize ourselves when He showers us with His beneficence; rather, we consider ourselves unworthy of G-d's special favor.

The trait of self-effacement is particularly critical for the Jewish people. Aware of the gravity of our mission, it is very easy to become overly impressed with our importance. Cultivating humility is therefore crucial.

This is not to imply that we should shy away from fulfilling our Divine task. On the contrary, we should continually seek to expand our influence, both over the less-than-holy aspects of our own selves and over the world in general. But we should be so enthralled and so absorbed with our mission that we feel insignificant in comparison to it.

Our self-effacement then enables us to be even more effective in accomplishing our Divine mission, inspiring us to de-emphasize our own selfhood even more. We thus enter a continuous spiral of greater effectiveness and greater self-effacement.[13]

13. *Likutei Sichot,* vol. 34, p. 49.

Eikev

Appreciation and Love

Deuteronomy 7:12–11:25

IN THE THIRD SECTION OF THE BOOK OF DEUTERONOMY,
Moses continues his second farewell address to the Jewish people. He urges them to observe even what appear to be minor
commandments, which a person would be likely to figuratively
trample with his heel (*Eikev*, in Hebrew). Moses then continues
his review of the events of the Jewish people's 40-year trek in the
desert, emphasizing the lessons they were to learn from them.

FIRST READING
Deuteronomy 7:12–8:10

Moses told the Jewish people that if they would be careful to perform all of G-d's commandments, even the seemingly minor ones, G-d would provide them with all the material means that they would need to fulfill His will.

Enlightenment and Sweetness

אֶרֶץ חִטָּה וּשְׂעֹרָה וְגֶפֶן וּתְאֵנָה וְרִמּוֹן אֶרֶץ זֵית שֶׁמֶן וּדְבָשׁ: (דברים ח, ח)

[Moses told the Jewish people, "G-d has given you] a land of wheat, barley, grapevines, figs, and pomegranates; a land of oil-producing olive and [date]-honey."

Wheat is primarily human food, barley primarily animal food. Wheat and barley therefore represent our work with our Divine and animal souls. Wine – the product of the grape – represents the joy with which we should approach this work. Since Adam and Eve's first clothes were made of fig leaves,[1] figs represent our efforts to refine the "garments" of our souls, i.e., thought, speech, and action. The seed-laden pomegranate symbolizes the multitude of Divine commandments[2] through which we refine the world around us.

Olives and dates signify the extra exertion required for our work during the exile. Olives produce their oil only when pressed hard; date palm trees take a long time to grow. But both olives and dates produce added benefits: light from oil and honey from dates. These allude to the revelations of the inner dimension of the Torah that will accompany the Messianic redemption.

Similarly, as each of us journeys toward our personal "promised land," the great efforts we make in attaining, sustaining, and spreading Divine consciousness will enlighten and sweeten our relationship with G-d and His Torah.[3]

1. Genesis 3:7.
2. *Berachot* 57a, et al.
3. *Sefer HaSichot 5752*, vol. 1, pp. 324–328.

SECOND READING

Deuteronomy 8:11–9:3

Moses told the Jewish people to remember G-d's protection.

The Spiritual Desert

הַמּוֹלִיכְךָ בַּמִּדְבָּר הַגָּדֹל וְהַנּוֹרָא נָחָשׁ שָׂרָף וְעַקְרָב וְצִמָּאוֹן וּגו': (דברים ח, טו)

[Moses told the Jewish people, "G-d] led you through the great and awesome desert, [filled with] snakes, vipers, scorpions, and thirst...."

The Torah here lists the stages through which we collectively and individually can descend into exile:

Great: The first stage is overestimating the power of the mundane world and underestimating the power of holiness. *Awesome:* This leads us to grant the mundane world dominion over the "religious" aspects of life as well. *[Filled with] Snakes:* This leads us to replace our natural religious fervor with enthusiasm for worldly pursuits. This fervor is symbolized by the snake's hot venom. *Vipers:* Eventually, our enthusiasm for worldly things will consume our religious fervor altogether; this is symbolized by the burning sting of the viper. *Scorpions:* But sooner or later, devotion to worldly pursuits will leave us bored, our enthusiasm for them spent. This leaves us cold and deadened to any kind of stimulation, symbolized by the scorpion's cold venom. *And thirst:* When G-d then tries to arouse us from this state with a thirst for true life, we will not be able to recognize what we are thirsting for. We will "thirst" but remain "parched."

The way to avoid all of this, then, is not to begin this process altogether – i.e., not overestimating the power of our environment. By fostering our awareness of the power of holiness within us, we can avoid the pitfalls of exile and live up to our true potential.[4]

---

4. *Likutei Sichot,* vol. 2, pp. 372–375.

THIRD READING

Deuteronomy 9:4–29

As an example of G-d's willingness to forgive the Jewish people for their misdeeds, Moses recounted the incident of the Golden Calf. After G-d gave Moses the Tablets of the Covenant on Mount Sinai, He told Moses to descend the mountain to see the Golden Calf that the people had made.

Leaders and Followers

וַיֹּאמֶר ה' אֵלַי קוּם רֵד מַהֵר מִזֶּה כִּי שָׁחֵת עַמְּךָ וְגוֹ': (דברים ט, יב)

[Moses said to the Jewish people,] "G-d said to me, 'Arise, descend quickly from here, for your people have become corrupt.... '"

When G-d told Moses to descend, He not only meant that he should descend the mountain; He also meant that on account of the people's misdeeds, Moses would have to descend from the exalted level of Divine consciousness to which he had ascended when he received the Torah directly from G-d.

Moses clearly did not participate in the people's misdeed. Moreover, he could not even be faulted for not protesting their actions, since he was not there. Nonetheless, he was adversely affected by their sin, because the nature of the bond between a true Jewish leader and his flock is such that when they ascend, he ascends too, and when they fall, he falls too.

We all are leaders, since we all have people whom we can influence. From this incident with Moses, we see how entwined our own personal success in life is with the success of those whom we can influence. The surest way to promote our own spiritual growth is by promoting the spiritual progress of others.[5]

5. _Likutei Sichot_, vol. 21, p. 175.

FOURTH READING
Deuteronomy 10:1–11

After Moses shattered the first set of tablets, he pleaded with G-d to forgive the Jewish people. G-d did forgive them, and instructed Moses to prepare two replacement tablets upon which G-d would inscribe the Ten Commandments again.

Living in the Past

פְּסָל לְךָ שְׁנֵי לוּחֹת אֲבָנִים כָּרִאשֹׁנִים וגו': (דברים י, א)

[G-d told Moses,] "Hew out two tablets
of stone like the first ones."

The relationship between G-d and the Jewish people that was embodied in the first tablets was more direct than the relationship that was embodied in the second tablets. Nonetheless, the relationship expressed in the second tablets was (and remains) potentially more intense.[6] Studying the Torah and properly extracting from it G-d's practical and spiritual instructions for living life would now require more mental exertion and moral dedication than was required when we possessed the first tablets. We must tap deeper reserves of power and inspiration than we needed to before. This requires that we demonstrate more of our inherent spiritual strength.

Similarly, we should realize that any apparent setback in life is in reality an opportunity for even greater progress waiting to be capitalized upon. On the cosmic level, this means that we can utilize the final moments of our present exile to elicit the infinite revelations of Divinity that will accompany the Messianic redemption.[7]

6. *Shemot Rabbah* 46:1.
7. *Hitva'aduyot 5742*, vol. 4, pp. 2002–2004.

FIFTH READING
Deuteronomy 10:12–11:9

Moses reminded the Jewish people about their participation in Korach's mutiny, and how the rebels were swallowed up by the earth.

Elevating Wealth

וַתִּבְלָעֵם ... וְאֵת כָּל הַיְקוּם אֲשֶׁר בְּרַגְלֵיהֶם וגו': (דברים יא, ו)

[Moses told the Jewish people, "The earth] swallowed up [the rebels] ... and all the property at their feet."

The sages point out that the reason why the Torah describes property as being "at their feet" is because our wealth is what enables us to stand on our own two feet, i.e., to be self-sufficient. The imagery of us standing on the wealth beneath our feet also teaches us that by elevating our wealth – by using some of it for charity – we elevate our entire being, as well.

The sages describe the period prior to the Messianic redemption as the era of "the heels of the Messiah,"[8] meaning the time when we can "hear his footsteps"[9] if we are properly attuned to the spiritual dimension of life.

The fact that the same metaphor ("feet") is used for wealth and the pre-Messianic era teaches us that at this time in particular we can elevate the materiality of the world – and thereby ourselves, as well – by giving charity generously.[10]

8. Based on Psalms 89:52.
9. See Psalms 77:20 for this usage of "heel."
10. *Igeret HaKodesh* 9; *Hitva'aduyot 5746*, vol. 2, p. 275.

SIXTH READING

Deuteronomy 11:10–21

Moses then told the Jewish people that they should express their love of G-d not only as individuals, but as a community, serving only Him.

Pledging Allegiance

הִשָּׁמְרוּ לָכֶם פֶּן יִפְתֶּה לְבַבְכֶם וְסַרְתֶּם וַעֲבַדְתֶּם אֱלֹהִים אֲחֵרִים וגו': (דברים יא, טז)

[Moses told the Jewish people,] "Beware, lest your heart be misled and you turn away and worship false gods."

The Ba'al Shem Tov interpreted this verse to mean that the moment a person turns away from G-d, he is already "serving idols" in some sense.[11]

Divine consciousness encompasses the awareness that G-d is the only true reality, and that everything else depends upon Him to exist. As soon as a person allows this consciousness to lapse, he is by that very fact tacitly ascribing at least some independent reality to creation. Having lost sight of the fact that G-d is the only independent force in the world, he succumbs to the illusion that he should respect lesser "deities" – whether these be celestial forces, natural forces (such as cause and effect), or societal forces (such as wealth, power, and prestige). This is a subtle but very real form of idolatry.

By periodically re-focusing on how G-d is the only true reality, we can ensure that our allegiance to true values remains pure.[12]

11. *Tzava'at HaRibash* (ed. Kehot) 76.
12. *Sichot Kodesh 5720*, pp. 392–393.

SEVENTH READING

Deuteronomy 11:22–25

Moses promised the Jewish people that if they would keep G-d's commandments, imitate His goodness, and cleave to the sages of the Torah, G-d would enable them to successfully drive out the nations that were occupying the Land of Israel.

Expanding Holiness

מִן הַנָּהָר נְהַר פְּרָת וְעַד הַיָּם הָאַחֲרוֹן יִהְיֶה גְּבֻלְכֶם: (דברים יא, כד)

[Moses told the Jewish people,] "Your border will be from the river – the Euphrates River – to the western sea."

The Hebrew word used in this verse for "west" (*acharon*) literally means "last." Thus, this verse can be understood to imply that in the Messianic future, the Land of Israel will spread over the entire world.[13] G-d is thus telling us in this verse that the ultimate goal of taking possession of the Land of Israel is that the revelation of Divinity it is uniquely suited to express should eventually spread over the entire globe.

Allegorically, this means that our spiritual growth (our conquest of the Land of Israel) is ultimately intended to affect the lowliest aspects of reality (to "annex" the mundane world to the holiness of the Land of Israel) by illuminating them with Divine consciousness.[14]

---

13. *Sifrei, Devarim*; *Pesikta Rabati, Shabbat veRosh Chodesh*; *Yalkut Shim'oni*, Isaiah §153.

14. *Sefer HaSichot 5750*, vol. 2, pp. 625–627.

Re'eih

Devotion to G-d

Deuteronomy 11:26–16:17

THE FOURTH SECTION OF THE BOOK OF DEUTERONOMY CON-
tinues Moses' second farewell address to the Jewish people. Moses
begins by urging the people to see (*Re'eih*, in Hebrew) that G-d
has given them the choice between a life of blessings or curses;
the choice is theirs.

FIRST READING

Deuteronomy 11:26–12:10

Moses urged the Jewish people to realize that G-d gives them the choice between good and evil. Their choice will result either in a life of blessings or one of curses.

Divine Blessing

רְאֵה אָנֹכִי נֹתֵן לִפְנֵיכֶם הַיּוֹם בְּרָכָה וּקְלָלָה: (דברים יא, כו)

[Moses told the Jewish people in G-d's Name,] "See, I set before you today a blessing and a curse."

G-d provides all His creatures with whatever they need to accomplish their purpose in this world. This includes both physical gifts (such as good health, prosperity, and talent) and mental gifts (such as courage, optimism, and sensitivity). However, even if G-d has designated the proper gifts for us, obstacles (such as various types of misbehavior) can sometimes prevent these Divine gifts from materializing in our lives, preventing them from descending from the realm of the potential into the realm of the actual.

In such cases, we need a "blessing." A blessing does not create new Divine beneficence; it simply allows us to receive what G-d has already intended for us. Thus, when G-d tells us that He has set before us "a blessing and a curse," He means that through the choices we make, we can determine the extent to which the beneficence He has stored away for us will become manifest in our lives.

Furthermore, the more we dedicate ourselves to fulfilling our Divine mission, the more means G-d provides us with in order to fulfill our goals. Thus, besides accessing what G-d has set aside for us, we can increase the Divine beneficence available to us, as well.[1]

---

1. *Likutei Torah* 4:19a; *Likutei Sichot,* vol. 10, p. 38; ibid., vol. 20, p. 137.

SECOND READING

Deuteronomy 12:11–28

Moses told the Jewish people that after they enter the Land of Israel, they must establish a centralized location for the sacrificial rites.

Jerusalem

וְהָיָה הַמָּקוֹם אֲשֶׁר יִבְחַר ה' אֱלֹקֵיכֶם בּוֹ לְשַׁכֵּן שְׁמוֹ שָׁם וגו': (דברים יב, יא)

[Moses told the Jewish people,] "Regarding the place to which G-d, your G-d, will choose to attach His Name...."

Jerusalem is "the place to which G-d chose to attach His Name" as the exclusive and eternal site of the holy Temple. Nevertheless, wherever we are, we can transform that location into a miniature, spiritual "Jerusalem" by serving G-d there, spiritually elevating and refining ourselves and our environment.[2]

This truth is reflected in the fact that wherever we pray, we face Jerusalem. By facing Jerusalem, we connect our local "Jerusalem" to Jerusalem itself, as our prayers ascend to heaven via the spiritual portal of the site of the holy Temple. Furthermore, by facing the real Jerusalem, we express our hope that G-d will soon redeem us from our exile, and we will, living in the Land of Israel, be able to experience the spiritual exaltation that will be available to us when the holy Temple is finally rebuilt.

By transforming our local environment into a spiritual "Jerusalem" while simultaneously yearning to serve G-d in Jerusalem itself, we can hasten the advent of our own personal redemption, as well as the ultimate, Messianic Redemption of humanity as a whole.[3]

2. *Sefer HaChayim* 5:1.
3. *Likutei Sichot*, vol. 2, pp. 617–619.

THIRD READING

Deuteronomy 12:29–13:19

Moses then told the Jewish people that when they are confronted with a challenge to their faith (such as the prosperity of the wicked or of false prophets), they must remember that G-d is testing their loyalty and commitment to Him.

Cleaving to G-d

אַחֲרֵי ה' אֱלֹקֵיכֶם תֵּלֵכוּ ... וְאֶת מִצְוֹתָיו תִּשְׁמֹרוּ וּבְקֹלוֹ
תִּשְׁמָעוּ וְאֹתוֹ תַעֲבֹדוּ וּבוֹ תִדְבָּקוּן: (דברים יג, ה)

[Moses told the Jewish people,] "You should follow G-d, your G-d . . . keep His commandments, heed His voice, worship Him, and cleave to Him."

If we are already "following G-d, keeping His commandments, heeding His voice, and worshipping Him," what is left to do in order to "cleave to Him?"

"Cleaving to G-d" means acting as He does, exhibiting kindness and concern for all creatures by helping them in their time of need. True, this type of behavior is largely included in "keeping His commandments," many of which require us to extend our help to others. But, in addition, the Torah is bidding us to identify with G-d so thoroughly, to merge our consciousness with His so totally, that we do what He does *naturally*, rather than out of the obligation of being commanded to do so.

The Torah is justified in this expectation inasmuch as we all possess a Divine soul, a "veritable part of G-d above."[4] The more we enable our Divine soul to express itself (by following G-d, keeping His commandments, heeding His voice, and worshipping Him), the more we can ultimately identify with G-d Himself.[5]

---

4. Job 31:2; *Tanya*, chapter 2 (6a).

5. *Likutei Sichot*, vol. 14, pp. 62–63.

FOURTH READING

Deuteronomy 14:1–21

Moses then instructed the Jewish people regarding how they must distinguish themselves from other peoples in order to remain true to their Divine mission. These instructions included the laws regarding *kashrut* (i.e., permitted vs. forbidden types of food).

Elevating Reality

אַךְ אֶת זֶה לֹא תֹאכְלוּ וגו': (דברים יד, ז)

[Moses told the Jewish people,] "But you must not eat [the following animals]."

G-d created everything for a purpose,[6] and it is our task to help each component of creation fulfill its purpose. In many cases, we accomplish this by making active use of the item in question – for example, by using it to fulfill some commandment. In other cases, however, we accomplish this goal passively – for example, by avoiding the item in question or not using it. In those cases, we elevate the object by avoiding it.

G-d commands us not to consume non-kosher animals since they originate in the realm of spirituality that is beyond our ability to elevate through eating. In their case, we elevate them by fulfilling G-d's commandment to abstain from eating them.

On the other hand, these animals can be elevated directly and actively by using them for purposes other than eating. For example, when a donkey or horse transports a person to perform a commandment, it, too, is infused with holiness.

By utilizing everything in our lives for fulfilling our Divine mission, we sanctify all aspects of reality with which Divine providence has put us in contact.[7]

---

6. *Avot* 6:11.
7. *Igrot Kodesh*, vol. 15, p. 281; *Hitva'aduyot 5743*, vol. 4, p. 1928.

FIFTH READING

Deuteronomy 14:22–29

Moses then taught the Jewish people that after they conquer the Land of Israel and begin working the land, G-d has obligated them to set aside a portion of their produce for the poor.

Charity and Wealth

וְהַגֵּר וְהַיָּתוֹם וְהָאַלְמָנָה אֲשֶׁר בִּשְׁעָרֶיךָ וְאָכְלוּ וְשָׂבֵעוּ לְמַעַן

יְבָרֶכְךָ ה' אֱלֹקֶיךָ בְּכָל מַעֲשֵׂה יָדְךָ אֲשֶׁר תַּעֲשֶׂה: (דברים יד, כט)

[Moses told the Jewish people, "You must give so] the convert, the orphan, and the widow who are in your cities may eat and be satisfied, so that G-d, your G-d, will bless you in all the work of your hand that you do."

We are taught in the Talmud that "the world stands on three pillars: the study of the Torah, the worship of G-d, and acts of loving kindness."[8] Thus, at all times, each of us has to engage in all three "pillars" in order to ensure that both the world in general and our personal, individual worlds stand on a firm basis.

Nonetheless, there were periods in Jewish history when our main focus was on the study of the Torah, and other periods when our main focus was on worship and prayer. In the present period, immediately preceding the final Redemption, our main focus is on charity – providing for the physical and spiritual needs of others.[9] We should even consider our study of the Torah, worship of G-d, and all the commandments and good deeds that we perform to be forms of charity, since their positive effects benefit the whole world, hastening the advent of the Messianic Redemption.[10]

8. *Avot* 1:2.
9. *Igeret HaKodesh* 9 (114a).
10. *Sefer Ma'amarim Melukat*, vol. 1, p. 109; *Igrot Kodesh*, vol. 11, p. 418, etc.

SIXTH READING
Deuteronomy 15:1–18

Moses then taught the Jewish people the law that the sabbatical year cancels loans. He warned them not to let this fact prevent them from loaning money.

Infinite Generosity

כִּי פָתֹחַ תִּפְתַּח אֶת יָדְךָ לוֹ: (דברים טו, ח)

[**Moses told the Jewish people, "Do not hesitate to give to someone;**] **rather, you must willingly open your hand for him."**

As finite beings living in a finite world, we are limited. This is especially clear with regard to charity. Our ability to give is limited by the resources that we have at our disposal. There is likewise a limit to the enthusiasm with which we can give, inasmuch as our enthusiasm results from our intellectual commitment and emotional involvement, which are also limited.

In contrast, there is relatively no limit to how much we can *want* something. Our will – relative to our ability to understand, feel, and act – is unlimited.

It is therefore crucial that we perform G-d's commandments willingly and wholeheartedly. Only then can the commandments we perform not be limited by the natural limitations of our abilities to understand, feel, and act. When we summon our unlimited willpower, we are capable of understanding, feeling, and acting far more than we originally thought.

By going beyond our natural limitations in performing G-d's will, especially with regard to charity, we elicit G-d's infinite beneficence. The ultimate expression of G-d's infinite beneficence will be the Messianic Redemption, in which the boundaries of nature – manifest as the constraints of exile – will be finally and irrevocably broken.[11]

11. *Likutei Sichot*, vol. 34, pp. 86–88.

SEVENTH READING
Deuteronomy 15:19–16:17

Moses then reviewed with the Jewish people the laws of the three "pilgrim" festivals – Passover, *Shavu'ot*, and *Sukkot* – which they were required to celebrate in the center that G-d would designate for centralized worship. Each festival must fall in a specific season.

Catching Up

שָׁמוֹר אֶת חֹדֶשׁ הָאָבִיב וְעָשִׂיתָ פֶּסַח לַה' אֱלֹקֶיךָ וְגו': (דברים טז, א)

[Moses told the Jewish people,] "Safeguard the month of ripening, when you must offer up the Passover offering to G-d, your G-d...."

The lunar year is approximately 11 days shorter than the solar year, so a month is added to the Jewish calendar every few years in order to make the lunar year "catch up" with the solar year. This ensures that the holidays – which always fall on a specific day of a specific lunar month – will also always fall in the correct season.

One of the lessons we can derive from this practice is that G-d always affords us an opportunity to "catch up," to complete whatever we left unfinished for whatever reason, and even to counteract the effects of not having utilized our time to the fullest extent.

Moreover, this feature of the Jewish calendar implies that by bettering our behavior, we can change not only our future, but our past – erasing its deficiencies and moving forward just as if these deficiencies never existed.

Furthermore, G-d empowers us to not only neutralize the deficiency of the lunar year but to even make some lunar years *longer* than the solar year. This is clearly an example of how G-d intends us to be His partner in creation, bringing the world to its true fulfillment.[12]

12. *Likutei Sichot*, vol. 34, pp. 338–341; *Igrot Melech*, vol. 1, pp. 428–433.

Shofetim

Leaders
Deuteronomy 16:18–21:9

THE FIFTH SECTION OF THE BOOK OF DEUTERONOMY CON-
tinues Moses' second farewell address to the Jewish people. It
opens as Moses instructs the Jewish people to appoint judges
(*Shofetim*, in Hebrew) throughout the Land of Israel to try cases
and uphold the law. It continues with Moses' instructions regarding the other leaders of the Jewish people: the king, the priests,
and the prophets.

FIRST READING

Deuteronomy 16:18–17:13

Moses instructed the Jewish people to appoint judges and sheriffs throughout the Land of Israel to try cases and uphold the law.

The Key to Objectivity

וְלֹא תִקַּח שֹׁחַד כִּי הַשֹּׁחַד יְעַוֵּר עֵינֵי חֲכָמִים וגו': (דברים טז, יט)

[Moses instructed the Jewish people to tell their judges,] "You must not accept a bribe, for bribery blinds the eyes of the sage...."

The problem with bribery is that aside from making us act immorally or irrationally, it distorts our sense of judgment, making us sincerely believe that our warped perception is indeed objective and just. The Torah therefore tells us that bribery "blinds the eyes of the sage," implying that even after accepting a bribe, the individual remains a sage – fully capable of logical reasoning – but that he has become blind to objective truth.[1]

It follows that besides the usual form of bribery – a monetary or other type of gift – there also exists a subtler form of bribery: our simple awareness of ourselves. If we seek to ascertain the truth about anything, we must approach it without any sense of selfhood, for even the slightest degree of self-awareness can cause our perception to be subjective, and therefore incorrect, even if only subtly.

In contrast, by cultivating true selflessness, we can be truly objective and see the unobstructed truth in all situations.[2]

1. *Hitva'aduyot 5747*, vol. 3, p. 232.
2. *Likutei Sichot*, vol. 23, p. 95.

SECOND READING
Deuteronomy 17:14–20

In addition to a system of judges and sheriffs, Moses instructed the Jewish people to appoint a king over them.

A Personal King

שׂוֹם תָּשִׂים עָלֶיךָ מֶלֶךְ וגו': (דברים יז, טו)

[Moses told the Jewish people,] "You may appoint a king over yourself...."

The Torah uses two terms for "king." The more common one is *melech*, meaning "ruler." The second is *nasi*, which means "someone who is aloof," and is also used for tribal heads.

This is because the king is intended to play two roles. His primary purpose is to be the nation's political leader, ensuring its military, economic, and social security by protecting it from foreign and domestic enemies, ensuring that the law is obeyed and that justice is served.

His secondary purpose is to lead the people spiritually – firstly by his own example of high moral conduct, and secondly by honoring Torah sages, or by teaching the Torah himself, if he is qualified.

Nowadays, we fulfill the Torah's directive to appoint a king by seeking our own, personal authorities, with whom we should consult for spiritual guidance. The two aspects of kingship described above teach us that we should consult our "kings" not only with regard to spiritual matters, but with regard to mundane matters as well, since there is a spiritual dimension to every aspect of life, and even mundane matters have an impact on our spiritual well-being.

By appointing our own personal "kings," we can hasten the advent of the Messiah, who will embody both aspects of kingship – leading the world to its material redemption and teaching us previously unrevealed dimensions of the Torah.[3]

3. *Likutei Sichot*, vol. 19, pp. 165–170.

THIRD READING

Deuteronomy 18:1–5

Moses then instructed the Jewish people to honor their priests, taking care to give them their allotments from their produce and flocks.

Assisting Our Inner Priest

רֵאשִׁית דְּגָנְךָ תִּירֹשְׁךָ וְיִצְהָרֶךָ וְרֵאשִׁית גֵּז צֹאנְךָ תִּתֶּן לוֹ: (דברים יח, ד)

[Moses told the Jewish people,] "You must give him the first of your grain, wine, and oil; and the first of the fleece of your sheep."

The difference between food and clothing is that the nutrients that we absorb from food nourish each part of our body differently, in accordance with the needs of that particular part, whereas clothing protects and warms the body in general. Food is therefore a metaphor for our intellect and emotions, which operate through specific organs (the brain and the heart), whereas clothing is a metaphor for our will and delight, which influence our bodies as a whole.

Thus, when the Torah tells us to give "the first of your grain, wine, and oil" to the priest, it is allegorically referring to our *specific* faculties. When it tells us to give him "the first fleece of your sheep," from which clothing is made, it is referring to our *general* faculties.

Our inner "priest" is our Divine soul, that part of us that is entirely devoted to spreading holiness in the world and helping us fulfill our Divine mission. By devoting the first and best aspects of our intellect, emotions, will, and delight to our Divine soul, we enable it to assist us in sanctifying ourselves and the world in general.[4]

4. *Likutei Sichot*, vol. 2, p. 326.

FOURTH READING

Deuteronomy 18:6–13

Moses then encouraged the Jewish people to turn only to G-d for all their needs, and not to seek ways to foretell the future.

Trusting in G-d

תָּמִים תִּהְיֶה עִם ה' אֱלֹקֶיךָ: (דברים יח, יג)

[Moses told the Jewish people,] **"Be wholehearted with G-d."**

In the course of fulfilling our Divine mission in life, we can sometimes wonder if we have properly ascertained what G-d wants of us in a specific situation. After all, we are only human, and we all know only too well how possible it is to misinterpret the meaning of messages.

The answer to this concern is to "be wholehearted with G-d," meaning to trust that G-d does not place us in situations that we are insufficiently equipped to handle. If, from our part, we make sure to enlist G-d's help and rely on it – ignoring whatever internal or external voices there may be that attempt to dissuade us – Divine providence will ensure that we possess all the knowledge and other qualities necessary to navigate life's challenges.[5]

---

5. *Likutei Sichot*, vol. 25, p. 341.

THURSDAY

FIFTH READING
Deuteronomy 18:14–19:13

Moses then warned the Jewish people not to listen to false prophets, and reviewed the laws of Cities of Refuge. When someone commits an accidental murder, this stroke of Divine providence indicates that the accidental murderer needs to be exiled to one of these cities in order to cure himself of some inner defect that would otherwise go unrectified. The victim's close relatives are allowed to kill the accidental murderer unless he has fled to one of these specially designated asylum cities.

The Power of Reframing

שָׁלוֹשׁ עָרִים תַּבְדִּיל לָךְ וגו': (דברים יט, ב)

[Moses told the Jewish people,] "You must designate three cities for yourself...."

Our Divine soul – our true source of optimism and positive energy – thrives on our good and holy deeds. When we allow ourselves to harbor negative thoughts, say negative words, or do negative acts, we drain vitality from our Divine souls, channeling this vitality instead into negativity. Allegorically, then, whenever we commit a misdeed, we are "killing" our Divine soul to some degree.

The Torah tells us that in such cases we have to take stock of our lives by going into "exile" in a "city of refuge," meaning that we have to uproot ourselves from our habitual misbehavior, reframing our lives in a better, more positive light.

In this way we can, at any time, remake ourselves into new, better human beings, starting life afresh with a positive outlook and a clean slate.[6]

6. *Likutei Sichot*, vol. 2, pp. 623–626.

SIXTH READING
Deuteronomy 19:14–20:9

Moses then began to instruct the Jewish people regarding how they were to conduct their conquest of the Land of Israel. Before battle, a specially appointed priest had to command the soldiers, in G-d's name, to be courageous.

Positive Thoughts

אַל יֵרַךְ לְבַבְכֶם אַל תִּירְאוּ וְאַל תַּחְפְּזוּ וְאַל תַּעַרְצוּ מִפְּנֵיהֶם: (דברים כ, ג)

[The priest must tell the soldiers,] "You must not let your heart become faint; you must not be afraid, you must not be alarmed, and you must not be terrified of them."

It is natural for people to be afraid on the frontlines of battle. The fact that G-d commanded these warriors not to be afraid teaches us that we have more control over our emotions – even natural, "gut" emotions – than we are accustomed to think we do. By choosing not to dwell on what is frightening, the soldiers can avoid becoming prey to fear.

Moreover, simply realizing that we can control our emotions to such an extent breaks their stranglehold over us.

G-d therefore encourages us to use our minds to influence our emotions proactively, inspiring ourselves to love Him and to fear Him. To be sure, our Divine souls innately love and fear G-d. But due to the overwhelming materiality of our day-to-day lives, these emotions are often submerged under more material loves and fears. By consciously choosing to think about the reality of G-d's presence in our lives, we manifest our otherwise hidden love and fear of Him, which enables us to live our lives in accordance with our higher values and truest desires.[7]

---

7. *Sefer HaMa'amarim Melukat*, vol. 2, p. 245.

SEVENTH READING
Deuteronomy 20:10–21:9

Moses told the Jewish people that unwitnessed, unsolved murder must be atoned for by a specific ritual performed by the judges of the high court (the Sanhedrin) and those of the city closest to the site of the murder.

Assuming Responsibility

וְיָצְאוּ זְקֵנֶיךָ וְשֹׁפְטֶיךָ וגו': (דברים כא, ב)

[Moses told the Jewish people,] "Your elders and judges must go out...."

The judges of the nearest city must absolve themselves of guilt in the case of an unsolved murder because they should have given the victim proper escort. Why, however, must the Sanhedrin, whose seat is in Jerusalem, travel to some far-flung outpost to participate in this ritual? Is it their fault that this crime occurred?

The answer is that since the Sanhedrin is responsible for the moral education of the nation, they are quite responsible for such a crime, even if indirectly.[8]

Allegorically, the slain person is anyone who is a victim of society's materialist outlook, which cuts him off from the Torah, our source of true life. The "Sanhedrin" – i.e., those of us with influence – must assume responsibility for such people. Specifically, the "local authorities" – those of us nearby – must give them the "escort" that will enable them to survive the spiritual threats along their journey in life, meaning that we must teach them the Torah and teach them to perform G-d's commandments.

If, on the other hand, we feel that we ourselves are the "slain" people in this analogy, then, if necessary, we must assume responsibility ourselves for our own spiritual welfare.[9]

8. *Tana d'vei Eliyahu* 11.
9. *Likutei Sichot*, vol. 24, pp. 129–131.

Teitzei

Expanding Divine Consciousness
Deuteronomy 21:10–25:19

THE SIXTH SECTION OF THE BOOK OF DEUTERONOMY CON-
tinues Moses' second farewell address to the Jewish people. Moses
continues to review many aspects of Jewish law, beginning with
the laws governing the behavior of Jewish soldiers when they "go
out" (*Teitzei*, in Hebrew) to war.

FIRST READING

Deuteronomy 21:10–21

Moses told the Jewish people that after they conquer the Land of Israel from its occupiers, they would be allowed, if necessary, to attack neighboring countries that posed a threat to their security.

The Peaceful War against Evil

כִּי תֵצֵא לַמִּלְחָמָה וגו': (דברים כא, י)

[Moses told the Jewish people,] "If you go out to [an optional] war...."

Our ability to succeed in our Divine mission to vanquish evil in the world at large is directly proportional to our success in vanquishing the evil within ourselves. The theater of our inner spiritual battle with evil is daily prayer, in which we strive to empower our Divine souls over our materialistic, animal drives.[1]

What, then, is the spiritual correlate to the "optional" war? Are we not obligated to confront every instance of evil we perceive within ourselves?

The answer is yes, but there is another way to vanquish our inner negativity besides confronting it directly in prayer: studying the Torah. Studying the Torah fills our consciousness with Divine awareness, and this awareness can largely dissipate the evil within us. Whereas the direct confrontation in prayer requires strenuous effort, the effect of Torah study is virtually effortless.

Thus, whenever there is an option to do away with evil through Torah study, taking the route of direct engagement in prayer becomes an "optional" war. Eliminating evil through Torah study renders the need to battle evil in prayer unnecessary, transforming prayer into the simple, serene expansion of Divine consciousness.[2]

---

1. See *Zohar* 3:243a. *Likutei Torah* 4:34c–35d.
2. *Likutei Sichot*, vol. 14, pp. 84–85.

SECOND READING

Deuteronomy 21:22–22:7

Moses then reviewed with the Jewish people the laws regarding inheritance, parental responsibility for their children's behavior, returning lost items, helping others, and cross-dressing.

Returning Lost Spirituality

לֹא תִרְאֶה אֶת שׁוֹר אָחִיךָ אוֹ אֶת שֵׂיוֹ נִדָּחִים וְהִתְעַלַּמְתָּ מֵהֶם הָשֵׁב תְּשִׁיבֵם לְאָחִיךָ: וְאִם לֹא קָרוֹב אָחִיךָ אֵלֶיךָ וְלֹא יְדַעְתּוֹ וַאֲסַפְתּוֹ אֶל תּוֹךְ בֵּיתֶךָ וְהָיָה עִמְּךָ עַד דְּרֹשׁ אָחִיךָ אֹתוֹ וַהֲשֵׁבֹתוֹ לוֹ: (דברים כב, א-ב)

[Moses told the Jewish people,] "You must not see your fellow's ox or sheep straying and ignore them; you must return them to your brother. If your fellow is not near you, or you do not know him, you must bring [the animal] into your house, where it must remain with you until your fellow seeks it out, whereupon you must return it to him."

Allegorically, the missing ox or sheep alludes to elements that are lacking from our fellow's observance of G-d's commandments and/or spiritual life in general. The Torah tells us here that we must not ignore such shortcomings in our fellows; we must help them reclaim their spiritual wealth.

This is true even if "your fellow is not near you, or you do not know him." Even in such cases, we must help our fellows retrieve whatever spiritual wealth they have lost due to their inadvertent over-involvement in the mundane affairs of the material world.

Furthermore, if, for some reason, our fellows do not consciously value their missing spirituality enough to seek it out, we must educate them to appreciate it – "until your fellow seeks it out" willingly.[3]

3. *Likutei Sichot*, vol. 24, pp. 284–285.

THIRD READING
Deuteronomy 22:8–23:7

Moses then reviewed with the Jewish people the laws regarding sending away a mother bird before taking her eggs, and the laws requiring them to build parapets on the roofs of their homes in order to prevent people from falling.

Boundaries

כִּי תִבְנֶה בַּיִת חָדָשׁ וְעָשִׂיתָ מַעֲקֶה לְגַגֶּךָ וגו': (דברים כב, ח)

[Moses told the Jewish people,] "When you build a new house, you must make a parapet for your roof."

Allegorically, "when you build a new house" means "when you set out to make this physical world into a home for G-d." This house is considered "new" because spiritualizing the physical is a reversal of the order of creation. G-d made the physical world appear consummately physical; by revealing its inner Divine essence, we make it a vehicle for spirituality.

"You must make a fence around the roof" means that in order to succeed in this mission and avoid being dragged into the materiality of the physical world, we must be sure to remain sufficiently aloof from the world. We accomplish this by setting appropriate boundaries that we do not cross. This shows that our involvement in the physical world is not for our own betterment or indulgence, but for selfless purposes.

This selflessness opens us up in turn to greater insights and to higher levels of the Divine consciousness.[4]

---

4. *Likutei Sichot*, vol. 2, pp. 384 ff; vol. 19, pp. 208 ff.

FOURTH READING

Deuteronomy 23:8–24

Moses also reviewed with the Jewish people the laws governing conduct in battle.

Courage, Confidence, and Clarity

כִּי ה' אֱלֹקֶיךָ מִתְהַלֵּךְ בְּקֶרֶב מַחֲנֶךָ לְהַצִּילְךָ

וְלָתֵת אֹיְבֶיךָ לְפָנֶיךָ וְגוֹ': (דברים כג, טו)

[**Moses told the Jewish people, "Your army
must conduct itself properly,**] **for G-d, your G-d,
accompanies you in the midst of your camp, to rescue
you and to deliver your enemies before you."**

The merit of those who actively protect our holy land and our people is very great, for they are assisting G-d, so to speak, in protecting us from our enemies. It is crucial that these individuals cultivate faith and trust in G-d, in order that they not fear the enemy or become disoriented.[5]

It is therefore particularly important that these individuals perform the commandment of *tefillin* – which are worn opposite the heart and over the head, indicating that they aid in subjecting the emotions and the mind to G-d. Subjecting our hearts and minds to G-d ensures that we will respond correctly – both emotionally and intellectually – to the challenges we face, i.e., with courage, confidence, and clarity. This, in turn, will elicit G-d's blessings in whatever we do and in our ability make the proper decisions.

In the specific case of the military, this translates into victory in battle. But for all of us, it means success in our Divine mission to make the world into G-d's ultimate home.[6]

---

5. See *Mishneh Torah, Melachim* 7:15.
6. Letter to the IDF after the *Yom Kippur* War, printed in *Igrot Kodesh*, vol. 29, pp. 10–11; *Likutei Sichot*, vol. 11, p. 203–204; and ibid., vol. 24, p. 449.

FIFTH READING

Deuteronomy 23:25–24:4

Moses also reviewed with the Jewish people the laws of divorce.

Spiritual Spouses

וְכָתַב לָהּ סֵפֶר כְּרִיתֻת וגו': (דברים כד, א)

[Moses told the Jewish people, "In order for a man to divorce his wife,] he must write her a bill of divorce."

Allegorically, each of us has a particular Divine mission, to which we are "married." This is within the greater context of our collective mission to refine the world and transform it into G-d's home.

Ideally, we should be happily "married" to our individual Divine mission. But we may sometimes feel that we have been mismatched, and might therefore consider abandoning our present Divine mission in favor of a new one.

In such cases, the traditional Jewish attitude of considering divorce a last resort teaches us that we should first try to persevere in our present Divine mission. It often happens that the problem is not with the mission but with ourselves: perhaps we are reluctant to make the effort required to continue, or we think that we deserve an easier or more glorious mission. As with marriage itself, maintaining "marital harmony" with our soul's mission-mate is often helped by consulting with experienced and sensitive counselors.

Again, as is the case with marriage itself, attaining proper "marital harmony" with our Divine mission is well worth the effort, for "when a man and woman merit, the Divine presence will rest between them,"[7] which allegorically means that we, through fulfilling our Divine mission, will indeed transform our portion of reality into G-d's true home.[8]

---

7. *Sotah* 17a.
8. *Likutei Sichot*, vol. 4, pp. 1121–1123.

SIXTH READING
Deuteronomy 24:5–13

Moses also reviewed with the Jewish people the laws regarding exemptions from military service. A man is exempt from military service during the first year of his marriage.

Fidelity to G-d

כִּי יִקַּח אִישׁ אִשָּׁה וְגו': (דברים כד, ה)

[Moses told the Jewish people,] "When a man takes a wife...."

In prophetic and Talmudic imagery, G-d and His chosen Jewish people are joined to each other like a husband and wife. In this allegorical context, the Biblical prohibition of a woman having more than one husband is analogous to the prohibition of worshipping other deities.

In a broader context, being "married" to G-d implies renouncing love for anything that "competes" with our love of Him. In particular, this means love for any aspect or element of the material world – such as sensual pleasure, wealth, influence, power, prestige, beauty, and so on. The Torah indeed allows us to enjoy these pursuits (as long as we partake of them in permitted ways), but encourages us to do so only as part of our appreciation of G-d's goodness, using them to intensify our love for Him. As soon as they become ends in themselves, they lose their legitimacy.

In human marriage, a couple can preserve, develop, and enhance their relationship by focusing their love on each other, renouncing all other relationships. Similarly, by focusing on the Divine dimension in everything – rather than its material aspect – we can develop and enhance our relationship with G-d, turning it into a true union.[9]

9. *Likutei Sichot*, vol. 19, pp. 217–218.

SEVENTH READING

Deuteronomy 24:14–25:19

Moses reviewed with the Jewish people the duty to remember how the nation of Amalek attacked them when they left Egypt.

The Antidote to Indifference

זָכוֹר אֵת אֲשֶׁר עָשָׂה לְךָ עֲמָלֵק ... אֲשֶׁר קָרְךָ בַּדֶּרֶךְ וְגוֹ': (דברים כה, יז-יח)

[Moses told the Jewish people,] "You must remember what Amalek did to you ... how they attacked you by surprise on the way.... "

The Hebrew word used in this verse for "attacked you by surprise" (קרך) can also be understood to mean "cooled you off." Thus, allegorically, Amalek represents the inner voice of apathy and indifference that tries to cool off our enthusiasm for holiness and goodness. A defining characteristic of a healthy spiritual life is periodically feeling inspired to leave "Egypt," i.e., to lift ourselves above the bondage and dictates of physical reality by aspiring to lead a higher, more spiritual life. But when we try to "leave Egypt," the voice of our inner Amalek attempts to distract us and discourage us.

The antidote to Amalek is to "remember"; to keep the holy words of the Torah in the forefront of our consciousness.[10]

The fact that the Torah commands us to "wipe out" Amalek implies that we can successfully do so. By continuously reminding ourselves of the Torah's eternal relevance, we can neutralize the ability of Amalek to "cool off" our relationship with G-d.[11]

10. *Sefer HaMa'amarim Kuntereisim*, vol. 2, p. 287a–288a.
11. *Sefer HaSichot 5749*, vol. 2, pp. 680–681.

Tavo

Entering the Covenant
Deuteronomy 26:1–29:8

THE SEVENTH SECTION OF THE BOOK OF DEUTERONOMY
concludes Moses' second farewell address to the Jewish people. It
contains Moses' completion of his review of the commandments,
beginning with one that would become relevant only after the
Jewish people would enter (*Tavo*, in Hebrew) the Land of Israel –
that of bringing the first fruits of each year's harvest to the holy
Temple. It then continues with Moses' review of the covenant
between G-d and the Jewish people.

FIRST READING

Deuteronomy 26:1–11

Moses taught the Jewish people the laws regarding the first fruits of the annual harvest, which they would be required to observe once they enter the Land of Israel.

A Descent that Leads to Ascent

וְהָיָה כִּי תָבוֹא אֶל הָאָרֶץ אֲשֶׁר ה' אֱלֹקֶיךָ נֹתֵן לְךָ וְגוֹ': (דברים כו, א)

[Moses told the Jewish people,] "When you enter the land that G-d, your G-d, is giving you...."

Allegorically, "coming into the land" refers to the descent of the soul into the body at birth. This descent is quite drastic, for when we leave our idyllic, spiritual abode, we find ourselves confronting a world whose physicality is so overwhelming that it totally obscures the Divinity within it.

Nevertheless, this new abode is a gift "that G-d, your G-d, is giving you." This is because before our descent into a body, we are capable of experiencing only the degree of Divine consciousness that characterizes our pre-birth level of spirituality. In contrast, in the course of fulfilling our mission in the physical world, we acquire the ability to experience much higher levels of Divine consciousness. Thus, our descent into this world leads to an ultimate ascent – a level of Divine revelation higher than we had ever known.

Being aware of this process helps us maximize the time we spend in this lifetime, inspiring us to live our lives in the fullest and best way possible.[1]

1. *Likutei Sichot*, vol. 9, p. 357.

SECOND READING

Deuteronomy 26:12–15

The Jewish farmer was required to take a portion of the produce of the first, second, fourth, and fifth years of every seven-year cycle and consume it in Jerusalem. While there, had had to recite a declaration that he had observed all the laws pertaining to his harvest, including those concerning the first fruits.

Elevating Physicality

וְגַם נְתַתִּיו לַלֵוִי וגו': (דברים כו, יג)

[Moses told the Jewish people, "You must declare,] 'I have given the Levite [his due], and also [the first fruits to the priests].'"

As opposed to most offerings brought in the Temple, the first fruits were not burned on the Altar, but given to a priest to eat. Although portions of those sacrifices that were burned on the Altar were also eaten or used by the priests, the first fruits were unique in that no part of them whatsoever was burned on the Altar. The priest only placed them in front of the Altar for a short time, and they were thus considered to have been given to G-d. After this, they were enjoyed entirely by human beings.

The reason for this is that while all sacrifices expressed how we strive to become closer to G-d in some way (this being the meaning of the Hebrew word for "sacrifice," *korban*), the first fruits chiefly expressed the attitude we are intended to have toward our involvement in the physical world. We are not meant to destroy physicality but to elevate it, so that its inherent holiness is revealed even while it retains its physical state.[2]

2. *Likutei Sichot*, vol. 9, p. 358.

THIRD READING

Deuteronomy 26:16–19

Moses then began to encourage the Jewish people to uphold their covenant with G-d that was forged at the Giving of the Torah on Mount Sinai. In return for keeping the covenant, G-d would hold them especially dear, above His love for all other people.

Disengaged Yet Involved

וַה׳ הֶאֱמִירְךָ הַיּוֹם לִהְיוֹת לוֹ לְעַם סְגֻלָּה … וּלְתִתְּךָ עֶלְיוֹן

עַל כָּל הַגּוֹיִם … וְלִהְיֹתְךָ עַם קָדֹשׁ: (דברים כו, יח-יט)

[**Moses told the Jewish people,**] "**G-d has set you apart today, to be His treasured people…to make you supreme above all the nations…a holy people.**"

The basis of our relationship with G-d is that He *chose* us as His "treasure," which means that He and we are bound together supra-rationally. This bond is hidden; it exists in our lives as an undercurrent, whose presence we rarely even sense. It is therefore necessary to bring this intrinsic bond to the surface by relating to G-d *actively*. We do this in two ways:

First, by being "a holy people," dedicating ourselves to G-d's purposes by studying His Torah and observing its commandments. This *separates* us from the materiality of the world, setting us apart as a holy nation.

Second, by being a "kingdom of nobles" who rule over the materiality of the world, co-opting its positive aspects into our Divine mission. This *engages* us in the materiality of the world.

By actualizing our bond with G-d in these two ways, we can develop the sensitivity that enables us to palpably feel our hidden, inherent relationship with Him.[3]

---

3. *Likutei Sichot*, vol. 18, pp. 21–23, 409–410; ibid., vol. 11, pp. 5–7.

FOURTH READING
Deuteronomy 27:1–10

In order to renew the covenant between G-d and the Jewish peo-
ple upon their entry into the Land of Israel, G-d instructed the
Jewish people to perform an elaborate ritual at Shechem, between
Mount Gerizim and Mount Eival.

Sanctifying the Secular

וְכָתַבְתָּ עַל הָאֲבָנִים אֶת כָּל דִּבְרֵי הַתּוֹרָה הַזֹּאת בַּאֵר הֵיטֵב: (דברים כז, ח)

**[Moses told the Jewish people, "When you reach
Shechem, you must erect an altar] and write upon the
stones all the words of this Torah very clearly...."**

We are taught[4] that the words "very clearly" imply that the Jews
were to translate the Torah into the 70 original languages of
humanity and to write these translations on this altar.

It is certainly preferable to study the Torah in the original
Hebrew, for the subtle nuances of meaning inherent in the text –
not to mention its allusive and mystical subtexts – can only be
noticed and appreciated in the original. Nevertheless, there is an
advantage in studying the Torah in secular languages, namely, that
using these languages to study the Torah elevates and sanctifies
them, at least while they are being used for this purpose. Furthermore, expressing the Torah's concepts in secular idioms allows
the sanctity and message of the Torah to permeate even those
layers of existence that are otherwise antithetical or antagonistic
to Divine consciousness.

Thus, by studying the Torah in other languages, we prepare
the world for its ultimate spiritual elevation and sanctification,
which will occur with the Messianic Redemption.[5]

4. Rashi on this verse.
5. *Likutei Sichot*, vol. 36, pp. 38–44; ibid., vol. 3, pp. 862–864.

FIFTH READING

Deuteronomy 27:11–28:6

Moses then added his own blessings and warnings to those given by G-d at Mount Sinai.

Being Pursued by G-d's Blessings

וּבָאוּ עָלֶיךָ כָּל הַבְּרָכוֹת הָאֵלֶּה וְהִשִּׂיגֻךָ כִּי
תִשְׁמַע בְּקוֹל ה' אֱלֹקֶיךָ: (דברים כח, ב)

**[Moses promised the Jewish people,] "All
the following blessings will pursue you and
overtake you, if you obey G-d, your G-d."**

This implies that even if we are foolish enough to flee from G-d's blessings, they will ultimately overtake us, and we will receive them even against our will![6]

---

6. *Hitva'aduyot 5742*, vol. 4, p. 2158.

SIXTH READING

Deuteronomy 28:7–69

Included in Moses' blessings was the promise that the Jewish people would be G-d's holy people if they follow His teachings.

Quantum Leaps

וְהָלַכְתָּ בִּדְרָכָיו: (דברים כח, ט)

[Moses told the Jewish people, "You will be G-d's people if] you walk in His ways."

Following G-d's path as outlined in the Torah enables us to "walk." Before our souls descend into our bodies, we experience G-dliness in a relatively static fashion. Any new level of Divine consciousness that we reach can be understood in the context of our previous level of spiritual understanding. Thus, our spiritual growth prior to birth is a limited, step-by-step process.

In contrast, once our souls have entered our bodies and we are able to study the Torah and perform G-d's commandments, we are able to move toward G-d with quantum leaps. This ability enables us to "walk," i.e., to make real progress in our relationship with G-d.

This knowledge can inspire us not to remain complacent regarding our spiritual lives, but to aspire to levels of Divine consciousness beyond what we can presently even imagine. We can achieve these levels through devoted study of the Torah and the performance of G-d's commandments.[7]

7. *Likutei Sichot*, vol. 4, p. 1132.

SHABBAT

SEVENTH READING
Deuteronomy 29:1–8

Moses then told the Jewish people that they should be confident in their ability to remain true to G-d's covenant and enjoy His protection.

Spiritual Maturity

וְלֹא נָתַן ה' לָכֶם לֵב לָדַעַת וְעֵינַיִם לִרְאוֹת וְאָזְנַיִם
לִשְׁמֹעַ עַד הַיּוֹם הַזֶּה: (דברים כט, ג)

**[Moses told the Jewish people,] "G-d did not give you a
heart to know, eyes to see, and ears to hear – until this day."**

Moses said this almost 40 years after G-d gave the Torah to the Jewish people. According to the sages, this teaches us that it takes time for students to internalize their teacher's methodology and analytical approach to knowledge. Only after observing how the teacher tackles subject after subject, challenge after challenge, will the teacher's methods crystallize into a coherent methodology in the students' minds. Once the students have acquired their teacher's thinking process, they will be able to apply it to any new subject matter that presents itself.

Thus, Moses meant that now that almost 40 years had elapsed since the Jewish people had first been exposed to the Torah and its worldview – and they had observed G-d's ways during all the intervening years – they were now "mature" enough to live their lives in full accordance with the Torah's intentions.

Similarly, as the Ba'al Shem Tov said,[8] we must cultivate the ability to discern G-d's lessons for us in every event that we witness or experience. This enables us to mature spiritually, learning how to respond to life's challenges and opportunities in the most effective, positive ways possible.[9]

---

8. *Keter Shem Tov* (ed. Kehot), addenda 127 ff.
9. *Likutei Sichot*, vol. 34, pp. 164–166.

Nitzavim

Sealing the Covenant
Deuteronomy 29:9–30:12

IN THE EIGHTH SECTION OF THE BOOK OF DEUTERONOMY, Moses begins his third and final farewell address to the Jewish people, which he delivered on the day he would die, 7 Adar 2488. He opens his address by telling the people that they are all standing (*Nitzavim*, in Hebrew) before him in order to seal the covenant between them and G-d.

FIRST READING

Deuteronomy 29:9–11

Moses told the Jewish people that G-d's covenant applies to each and every one of them.

Beginning with the Foundation

אַתֶּם נִצָּבִים הַיּוֹם כֻּלְּכֶם לִפְנֵי ה' אֱלֹקֵיכֶם רָאשֵׁיכֶם שִׁבְטֵיכֶם

זִקְנֵיכֶם ... טַפְּכֶם ... לְעָבְרְךָ בִּבְרִית ה' אֱלֹקֶיךָ: (דברים כט, ט-יא)

[**Moses said to the Jewish people,**] "**You are all standing today before G-d, your G-d: your leaders ... elders ... young children ... in order that you enter into a covenant with G-d.**"

In these verses, G-d tells us that He made His covenant with all of us – with every type of Jew, regardless of status, gender, or age.

Inasmuch as the chief instrument of this covenant is the Torah, this means that every word of the Torah is relevant to every Jew, containing a lesson for even the youngest and uninitiated. Of course, every word of the Torah also contains infinitely more insights, of infinite sophistication and depth, which can only be understood by those with the requisite background. But these deeper levels of meaning are additional to the Torah's basic, simple meaning and lessons.

Thus, regardless of our background, the entire Torah is relevant to each of us in a way that we can immediately understand and appreciate. The deeper meanings of the Torah's words indeed beckon us, but we must always first and foremost seek to understand the Torah's message for us implicit in its simplest, most accessible meaning.[1]

---

1. *Sichot Kodesh 5739*, vol. 1, pp. 235–236.

SECOND READING
Deuteronomy 29:12–14

Moses told the Jewish people that G-d was sealing His covenant not only with them but with all future generations of Jews.

Our Covenant with G-d

וְאֵת אֲשֶׁר אֵינֶנּוּ פֹּה עִמָּנוּ הַיּוֹם: (דברים כט, יד)

[Moses told the Jewish people that G-d was sealing His covenant not only with them, but also] "with those who are not here with us today."

The first covenant that G-d made with the Jewish people, at Mount Sinai, transformed only that generation into G-d's chosen people. In order for all Jews for all time to become G-d's chosen people, a second covenant was required. Moses made this covenant between G-d and the Jewish people 40 years later, on the day of his death.

The first covenant was contingent upon the people's loyalty to G-d, as is clear from the fact that it had to be renewed after the incident of the Golden Calf. This second covenant, however, is absolute. It cannot be nullified or canceled by any inconsistencies in our behavior.

The Jews who stood before Moses when he established this covenant with G-d were our proxies. Thus, each of us, rather than being obligated to observe the commandments and being privileged to enjoy the accompanying unique relationship with G-d only indirectly (by virtue of being a descendant of past parties to G-d's covenant) is a *direct* party to G-d's covenant.[2]

2. *Likutei Sichot*, vol. 19, pp. 266–272; ibid., vol. 24, pp. 188–191.

THIRD READING
Deuteronomy 29:15–28

Moses told the Jewish people that inasmuch as they had seen the idolatrous practices of Egypt, some of them might be enticed to imitate the Egyptian way of life. It was therefore necessary to renew and strengthen the covenant that G-d first forged with the Jewish people at Mount Sinai.

The Gift of Freedom

כִּי אַתֶּם יְדַעְתֶּם אֵת אֲשֶׁר יָשַׁבְנוּ בְּאֶרֶץ מִצְרָיִם וְגוֹ': (דברים כט, טו)

[Moses told the Jewish people,] "You know how we dwelt in Egypt."

G-d wants us to constantly recall that we were slaves in Egypt and that He freed us from this slavery.[3]

The word for "Egypt" in Hebrew (*Mitzrayim*) means "constraints" (*meitzarim*). Allegorically, then, "Egypt" signifies our personal and collective spiritual constraints. G-d wants us to also constantly[4] feel how He continuously frees us from our personal and collective "Egypts."

Conscious of our absolute, G-d-given freedom, we will never be slaves to any form of negativity or evil. We can freely choose to ignore the voices – both from within and from without – that urge us to go against G-d's will or to conform with any of the negative norms of our society.[5]

---

3. *Pesachim* 10:5 (116b).
4. *Tanya*, chapter 47.
5. *Hitva'aduyot 5745*, vol. 5, pp. 2989–2990.

FOURTH READING

Deuteronomy 30:1–6

Moses then informed the Jewish people that in the future, they would undergo periods of infidelity to G-d's covenant, and suffer as a result. Nonetheless, even then, the path of return to G-d would always be open.

G-d Is Always Accessible

וְשָׁב ה' אֱלֹקֶיךָ אֶת שְׁבוּתְךָ וְגוֹ': (דברים ל, ג)

[Moses told the Jewish people,] "G-d, your G-d, will bring back your exiles."

This phrase may also be read, "G-d, your G-d, will return *together with* your exiles," implying that G-d, so to speak, accompanies us into exile.

This notion may be likened to the law that stipulates that when a student commits an act of unintentional murder, requiring him to be exiled to a city of refuge,[6] his teacher must accompany him.[7] G-d is our teacher and we are His students;[8] thus, when we go into exile, G-d must go into exile along with us.

This means that G-d is just as accessible to us in exile as He was before we were exiled and as He will be after the Redemption. This includes all our states of personal "exile" – i.e., situations in which we feel estranged from holiness or apathetic to it. Even at such times, G-d is nearby; opening the lines of communication is entirely up to us.[9]

6. See Exodus 21:13; Numbers 35:6–34; Deuteronomy 4:41–43, 19:1–13.

7. *Makot* 10a.

8. Isaiah 54:13.

9. *Likutei Sichot*, vol. 29, p. 38.

FIFTH READING
Deuteronomy 30:7–10

Moses then promised the Jewish people that in the future they would indeed enjoy the fulfillment of all of G-d's blessings.

Transforming Troubles

כִּי תָשׁוּב אֶל ה' אֱלֹקֶיךָ בְּכָל לְבָבְךָ וּבְכָל נַפְשֶׁךָ: (דברים ל, י)

[**Moses told the Jewish people, "G-d will once again bless you with abundance and rejoice over you,**] **when you return to G-d with all your heart and soul."**

The Ba'al Shem Tov taught us that by returning to G-d during times of trouble, we can transform the trouble itself into Divine revelation. "Returning to G-d" in this context means understanding our suffering to be a cue from G-d that He wants us to become closer to Him. This can involve either correcting the negative or re-emphasizing the positive – in other words, either renouncing some form of misbehavior or simply intensifying our study of the Torah, our prayers, or our performance of G-d's commandments – or both.

This awareness can inspire us to look at troublesome times not as causes for depression or annoying nuisances, but as tremendous opportunities for spiritual growth.[10]

10. *Sefer HaMa'amarim 5699*, p. 161; *Likutei Sichot*, vol. 2, p. 352; *Keter Shem Tov* (ed. Kehot), addendum 10.

SIXTH READING

Deuteronomy 30:11–14

Moses assured the Jewish people that they would always be able to know what G-d expects of them by studying the Torah.

Our Innate Love of G-d

כִּי הַמִּצְוָה הַזֹּאת . . . וְלֹא רְחֹקָה הִוא: (דברים ל, יא)

[Moses said to the Jewish people, regarding the study of the Torah,] "This commandment is not remote from you."

All of us have the power to train our hearts to become emotionally involved with G-d through studying His Torah and observing His commandments. We possess this power in the form of an inherent, deep-seated love for G-d that is innate to our Divine soul.

This love is initially "hidden," i.e., we are not conscious of it. However, we can easily access it by means of a number of rather simple exercises in contemplating Divine providence, the vastness and beauty of creation, and so on.

We therefore do not have to "manufacture" love of G-d or force ourselves, against our nature, to love Him. We already naturally love Him; all we have to do is open ourselves up to this love, allowing it to manifest itself.[11]

11. *Likutei Sichot*, vol. 34, pp. 173–178.

SEVENTH READING

Deuteronomy 30:15–20

Moses then told the Jewish people that G-d is presenting them with the free choice to choose between good and evil.

Choosing Life

רְאֵה נָתַתִּי לְפָנֶיךָ הַיּוֹם אֶת הַחַיִּים וְאֶת הַטּוֹב וְאֶת הַמָּוֶת

וְאֶת הָרָע ... וּבָחַרְתָּ בַּחַיִּים וְגוֹ': (דברים ל, טו-יט)

[Moses told the Jewish people,] "Behold, I have set before you today life and good and death and evil. Choose life!"

The basic understanding of this verse is that good leads to life and evil leads to death. On a deeper level, however, this verse alludes to four distinct levels of reality:

- "Death" refers to the physical universe, since it possesses no intrinsic life-force.
- "Evil" refers to that which diverts our attention from G-d, i.e., our inborn attraction for both permitted and prohibited sensual indulgences.
- "Life" refers to the vitality that we perceive in all living beings, which originates in the Divine life-force that exists within all creation – whether animate or inanimate.
- "Good" refers to the more sublime Divine energy, which exists outside of the context of creation.

In this context, G-d is enjoining us in this verse to choose a life that leads to Divine revelation, rather than a life that is devoted to materiality and that opposes the propagation of Divine consciousness.

Making this choice enables us to live our lives to the fullest, as the verse continues, "in order that you and your descendants may live!"[12]

12. *Likutei Sichot*, vol. 25, p. 7; *Sefer HaMa'amarim 5670*, p. 20.

Vayeilech

Recording and Sealing the Covenant
Deuteronomy 31:1–30

THE NINTH SECTION OF THE BOOK OF DEUTERONOMY CON-
tinues the description of Moses' third and final farewell address
to the Jewish people. It begins with the account of how Moses
went (*Vayeilech*, in Hebrew) and installed Joshua as his successor,
and continues with the account of how Moses wrote down the
Torah and commanded the Jewish people to assemble every seven
years to hear it read in the holy Temple.

FIRST READING
Deuteronomy 31:1–3

Moses informed the Jewish people that this day, 7 Adar, was his 120th birthday, and would also be the day that he would die.

An Insatiable Thirst

וַיֹּאמֶר אֲלֵהֶם ... לֹא אוּכַל עוֹד לָצֵאת וְלָבוֹא וגו': (דברים לא, ב)

[Moses] said to [the people,] "I can no longer go and come."

With these words, Moses meant that his ability to expound and explain the Torah had been curtailed. He understood this as a clear Divine indication that his term as leader was ending.

Although none of us can compare to Moses, we can nonetheless learn an important lesson from this. We should consider every iota of knowledge of the Torah that we can possibly absorb to be essential to the effective fulfillment of our Divine mission. To that end, we should strive to make the Torah part and parcel of our very being, and conversely, try to avoid forgetting even the smallest bit of knowledge that we have learned, or squandering any opportunity to add to our knowledge of the Torah.

Each time we enhance our knowledge of the Torah, our observance of G-d's commandments, or our heartfelt connection to G-d, we become more alive and energized, having enhanced our connection to the source of life. This renders us better able both to fulfill our Divine mission and to help others fulfill theirs, as well.[1]

1. *Likutei Sichot*, vol. 29, pp. 193–194.

SECOND READING

Deuteronomy 31:4–6

Moses reassured the Jewish people that G-d would always be with His people. They therefore had nothing to fear from the nations then occupying the Land of Israel, which they were about to enter and conquer.

Divine Assistance

חִזְקוּ וְאִמְצוּ ... כִּי ה' אֱלֹקֶיךָ הוּא הַהֹלֵךְ עִמָּךְ
לֹא יַרְפְּךָ וְלֹא יַעַזְבֶךָ: (דברים לא, ו)

[Moses told the people,] "Neither fear nor be discouraged ... for G-d, your G-d, is the one who goes with you; He will neither fail you nor forsake you."

In both Moses' time and our own, the Jewish people witnessed how they have survived miraculously in the face of seemingly insurmountable odds. We have seen how "G-d is the one who goes with you; He will neither fail you nor forsake you." We must, of course, employ every natural means at our disposal to outsmart and outfight our enemies, but in the final analysis we must not deny G-d's openly miraculous assistance and protection.

This holds true on the personal level, as well, as we each fight our own battles against our inner and outer enemies. No matter how formidable our demons may seem to us, we should recall that these challenges were put in place by G-d in order to test our faith in Him. Consciously or not, they are waiting for us to resist them, and once we do, they will be transformed into our allies.

All of this will lead to the ultimate victory of good over evil, of right over wrong, and of holiness over materialism, hastening the advent of the final Redemption of all reality.[2]

2. *Sichot Kodesh 5738*, vol. 1, pp. 25–26, 31–34, 37–41.

THIRD READING

Deuteronomy 31:7–9

Moses then summoned Joshua and appointed him as his successor in the presence of the entire Jewish people.

Our Right to the Land

וַיִּקְרָא מֹשֶׁה לִיהוֹשֻׁעַ וַיֹּאמֶר אֵלָיו ... כִּי אַתָּה תָּבוֹא אֶת הָעָם הַזֶּה
אֶל הָאָרֶץ אֲשֶׁר נִשְׁבַּע ה' לַאֲבֹתָם לָתֵת לָהֶם וְגוֹ': (דברים לא, ז)

**Moses summoned Joshua and said to him ... "You
must come with this people into the land
that G-d swore to their forefathers."**

The Torah begins relating its instructions for humanity in general and the Jewish people in particular only halfway through its second book, the Book of Exodus. Before this, it describes the early history of the world and the origins of the Jewish people. This lengthy preface is required in order to explain how the task of fulfilling G-d's purpose on earth eventually necessitated the existence of a unique nation among humanity – the Jewish people – living life according to the specific Divine commandments in the context of a specific homeland – the Promised Land of Israel.

The creation account establishes G-d, the Creator, as the true "owner" of the entire world. This sovereignty allowed Him, when the time came, to expropriate the intended Jewish homeland from the people whom He had allowed to occupy it in the meantime.

This is the sole justification necessary – and the sole justification that is ultimately effective – for the renewal of Jewish presence in the Holy Land. The Land of Israel is ours solely because this is G-d's intention, and we should say so unequivocally and proudly.[3]

---

3. *Likutei Sichot*, vol. 5, pp. 1–15; ibid. vol. 20, p. 541; ibid., vol. 10, pp. 1–6.

FOURTH READING
Deuteronomy 31:10–13

Moses then conveyed G-d's command to the Jewish people that they assemble once every seven years, during the festival of *Sukkot*, in order to hear their king read specific passages from the Torah. Although they were commanded to study the Torah in any case, this ceremony was designed to instill renewed commitment to G-d's covenant with them.

Inspiring Ourselves and Others

הַקְהֵל אֶת הָעָם ... לְמַעַן יִשְׁמְעוּ וּלְמַעַן יִלְמְדוּ
וְיָרְאוּ אֶת ה' אֱלֹקֵיכֶם וגו': (דברים לא, יב)

[**Moses told the Jewish people, "Every seven years]
assemble the people . . . in order that they hear and
in order that they learn to revere G-d, your G-d."**

The commandment to assemble every seven years differs from most other commandments in that its content and meaning are not just the intention *behind* its performance or even the intended *result* of its performance, but *an integral component* of its performance.

In this way, the septennial assembly is similar to prayer. The content of our prayers is an integral component of them. Pronouncing the words of prayer and going through the body-motions without paying attention to what we are saying is not true prayer.

Nowadays, we fulfill the commandment to convene a septennial assembly by gathering others in order to inspire them to advance and enhance their relationship with G-d. By doing so, we hasten the advent of the Redemption, when the Messiah will assemble us all and we will listen to him read the Torah in the rebuilt Temple, inspiring us to continuously advance and enhance our relationship with G-d by making the world into His true home.[4]

4. *Likutei Sichot*, vol. 34, pp. 211–216.

FIFTH READING

Deuteronomy 31:14–19

G-d then informed Moses that He was going to dictate a poem to him that he should teach the Jewish people. The purpose of the poem was to inspire the Jewish people to remain loyal to G-d throughout any misfortunes that might befall them as a result of their misdeeds.

Double Darkness; Double Light

וְאָנֹכִי הַסְתֵּר אַסְתִּיר פָּנַי בַּיּוֹם הַהוּא וְגו': (דברים לא, יח)

[G-d instructed Moses to tell the Jewish people,] "I will hide My face on that day."

In this verse, the Hebrew verb for "hide" is intensified by a grammatical repetition. According to the Ba'al Shem Tov, this teaches us that toward the end of the exile, G-d's hiddenness will itself be hidden from us.[5] In other words, having become accustomed to spiritual darkness, we will view it as natural.

However, we have also been taught that all of the Torah's threats are really blessings that are too intense or too sublime to be revealed to us as blessings. In this case, the double darkness of our present exile is the external manifestation of a double light that we are indeed bathed in but cannot perceive. This double light is the awareness that G-d is not only beyond anything that we can conceive, but beyond anything that we can conceive of conceiving.

This double inconceivability of G-d allows us to believe that He can extricate us from the double darkness of exile, inconceivable as it may seem to us. This awareness can inspire us to redouble our dedication to G-d and to our Divine mission.[6]

5. *Toledot Ya'akov Yosef, Bereishit* (22a).
6. *Likutei Sichot*, vol. 9, pp. 193–195.

SIXTH READING
Deuteronomy 31:20–24

G-d then addressed Joshua from the cloud at the entrance to the Tabernacle, charging him with the mission of leading the Jewish people into the Land of Israel.

A Land of Milk

כִּי אֲבִיאֶנּוּ אֶל הָאֲדָמָה . . . זָבַת חָלָב וּדְבַשׁ וְגוֹ': (דברים לא, כ)

[G-d instructed Moses to tell the Jewish people,] "When I bring them into the land . . . flowing with milk and honey. . . . "

In general, the Torah allows us to consume part of an animal only when the animal has first been properly ritually slaughtered. Milk, however, issues from the animal before slaughtering, so on this account milk should be forbidden. Nevertheless, the Torah does permit the consumption of milk, as evidenced in this verse and in the many others where this expression occurs.[7]

The permissibility of milk, which should seemingly be forbidden, alludes to the process of repentance. Through repentance, we transform something forbidden – a sin – into something positive. The sin itself becomes the impetus for renewing and strengthening our bond with G-d, just as milk possesses nutrients that enliven and strengthen us.[8]

---

7. *Bechorot* 6b; *Responsa Noda Bihudah*, second series, *Yoreh Dei'ah* 36;. See *Encyclopedia Talmudit*, s.v. *Chalav*.
8. *Likutei Sichot*, vol. 17, pp. 19–21.

SHABBAT

SEVENTH READING
Deuteronomy 31:25–30

Moses then instructed the Levites to place the Torah scroll that he would soon write in the Ark of the Covenant, together with the Tablets of the Covenant that he received at Mount Sinai.

Common and Personal Paths

לָקֹחַ אֵת סֵפֶר הַתּוֹרָה הַזֶּה וְשַׂמְתֶּם אֹתוֹ מִצַּד

אֲרוֹן בְּרִית ה' אֱלֹקֵיכֶם וְגוֹ': (דברים לא, כו)

[Moses told the Levites,] "Take this Torah scroll and place it alongside the Ark of the Covenant of G-d, your G-d...."

Moses wrote 13 copies of the Torah: one for each of the 12 tribes, and one to be placed alongside the Tablets of the Covenant, to serve as a standard by which other copies of the Torah could always be checked for accuracy.[9]

The fact that Moses wrote a copy of the Torah for each tribe teaches us that each tribe possesses its unique reflection of the Torah. This is manifest nowadays in how observance of the Torah has flowered into a beautiful assortment of regional and cultural variations in Jewish practice, all of which are based on the Torah's original teachings.

But just as there was a thirteenth, "general" Torah scroll, the "general" path of Jewish practice, spiritual life, and prayer, was worked out by the founder of Chabad Chasidism, Rabbi Shneur Zalman of Liadi.[10] Those of us who have difficulty identifying which "tribal" path of observance and prayer is uniquely suited to our individual soul can make use of this "general" path.[11]

9. *Devarim Rabbah* 9:9; *Midrash Tehilim* 90:3; cf. Rashi on Deuteronomy 29:3.
10. I.e., his update of the *Shulchan Aruch,* the *Tanya,* and his version of the liturgy.
11. *Likutei Sichot,* vol. 4, pp. 1148–1149.

Ha'azinu

The Poem of Testimony

Deuteronomy 32:1–52

THE TENTH SECTION OF THE BOOK OF DEUTERONOMY IS composed almost entirely of the Poem of Testimony that G-d taught Moses and instructed him to teach the Jewish people. In it, Moses bids the Jewish people to hearken (*Ha'azinu*, in Hebrew) to his words as he reviews their history and informs them of the consequences of their future conduct, whether good or bad.

FIRST READING
Deuteronomy 32:1–6

Moses called upon both heaven and earth to bear witness to the message he was about to deliver to the Jewish people. He began by comparing the Torah to rain and dew.

The Dew of the Torah

יַעֲרֹף כַּמָּטָר לִקְחִי תִּזַּל כַּטַּל אִמְרָתִי וגו': (דברים לב, ב)

[Moses told the Jewish people,] "My doctrine will drop like the rain; my speech will flow like the dew."

The extent to which rain falls depends on our merits, whereas the extent to which dew condenses does not. Thus, rain and dew allude to the two aspects of Divine revelation that we receive when we study the Torah: one is commensurate with our efforts, whereas the second is a Divine gift.

These two aspects of Divine revelation are present in the study of any part of the Torah. Studying any part of the Torah is an encounter with the Giver of the Torah, who reveals Himself subliminally within the words we utter and the ideas we study.

In the narrower sense, however, we elicit the "rain" of Torah by studying the Torah's laws and their derivation, and the "dew" of Torah by studying its inner dimension.

The full revelation of the Torah's inner dimension will occur as part of the future Redemption. As we approach the advent of this Redemption, we are granted a taste of this future revelation. Thus, studying the inner dimension of the Torah enables us to live life on a higher, more spiritually developed level.

This "taste" of the future Redemption inspires us to redouble our efforts to hasten its advent.[1]

1. *Sefer HaMa'amarim Melukat*, vol. 1, pp. 457–464; ibid., vol. 4, pp. 386–387; ibid., vol. 5, pp. 38–40.

SECOND READING
Deuteronomy 32:7–12

G-d told Moses to encourage the Jewish people to remember their history, recalling how G-d chose them to be His people, gave them the Torah, and shepherded them through the desert on their way from Egypt to the Land of Israel.

Finding Faith

יִמְצָאֵהוּ בְּאֶרֶץ מִדְבָּר וגו': (דברים לב, י)

[Moses said, "G-d] found [the Jewish people] in a desert land."

A "find" is something we come upon unexpectedly, rather than as the result of any efforts we have expended to earn it. When G-d gave us the Torah at Mount Sinai, we undertook to relate to Him beyond the dictates of reason or logic, that is, with pure faith. Faith, being by definition beyond the reach of intellect and therefore unattainable by unaided human effort, can truly be categorized as a "find."

Thus, the use of the verb "to find" in describing G-d's encounter with the Jewish people at Mount Sinai indicates that, in return for us binding ourselves to Him on pure faith, beyond reason and logic, G-d bound Himself to us similarly, transcending reason and logic.

Inasmuch as G-d gives us the Torah anew each day, this lesson inspires us to renew our pure faith in Him daily, as well.[2]

---

2. *Likutei Sichot*, vol. 34, p. 210.

THIRD READING

Deuteronomy 32:13–18

After shepherding the Jewish people through the desert, G-d provided them with material bounty in the Land of Israel.

Being Above and Beyond

יַרְכִּבֵהוּ עַל בָּמֳתֵי אָרֶץ וְגוֹ': (דברים לב, יג)

**[Moses said, "G-d] made [the Jewish people] ride
on the highest place on earth.... He nurtured them
with honey from a rock, and oil from a flint-stone."**

The significance of making the Jewish people "ride on the highest place on earth" is that G-d has rendered the collective Jewish people, as well as each individual Jew, above the limitations of physical reality. This implies that by nature, the Jewish people and each individual Jew is able to influence and affect the world.

The way we manifest this innate power is stated in the second half of this verse: "He nurtured them with honey from a rock, and oil from flint-stone." Honey and oil allude to the inner dimension of the Torah.[3] It is by studying the inner dimension of the Torah and enhancing our relationship with G-d through these teachings that we actualize our power to influence and affect the world from our vantage point far above it.

Furthermore, the Torah's inner teachings inspire us with the sense of responsibility to use our G-d-given powers to influence the world positively, ultimately transforming it into His true home.[4]

3. *Imrei Vinah, Sha'ar HaKeri'at Shema* 54 ff; *Chagigah* 13a.
4. *Hitva'aduyot 5749*, vol. 1, p. 76.

FOURTH READING

Deuteronomy 32:19–28

G-d also cautioned the Jewish people that should they overin-dulge in their wealth, it would cause them to rebel against Him. He would punish them for these misdeeds, but would nonetheless never forsake them.

The Inspiration of Being Eternal

חִצַּי אֲכַלֶּה בָּם: (דברים לב, כג)

[Moses said that G-d would say,] "I will use up My arrows on them."

Although this statement is a threat, it is also – as Rashi points out – a blessing: "My supply of arrows will come to an end, but nevertheless the Jewish people will not come to an end." In other words, implicit in this verse is an affirmation of the eternity of the Jewish people. Our perpetuity is derived from G-d's perpetuity; inasmuch as we are part of Him, so to speak, we share something of His eternity.

Now that we have survived all the horrors of exile, we can be sure that we have fulfilled whatever requirements there may have been to experience negativity throughout our long history. We are on the threshold of redemption and can confidently look forward to nothing but the brightest future, and should therefore prepare ourselves accordingly.[5]

5. *Hitva'aduyot 5748*, vol. 4, p. 123.

FIFTH READING
Deuteronomy 32:29–39

G-d told Moses to reassure the Jewish people that He will eventually comfort them for their suffering during their exile.

Future Revelations

רְאוּ עַתָּה כִּי אֲנִי אֲנִי הוּא וְגוֹ': (דברים לב, לט)

[G-d said,] "See, now, it is I, it is I . . . . "

G-d refers to Himself many times throughout the Torah, but this is the only time He does so doubly. This repetition alludes to the two ways in which G-d's presence is manifest in the world.

The first "I" refers to the Divine life-force that gives each aspect of creation its *identity*. This life-force is different for every creature, each one receiving the amount and quality of life-force it needs in order to function as the creature it was created to be.

The second "I" refers to the Divine life-force that gives each aspect of creation its *existence*. This life-force is the same for every creature, since existence is an "on-off" quality – something either exists or it doesn't.

Presently, we are aware of the first Divine "I" but not the second. Although we are indeed aware that we exist, we are not aware of being brought into existence constantly by any Divine life-force. We will become fully aware of this Divine life-force only in the Messianic future.

Yet, this verse says, "See *now* that it is I, it is I," meaning that even now, we can savor a taste of this revelation by fulfilling our Divine mission to refine the world, revealing the Divine potential of all aspects of life. This, in turn, will prepare us for the ultimate revelation of Divinity that will occur with the final, Messianic Redemption.[6]

6. *Sefer HaMa'amarim Melukat*, vol. 1, pp. 55–58.

SIXTH READING
Deuteronomy 32:40–43

G-d then told Moses to inform the Jewish people that eventually the non-Jewish nations would appreciate them and praise them for remaining true to their covenant with G-d.

G-d is Always Present

כִּי אֶשָּׂא אֶל שָׁמַיִם יָדִי וְאָמַרְתִּי חַי אָנֹכִי לְעֹלָם: (דברים לב, מ)

[Moses said that G-d would say,] "For I raise My hand to heaven [in order to swear,] and say, 'I live forever.... '"

The Hebrew word for "forever" literally means "for the world," i.e., "as long as the world exists." In other words, G-d is here vowing that, no matter what the circumstances, His presence will always be "in the world," accompanying the Jewish people. Whatever our tribulations, He will never forsake us.

We should therefore never fall into the conceptual trap known as "deism" – the assumption that G-d, after having created the world, retreated into heaven, from where He merely passively observes the world running according to the brute laws of nature.

Rather, this verse tells us to remain confident that G-d is involved in our lives. He feels the pain of our exile, and – as He promises in the verses that follow this one – He will soon redeem us and the whole world.[7]

7. *Sichot Kodesh 5736*, vol. 1, pp. 39–44.

SEVENTH READING
Deuteronomy 32:44–52

After Moses finished conveying the Poem of Testimony to the Jewish people, he encouraged them to pay heed to all its lessons, as well as to the Torah in general.

The Challenge of Greatness

וַיָּבֹא מֹשֶׁה וַיְדַבֵּר אֶת כָּל דִּבְרֵי הַשִּׁירָה הַזֹּאת

... הוּא וִהוֹשֵׁעַ בֶּן נוּן: (דברים לב, מד)

Moses came and recited this entire poem ... himself and [then had Joshua, who was originally known as] Hoshea son of Nun, [repeat it].

As Rashi tells us, Moses did a number of things on the last day of his life in order to demonstrate that the leadership was now passing to Joshua. In certain respects, Moses made Joshua his equal on this day. Nonetheless, the Torah refers to Joshua by his original name, Hoshea, in order to teach us that his ascent to greatness did not cause him to become haughty. On the contrary, he continued to act modestly – as if he were still the novice he was before Moses renamed him Joshua.

G-d has blessed us all with unique talents, sensibilities, and gifts. If we utilize these gifts properly – as we should – we will thereby rise to a position of greatness or leadership in some aspect of life. When this happens, it is tempting to focus on how we achieved our position in the merit of our own qualities, forgetting that they were given to us by G-d. It is at this point that we need to follow Joshua's example, remaining humble.

This humility will in fact enable us to succeed in our position of leadership and remain successful leaders.[8]

---

8. *Likutei Sichot*, vol. 29, pp. 201–202.

VeZot HaBerachah

The Final Blessing

Deuteronomy 33:1–34:12

THE ELEVENTH AND FINAL SECTION OF THE BOOK OF DEU-
teronomy concludes Moses' third and final farewell address to the
Jewish people. It begins with the blessings (*VeZot HaBerachah*,
in Hebrew) that he pronounced to each of the twelve tribes, and
concludes with his death.

FIRST READING
Deuteronomy 33:1–7

Moses began by noting that G-d's blessings can only truly rest on the Jewish people when they are united in their devotion to Him.

Jewish Unity

יַחַד שִׁבְטֵי יִשְׂרָאֵל: (דברים לג, ה)

[Moses said to G-d, "You are the King of the Jewish people] when the tribes of Israel are united."

Unity does not require that all members of a group be alike, but that each one fulfill his or her unique purpose while acknowledging the necessary contribution of all other members of the group. Furthermore, each member can function fully only when all the other members are functioning fully. Thus, the proper functioning of each member not only affects his or her own effectiveness and the overall effectiveness of the body as a whole, but also the effectiveness of every other member individually.

Thus, Jewish unity should ideally be more than the simple dedication to a common goal (although that is a worthy aim in its own right), and more than a relationship by which each of us completes the other (although this, too, is a worthy aim). Unity should be an awareness that all of us, together, form one whole. All aspects of all of us are part of one "body," meaning that every facet of our individual lives has an impact on every facet of the life of every other Jew.

Conversely, just as the body's completeness is dependent upon the individual completeness of each of its parts, so is it crucial that we all develop our individuality, living up to our unique potential.[1]

1. *Likutei Sichot*, vol. 4, pp. 1141–1143.

SECOND READING
Deuteronomy 33:8–12

Moses then blessed each tribe separately, emphasizing each one's unique contribution to the collective mission of the Jewish people. He blessed the tribe of Levi to be worthy of their role as the priests and Levites serving in the holy Temple, and of their duty to teach the Torah to the rest of the Jewish people.

Joy

וּלְלֵוִי אָמַר . . . יוֹרוּ מִשְׁפָּטֶיךָ לְיַעֲקֹב וְתוֹרָתְךָ לְיִשְׂרָאֵל וְגוֹ׳: (דברים לג, ח-י)

[Moses] said regarding Levi, ". . . They will teach Your ordinances to [the descendants of] Jacob and Your Torah to Israel."

The Levites infused the Temple service with joy, by accompanying the daily and festival sacrifices with music and songs praising G-d.[2]

This verse demonstrates how the Levites also infused the study of the Torah with joy, by rendering authoritative legal judgments, instructing the people exactly how they should act. Knowing what our obligations are, clearly and definitively, dispels doubt and fills us with joyful confidence in our path in life.

The quality that enabled the tribe of Levi to achieve this joy was their absolute devotion to G-d – even to the extent of self-sacrifice.[3] Selfless devotion to G-d enables us to ascertain His will unencumbered by personal agendas or predispositions.

We can all learn from the Levites' example how selfless devotion to G-d infuses joy into our Divine mission and our study of the Torah.[4]

---

2. *Zohar* 1:148b.
3. As is mentioned in v. 9, referring to how the Levites endangered their lives by fighting those who worshipped the Golden Calf.
4. *Hitva'aduyot 5742*, vol. 1, pp. 210–211.

THIRD READING
Deuteronomy 33:13–17

Moses blessed the tribes of Ephraim and Manasseh that they would be populous.

Supernatural Success

וְהֵם רִבְבוֹת אֶפְרַיִם וְהֵם אַלְפֵי מְנַשֶּׁה: (דברים לג, יז)

[Moses said,] "These are the myriads of Ephraim and the thousands of Manasseh."

Ephraim's name refers to how Joseph prospered in Egypt despite all odds, while Manasseh's name refers to how Joseph's prosperity enabled him to forget his pain over the loss of the past that he enjoyed with his parents and siblings.[5]

In terms of our approach to our Divine mission, Manasseh symbolizes our awareness of our origins – our natural limitations as human beings – and our awareness that, on account of our limitations, we have to negotiate life's challenges delicately in order to succeed in our mission.

In contrast, Ephraim symbolizes our awareness of how G-d has blessed us with powers beyond those with which we are endowed naturally, how He has granted us supernatural success in the past and will continue to do so. This awareness enables us to face life's challenges head-on, ignoring apparent obstacles.

Thus, the reward we can expect for facing life like a "Manasseh" is "thousands" – an abundance, to be sure, for it is no small thing to accomplish our purpose despite the odds. Yet if we face life like an "Ephraim," the reward is "myriads" – tenfold and more, since this approach enables us to accomplish so much more. Our confidence in G-d's supernatural assistance elicits His infinite bounty, which we draw both into the world and into our own lives.[6]

5. Genesis 41:51–52.
6. *Sichot Kodesh 5741*, vol. 1, pp. 118–121.

FOURTH READING
Deuteronomy 33:18–21

The tribe of Zebulun took upon themselves the task of supporting the tribe of Issachar, freeing the latter to devote themselves to the study of the Torah full-time. Moses therefore blessed Zebulun with success in commerce and Issachar with success in wisdom.

Work and Study

וְלִזְבוּלֻן אָמַר שְׂמַח זְבוּלֻן בְּצֵאתֶךָ וְיִשָּׂשכָר בְּאֹהָלֶיךָ: (דברים לג, יח)

**[Moses] said regarding Zebulun, "Rejoice, Zebulun,
in your departure [for business pursuits], and
Issachar, in your tents [of Torah study]."**

Zebulun is mentioned first in this verse by virtue of the intrinsic merit of working for a living over a life dedicated to full-time Torah study.

As we know, our Divine mission consists of making the physical and materialistic world into G-d's home. Although both studying the Torah and sanctifying the material world accomplish this goal, it is mainly achieved by the latter. Therefore, those who work for a living have a far greater opportunity to fulfill life's purpose than do those who study full-time.

There is, of course, an advantage to full-time study, and Jewish law insists that those who are both capable of studying the Torah full-time and who do not have to work for a living devote themselves to full-time study.[7] But with respect to refining the world and thereby transforming it into G-d's home, pride of place belongs to work.[8]

---

7. *Shulchan Aruch, Yoreh Dei'ah* 245:22; *Shulchan Aruch HaRav, Hilchot Talmud Torah* 3–4.
8. *Likutei Sichot,* vol. 30, pp. 136–137.

FIFTH READING
Deuteronomy 33:22–26

Moses blessed the tribe of Naphtali with the abundance of fish they would catch from Lake Kinneret, located in their territory.

The Virtue of Selflessness

וּלְנַפְתָּלִי אָמַר ... יָם וְדָרוֹם יְרָשָׁה: (דברים לג, כג)

[Moses] said regarding Naphtali ... "Take possession of the lake and the south."

"Lake" in the Torah also means "the west" (since the western border of the Land of Israel is the Mediterranean Sea). Thus, this phrase can be translated: "take possession of the west and the south."

The west alludes to the Divine energy manifest throughout creation. The daily setting of the heavenly bodies in the west is understood as their ongoing prostration before the Divine Presence.[9] Similarly, the Holy of Holies was the westernmost part of the Sanctuary.[10]

The south alludes to Divine energy that remains beyond creation. In the northern hemisphere, the sun shines strongest from the south. The sun allegorically represents the Name of G-d (*Havayah*) that is associated with this Divine energy.[11]

The tribe of Naphtali, as part of the camp of the tribe of Dan,[12] traveled at the rear of the Israelites' military formation in the desert.[13] The rear position alludes to the least illustrious aspect of our psyches – our simple, selfless submission to G-d's will. By cultivating this selfless submission, we can, like the tribe of Naphtali, "take possession of the west and the south."[14]

9. *Bava Batra* 25a.
10. Exodus 26:33.
11. Psalms 84:12; *Sha'ar HaYichud VehaEmunah* 4 (78a).
12. Numbers 2:29–30.
13. Numbers 10:25.
14. *Likutei Sichot*, vol. 1, pp. 103–107.

SIXTH READING
Deuteronomy 33:27–29

After blessing each of the tribes individually, Moses blessed the Jewish people collectively, contrasting their role in the world with that of all other nations.

A Light to the Nations

וַיִּשְׁכֹּן יִשְׂרָאֵל בֶּטַח בָּדָד וְגוֹ': (דברים לג, כח)

[Moses said of the Jewish people,] "Israel will dwell safely and individually."

This does not mean that in the future the Jewish people will be totally isolated. It is part of the mission of the Jewish people to guide and educate the non-Jewish world how to live a G-dly life, in particular by convincing them to fulfill the commandments they are obligated to fulfill, known as the Noahide laws.

Even when the non-Jewish world has been elevated to the highest possible levels of civilization and spiritual refinement, the Jewish people will still be obligated to instruct them in G-d's ways. This is alluded to later in this passage, in which we are told, "you will tread upon their heights,"[15] meaning that we must not shirk our obligation to assume our role as their teachers, even when they have reached the "heights" of human achievement.

As G-d's appointed purveyors of His message to humanity, we must always realize that the infinite depths of the Torah will always contain directions for further progress and growth, not only for us as Jews but for our non-Jewish charges.[16]

15. V. 29.
16. *Hitva'aduyot 5745*, vol. 1, pp. 246–247.

SEVENTH READING
Deuteronomy 34:1–12

After Moses concluded his farewell address, G-d instructed him to ascend Mount Nebo to die.

The Key to Immortality

וַיָּמָת שָׁם מֹשֶׁה עֶבֶד ה' וְגו': (דברים לד, ה)

Moses, the servant of G-d, died.

All righteous people are considered to "live on" after their physical death, because their spiritual influence continues. However, we still refer to them as having died, for their physical presence in this world has ceased. In Moses' case, however, the Talmud records an opinion according to which Moses did not die, but remains alive to this day.[17]

Moses' continued existence in this world is embodied in the Jewish religious leaders of each generation, whose bodies house a manifestation of his soul.[18] He lives on even after his "death" because he, like Jacob, embodied the attribute of truth,[19] meaning unchanging incorruptibility. Jacob was able to weather all the tribulations of his life unflinchingly, and Moses survived the most difficult trials in the course of his leadership. Furthermore, both Jacob and Moses personified the ideal of devotion to studying and teaching the Torah, which demand uncompromising dedication to truth. The incorruptibility they expressed in their lives made them both immune to death.

By devoting ourselves to the truth, embodied in G-d's Torah, we too can partake of the immortality of Moses and Jacob as we transform the finite world into a home for the infinite presence of G-d.[20]

---

17. *Sotah 13b*; *Zohar* 1:37b.
18. *Tikunei Zohar 69* (112a, 114a); *Tanya*, chapter 44 (63a).
19. Moses: *Bava Batra 74a*; Jacob: Micah 7:20.
20. *Likutei Sichot*, vol. 26, pp. 6–9.

APPENDIX

ANNUAL TORAH STUDY CALENDAR

As explained in the introduction, it is customary to study a portion of the weekly Torah section each day. The schedule for this study program is given below. This calendar applies to the Diaspora. For the calendar for the Land of Israel, as well as for additional years, see www.chabadhousepublications.org

Section	Pages	2018–2019	2019–2020	2020–2021	2021–2022	2022–2023	2023–2024	2024–2025	2025–2026
GENESIS									
Bereishit	3–10	Oct 2–6 '18*	Oct 22–26 '19*	Oct 11–17 '20*	Sep 29–Oct 2 '21*	Oct 18–22 '22*	Oct 8–14 '23*	Oct 25–26 '24*	Oct 15–18 2025*
Noach	11–18	Oct 7–13	Oct 27–Nov 2	Oct 18–24	Oct 3–9	Oct 23–29	Oct 15–21	Oct 27–Nov 2	Oct 19–25
Lech Lecha	19–26	Oct 14–20	Nov 3–9	Oct 25–31	Oct 10–16	Oct 30–Nov 5	Oct 22–28	Nov 3–9	Oct 26–Nov 1
Vayeira	27–34	Oct 21–27	Nov 10–16	Nov 1–7	Oct 17–23	Nov 6–12	Oct 29–Nov 4	Nov 10–16	Nov 2–8
Chayei Sarah	35–42	Oct 28–Nov 3	Nov 17–23	Nov 8–14	Oct 24–30	Nov 13–19	Nov 5–11	Nov 17–23	Nov 9–15
Toledot	43–50	Nov 4–10	Nov 24–30	Nov 15–21	Oct 31–Nov 6	Nov 20–26	Nov 12–18	Nov 24–30	Nov 16–22
Vayeitzei	51–58	Nov 11–17	Dec 1–7	Nov 22–28	Nov 7–13	Nov 27–Dec 3	Nov 19–25	Dec 1–7	Nov 23–29
Vayishlach	59–66	Nov 18–24	Dec 8–14	Nov 29–Dec 5	Nov 14–20	Dec 4–10	Nov 26–Dec 2	Dec 8–14	Nov 30–Dec 6
Vayeishev	67–74	Nov 25–Dec 1	Dec 15–21	Dec 6–12	Nov 21–27	Dec 11–17	Dec 3–9	Dec 15–21	Dec 7–13
Mikeitz	75–82	Dec 2–8	Dec 22–28	Dec 13–19	Nov 28–Dec 4	Dec 18–24	Dec 10–16	Dec 22–28	Dec 14–20
Vayigash	83–90	Dec 9–15	Dec 29–Jan 4 '20	Dec 20–26	Dec 5–11	Dec 25–31	Dec 17–23	Dec 29–Jan 4 '25	Dec 21–27
Vaichi	91–98	Dec 16–22	Jan 5–11	Dec 27–Jan 2 '21	Dec 12–18	Jan 1–7 '23	Dec 24–30	Jan 5–11	Dec 28–Jan 3 2026
EXODUS									
Shemot	101–108	Dec 23–29	Jan 12–18	Jan 3–9	Dec 19–25	Jan 8–14	Dec 31–Jan 6 '24	Jan 12–18	Jan 4–10
Va'eira	109–116	Dec 30–Jan 5 '19	Jan 19–25	Jan 10–16	Dec 26–Jan 1 '22	Jan 15–21	Jan 7–13	Jan 19–25	Jan 11–17
Bo	117–124	Jan 6–12	Jan 26–Feb 1	Jan 17–23	Jan 7–8	Jan 22–28	Jan 14–20	Jan 26–Feb 1	Jan 18–24
Beshalach	125–132	Jan 13–19	Feb 2–8	Jan 24–30	Jan 9–15	Jan 29–Feb 4	Jan 21–27	Feb 2–8	Jan 25–31
Yitro	133–140	Jan 20–26	Feb 9–15	Jan 31–Feb 6	Jan 16–22	Feb 5–11	Jan 28–Feb 3	Feb 9–15	Feb 1–7
Mishpatim	141–148	Jan 27–Feb 2	Feb 16–22	Feb 7–13	Jan 23–29	Feb 12–18	Feb 4–10	Feb 16–22	Feb 8–14
Terumah	149–156	Feb 3–9	Feb 23–29	Feb 14–20	Jan 30–Feb 5	Feb 19–25	Feb 11–17	Feb 23–Mar 1	Feb 15–21
Tetzaveh	157–165	Feb 10–16	Mar 1–7	Feb 21–27	Feb 6–12	Feb 26–Mar 4	Feb 18–24	Mar 2–8	Feb 22–28
Tisa	165–172	Feb 17–23	Mar 8–14	Feb 28–Mar 6	Feb 13–19	Mar 5–11	Feb 25–Mar 2	Mar 9–15	Mar 1–7
Vayakheil	173–180	Feb 24–Mar 2	Mar 15–21**	Mar 7–13**	Feb 20–26	Mar 12–18**	Mar 3–9	Mar 16–22	Mar 8–14**
Pekudei	181–188	Mar 3–9	Mar 15–21**	Mar 7–13**	Feb 27–Mar 5	Mar 12–18**	Mar 10–16	Mar 23–29	Mar 8–14**
LEVITICUS									
Vayikra	191–198	Mar 10–16	Mar 22–28	Mar 14–20	Mar 6–12	Mar 19–25	Mar 17–23	Mar 30–Apr 5	Mar 15–21
Tzav	199–206	Mar 17–23	Mar 29–Apr 4	Mar 21–27	Mar 13–19	Mar 26–Apr 1	Mar 24–30	Apr 6–12	Mar 22–28
Shemini	207–214	Mar 24–30	Apr 5–18***	Mar 28–Apr 10***	Mar 20–26	Apr 2–15***	Mar 31–Apr 6	Apr 13–26***	Mar 29–Apr 11***

Portion	Pages								
Tazri'a	215–222	Mar 31–Apr 6	Apr 19–25**	Apr 11–17**	Mar 27–Apr 3	Apr 16–22**	Apr 7–13	Apr 27–May 3**	Apr 12–18**
Metzora	223–230	Apr 7–13	Apr 19–25**	Apr 11–17**	Apr 4–9	Apr 16–22**	Apr 14–20	Apr 27–May 3**	Apr 12–18**
Acharei	231–238	Apr 14–May 4***	Apr 26–May 2**	Apr 18–24**	Apr 10–30***	Apr 23–29**	Apr 21–May 4***	May 4–10**	Apr 19–25**
Kedoshim	239–246	May 5–11	Apr 26–May 2**	Apr 18–24**	May 1–7	Apr 23–29**	May 5–11	May 4–10**	Apr 19–25**
Emor	247–254	May 12–18	May 3–9	Apr 25–May 1	May 8–14	Apr 30–May 6	May 12–18	May 11–17	Apr 26–May 2
Behar	255–262	May 19–25	May 10–16**	May 2–8**	May 15–21	May 7–13**	May 19–25	May 18–24**	May 3–9**
Bechukotai	263–270	May 26–Jun 1	May 10–16**	May 2–8**	May 22–28	May 7–13**	May 26–Jun 1	May 18–24**	May 3–9**
NUMBERS									
Bemidbar	273–280	Jun 2–8	May 17–23	May 9–15	May 29–Jun 4	May 14–20	Jun 2–8	May 25–31	May 10–16
Naso	281–288	Jun 9–15	May 24–Jun 6***	May 16–22	Jun 5–11	May 21–Jun 3***	Jun 9–15	Jun 1–7	May 17–30***
Beha'alotecha	289–296	Jun 16–22	Jun 7–13	May 23–29	Jun 12–18	Jun 4–10	Jun 16–22	Jun 8–14	May 31–Jun 6
Shelach	297–304	Jun 23–29	Jun 14–20	May 30–Jun 5	Jun 19–25	Jun 11–17	Jun 23–29	Jun 15–21	Jun 7–13
Korach	305–312	Jun 30–Jul 6	Jun 21–27	Jun 6–12	Jun 26–Jul 2	Jun 18–24	Jun 30–Jul 6	Jun 22–28	Jun 14–20
Chukat	313–320	Jul 7–13	Jun 28–Jul 4**	Jun 13–19	Jul 3–9	Jun 25–Jul 1**	Jul 7–13	Jun 29–Jul 5	Jun 21–27**
Balak	321–328	Jul 14–20	Jun 28–Jul 4**	Jun 20–26	Jul 10–16	Jun 25–Jul 1**	Jul 14–20	Jul 6–12	Jun 21–27**
Pinchas	329–336	Jul 21–27	Jul 5–11	Jun 27–Jul 3	Jul 17–23	Jul 2–8	Jul 21–27	Jul 13–19	Jun 28–Jul 4
Matot	337–344	Jul 28–Aug 3**	Jul 12–18**	Jul 4–10**	Jul 24–30**	Jul 9–15**	Jul 28–Aug 3**	Jul 20–26**	Jul 5–11**
Mas'ei	345–352	Jul 28–Aug 3**	Jul 12–18**	Jul 4–10**	Jul 24–30**	Jul 9–15**	Jul 28–Aug 3**	Jul 20–26**	Jul 5–11**
DEUTERONOMY									
Devarim	355–362	Aug 4–10	Jul 19–25	Jul 11–17	Jul 31–Aug 6	Jul 16–22	Aug 4–10	Jul 27–Aug 2	Jul 12–18
Va'etchanan	363–370	Aug 11–17	Jul 26–Aug 1	Jul 18–24	Aug 7–13	Jul 23–29	Aug 11–17	Aug 3–9	Jul 19–25
Eikev	371–378	Aug 18–24	Aug 2–8	Jul 25–31	Aug 14–20	Jul 30–Aug 5	Aug 18–24	Aug 10–16	Jul 26–Aug 1
Re'eih	379–388	Aug 25–31	Aug 9–15	Aug 1–7	Aug 21–27	Aug 6–12	Aug 25–31	Aug 17–23	Aug 2–8
Shofetim	387–394	Sep 1–7	Aug 16–22	Aug 8–14	Aug 28–Sep 3	Aug 13–19	Sep 1–7	Aug 24–30	Aug 9–15
Teitzei	395–402	Sep 8–14	Aug 23–29	Aug 15–21	Sep 4–10	Aug 20–26	Sep 8–14	Aug 31–Sep 6	Aug 16–22
Tavo	403–410	Sep 15–21	Aug 30–Sep 5	Aug 22–28	Sep 11–17	Aug 27–Sep 2	Sep 15–21	Sep 7–13	Aug 23–29
Nitzavim	411–418	Sep 22–28	Sep 6–12**	Aug 29–Sep 4	Sep 18–24	Sep 3–9**	Sep 22–28**	Sep 14–20	Aug 30–Sep 5**
Vayeilech	419–426	Sep 29–Oct 5	Sep 6–12**	Sep 5–11	Sep 25–Oct 1	Sep 3–9**	Sep 22–28**	Sep 21–27	Aug 30–Sep 5**
Ha'azinu	427–434	Oct 6–12	Sep 13–26***	Sep 12–18	Oct 2–8	Sep 10–23***	Sep 29–Oct 5	Sep 28–Oct 4	Sep 6–19***
Vezot Haberachah	435–442	Oct 13–22*	Sep 27–Oct 11*	Sep 19–29*	Oct 9–18*	Sep 24–Oct 8*	Oct 6–25*	Oct 5–15*	Sep 20–Oct 4*

*Vezot Haberachah/Bereishit: On *Simchat Torah*, the remaining portions of the section *Vezot Haberachah* are studied; on the following day, the section *Bereishit* is studied up to the portion of that day of the week.

**Double section: The first section is studied during the first half of the week and the second during the second half of the week.

***Study of weekly section is repeated due to holiday schedule.

The Jewish Calendar

Month	Natural Order	Torah Order	Gregorian Equivalent
Tishrei	1	7	September–October
Marcheshvan	2	8	October–November
Kislev	3	9	November–December
Tevet	4	10	December–January
Shevat	5	11	January–February
Adar	6	12	February–March
Nisan	7	1	March–April
Iyar	8	2	April–May
Sivan	9	3	May–June
Tamuz	10	4	June–July
Menachem-Av	11	5	July–August
Elul	12	6	August–September

Bibliography

1. CHABAD CHASIDIC WORKS

The Rebbe, Rabbi Menachem Mendel Schneerson (1902–1994)
    Likutei Sichot (39 volumes)
    Hitva'aduyot (*Torat Menachem,* cited by year; 94 volumes)
    Igrot Kodesh (30 volumes)
    Reshimot
    Sichot Kodesh (cited by year; 49 volumes)
    Sefer HaMa'amarim Melukat (6 volumes)
    Sefer HaMa'amarim (cited by year; 40 volumes)
    Sefer HaSichot (cited by year; 12 volumes)
    Igrot Melech

Rabbi Shneur Zalman of Liadi (1745–1812)
    Tanya (*Likutei Amarim, Sha'ar HaYichud VeHaEmunah,*
        Igeret HaTeshuvah, Igeret HaKodesh)
    Torah Or
    Likutei Torah
    Ma'amarei Admor HaZakein (32 volumes)

Rabbi Dovber Shneuri (1773–1827)
    Ma'amarei Admor HaEmtza'i (19 volumes)
    Siddur im Dach
    Bi'urei HaZohar
    Torat Chaim
    Imrei Vinah

Rabbi Menachem Mendel Schneersohn of
    Lubavitch (1789–1866)
    Derech Mitzvotecha
    Or HaTorah (38 volumes)
    Bi'urei HaZohar
    Yaheil Or

Rabbi Shmuel Schneersohn of Lubavitch (1834–1882)
    Torat Shmuel (30 volumes)

Rabbi Shalom Dovber Schneersohn of Lubavitch (1860–1920)
  BeSha'ah sheHikdimu 5672
  Kuntres Umayan
  Kuntereis Eitz HaChayim
  Sefer HaMa'amarim (35 volumes)
  Yom Tov shel Rosh HaShanah 5666
  Sefer HaSichot Torat Shalom

Rabbi Yosef Yitzchak Schneersohn of Lubavitch (1880–1950)
  HaYom Yom
  Igrot Kodesh Mehorayatz (15 volumes)
  Likutei Diburim (4 volumes)
  Sefer HaMa'amarim (cited by year; 29 volumes)
  Sefer HaSichot (cited by year; 12 volumes)

2. OTHER WORKS

Note: Words preceded by an asterisk (*) have their own entries.

Arachin: a tractate of the *Talmud.

Avodah Zarah: a tractate of the *Talmud.

Avot: a tractate of the *Talmud.

Avot d'Rabbi Natan: a minor tractate of the *Talmud.

Ba'alei HaNefesh: Rabbi Avraham ben David of Posquières (c. 1125–1198). Laws and ethics.

Bartenura: see Commentary on the *Mishnah.

Bava Batra: a tractate of the *Talmud.

Bava Kama: a tractate of the *Talmud.

Bava Metzia: a tractate of the *Talmud.

Bechorot: a tractate of the *Talmud.

Bemidbar Rabbah: see Midrash.

Berachot: a tractate of the *Talmud.

Bereishit Rabbah: see Midrash.

Bible: the written *Torah. The Bible comprises 24 books, divided into three sections:

(1) the Torah (תּוֹרָה, "teaching"), comprising the five books of Moses;

(2) the eight books of the Prophets (נְבִיאִים – the first and second books of Samuel and Kings are considered one book, as are the twelve "minor" prophets);

(3) the eleven books of the Writings (כְּתוּבִים – the books of Ezra and Nehemiah are considered one book, as are the two books of Chronicles).

The Bible is therefore known in Hebrew as the Tanach (תַּנַ"ךְ), the abbreviation formed by the first letters of the names of these three sections.

Chidushei Agadot: Rabbi Shmuel Eidels (1555–1631). Commentary on the *Talmud.

Chronicles: a book of the *Bible.

Chulin: a tractate of the *Talmud.

*Commentary on the *Bible*: Rabbi Bachye ben Asher Ibn Chelaveh (?–1340).

*Commentary on the *Bible*: Rabbi Moshe ben Nachman (Ramban, Nachmanides, 1194–1270).

*Commentary on the *Bible*: Rabbi Shlomo ben Yitzchak (Rashi, 1040–1105).

*Commentary on the *Bible*: Rabbi Shmuel ben Meir (Rashbam, c. 1085–1174).

*Commentary on the *Mishnah*: Rabbi Ovadiah ben Avraham of Bartenura [Bertinoro] (c. 1445 – c. 1515).

*Commentary on *Mishneh Torah*: Rabbi David ben Zimra (c. 1479–1573).

*Commentary on the *Talmud*: Rabbeinu Asher (the Rosh) (1259–1327).

*Commentary on the *Torah*: Rabbi Shimshon Raphael Hirsch (1808–1888).

Degel Machaneih Ephraim: Rabbi Moshe Chaim Ephraim of Sudilkov (1748–1800). Chasidic teachings.

Deuteronomy: a book of the *Bible.

Encyclopedia Talmudit ("Talmudic Encyclopedia"): first editor: Rabbi Shelomo Yoseif Zevin (1886–1978).

Exodus: a book of the *Bible.

Ezekiel: a book of the *Bible.

Genesis: a book of the *Bible.

Gur Aryeh: Rabbi Yehudah Leowe ben Betzalel of Prague (1512–1609). Super-commentary on *Rashi's commentary on the Torah.

Hosea: a book of the *Bible.

Isaiah: a book of the *Bible.

Jeremiah: a book of the *Bible.

Job: a book of the *Bible.

Joshua: a book of the *Bible.

Keli Yekar: Rabbi Shelomo Ephraim of Luntschitz (1550–1619). Commentary on the *Torah.

Keter Shem Tov: Rabbi Yisrael Ba'al Shem Tov (1698–1760). Chasidic teachings.

Ketubot: a tractate of the *Talmud.

Kidushin: a tractate of the *Talmud.

Leviticus: a book of the *Bible.

Likutei Levi Yitzchak: Rabbi Levi Yitzchak Schneerson (1878–1944). Chasidic teachings.

Likutei Torah (Arizal): Kabbalistic teachings of Rabbi Yitzchak Luria (1534–1572) as recorded by Rabbi Chaim Vital (1542–1620).

Machzor Vitri: Rabbi Simchah ben Shmuel of Vitri (?-1105). Commentary on the liturgy.

Makot: a tractate of the *Talmud.

Mechilta: halachic *Midrash to the book of *Exodus.

Megaleh Amukot: Rabbi Natan Nata Shapiro (1585–1633). Kabbalistic commentary on the *Torah.

Megilah: a tractate of the *Talmud.

Menachot: a tractate of the *Talmud

Micah: a book of the *Bible.

Midrash: the second major body of the Oral *Torah (after the *Talmud), consisting of halachic or homiletic material couched as linguistic analyses of the Biblical text.

Midrash Lekach Tov: Rabbi Toviyah ben Eliezer (11th century). A *Midrash on the *Torah and the Books of Song of Songs, Ruth, Lamentations, Ecclesiastes, and Esther. Also known as *Pesikta Zutarta*.

Midrash Tanchuma: a *Midrash on the *Torah.

MiMa'ainei HaChasidut: Rabbi Alter Eliyahu Friedman. Collection of Chasidic teachings on the *Torah.

Mishnah: see Talmud.

Mishneh Torah: Rabbi Moshe ben Maimon (Maimonides, 1135–1205). Codification of Jewish law.

Mo'ed Katan: a tractate of the *Talmud.

Nachmanides: see *Commentary on the Bible*.

Nedarim: a tractate of the *Talmud.

Nega'im: a tractate of the *Talmud.

Numbers: a book of the *Bible.

Or HaChaim: Rabbi Chaim ben Atar (1696–1743). Commentary on the *Torah.

Or HaMei'ir: Rabbi Ze'ev Wolf of Zhitomer (1740–1800). Chasidic Teachings.

Peri Etz Chaim: Kabbalistic teachings of Rabbi Isaac Luria (1534–1572), edited by Rabbi Meir Popperos (1624–1662).

Pesachim: a tractate of the *Talmud.

Pesikta d'Rav Kahana: a *Midrash.

Pesikta Rabati: a *Midrash.

Pirkei d'Rabbi Eliezer: a *Midrash.

Proverbs: a book of the *Bible.

Psalms: a book of the *Bible.

Rabbeinu Asher: see *Commentary on the Talmud*.

Rabbeinu Bachye: see *Commentary on the Bible*.

Rashbam: see *Commentary on the Bible*.

Rashi: see *Commentary on the Bible*.

Responsa Noda Bihudah: Rabbi Yechezkel Landau (1713–1793).

Ruth: a book of the *Bible.

Samuel: a book of the *Bible.

Sanhedrin: a tractate of the *Talmud.

Sefer HaBahir: Rabbi Nechunyah ben HaKanah (1st century). Early work of Kabbalah.

Sefer Chareidim: Rabbi Elazar Azikri (1533–1600). Ethics.

Sefer HaChinuch: Rabbi Aharon (?) HaLevi (13th–14th century). Legal and ethical exposition of the 613 commandments.

Shabbat: a tractate of the *Talmud.

Shekalim: a tractate of the *Talmud.

Shemot Rabbah: a *Midrash.

Shir HaShirim Rabbah: a *Midrash.

Shulchan Aruch HaRav: Rabbi Shneur Zalman of Liadi (1745–1812). An update of the *Shulchan Aruch*, the Code of Jewish Law by Rabbi Yosef Karo (1488–1575).

Sifra: halachic *Midrash to the Book of *Leviticus.

Sifrei: halachic *Midrash to the Books of *Numbers and *Deuteronomy.

Siftei Cohen: Rabbi Mordechai HaKohen (16th century). Kabbalistic commentary on the *Torah.

Song of Songs: a book of the *Bible.

Sotah: a tractate of the *Talmud.

Ta'anit: a tractate of the *Talmud.

Talmud: the written version of the greater part of the Oral *Torah, comprising mostly legal but also much homiletic and even some explicitly mystical material. The Talmud comprises the *Mishnah* (מִשְׁנָה, "repetition") and the *Gemara* (גְּמָרָא, "study"). The Mishnah is the basic compendium of the laws (each known as a *mishnah*) comprising the Oral Torah, redacted by Rabbi Yehudah the Prince in the second century CE. The *Mishnah* was elaborated upon over the next few centuries in the academies of the Holy Land and Babylonia; this material is the *Gemara*. There are thus two Talmuds: the one composed in the Holy Land, known as the *Talmud Yerushalmi* ("The Jerusalem Talmud"), completed in the third century, and the one composed in Babylonia, known as the *Talmud Bavli* ("The Babylonian Talmud"), completed in the sixth century. References to tractates of the Talmud refer to the versions in the Babylonian Talmud, unless preceded by the word *Yerushalmi*.

Tana d'vei Eliyahu: a *Midrash.

Targum ("Translation"): the Aramaic translation of the Bible. The authoritative Aramaic translation of the Five Books of Moses is that of Onkelos (2nd century). There is also a second Aramaic translation of the Five Books of Moses known as *Targum Yerushalmi I*.

Targum Yerushalmi: see *Targum.

Tikunei Zohar: Additions to the *Zohar.

Toledot Ya'akov Yosef: Rabbi Yaakov Yosef of Polnoye (1710– 1784). Chasidic teachings.

Torah ("teaching"): G-d gave the Torah in two parts: the Written Torah and the Oral Torah. The Written Torah originally consisted of the Five Books of Moses (the "Pentateuch"), the other books being added later (see Bible). The Oral Torah was communicated together with the Five Books of Moses as an explanation of the laws and lore included in it. This material was later written down in the form of the *Talmud, the *Midrash, and the *Zohar. (All references to the "sages" in this book refer to the sages who transmitted the Oral Torah as recorded in these works.)

Torat Moshe: Rabbi Moshe Alsheich (1505–1593). Commentary of the *Torah.

Tur: Rabbi Yaakov ben Asher (c. 1275–c. 1340). Legal code; the *Shulchan Aruch* is based on the *Tur*. Cited by volume name (*Orach Chayim, Even HaEzer, Yoreh Dei'ah,* and *Choshen Mishpat*).

Tzava'at HaRibash: Rabbi Yisrael Ba'al Shem Tov (1698–1760). Chasidic teachings.

Tzeror HaMor: Rabbi Avraham Sebb (1440–1508). Commentary on the *Torah.

Vayikra Rabbah: *Midrash on the Book of Leviticus.

Yalkut Shim'oni: Rabbi Shimon Ashkenazi (14th century). Compendium of midrashic material, including material missing from older midrashic collections.

Yerushalmi: see *Talmud.

Yevamot: a tractate of the *Talmud.

Yoma: a tractate of the *Talmud.

Zechariah: a book of the *Bible.

Zevachim: a tractate of the *Talmud.

Zohar: Rabbi Shimon bar Yochai (2nd century). One of the basic texts of the Oral *Torah and Kabbalah.

Index

נדפס לזכות

הרה"ח הרה"ת **משה מאיר** הכהן
וזוגתו **פנינה** שיחיו
בניהם ובנותיהם
מנחם מענדל הכהן, **יאכא גאלדע, גיטל,**
לוי יצחק הכהן, **ודבורה לאה**
שיחיו
ליפשיץ

שלוחי כ"ק אדמו"ר נשיא דורנו
בעיר פורט לודרדייל, פלורידה

לברכה והצלחה רבה, בכל אשר יפנו
בגשמיות וברוחניות

RABBI MENACHEM MENDEL SCHNEERSON (1902–1994), one
of the great Jewish leaders of the 20th century, changed the map
of world Judaism and deeply affected both Jews and non-Jews
throughout the world. His written works span over 200 volumes,
many of which are still being published. His students continue
to disseminate his teachings in many varied forms, while his
global network of emissaries continues to spread his message
of goodness and kindness, a message that informs every page of
Daily Wisdom.